CONFUCIAN SPIRITUALITY
Volume One

D1564483

World Spirituality

An Encyclopedic History of the Religious Quest

1. Asian Archaic Spirituality
2. European Archaic Spirituality
3. African Spirituality
4. South and Meso-American Spirituality
5. North American Indian Spirituality
6. Hindu Spirituality: Vedas through Vedanta
7. Hindu Spirituality: Postclassical and Modern
8. Buddhist Spirituality: Indian, Sri Lankan, Southeast Asian
9. Buddhist Spirituality: Chinese, Tibetan, Japanese, Korean
10. Taoist Spirituality
11A. Confucian Spirituality I
11B. Confucian Spirituality II
12. Ancient Near Eastern Spirituality: Zoroastrian, Sumerian, Assyro-Babylonian, Hittite
13. Jewish Spirituality: From the Bible to the Middle Ages
14. Jewish Spirituality: From the Sixteenth-Century Revival to the Present
15. Classical Mediterranean Spirituality: Egyptian, Greek, Roman
16. Christian Spirituality: Origins to the Twelfth Century
17. Christian Spirituality: High Middle Ages and Reformation
18. Post-Reformation and Modern
19. Islamic Spirituality: Foundations
20. Islamic Spirituality: Manifestations
21. Modern Esoteric Movements
22. Spirituality and the Secular Quest
23. Encounter of Spiritualities: Past to Present
24. Encounter of Spiritualities: Present to Future
25. Dictionary of World Spirituality

Volume 11A of
World Spirituality:
An Encyclopedic History
of the Religious Quest

CONFUCIAN SPIRITUALITY

VOLUME ONE

Edited by
Tu Weiming
and
Mary Evelyn Tucker

A Herder and Herder Book
The Crossroad Publishing Company
New York

The Crossroad Publishing Company
481 Eighth Avenue, Suite 1550, New York, NY 10001

Printed in the United States of America

Library of Congress Cataloging-in-Publication Data

Confucian spirituality / Edited by Tu Weiming and Mary Evelyn Tucker.
    p. cm.
  "A Herder and Herder Book."
  Includes bibliographical references and index.
  ISBN 0-8245-2111-0 (alk. paper)
  1. Confucianism. 2. Confucian ethics. 3. Philosophy, Confucian. I.
Tu, Wei-ming. II. Tucker, Mary Evelyn. III. Title.
BL1855.C66 2003
299'.512—dc21
                                          2003005752

1   2   3   4   5   6   7   8   9   10   06   05   04   03

Contents

PREFACE TO THE SERIES   xi

ACKNOWLEDGMENTS   xii

INTRODUCTION, *by Mary Evelyn Tucker*   1

Part One:
Synoptic Overview

1   Individualism and Holism in Chinese Tradition:
     The Religious Cultural Context
     Thomas Berry   39

2   The Ethical and the Meta-Ethical in Chinese
     High Cultural Thought
     Benjamin I. Schwartz   56

3   Between the Heavenly and the Human
     Ying-shih Yü   62

4   What Is Confucian Spirituality?
     Julia Ching   81

5   Affectivity in Classical Confucian Tradition
     Thomas Berry   96

6   Classical Chinese Views of Reality and Divinity
     Chung-ying Cheng   113

7   Virtues and Religious Virtues in the Confucian
     Tradition
         Lee H. Yearley   134

                         **Part Two:
         The Formation of the Confucian Tradition:
     Sagely Learning, Ritual Practice, Political Morality**

8   *Li* and the A-theistic Religiousness of Classical
     Confucianism
         Roger T. Ames   165

9   Is There a Universal Path of Spiritual Progress
     in the Texts of Early Confucianism?
         Henry Rosemont, Jr.   183

10   Ritual and Sacrifice in Early Confucianism:
     Contacts with the Spirit World
         Deborah Sommer   197

11   Death and Dying in the *Analects*
         Philip J. Ivanhoe   220

12   Practicality and Spirituality in the *Mencius*
         Irene Bloom   233

13   The Ethical and the Religious Dimensions of *Li*
         A. S. Cua   252

14   Xunzi's Piety
         Paul Rakita Goldin   287

15   The Way of the Unadorned King: The Classical
     Confucian Spirituality of Dong Zhongshu
         Sarah A. Queen   304

16   Determining the Position of Heaven and Earth:
       Debates over State Sacrifices in the
       Western Han Dynasty
         Michael Puett   318

GLOSSARY, *compiled by John Berthrong*   335

GENERAL BIBLIOGRAPHY, *compiled by John Berthrong*   339

CONTRIBUTORS   365

PHOTOGRAPHIC CREDITS   369

INDEX   371

Preface to the Series

THE PRESENT VOLUME is part of a series entitled World Spirituality: An Encyclopedic History of the Religious Quest, which seeks to present the spiritual wisdom of the human race in its historical unfolding. Although each of the volumes can be read on its own terms, taken together they provide a comprehensive picture of the spiritual strivings of the human community as a whole—from prehistoric times, through the great religions, to the meeting of traditions at the present.

Drawing upon the highest level of scholarship around the world, the series gathers together and presents in a single collection the richness of the spiritual heritage of the human race. It is designed to reflect the autonomy of each tradition in its historical development, but at the same time to present the entire story of the human spiritual quest. The first five volumes deal with the spiritualities of archaic peoples in Asia, Europe, Africa, Oceania, and North and South America. Most of these have ceased to exist as living traditions, although some perdure among tribal peoples throughout the world. However, the archaic level of spirituality survives within the later traditions as a foundational stratum, preserved in ritual and myth. Individual volumes or combinations of volumes are devoted to the major traditions: Hindu, Buddhist, Taoist, Confucian, Jewish, Christian, and Islamic. Included within the series are the Jain, Sikh, and Zoroastrian traditions in order to complete the story, the series includes traditions that have not survived but have exercised important influence on living traditions—such as Egyptian, Sumerian, classical Greek and Roman. A volume is devoted to modern esoteric movements and another to modern secular movements.

Having presented the history of the various traditions, the series devotes two volumes to the meeting of spiritualities. The first surveys the meeting of spiritualities from the past to the present, exploring common themes

A longer version of this preface may be found in Christian Spirituality: Origins to the Twelfth Century, *the first published volume in the series.*

that can provide the basis for a positive encounter, for example, symbols, rituals, techniques. The second deals with the meeting of spiritualities in the present and future. Finally, the series closes with a dictionary of world spirituality.

Each volume is edited by a specialist or a team of specialists who have gathered a number of contributors to write articles in their fields of specialization. As in this volume, the articles are not brief entries but substantial studies of an area of spirituality within a given tradition. An effort has been made to choose editors and contributors who have a cultural and religious grounding within the tradition studied and at the same time possess the scholarly objectivity to present the material to a larger forum of readers. For several years some five hundred scholars around the world have been working on the project.

In the planning of the project, no attempt was made to arrive at a common definition of spirituality that would be accepted by all in precisely the same way. The term "spirituality," or an equivalent, is not found in a number of the traditions. Yet from the outset, there was a consensus among the editors about what was in general intended by the term. It was left to each tradition to clarify its own understanding of this meaning and to the editors to express this in the introduction to their volumes. As a working hypothesis, the following description was used to launch the project:

> The series focuses on that inner dimension of the person called by certain traditions "the spirit." This spiritual core is the deepest center of the person. It is here that the person is open to the transcendent dimension; it is here that the person experiences ultimate reality. The series explores the discovery of this core, the dynamics of its development, and its journey to the ultimate goal. It deals with prayer, spiritual direction, the various maps of the spiritual journey, and the methods of advancement in the spiritual ascent.

By presenting the ancient spiritual wisdom in an academic perspective, the series can fulfill a number of needs. It can provide readers with a spiritual inventory of the richness of their own traditions, informing them at the same time of the richness of other traditions. It can give structure and order, meaning and direction to the vast amount of information with which we are often overwhelmed in the computer age. By drawing the material into the focus of world spirituality, it can provide a perspective for understanding one's place in the larger process. For it may well be that the meeting of spiritual paths—the assimilation not only of one's own spiritual heritage but of that of the human community as a whole—is the distinctive spiritual journey of our time.

EWERT COUSINS

Acknowledgments

T HE EDITORS would like to thank the East-West Cultural Centre in Singapore for making possible the initial Harvard conference in August 1997 from which these volumes on Confucian Spirituality arose. Laura Epperson of the Harvard-Yenching Institute was most gracious in helping to organize the conference at the Harvard Center for the Study of World Religions.

Gratitude is also due to Deborah Sommer for providing the pictures for these volumes, to John Berthrong for the glossary, to Man Lung Cheng and Li Ruohong for assistance with the photos, and to Ronald Suleski for myriad contributions.

Special thanks is extended to Ewert Cousins for his tireless efforts on behalf of the World Spirituality series.

This book is dedicated to our teachers, Wing-tsit Chan, Wm. Theodore de Bary, and Thomas Berry.

Introduction

MARY EVELYN TUCKER

THE ART OF CONFUCIAN SPIRITUALITY might be described as discovering one's cosmological being amidst daily affairs. For the Confucian the ordinary is the locus of the extraordinary; the secular is the sacred; the transcendent is in the immanent. What distinguishes Confucian spirituality among the world's religious traditions is an all-encompassing cosmological context that grounds its world-affirming orientation for humanity. This is not a tradition that seeks liberation outside the world, but rather one that affirms the spirituality of becoming more fully human within the world. The way of immanence is the Confucian way.[1]

The means of self-transformation is through cultivation of oneself in relation to others and to the natural world. This cultivation is seen in connection with a tradition of scholarly reflection embedded in a commitment to the value of culture and its myriad expressions. It aims to promote flourishing social relations, effective educational systems, sustainable agricultural patterns, and humane political governance within the context of the dynamic, life-giving processes of the universe.

One may hasten to add that, while subject to debate, aspects of transcendence are not entirely absent from this tradition, for example, in the idea of Heaven in classical Confucianism or the Supreme Ultimate in later Neo-Confucianism.[2] However, the emphasis of Confucian spirituality is on cultivating one's Heavenly-endowed nature in relation to other humans and to the universe itself. There is no impulse to escape the cycles of samsaric suffering as in Hinduism or Buddhism or to seek otherworldly salvation as in Judaism, Christianity, or Islam. Rather, the microcosm of the self and

1

the macrocosm of the universe are implicitly and explicitly seen as aspects of a unified but ever-changing reality.

The seamless web of immanence and transcendence in this tradition thus creates a unique form of spiritual praxis among the world's religions. There is no ontological split between the supernatural and the natural orders. Indeed, this may be identified as one of the distinctive contributions of Confucian spirituality, both historically and in its modern revived forms.

How to describe this form of spirituality is part of the challenge of these two volumes, which are intended to give the reader an overview of the remarkable array of Confucian spirituality from the classical period to the contemporary period. This is the first time such a comprehensive collective perspective has been offered to Western readers interested in exploring the varied dimensions of Confucian spirituality. We hope that by examining these distinctive forms of Confucian spirituality the very notion of spirituality in the larger human community will be broadened and enriched.

These essays are intended as an invitation for further research into the religious and spiritual dimensions of Confucianism. We trust that future research on East Asia, in both its premodern and modern phases, will include more extensive interdisciplinary collaborative reflection on the significant topic of the multiform spiritual dimensions of Confucianism.

What Is Confucian Spirituality?

Among the world's religious traditions Confucianism has the distinction of being the tradition that is least understood as having religious or spiritual aspects. Part of the complexity of the problem regarding the religious nature of Confucianism lies in sorting out a series of interlocking questions. Foremost among them is how one defines Confucianism—as a political system, as ethical teachings, as social norms, as a humanistic philosophy, or as a religious worldview.[3] We acknowledge all of these features as being part of Confucianism. However, we aim here to explore Confucianism not necessarily as a "religion" per se, but as a religious worldview with distinctive spiritual dimensions.

We are refraining from using the term "religion" to describe Confucianism, as "religion" tends to be associated with formal institutional structures and most often with characteristics of Western religions such as theism, personal salvation, and natural/supernatural dichotomies.[4] The term "religion" may thus obscure rather than clarify the distinctive religious and spiritual dimensions of Confucianism.[5] Therefore, instead of claiming Confucianism as a religion (which is problematic in itself for many people), we are suggesting that Confucianism manifests a religious worldview in its cosmological orientation.[6] This cosmological orientation is realized in the connection of the microcosm of the self to the macrocosm of the universe through spiritual practices of communitarian ethics, self-transformation, and ritual relatedness.

A religious worldview is that which gives humans a comprehensive and defining orientation to ultimate concerns.[7] Spirituality is that which provides expression for the deep yearnings of the human for relatedness to these ultimate concerns. While a religious worldview may be assumed as part of a given set of cultural ideals and practices into which one is born, spirituality is the vehicle of attainment of these ideals. The Confucian religious worldview is distinguished by its cosmological context, in which humans complete the triad of Heaven and Earth. Confucian spirituality requires discipline and practice along with spontaneity and creativity. Confucian spirituality establishes different ethical responsibilities for specific human relations, deepens subjectivity in its methods of self-cultivation, and celebrates communion of cosmic and human forces in its ritual connections. It aims to situate human creativity amidst concentric circles of interdependent creativity from the person to the larger universe.

One way to appreciate the distinctiveness of the Confucian religious worldview and its spiritual expressions is to observe broad characteristics of religions with a common geographical place of origin. In this spirit it is significant to note that the flowering of the world's religions that took place in the sixth century B.C.E. was labeled by Karl Jaspers as the Axial Age.[8] This period of flowering can be characterized as having three major centers of origin: those in West Asia—Judaism, Christianity, Islam; those in South Asia—Hinduism, Jainism, Buddhism; and those in East Asia—Confucianism and Daoism. The first can be described as prophetic and historically based religions; the second can be seen as mystical religions and religions of liberation; the third can be understood as religious worldviews of cosmic and social harmony.[9] It is precisely the interaction of the cosmic and social that underlies the spiritual dynamics of Confucianism.

The Dimensions of Confucian Spirituality

The cosmological orientation of Confucianism provides a holistic context for its spiritual dimensions, namely, communitarian ethics, modes of self-transformation, and ritual practices. The integrating impetus of these spiritual practices can be described as celebrating the generativity and creativity of the cosmos in the midst of changing daily affairs. These three forms of spirituality are interrelated, and they set in motion patterns of relational resonance between humans and the ever-expanding, interconnected circles of life.

The *cosmological orientation* of the Confucian religious worldview has been described as encompassing a continuity of being between all life forms without a radical break between the divine and human worlds.[10] Heaven, Earth, and humans are part of a continuous worldview that is organic, holistic, and dynamic. Tu Weiming has used the term "anthropocosmic" to describe this integral relatedness of humans to the cosmos.[11] The flow of life and energy is seen in *qi* (material force or vital energy), which unifies the plant, animal, and human worlds, and pervades all the elements of reality. The identification of the microcosm and the macrocosm in Confucian thought is a distinguishing feature of its cosmological orientation.[12]

Humans are connected to one another and to the larger cosmological order through an elaborate system of *communitarian ethics*. The five relations of society are marked, for example, by virtues of mutual exchange along with differentiated respect.[13] Reciprocity is a key to Confucian ethics and the means by which Confucian societies develop a communitarian basis so that they can become a bonded "fiduciary community."[14] Moreover, the cultivation of virtue in individuals is the basis for the interconnection of self, society, and the cosmos. As P. J. Ivanhoe observes, the activation of virtue evokes response: "This mutual dynamic of *de* 'virtue' or 'kindness' and *bao* 'response' was thought to be in the very nature of things; some early thinkers seemed to believe it operated with the regularity and force of gravity."[15]

In all of this, Confucian spirituality aims at moral *transformation* of the human so that individuals can realize their full personhood. Each person receives a Heavenly-endowed nature, and thus the potential for full authenticity or even sagehood is ever present. Nonetheless, to become a noble person (*junzi*) is an achievement of continual self-examination, rigorous discipline, and the cultivation of virtue. This process of spiritual self-transformation is a communal act.[16] It is not an individual spiritual path aimed at personal salvation. It is, rather, an ongoing process of rectification so as to cultivate one's "luminous virtue."[17] The act of inner cultivation implies reflecting on the constituents of daily experience and bringing that experience into accord with the insights of the sages. The ultimate goal of such self-cultivation is the realization of sagehood, namely, the attainment of one's cosmological being.[18]

Attainment of one's cosmological being means that humans must be attentive to one another, responsive to the needs of society, and attuned to the natural world through *rituals* that establish patterns of relatedness. In the Confucian context there were rituals performed at official state ceremonials as well as rituals at Confucian temples. However, the primary emphasis of ritual in the Confucian tradition was not liturgical ceremonies connected with places of worship (as in Western religions), but rituals involved in daily interchanges and rites of passage intended to smooth and elevate human relations. For the early Confucian thinker Xunzi, rituals are seen as vehicles for expressing the range and depth of human emotion in appropriate contexts and in an adequate manner.[19] Rituals thus become a means of affirming the emotional dimensions of human life. Moreover, they link humans to one another and to the other key dimensions of reality—the political order, nature's seasonal cycles, and the cosmos itself. Thus Confucian rituals are seen to be in consonance with the creativity of the cosmic order.

Confucian spirituality, then, might be seen as a means of integrating oneself into the larger patterns of life embedded in society and nature. P. J. Ivanhoe describes this effort succinctly when he observes that the Confucians believed "that a transformation of the self fulfilled a larger design, inherent in the universe itself, which the cultivated person could come to discern, and that a peaceful and flourishing society could only arise and be sustained by realizing this grand design. Cultivating the self in order to take one's place in this universal scheme describes the central task of life."[20]

The Appeal of Confucian Spirituality

Scholars in the field of religious studies may be able to make certain helpful clarifications toward elucidating the rich and varied nature of Confucian spirituality. While historians in the last fifty years have analyzed the development of Confucian texts, lineages, and institutions, and while social scientists have examined individual, family, and political patterns of Confucian-influenced behavior, only a few scholars have as yet explored the religious and philosophical dimensions of the Confucian tradition.[21] Further interpretations of the religious and philosophical nature of Confucianism may be important for understanding the endurance and appeal of Confucianism across East Asia, both traditionally and in the modern period.[22]

As David Keightley observes: "The strength and endurance of the Confucian tradition, ostensibly secular though its manifestations frequently were, cannot be fully explained, or its true nature understood, unless we take into account the religious commitment which assisted at that tradition's birth and which continued to sustain it."[23] Clearly, Confucian thought had an appeal to individuals and groups in East Asia for centuries beyond its political or ideological uses. Individual scholars and teachers engaged in the study and practice of Confucianism for intellectual inspiration, personal edification, spiritual growth, and ritual expression. We can see this in the spread of Confucianism to Korea, Japan, and Vietnam. This was especially evident in Japan, where there was no civil service examination system to advance personal careers. In the Tokugawa period (1603-1868), for example, many Japanese scholars and teachers studied Confucianism for its inherent value and assisted its spread in the society by establishing schools.[24]

Confucianism is more than the conventional stereotype of a model for creating social order and political stability sometimes used for oppressive or autocratic ends. While Confucianism aimed to establish stable and harmonious societies, it also encouraged personal and public reform, along with the reexamination of moral principles and spiritual practices appropriate to different contexts.[25] This is evident in Confucian moral and political theory, from the early classical concept of the rectification of names in the *Analects* to Mencius's qualified notion of the right to revolution. It is likewise seen in the later Neo-Confucian practice of delivering remonstrating lectures to the emperor and, when necessary, withdrawing one's services from an unresponsive or corrupt government.

On a personal level, the whole process of self-cultivation in Confucian spiritual practice was aimed at achieving authenticity and sincerity through conscientious study, critical self-examination, continual effort, and a willingness to change oneself.[26] "Learning for oneself," not simply absorbing ideas uncritically or trying to impress others, was considered essential to this process.[27] Thus, authenticity could only be realized by constant transformation so as to bring oneself into consonance with the creative and generative powers of Heaven and Earth.[28] These teachings sought to inculcate a process in tune with the dynamic, cosmological workings of nature. It thus affirmed change as a positive force in the natural order and in human affairs. This process of harmonizing with changes in the universe can be identified as a major wellspring of Confucian spirituality expressed in various forms of self-cultivation.

This focus on the positive aspects of change can be seen in each period of Confucianism as well as in its spread to other geographical contexts. Change in self, society, and cosmos was affirmed and celebrated from the early formative period, which produced the *Classic of Changes* (*Yijing*). Later Han Confucianism emphasized the vitality of correspondences between the human and the various elements in nature.[29] Eleventh- and twelfth-century Song Neo-Confucianism stressed the creativity of Heaven and Earth. Confucian spirituality in all its diverse expressions was seen in

East Asia as a powerful means of personal transformation. Furthermore, it was a potential instrument of establishing social harmony and political order through communitarian ethics and ritual practices. It emphasized moral transformation that rippled outward across concentric circles rather than the external imposition of legalistic and bureaucratic restraints. It was precisely this point that differentiated the Confucian aspirations and ideals from those of the Legalists, such as Han Fei Tzu, who felt humans could be restrained by law and changed by punishment.[30] It is a tradition that has endured for more than two and a half millennia in varied historical, geographical, and cultural contexts and is still undergoing transformation and revitalization in its contemporary forms.[31]

Overview of the Historical Development of the Confucian Tradition

The Confucian tradition has assumed distinctive expressions in China, Korea, Japan, Vietnam, Hong Kong, Taiwan, and Singapore. Viewing Confucianism as a singular tradition is problematic because of its geographic spread, its historical development, and its varied forms, ranging from Imperial State Confucianism to local and familial Confucianism. Nonetheless, this overview will try to make some distinctions in the various kinds of Confucianism in order to highlight its religious dimensions.[32]

While originating in the first millennium B.C.E. in China, the tradition includes the transmission and transformation of Confucianism that took place in different East Asian cultural and geographical contexts. In examining the reasons for its spread and its appeal, it is important to highlight the spiritual dynamics of the tradition and the ways in which it interacted with native traditions in China and across East Asia. Confucianism, for example, responded to and mingled with Daoism and Buddhism in China, with shamanism in Korea, and with Shinto in Japan.[33] Thus, although these two volumes explore the nature of Confucian spirituality, the borrowing and creative interaction among the various religious traditions in East Asia need to be underscored. Indeed, the so-called unity and syncretism of the three traditions of Confucianism, Daoism, and Buddhism in China should be noted. This was especially pronounced in the Ming (1368–1644) and Qing (1644–1911) periods.[34]

While recognizing this dynamic cross-fertilization of religious traditions in East Asia, we can also identify historically four major periods of Confucian thought and practice. The first stage in China is that of classical Confucianism, which ranges from approximately the sixth century B.C.E. to the second century before the common era. This is the period of the flourishing of the early Confucian thinkers, namely, Confucius and Mencius. The second period is that of Han Confucianism, when the classical tradition was shaped into a political orthodoxy under the Han empire (202 B.C.E.–220 C.E.) and began to spread to other parts of East Asia. This period saw the development of the theory of correspondences of the microcosm of the human world with the macrocosm of the natural world. The third major period is the Neo-Confucian era from the eleventh to the early twentieth century. This includes the comprehensive synthesis of Zhu Xi in the eleventh century and the distinctive contributions of Wang Yangming in the fifteenth and sixteenth centuries. The influence of Confucianism as an educational and philosophical system was felt throughout many parts East Asia during this period. The last phase is that of New Confucianism in the twentieth century, which represents a revival of the tradition under the influence of scholars who came to Taiwan and Hong Kong after Mao's ascendancy in 1949.[35] Four decades later, in October 1989, the International Confucian Society held two major conferences in Beijing and in Confucius's birthplace, Qufu, to explore the future of the Confucian Way. These conferences were intended to mark the 2540th anniversary of Confucius' birth and they both signified the interest of Confucian practitioners in looking toward the future.

The acknowledged founder of the Confucian tradition was known as the sage-teacher Kongzi (551–479 B.C.E.).[36] His name was Latinized by the Jesuit missionaries as Confucius. Born into a time of rapid social change, Confucius was concerned with the goal of reestablishing political and social order. He taught that this could be done through rectification of the individual and the state. This involved a program embracing both political and religious components. As a creative transmitter of earlier Chinese traditions, Confucius, according to legend, compiled the Appendices to the *Classic of Changes* and compiled the other Classics, namely, the *Classic of Documents, Poetry, Rites,* and the *Spring and Autumn Annals.*[37]

The principal sayings and teachings of Confucius are contained in his conversations recorded in the *Analects.* Here he emphasized the cultivation of moral virtues, especially humaneness (*ren*) and the practice of civility or ritual decorum (*li*), which entails the practice of filiality (*xiao*).[38] Virtue and civility were exemplified by the noble person (*junzi*) particularly within the five relations, namely, between ruler and minister, parent and child, husband and wife, older and younger siblings, and friend and friend. The essence of Confucian thinking was that to establish order in society one had to begin with individual cultivation and then create harmony, filiality, and decorum in the family. Like concentric circles, the effect of virtue would thus reach outward from the individual and family to society. Likewise, if the ruler was moral, it would have a "rippling out" effect to the whole country.

At the heart of this classical Confucian worldview was a profound commitment to humaneness and civility. These two virtues defined the means of human relatedness as a spiritual path. Through civility, beginning with filiality, one could repay the gifts of life to one's parents, to one's ancestors, and to the whole natural world. Through humaneness one could extend this sensibility to other humans and to all living things. In doing so one became more fully human. The root of practicing humaneness was considered to be filial relations. The extension of these relations from one's family and ancestors to the human family and to the cosmic family was the means whereby these primary biological ties provided a person with the roots, trunks, and branches of an interconnected spiritual path.

The personal and the cosmic were joined in the stream of filiality. From the lineages of ancestors to future progeny intergenerational connections and ethical bonding arose. Through one's parents and ancestors one became part of human life. Reverence and reciprocity were considered a natural response to this gift of life and a means of participating in its creativity. Great sacrifices were made for the family, and utmost loyalties were required in this spiritual path.[39] Analogously, through developing reverence for Heaven and Earth as the great parents of all life, one came to realize one's full cosmological being.

Confucian thought was further developed in the writings of Mencius (385?–312? B.C.E.) and Xunzi (310?–219? B.C.E.), who debated whether human nature was intrinsically good or evil and what were the consequences for the development of the human. Mencius's argument for the inherent goodness of human nature gained dominance among Confucian thinkers and gave an optimistic flavor to Confucian educational philosophy and political theory. This perspective influenced the spiritual aspects of the tradition as well because self-cultivation was seen as a natural means of uncovering this innate good nature. Mencius contributed an understanding of the process required for self-cultivation. He did this by identifying the four seeds of virtues he believed are innate in every human. He then suggested ways in which these seeds could be cultivated toward their full flowering as virtues. Analogies taken from the natural world (like the seeds and the stories of the man from Song and Ox mountain[40]) extended the idea of self-cultivation of the individual for the sake of family and society to a wider frame of reference that also encompassed the natural environment. This can be described as a path of botanical cultivation, where images of nurturing, tending, weeding, gathering, and harvesting are used to illustrate how spiritual practices of self-cultivation are analogous to agricultural rhythms.[41]

Xunzi, on the other hand, contributed a strong sense of the importance of ritual practice as a means of self-cultivation. He noted that human desires need to be satisfied and emotions such as joy and sorrow need to be expressed in the appropriate degree. Rituals provide the form for such expression in daily human exchange as well as in rites of passage such as marriage and death. Moreover, because Xunzi saw human nature as innately flawed, he emphasized the need for education to shape human nature toward the good. Finally, he had a highly developed sense of the interdependent triad of Heaven, Earth, and humanity, which was emphasized also by many later Confucian thinkers. He writes: "Heaven has its seasons; Earth has its riches; humans have their government."[42]

Confucianism blossomed in a Neo-Confucian revival in the eleventh and twelfth centuries, which resulted in a new synthesis of the earlier teachings. The major Neo-Confucian thinker, Zhu Xi (1130–1200), designated four texts from the canon of historical writings as containing the central ideas of Confucian thought. These were two chapters from the *Classic of Rites*, namely, the *Great Learning* and the *Mean*, as well as the *Analects* and the *Mencius*. He elevated these Four Books to a position of prime importance over the Five Classics mentioned earlier. These texts and Zhu Xi's commentaries on them became, in 1315, the basis of the Chinese civil service examination system, which endured for nearly six hundred years until 1905. Every prospective government official had to take the civil service exams based on Zhu Xi's commentaries on the Four Books. The idea was to provide educated, moral officials for the large government bureaucracy which ruled China. The influence, then, of Neo-Confucian thought on government, education, and social values was extensive.

Zhu Xi's synthesis of Neo-Confucianism was recorded in his classic anthology, *Reflections on Things at Hand* (*Jinsilu*), which he co-edited with Lu Zuxian (1137–1181).[43] In this work he provided, for the first time, a comprehensive metaphysical basis for Confucian thought and practice. In response to the Buddhists' metaphysics of emptiness and their perceived tendency toward withdrawal from the world in meditative practices, Zhu formulated a this-worldly spirituality based on a balance of cosmological orientation, ethical and ritual practices, scholarly reflection, and political participation. The aim was to balance inner cultivation with outward investigation of things. Zhu used the *Explanation of the Diagram of the Supreme Polarity* (*Taijitu shuo*) as a cosmological framework to orient spiritual practice and self-cultivation.[44]

Unlike the Buddhists, who saw the world of change as the source of suffering, Zhu Xi, and the Neo-Confucians after him, affirmed change as the source of transformation in both the cosmos and the person. Thus Neo-Confucian spiritual discipline involved cultivating one's moral nature so as to bring it into harmony with the larger pattern of change in the cosmos. Each moral virtue had its cosmological component.[45] For example, the central virtue of humaneness was seen as the source of fecundity and growth in both the individual and the cosmos. By practicing humaneness, one could effect the transformation of things in oneself, in society, and in the cosmos. In so doing, one's deeper identity with reality was recognized as forming one body with all things, thus actualizing one's cosmological being. As the *Mean* stated it: "being able to assist in the transforming and nourishing powers of Heaven and Earth, one can form a triad with Heaven and Earth."[46] All of this for Zhu was part of a dynamic process of the mutual interaction of the *qi* of the person interacting with the *qi* of the cosmos. As Zhu put it: "Once a person's mind has moved, it must reach the *qi* [of Heaven and Earth] and mutually stimulate and interact with this [*qi*] that contracts and expands, goes and comes."[47]

To realize one's cosmological being, a rigorous spiritual practice was needed. This involved a development of poles present in earlier Confucian thought, namely, a balancing of religious reverence within and ritual propriety manifested in daily life. For Zhu Xi and later Neo-Confucians such spiritual practices were a central concern. Interior meditation became known as "quiet-sitting," "abiding in reverence," or "rectifying the mind." Moral self-discipline was known as "making the will sincere," "controlling the desires," and "investigating principle."[48] All of this was expressed in a broad understanding of spiritual cultivation known as the "learning of the mind-and-heart" which became a primary instrument of the transmission of Confucianism throughout East Asia.[49]

Through conscientious spiritual effort and study one could become a noble person (*junzi*) or even a sage (*sheng*) who was able to participate in society and politics most effectively. While in the earlier Confucian view the emphasis was on the ruler as the prime moral leader of society, in Neo-Confucian thought this duty was extended to all people, with a particular responsibility placed on teachers and government officials. While ritual was primary in earlier Confucianism, spiritual discipline became even more significant in Neo-Confucian practice. In both the early and later tradition, major emphasis was placed on mutual respect and reciprocity in basic human relations. Zhu Xi helped to identify the dimensions of family rituals that were essential for the flourishing of the Confucian family.[50]

Confucian thought and practice spread to Vietnam, Korea, and Japan, where it had a profound effect on their respective cultures. Confucianism was transmitted to Korea as early as the Three Kingdoms period (57 B.C.E.–935 C.E.) where its political and educational ideas were utilized, especially as a philosophy to encourage unification of the disparate political groups on the peninsula. A Royal Academy based on Confucian texts was established in 651, and government civil service examinations were instituted in 788. While Buddhism was a major influence during the Koryo dynasty (918–1392), at the same time a strong central government with a civil bureaucracy emerged based on Confucian principles. With the founding of the Yi dynasty (1392–1910), Neo-Confucian ideas reached a new peak of influence in politics, society, and education.[51] A nationwide system of public schools was established and local associations were set up to propagate Confucian ethics. Moreover, there were widespread intellectual debates on Neo-Confucian philosophy, especially regarding the nature of principle (*li*) and material force (*qi*). This debate was the focus of the two leading Neo-Confucian thinkers, Yi T'oegye (1501–1570) and Yi Yulgok (1536–1584).[52]

Confucianism gained official recognition in Japan at the end of the third century, when a Korean official brought the *Analects* to the emperor Oji. With the adoption of Prince Shotoku's constitution in 604 and with the Taika Reforms of 645 and 646, Confucianism became a useful political philosophy to overcome the clan-based politics of the earlier period. During the Kamakura (1185–1336) and Muromachi (1336–1598) periods, Confucianism was closely tied to the Zen monasteries, where it was carefully studied by the Zen monks, who were attracted by its sophisticated forms of Chinese learning. During the Tokugawa era (1603–1868) Confucianism flourished primarily in the world of scholarship and education, in addition to its political uses.[53] One of the leading thinkers of this period was Kaibara Ekken (1630–1714), who passed on the learning of the mind-and-heart through texts written for wide distribution.[54] Ekken also continued the debate regarding the nature of the relationship of *li* and *qi* as a means of both grounding spiritual self-cultivation and investigating the natural world.

In the modern period, Confucianism continues to have a major influence in many aspects of East Asian society, including the importance given to education and to social mores. Despite the effects of modernization on traditional ways, Confucianism persists as a cultural DNA passed on in the family. Its influence extends to political attitudes, to how businesses operate, and even to broad-based economic policies. Indeed, earlier studies have suggested that the success of the Japanese in modernizing after the Meiji Restoration of 1868 and in achieving rapid economic development after

World War II, may have been due in part to the Confucian values, which emphasized particular social obligations and duties and helped shape the educational system. Similar arguments have been made for the economic achievements of the other "four mini dragons," which have also been influenced by Confucianism, namely, South Korea, Taiwan, Hong Kong, and Singapore. Some of this thinking is being revised in light of the economic crises in the region in the 1990s.

After 1949 the government of the People's Republic of China repudiated Confucianism, especially during the Cultural Revolution of the 1960s and 1970s. However, the Confucian tradition is currently being reexamined in China, often relying on publications of European and American scholars. Several conferences have been held in recent years in China on the thought of Confucius, Zhu Xi, and Wang Yangming and an official Confucian association has been formed. The direction and outcome of this revival of interest in Confucianism remain to be seen. This is in large part because of the contested nature of the tradition in China and because of the disruptive impact of westernization and modernization in the region over the last century.

Reinterpreting Confucianism: From Repudiation to Reevaluation

Even before the Maoist era, the nature and uses of Confucianism were subject to significant debate, especially in the nineteenth and twentieth centuries in both East Asia and the West. For Chinese intellectuals struggling with the burden of tradition in relation to Western imperialism in the nineteenth century and modernization in the twentieth century, the legacy of Confucianism has been seriously reevaluated. From the late-nineteenth-century reforms to the May Fourth movement of 1919, from the New Culture movement of the 1920s to the New Confucianism of the post-Mao era, the reinterpretation of the Confucian legacy has been a paramount concern for Chinese intellectuals as well as for Western scholars of China.[55]

In this struggle between traditional and modern values in East Asia, the question arises as to whether Confucianism should be regarded as simply a hierarchical, "feudal" system to be set aside in favor of Western individualistic values, scientific methods, democratic principles, and free market capitalism. Many feel that the two approaches to social organization and economic exchange are mutually incompatible. Some of the leading lines of argument are whether Confucianism should be seen primarily as a political ideology often fostering authoritarianism or whether it can accurately be viewed as a humanistic ethical system capable of supporting individual

autonomy and democratic processes.[56] This is often linked to the debate as
to whether Confucianism has, in fact, contributed positively or negatively
to economic growth and modernization in East Asia.[57] Furthermore, there
has been reflection on whether a distinctive form of modern Confucianism
may still be emerging in East Asia.[58] Of particular interest for these two
volumes is the fact that the religious and spiritual dimensions of Confucianism are being rediscovered in East Asia and in the west at the same time
as contemporary scholars are reexamining the varied political, economic,
and social roles of Confucianism.[59]

There are many related questions regarding Confucianism that have
been raised by these scholars and deserve further examination. These
include: What are the problematic aspects of Confucianism which may
have hindered individualism or dissent from authoritarian structures?
What can be learned from the failures of Confucianism, especially in the
challenges to building infrastructures to support civil society?[60] How can
we evaluate the human cost of modernization for many individuals and
groups in East Asia? What can be said about the clash of traditional and
modern values in East Asia in the face of growing environmental degrada-
tion that industrial processes have helped to create? What accounts for the
different rates of economic development in East Asian countries? Has Confucianism helped or hindered this process, or both assisted and obstructed
this process? Are there positive features of Confucianism that have encouraged education and the development of human resources in contemporary
East Asia? Are human rights recognized within Confucian cultures?[61]
What role has Confucianism played in fostering "Asian values"? Can Confucianism contribute to a broader understanding of environmental ethics?[62]

These topics are clearly vast, singularly important, and frequently inter-
locked. In acknowledging the complexity of the arguments involved and
the growing literature on these subjects, it would appear that various multi-
disciplinary efforts will be required to sift through the data, the texts, and
the historical record before any satisfactory solutions to some of these
questions might emerge. In addition, a more complex understanding of the
production and uses of ideology will be needed, as well as greater attention
to texts, contexts, and intertextuality.[63] Both in China and in the West,
twentieth-century intellectuals have been preoccupied with understanding
the nature of ideology as an oppressive force as a result of the rise of totali-
tarianism and fascism that led to the world wars and imperialist conquest.
In this reading, religion has often been relegated to the category of ideology, and thus the appreciation for religion and for spirituality as potentially liberating forces has been eclipsed.[64]

Furthermore, an understanding of the religious dimensions of Confucianism has been obscured by the absence of or ambivalence regarding the term "religion" in East Asia and by a circumscribed view in the West of the nature and function of religion in other cultures. It is important to note that there was no term for "religion" in the Chinese language before it was introduced by the Japanese in the late nineteenth century through translations of European works. This was picked up by one of the leading reformers of late nineteenth century China, Kang Youwei (1858–1927). Kang used the term *kong jiao/k'ung chiao* (meaning the teaching or lineage of Confucius) to indicate Confucianism as a religion.[65] The term that came to be used for religion in general was *zong jiao/tsung chiao*. Similarly, there was no term for philosophy until *zhexue/che hsueh* was adopted under Western influence in the late nineteenth century. Instead, it was customary simply to use *jiao/chiao* (meaning teaching or philosophical school) to represent broad philosophical or religious lineages such as Confucianism, Daoism, and Buddhism. Moreover, there was no fundamental distinction in Chinese thought between religion and philosophy. In addition, the three dominant traditions in China interacted in complex ways, often resulting in creative syncretism or in claims that the three traditions were one. The exclusive separation of religious traditions, such as we see in the West, was not operative in the same way in East Asia. Within the Neo-Confucian tradition, particular lineages or schools of thought become distinguished, such as the School of Principle (*li-xue*), associated with Zhu Xi, and the School of Mind (*hsin-xue*), associated with Wang Yangming.[66]

Confucianism in this context has thus been viewed by Westerners as either simply a humanistic ethical system or as a religious cult connected to state rituals. For widely divergent reasons, seventeenth-century European Christian missionaries, eighteenth-century French *philosophes,* and nineteenth-century translators such as James Legge[67] interpreted Confucianism as a rationalistic and ethical system without an idea of a personal God and without institutional structures such as were evident in Christianity.[68] Confucius was seen as agnostic, and Confucianism was not viewed as particularly religious. Herrlee Creel noted, however, that the view of Confucius as agnostic was most likely a result of the influence of post-Enlightenment valuing of rationalism by Western scholars which was also appropriated by Chinese intellectuals.[69] Consequently, Confucianism was understood to be a humanistic, rational, bureaucratic, political system, perpetuated by civil service examinations[70] and linked to a state cult. Elements of the tradition that might be viewed as spiritually enriching and personally transformative were overlooked or ignored.

In the twentieth century, Chinese intellectuals such as Hu Shi (1891–1962) tried to distinguish nonreligious from religious Confucianism so as to identify the dimensions of Confucianism that might be capable of contributing to the modernization of China. Hu saw the religious aspects of Confucianism, which he associated with the state cult, as being backward and feudalistic. He especially condemned the attempted revival of religious Confucianism by President Yuan Shikai after the reestablishment of the Republic in 1912. On the other hand, the sociologist of religion C. K. Yang accepted the dichotomy of two distinct systems of belief and practice and described the coexistence of Confucian thought with Chinese religion. He categorized the former as rational and ethical and the latter as supernaturally oriented and popularly based. He suggested that a dominant–subordinate working relationship existed between these two areas.[71] For twentieth-century Chinese, the legacy of Confucianism was clearly mixed, and its role as a religious tradition was far from clear in its function or efficacy.

This is especially true because of the destructive impact of Western imperialism in nineteenth-century China and the seductive power of modernization and westernization in twentieth-century China. The preoccupation of many nineteenth-century reformers throughout East Asia was whether one could effectively combine "Eastern morality," especially Confucian thought, as substance (*ti*) with Western technology as function (*yong*). The elaborate and at times anguished debates on this subject reflect an important new stage of the Confucian legacy in China, Korea, and Japan. Over the last one hundred years Confucianism has been seen by some interpreters, both in East Asia and in the West, as an ideology used to enforce class hierarchy, subservience, and conformity. Indeed, Confucianism has sometimes been identified with an *ancien régime* style of political order or solely with conservative modes of thinking. As a support for a repressive feudal past, it has been regarded by some as unenlightened at best and autocratic at worst. In short, for many individuals in East Asia and in the West, it appeared that modernity would proceed most effectively after the abandonment of Confucian-dominated thinking and the adaptation of Western scientific, political, and social values.[72]

This was particularly true of the New Culture movement leaders in the early part of the twentieth century. The movement was inspired by the writings of Chen Duxiu (1879–1942) and Hu Shi (1891–1962) and was joined by those embracing the slogan "Destroy the old curiosity shop of Confucianism." Its adherents championed science and democracy along with pragmatism and individualism. Yet this was also mingled with a swing toward disillusionment with the West, especially after World War I. This was especially true with the materialism and decadence of European society in evidence. Skepticism toward aspects of both Western and Confucian thought has been part of the complex legacy of Chinese intellectuals.

In the second half of the twentieth century a reevaluation of the role and relevance of Confucianism has been a major preoccupation of several philosophers in China as well as among the New Confucians in Hong Kong and Taiwan and the West.[73] Xiong Shili (1895–1968) is considered to be a primary inspiration of the New Confucian movement. Drawing on the *Classic of Changes* and the notion of the continuing creativity of the universe, he emphasized the virtue of humaneness, which forms one body with all things. Another important philosopher who remained in China during the Maoist regime was Liang Shuming (1893–1988). He published a comparative study of Chinese and Western civilization that celebrated Confucian moral values rather than the indiscriminate adoption of Western values and institutions. Both Xiong and Liang survived the attacks on Confucianism under Mao and persisted in writing on the philosophical and religious dimensions of Neo-Confucian thought.[74]

They were joined in this effort by the New Confucian philosophers who had escaped to Hong Kong and Taiwan after Mao's ascendancy. These included Zhang Junmai, Tang Junyi, Xu Fuguan, and Mou Zongsan. The publication of their "Manifesto for a Reappraisal of Sinology and the Reconstruction of Chinese Culture" in 1958 was a watershed moment for the revival of Confucianism in the modern period.[75] Some New Confucians also called for a more comprehensive understanding of the religious dimensions of Confucianism. This is true, for example, of Mou Zongsan, who affirmed Confucianism as one of the world's great religions. [76]

Categories for the Study of Confucianism

It may be helpful to distinguish various kinds of Confucianism so as to reframe the questions surrounding the emergence and manipulation of political ideologies and separate them from the spiritual dimensions of Confucianism. At the same time, we can acknowledge the ambiguous nature of many religions or philosophies in their frequent appropriation for manipulative or distorted ends.

Gilbert Rozman has proposed several types of Confucianism in his analysis of the "Confucian heritage and its modern adaptation" in East Asia.[77] He suggests a hierarchical categorization following the stratification of East Asian societies, which may include some overlap. At the top is *imperial Confucianism,* involving ideology and ritual surrounding the emperor. While this has often been seen as authoritarian, *reform Confucian-*

ism has been regarded as invoking principles of renewal or dissent to bene-fit society. This may intersect at times with *elite Confucianism,* which reflects the interests and concerns of the educated scholar-official class. Next is *merchant-house Confucianism,* which includes business groups in both the premodern and modern periods. Finally, there is *mass Confucian-ism* which embraces the vast numbers of peasants and ordinary citizens in East Asian societies.

Another classification of types of Confucianism has been made by Kim Kyong-Dong.[78] He speaks of the *religious aspects* in reference to ideas of Heaven and rituals of ancestor worship or veneration of the sages. Next he cites Confucianism as a *philosophical system* that includes cosmology and metaphysics, theories of human nature, ways of knowing, and ethics. Con-fucianism, he notes, also embraces *visions of governance* based on political theories and *social norms* guiding human relations. Finally, Confucianism can be seen as a system of *personal cultivation* aimed at achieving inner equanimity and thus extending harmony to the world.

While Rozman's categories are quite apposite, they are limited by the perspective of social classification and may be appropriated by those who see Confucianism only as a political ideology. Similarly, Kim's categories are fitting but curiously separate the religious and philosophical aspects from social norms and personal cultivation. In evaluating the complex role of Confucianism as a religious worldview from a more comprehensive per-spective than social classifications or ideology, we will first identify four broad categories of Confucianism as having had a significant impact on East Asian history and society. Then we will discuss the religious world-view of Confucian cosmology and its expression in three distinctive forms of spirituality previously described, namely, *communitarian ethics, modes of self-transformation,* and *ritual practices.*

It should be clear that these broad categories of Confucian spirituality are intended to be suggestive and illustrative, not exhaustive or rigid classi-fications. Other dimensions may be identified in the future as more schol-ars become engaged in the study of Confucian spirituality. One should thus allow for the inevitable and often fruitful overlapping in the categories that are proposed here. Despite their limitations, the usefulness of these categories is in describing distinctive strands of Confucian spirituality which coexist and are used in different periods for distinctive ends.

Let us turn first to identify some broad descriptive categories of Confu-cian spirituality that are distinct from, yet overlap with, religious Confu-cianism:

1. *Political Confucianism* refers to state or imperial Confucianism, espe-cially in its Chinese form, and involves such institutions as the civil service

examination system and the larger government bureaucracy from the local level to the various ranks of court ministers. In Korea, Confucian bureaucratic government was adapted in the Koryo dynasty, and in 958 the civil service examination system was adopted as a means of selecting officials. Confucianism was further established as official orthodoxy under the Yi dynasty in 1392, and civil service examinations were inaugurated. In Japan there were no civil service examinations, but Confucian ideas were used in the Nara government and in Prince Shotoku's "constitution" of 719, as well as in legitimizing the Tokugawa Shogunate and later in the Meiji government's "Imperial Rescript on Education."

2. *Social Confucianism* alludes to what one might call family-based or human relations–oriented Confucianism. This involves the complex interactions of individuals with others both within and outside of the family. It has been described by Thomas Berry as a cultural coding and by Tu Weiming as a cultural DNA, or "habits of the heart" passed on from one generation to the next through the family. These interactions both reflect and create the intricate patterns of obligations and responsibilities that permeate East Asian society. In Japan, for example, these patterns are expressed in concepts such as *on* and *giri* (mutual obligations and debts requiring repayment).

3. *Educational Confucianism* encompasses public and private learning in schools, in families, and by individual scholars and teachers. It refers, although not exclusively, to the curriculum of study of the Four Books— the *Great Learning,* the *Mean,* the *Analects,* and the *Mencius*—selected as the canon by Zhu Xi. This was used as the basis of the civil service examination system in China and Korea. Educational Confucianism incorporates the adaptation of that curriculum to other educational institutions and venues in East Asia. In Japan and Korea, for example, it includes the various schools set up both privately and by national and provincial governments, especially in Yi-dynasty Korea and Tokugawa Japan. In addition, it refers to some of the moral training that continued to be part of the educational system in Korea and Japan in the twentieth century.[79] Educational Confucianism can be said to go beyond schools, institutions, and curriculum to include at its heart the notion of learning as a means of self-cultivation, an approach that is emphasized in the *Analects* and *Mencius.*[80]

4. *Economic Confucianism* describes business company forms of Confucianism in the modern period and merchant-related Confucianism in the premodern period, especially in Qing China, Yi Korea, and Tokugawa Japan.[81] It includes the idea of familialism and loyalty as critical principles for the transmission of family-based Confucian values into organizational

structures within the business community. This seems to be particularly widespread in East Asia, especially in the last fifty years.[82] It also includes the transmission across society of values often associated with Confucianism such as frugality, loyalty, and industriousness.

Religious Confucianism and Its Forms of Spirituality

As described earlier, a Confucian religious worldview is distinguished by its cosmological orientation. This is realized through the three dimensions of Confucian spirituality, namely, communitarian ethics, modes of self-transformation, and ritual practices.[83] The essays in these volumes represent a rich cross section of discussion concerning these interrelated topics.

The *cosmological orientation* of the Confucian religious worldview involves the recognition that humans are embedded in and dependent on the larger dynamics of nature. The fecundity of cosmic processes is not simply a static background but a fundamental context in which human life flourishes and finds its richest expression. To harmonize with the creativity and changes in the universe is the task of the human in forming one body with all things. This is the anthropocosmic vision that Tu Weiming has articulated:

> Human beings are . . . an integral part of the "chain of being," encompassing Heaven, Earth, and the myriad things. However, the uniqueness of being human is the intrinsic capacity of the mind to "embody" (*ti*) the cosmos in its conscience and consciousness. Through this embodying, the mind realizes its own sensitivity, manifests true humanity and assists in the cosmic transformation of Heaven and Earth.[84]

To activate these dimensions of one's cosmological being spiritual practice is necessary through ethics, cultivation, and ritual.

The *ethical dimensions* emphasize the communitarian nature of Confucian moral philosophy. The individual is always seen in relation to others, not as an isolated, atomistic individual. The embeddedness of a person in a web of relationships involves mutual obligations and responsibilities rather than individual rights. A series of relationships expressed as correspondences is thus established between the person, the family, the larger society, and the cosmos itself. Humans are considered to be in relational resonance with other humans as well as with animals and plants, the elements and the seasons, colors and directions. Communitarian ethics thus involves an elaborate patterning that binds together the society and the cosmos. There is a rich moral continuity between persons and the universe at large.

The *self-transformational dimensions* of Confucian spirituality entail various modes of personal cultivation. These include a variety of practices ranging from the aesthetic arts of music, poetry, painting, and calligraphy to spiritual disciplines such as quiet sitting, abiding in reverence, and being mindful when alone. One is encouraged to observe one's inner state of tranquillity before the emotions arise (centrality) and to achieve the appropriate balance in expressing emotions (harmony).[85] One cultivates the inner life so as to return to the original mind-and-heart of a child, thus expressing the deepest spontaneities and clearest responses of the human to others and to the larger cosmos. Tu Weiming has described such cultivation as "self-transformation as a communal act."[86] One of the main concerns of religious Confucianism is with moral and spiritual cultivation for the benefit of self, society, and the cosmos. This process of learning, reflection, and spiritual discipline is based on the understanding that to be fully human one aims to be a noble person (*junzi*) who is in harmony with the creative powers of Heaven and Earth and in accord with the larger human community. The goal of becoming a sage is an overarching goal of Confucian self-cultivation,[87] but always with the larger purpose of being of service to society and participating in the cosmological processes of the universe. Thus Confucian spirituality encompasses forms of practice that are attentive to the intersection of nature, of community, and of the self.

The *ritual dimensions* of Confucian spirituality involve the ties that link these intersections. Thus individuals and groups are joined together for a larger sense of social harmony, political coherence, and cosmological relationship. In China, state rituals at the altars of Heaven and Earth were a central component of this category, as were rituals at Confucian temples and in educational institutions. In addition to these forms of public display, private rituals were carried out at ancestral altars as well as within families and even between individuals. These included rituals for rites of passage such as birth, marriage, death, and mourning. From the more public state ceremonies to the more private family interactions, these ritual structures became a means of reflecting the patterns of the cosmos, linking to the world of the ancestors and binding individuals to one another.[88]

Spiritual Dimensions of Confucianism

It is appropriate to turn now to a fuller discussion of the religious worldview of Confucian cosmology as a way of appreciating its distinctive spiritual dynamics. This discussion is important for three reasons. First, it may help to shed some light on the varied roles and appeal of Confucianism in East Asia. Second, it is a valuable area of research because Confucianism is so little studied or understood within the discipline of the history of religions or comparative religions. Third, by elucidating the spiritual dimensions of Confucianism we may be able to broaden our understanding of the nature of spirituality in the human community at large.

Confucianism does not fit into the conventional definitions of religion, which have arisen from within the framework of the Western theistic traditions. As has been noted by various scholars, the absence of a personal Creator God in Confucianism and the lack of a strong distinction between the transcendent and immanent realms are just two examples of how Confucianism differs from western religions. Consequently, for many people Confucianism would not be characterized as a religion.[89] However, if we broaden our understanding of religion and place Confucianism in a comparative context, we will see more clearly the interaction of the Confucian religious worldview as a comprehensive cosmological orientation with particular dimensions of spiritual practice.

A fruitful way to illustrate this understanding of Confucianism is through Clifford Geertz's concept of "Religion as a Cultural System."[90] Geertz speaks of religion as consisting of a people's worldview and ethos, which become mutually reinforcing entities. The mediating relationship between cosmology and ethics is seen as crucial to an understanding of religion in different cultural contexts. As a cultural anthropologist, Geertz straddles the views of those concerned with analyzing religious experience (e.g., Rudolf Otto) and those more focused on a sociological analysis (e.g., Emile Durkheim). He acknowledges his debt to Max Weber, who was interested in studying not just social interactions but their underlying significance and cultural import as well. Likewise, he cites Wilfred Cantwell Smith as an influence in his formulation of religion as both faith and cumulative tradition, thus linking it to persons and culture.[91] These three areas of concern, namely, meaning, persons, and culture, are keys to Geertz's view of the role of religion.

Geertz observes that religion as a symbolic system cannot exist apart from a cultural context. Symbols, he suggests, mutually shape and are shaped by worldviews and ethos. When these two dimensions reinforce each other, there is a sense of coherence and order in a society. When they no longer function as patterns of meaning, a crisis of belief and practice occurs. Geertz points out that this is one way in which modern societies are in conflict with traditional beliefs and practices. In such circumstances, long-standing religious symbols appear to be unable to validate human action or substantiate a cosmology.

Geertz summarizes his concept of people's worldview and ethos, their cosmology and their spiritual practices, as mutually confirming entities expressed in symbols and ritual, in the following statement:

> As we are to deal with meaning, let us begin with a paradigm: viz., that sacred symbols function to synthesize a people's ethos—the tone, character and quality of their life, its moral and aesthetic style and mood—and their world-view—the picture they have of the way things in sheer actuality are, their most comprehensive ideas of order. In religious belief and practice a group's ethos is rendered intellectually reasonable by being shown to represent a way of life ideally adapted to the actual state of affairs the world-view describes, while the world-view is rendered emotionally convincing by being presented as an image of an actual state of affairs peculiarly well arranged to accommodate such a way of life.[92]

The religious worldview of Confucianism is evident in its dynamic cosmology interwoven with dimensions of spirituality, namely, communitarian harmony of society, moral cultivation of the individual, and public and private ritual expressions. This linking of self, society, and cosmos was effected through elaborate theories of correspondences.[93] Geertz's conceptual framework of worldview and ethos helps to elucidate further the interaction of Confucian cosmology and Confucian spirituality.

Worldview and Ethos:
Organic Cosmology and Communitarian Ethics

The Confucian religious worldview, while by no means singular or uniform, is one that can be described as having an organismic cosmology[94] characterized as a "continuity of being"[95] within an "immanental cosmos."[96] There is no clear separation, as in the Western religions, between a transcendent, otherworldly order and an immanent, this-worldly orientation. As the *Mean* (*Zhongyong*) states: "The Way of Heaven and Earth can be described in one sentence: They are without any doubleness and so they produce things in an unfathomable way. The Way of Heaven and Earth is extensive, deep, high, brilliant, infinite, and lasting."[97]

Without an ontological gap between this world and an other world there emerges an appreciation for the seamless interaction of humans with the universe. The Confucian cosmological worldview is one that embraces a fluid and dynamic continuity of being. In terms of ethos or ethics this involves working out the deep interconnections of Heaven, Earth, and humans. This profound symbolic expression of the triadic intercommunion of an immanental cosmos is invoked repeatedly in both the Confucian and Neo-Confucian texts cited across East Asia.[98] As Tu Weiming notes, this cosmology is neither theocentric nor anthropocentric, but rather anthropocosmic.[99] In this sense the emphasis is not exclusively on the divine or on humans, as is the prevailing model in the west. Rather, the comprehensive interaction of Heaven, Earth, and humans is what is underscored by the term anthropocosmic. Thus the worldview of an organic cosmology creates a context for the intricate communitarian model of social ethics that distinguishes East Asian societies.

The mutual attraction of things for one another in both the human and natural worlds gives rise to an embedded ethical system of reciprocal relationships. The instinctive qualities of the human heart toward commiseration and empathy is what is nurtured and expressed in human relations and ritual practices (*Mencius* 2A:6). The human is not an isolated individual in need of redemption by a personal God, but is deeply embedded in a network of life-giving and life-sustaining relationships and rituals. Within this organic universe the human is viewed as a microcosm of the macrocosm where one's actions affect the larger whole, like ripples in a pond, as expressed in the *Great Learning*. Thus, there is a relational resonance of personal and cosmic communion animated by authenticity (*cheng*), as illustrated in the *Mean*.[100] The individual is intrinsically linked via rituals to various communities, beginning with the natural bonding of the family and stretching out to include the social-political order and to embrace the symbolic community of Heaven and Earth.[101] Humans achieve their fullest identity as members of the great triad with Heaven and Earth. Within this triad Heaven is a guiding moral presence, Earth is a vital moral force, and humans are co-creators of a humane and moral social-political order.

Cosmology and Cultivation: Creativity of Heaven and Transformation of Humans

The Confucian organic cosmological order is distinguished by the creativity of Heaven as a life-giving force that is ceaselessly self-generating.[102] Similar to Whiteadian process thought, the Confucian universe is seen as an unfolding, creative process, not as a static, inert mechanistic system controlled by an absent or remote deity.[103] As a protecting, sustaining, and transforming force, Heaven helps to bring all to their natural fulfillment as cosmological. This is because humans are imprinted with a Heavenly-endowed nature that enables them to transform themselves through self-cultivation.[104]

The ethos, then, of this creative cosmology is one that encourages education, learning, and self-transformation. The optimistic view of humans as receiving a Heavenly nature results in a Confucian educational and family

ethos that ideally create a value system for nurturing innate human goodness and the creative transformation of individual potential. This ethos is
one that encourages a filial sense of repayment to Heaven for the gift of life
and for a Heavenly-bestowed nature. The way to repay these gifts is
through ongoing moral cultivation for the betterment of self and society.
The symbol or model that joins this aspect of the worldview and ethos
together is the noble person (*junzi*), or the sage (*sheng*), who "hears" the
will of Heaven and is able to embody it naturally in the ongoing process of
learning and self-cultivation. The sage is thus the highest embodiment of
the spiritual aspirations of the Confucian tradition.[105]

Vitalism of the Earth and Co-creativity of Humans: Cosmological Correspondences and Human Ritual

The creativity of Heaven in the Confucian cosmological worldview is paralleled by the vitalism of the natural world. From the early text of the *Classic of Changes* (*Yijing*), through the Neo-Confucian reappropriation of this
classic, the sense of the vitality of the natural world infuses many of the
Confucian writings.[106] This vitality is understood as part of the seasonal
cycles of nature, rather than as the developmental, evolving universe discussed by contemporary process philosophers and theologians. It is
expressed in an elaborate series of correspondences (seasonal, directional,
elemental) and rituals that in Han Confucianism were seen as patterns suggestive of the careful regulation needed in the social and political realms.[107]
This cosmological view of the integral cycles of nature reinforces an ethos
of cooperating with those processes through establishing a harmonious
society and government with appropriate ritual structures. The rituals
reflect the patterned structures of the natural world and bind humans to
one another, to the ancestral world, and to the cosmos at large.

The vital material force (*qi*) of the universe is that which joins humans
and nature, unifying their worldview and ethos and giving humans the
potential to become co-creators with the universe.[108] As Mencius notes, it
is *qi* that unites rightness (ethos) and the Way (worldview), filling the
whole space between Heaven and Earth.[109] The moral imperative of Confucianism, then, is to make appropriate ethical and ritual choices linked to
the creative powers of the Way and thus contribute to the betterment of
social and political order.

The Confucian worldview, then, affirms change, as is manifest in the creativity of Heaven and in the vitality of Earth. In particular, the varied and
dynamic patterns of cosmological change are celebrated as part of a life-giving universe. Rituals and music are designed to harmonize with these cos-

mic changes and to assist the process of personal transformation. Rituals help to join the worldview of cosmic change with the ethos of human changes in society, thus harmonizing the natural and human orders. Rituals and music are a means of creating grace, beauty, and accord. Thus, the natural cosmological structures of the Earth provide a counterpoint for an ethos of social patterns expressed in ritual behavior and music. Harmonizing with the universe in a cosmological sense is balanced by an ethos of reciprocal resonance in human relations and is expressed in the patterned behavior of rituals.

Conclusion

The religious worldview of Confucianism encompasses a dynamic cosmological orientation that is interwoven with spiritual expressions in the form of communitarian ethics of society, self-cultivation of the person, and ritual expressions integrating self, society, and cosmos. This tapestry of spiritual integration, which has had a long and rich history in China and in other countries of East Asia, deserves further study. These volumes are a contribution to such investigations. We trust they will also point the way toward future forms of Confucian spirituality in new and creative expressions.

Notes

1. In this introduction, except where noted, we are using the term Confucian and Confucianism to refer to the tradition in a broad sense without necessarily distinguishing between the early classical Confucian expressions and the later Neo-Confucian forms in China, Korea, and Japan.

2. As Tu Weiming puts it, "Despite the difficulty of conceptualizing transcendence as radical otherness, the Confucian commitment to ultimate self-transformation necessarily involves a transcendent dimension" (*Confucian Thought: Selfhood as Creative Transformation* [Albany, N.Y.: State University of New York Press, 1985] 137). This is not "radical transcendence but immanence with a transcendent dimension" (*Centrality and Commonality: An Essay on Confucian Religiousness* [Albany, N.Y.: State University of New York Press, 1989], 121). See similar arguments made earlier by Liu Shu-hsien, "The Confucian Approach to the Problem of Transcendence and Immanence," *Philosophy East and West* 22, no. 1 (1972): 45–52. Roger Ames and David Hall have argued that the Confucian tradition, especially in its classical forms does not focus on transcendence. See their books *Thinking Through Confucius* (Albany, N.Y.: State University of New York Press, 1987) and *Thinking from the Han: Self, Truth and Transcendence in Chinese and Western Culture* (Albany, N.Y.: State University of New York Press, 1998). See also Roger

Ames, "Religiousness in Classical Confucianism: A Comparative Analysis," in *Asian Culture Quarterly* 12, no. 2 (1984): 7–23.

3. Liu Shu-shien and others have observed that Confucianism as a cultural ideal embodying certain spiritual values and aspirations should be differentiated from Confucianism as embedded in social and political ideologies and institutions. See his chapter in Tu Weiming, *Confucian Traditions in East Asian Modernity: Moral Education and Economic Culture in Japan and the Four Mini Dragons* (Cambridge, Mass.: Harvard University Press, 1996). See also Liu Shu-sien, *Understanding Confucian Philosophy: Classical and Sung-Ming* (Westport, Conn.: Praeger, 1998).

4. While one could utilize certain Western definitions of religion to illustrate that Confucianism is a religion, these definitions may limit the understanding of the nature of Confucian spirituality. For example, we can draw on both Paul Tillich's and Frederick Streng's definitions of religion. For Tillich, religion focuses on ultimate concern, while Streng suggests that religion is a means of ultimate transformation. See Paul Tillich, *The Dynamics of Faith* (New York: Harper & Row, 1957); idem, *The Courage to Be* (New York: Harper & Row, 1952); and Frederick Streng, *Understanding Religious Life* (Belmont, Calif.: Wadsworth Publishing Co., 1985).

Both of these broad definitions are applicable to Confucianism. Ultimate concern in Confucianism is evident when a person is responding to the will of Heaven that is discovered in one's Heavenly-endowed nature and manifest in temporal affairs. Ultimate transformation in Confucianism involves modes of self-cultivation that are intellectual, spiritual, and moral. The goal here is to become more fully human, namely, more deeply empathetic and more comprehensively compassionate. Ultimate transformation leads one toward sagehood. Still, this attainment is within the phenomenal world, not apart from it, and for the benefit of the larger society, not for one's salvation alone. This distinguishes Confucian religiosity from Western forms of religion. See also Wilfred Cantwell Smith, *The Meaning and End of Religion* (New York: Macmillan, 1963) for a discussion of the nature of religion.

Articulating the Confucian worldview (both philosophically and religiously) apart from Western categories has been the concern of Roger Ames and David Hall, who suggest that Confucianism is at once nontheistic and profoundly religious. See their commentary on the *Mean* in *Focusing the Familiar* (Albany, N.Y.: State University of New York, 2001).

5. Tu Weiming has observed: "The problem of whether Neo-Confucianism is a religion should not be confused with the more significant question: what does it mean to be religious in the Neo-Confucian community? The solution to the former often depends on the particular interpretive position we choose to take on what constitutes the paradigmatic example of a religion, which may have little to do with our knowledge about Neo-Confucianism as a spiritual tradition" ("Neo-Confucian Religiosity and Human-Relatedness," in *Confucian Thought*, 132).

6. I am indebted to the work of Wm. Theodore de Bary and Tu Weiming in this area. For one of the first comprehensive discussions of the religious dimen-

sions of Confucianism, see de Bary's introduction to *The Unfolding of Neo-Confucianism* (New York: Columbia University Press, 1975). Similarly see Tu Weiming, *Centrality and Commonality*. In addition, the work of P. J. Ivanhoe and Roger Ames and David Hall has been significant. See P. J. Ivanhoe, *Confucian Moral Self Cultivation* (Indianapolis: Hackett, 2000); and Roger Ames and David Hall's numerous books including their most recent, *Focusing the Familiar*.

7. We are using worldview here in its singular form, yet we recognize worldviews as having various formative components.

8. Karl Jaspers, *Origin and Goal of History* (London: Routledge & Kegan Paul, 1953).

9. John Berthrong, *All Under Heaven: Transforming Paradigms in Confucian-Christian Dialogue* (Albany, N.Y.: State University of New York Press, 1994), 216.

10. See Tu Weiming, "The Continuity of Being: Chinese Visions of Nature" in *Confucian Thought*.

11. Ibid., 137–38.

12. See, e.g., John Henderson, *The Development and Decline of Chinese Cosmological Thought* (New York: Columbia University Press, 1984); *Explorations of Early Chinese Cosmology*, ed. Henry Rosemont (Missoula, Mont.: Scholars Press, 1984); Charles LeBlanc, *Huai-nan tzu: Philosophical Synthesis in Early Han Thought* (Hong Kong: Hong Kong University Press 1985).

13. The five relations are between ruler and minister, parent and child, husband and wife, older and younger siblings, and friend and friend.

14. Tu Weiming, *Centrality and Commonality*.

15. Ivanhoe, *Confucian Moral Self Cultivation*, xii.

16. Tu Weiming, *Centrality and Commonality*, 94–96.

17. This is from the *Great Learning* (*Daxue*). See *Sources of Chinese Tradition*, ed. Wm. Theodore de Bary and Irene Bloom (New York: Columbia University Press, 1999), 330.

18. For discussion of sagehood as the goal of Confucian spiritual practice, see Rodney Taylor, *The Religious Dimensions of Confucianism* (Albany, N.Y.: State University of New York Press, 1989); and Rodney Taylor, *The Cultivation of Sagehood as a Religious Goal in Neo-Confucianism: A Study of Selected Writings of Kao P'an-lung (1562–1626)* (Missoula, Mont.: Scholars Press, 1978). For an insightful discussion of the various models of self-cultivation in the Confucian and Neo-Confucian tradition, see Ivanhoe, *Confucian Moral Self Cultivation*.

19. *Hsun Tzu, Basic Writings*, trans. Burton Watson (New York: Columbia University Press, 1963). The importance of ritual practice for the Confucian spiritual path has been emphasized by Robert Neville; see especially his *Boston Confucianism: Portable Tradition in the Late-Modern World* (Albany, N.Y.: State University of New York Press, 2000). Edward Machle sees Xunxi's sense of ritual as reflecting a kind of cosmic dance; see his *Nature and Heaven in the Xunzi: A Study of the Tain Lun* (Albany, N.Y.: State University of New York Press, 1993).

20. Ivanhoe, *Confucian Moral Self Cultivation*, xiv.

21. Some of this work has been led by the New Confucians in Hong Kong and

Taiwan such as Tang Junyi and Mou Zongsan and their students, such as Tu Weiming and Liu Shu-shien. Scholars who have especially focused on the religious and philosophical dimensions of Confucianism include Roger Ames, John Berthrong, Julia Ching, Cheng Chung-ying, Antonio Cua, Wm. Theodore de Bary, David Hall, P. J. Ivanhoe, Young Chan Ro, Rodney Taylor, Mary Evelyn Tucker, and Lee Yearley. See especially the multiple volumes of David Hall and Roger Ames as well as John Berthrong, "Trends in the Interpretation of Confucian Religiosity, in *All Under Heaven;* Julia Ching, *Chinese Religions* (Maryknoll, N.Y.: Orbis Books, 1993); Liu Shu-hsien, "The Religious Import of Confucian Philosophy: Its Traditional Outlook and Contemporary Significance," in *Philosophy East and West* 21, no. 2 (1971): 157–75; Tang Chun-I, "The Development of Ideas of Spiritual Value in Chinese Philosophy," in *The Chinese Mind,* ed. Charles Moore (Honolulu: University Press of Hawaii, 1967); Taylor, *Religious Dimensions of Confucianism;* Tu Weiming, *Confucian Thought;* idem, *Centrality and Commonality.*

22. See Wm. Theodore de Bary, *The Trouble With Confucianism* (Cambridge, Mass.: Harvard University Press, 1991). The work of philosophers and Sinologists such as Roger Ames and P. J. Ivanhoe, is especially important in this regard.

23. David Keightley, "The Religious Commitment: Shang Theology and the Genesis of Chinese Political Culture," *History of Religions* 117 (1978): 224.

24. See Richard Rubinger, *Private Academies of Tokugawa Japan* (Princeton: Princeton University Press, 1982).

25. Wm. Theodore de Bary, "A Reappraisal of Neo-Confucianism," in *Studies in Chinese Thought,* ed. Arthur Wright, *The American Anthropological Association* 55, no. 5, part 2, memoir no. 75 (December 1953).

26. See Wm. Theodore de Bary, *Learning for One's Self: Essays on the Individual in Neo-Confucian Thought* (New York: Columbia University Press, 1991).

27. See de Bary, *Learning for One's Self.*

28. See Tu Weiming's discussion of this in *Centrality and Commonality.*

29. It is important to note that this ordering of cosmos and society can have both life-enhancing and life-constraining dimensions. When used as political ideology in the Han period the record becomes more mixed.

30. The Confucians were, however, caught in matters of pragmatic politics of governance that often required not only an appeal to personal moral transformation and ritual practice as a means of restraint, but also recognized that law and punishment had their function, although as a secondary measure.

31. Many of the writings of Western Confucian scholars are being translated into Chinese as part of the renewed interest in Confucianism in China. These include works by Wm. Theodore de Bary, Tu Weiming, Roger Ames and David Hall, Robert Neville, John Berthrong, and these two volumes on Confucian spirituality.

32. Clearly, the tension of acknowledging the historical particularity of Confucianism along with identifying certain overarching religious elements in the tradition is present here.

33. For example, in Japan Confucianism linked itself to Shinto during the seventeenth century, was separated from it by the nativists of the eighteenth century, and was rejoined to Shinto again in the late nineteenth century. Japanese Confucianism as a worldview and as a form of spiritual cultivation is still part of many of the new religions in Japan and deserves further study. See Helen Hardacre's discussion of "The World View of the New Religions," in *Kurozumikyo and the New Religions of Japan* (Princeton: Princeton University Press, 1986), ch. 1.

34. See Judith Berling, *The Syncretic Religion of Lin Chao-en* (New York: Columbia University Press, 1980).

35. Tu Weiming speaks of the New Confucians as the "Third Epoch of Confucian Humanism" after the classical and Neo-Confucian periods; see *Confucianism: The Dynamics of Tradition*, ed. by Irene Eber (New York: Macmillan, 1986), 3–21. John Berthrong has outlined six periods of Confucianism which separate out the Han, Tang, and later Qing Evidential Learning; see *All Under Heaven*, 77–83, 191–92.

36. The following nine paragraphs have appeared in slightly different form in "An Ecological Cosmology: The Confucian Philosophy of Material Force," in *Ecological Prospects: Scientific. Religious and Aesthetic Perspectives*, ed. Christopher Chapple (Albany, N.Y.: State University of New York Press, 1994).

37. The actual compilation and editing of these texts is the subject of numerous scholarly debates.

38. John Berthrong has translated *li* not only as "ritual" but as "civility," so as to encompass the area of politics and human rights (*All Under Heaven*).

39. Likewise, often great distortions were demanded by parents or in-laws and, this dark side of Confucianism was highlighted in the New Culture movement of the twentieth century. See, e.g., the novel *Family*, by Ba Jin.

40. The fours seeds or four beginnings (pity and compassion, shame and aversion, modesty and compliance, sense of right and wrong) in *Mencius* 2A:6 contain incipient tendencies toward the four virtues in all humans (humaneness, rightness, propriety, wisdom). The man of Song in *Mencius* 2A:2 describes a man who tried to help his seedlings to grow by pulling them up. Ox Mountain in *Mencius* 6A:8 describes a mountain that has been deforested as comparable to one's innate good nature that languishes because it is not cultivated.

41. See a discussion of this in Julia Ching, *The Religious Thought of Chu Hsi* (New York: Oxford University Press, 2000), 124–25. See also Sarah Allan, *The Way of Water and Sprouts of Virtue* (Albany, N.Y.: State University of New York Press, 1997).

42. *Hsun Tzu, Basic Writings*, trans. Watson, 80. Publications on Hsun Tzu (Xunzi) have grown in recent years. See Machle, *Nature and Heaven in the Xunzi*; Paul Ratika Goldin, *Rituals of the Way: The Philosophy of Xunzi* (LaSalle, Ill.: Open Court, 1995); T. C. Kline and P. J. Ivanhoe, *Virtue, Nature and Moral Agency in the Xunzi* (Indianapolis: Hackett, 2000). See also Eric Hutton, "Virtue and Reason in Xunxi" (Ph.D. diss., Stanford University, 2001).

43. Wing-tsit Chan, trans. *Reflections on Things at Hand* (New York: Columbia University Press, 1967).

44. For a comprehensive discussion see Ching, *Religious Thought of Chu Hsi*. See also Wing-tsit Chan, *Chu Hsi: Life and Thought* (New York: St. Martin's Press, 1987), especially 139–61 ("Chu Hsi's Religious Life").

45. This appears in the *Classified Conversations of Chu Hsi* (*Chu-tzu yu-lei* 94:12a); see Ching, *Religious Thought of Chu Hsi*, 95.

46. The *Mean* (*Zhongyong*) ch. 22 in *Sources of Chinese Tradition*, ed. de Bary and Bloom, 338.

47. Yung Sik Kim, *The Natural Philosophy of Chu Hsi 1130–1200* (Philadelphia: American Philosophical Association, 2000), 219.

48. For a discussion of Neo-Confucian spiritual practice, see Wm. Theodore de Bary, "Neo-Confucian Cultivation and Enlightenment," in *The Unfolding of Neo-Confucianism*, ed. Wm. Theodore de Bary (New York: Columbia University Press, 1975). See also Ivanhoe, *Confucian Moral Self Cultivation*.

49. This is the important thesis of Wm. Theodore de Bary in *Neo-Confucian Orthodoxy and the Learning of the Mind-and-Heart* (New York: Columbia University Press, 1981).

50. Patricia Ebrey, trans., *Chu Hsi's Family Rituals: A Twelfth-Century Manual for the Performance of Cappings. Weddings. Funerals, and Ancestral Rites* (Princeton: Princeton University Press, 1991).

51. On Korean Neo-Confucianism, see *The Rise of Neo-Confucianism in Korea*, ed. Wm. Theodore de Bary and Ja Hyun Kim Habush (New York: Columbia University Press, 1985).

52. See Michael Kalton, trans. and ed., *To Become a Sage: The Ten Diagrams on Sage Learning by Yi T'oegye* (New York: Columbia University Press, 1988); and Young-Chan Ro, *The Korean Neo-Confucianism of Yi Yulgok* (Albany, N.Y.: State University of New York Press, 1989).

53. For an excellent survey of the history of Japanese Confucianism, see Martin Collcutt, "The Legacy of Confucianism in Japan," in *The East Asian Region*, ed. Gilbert Rozman (Princeton: Princeton University Press, 1991), 111–54. See also Wm. Theodore de Bary and Irene Bloom, *Principle and Practicality: Essays in Neo-Confucianism and Practical Learning* (New York: Columbia University Press, 1979); *Confucianism and Tokugawa Culture*, ed. Peter Nosco (Princeton: Princeton University Press, 1984); and Mary Evelyn Tucker, "Confucianism in Japan," in *Encyclopedia of Chinese Philosophy, ed.* Antonio Cua (Westport, Conn.: Garland Publications, 2002).

54. See Mary Evelyn Tucker, *Moral and Spiritual Cultivation in Japanese Neo-Confucianism: The Life and Thought of Kaibara Ekken (1630-1714)* (Albany, N.Y. State University of New York Press, 1989).

55. One of the richest discussions of this reinterpretation of the Confucian legacy in light of Social Darwinism occurs in James Pusey's book *China and Charles Darwin* (Cambridge, Mass.: Council for East Asia Studies and Harvard University Press, 1983).

56. This debate has been explored by Wm. Theodore de Bary in *Trouble With Confucianism;* and in his book *The Liberal Tradition in China* (New York: Columbia Press, 1983).

57. This discussion was in part initiated by Max Weber's critique of Confucianism as an inhibiting force in the modernization process. See *The Religion of China: Confucianism and Daoism,* trans. Hans H. Gerth (Glencoe, Ill: Free Press, 1951). The view of Confucianism as a static tradition has been challenged by Wm. Theodore de Bary and others. See, e.g., de Bary's introduction to *Unfolding of Neo-Confucianism;* and Thomas Metzger, *Escape from Predicament: Neo-Confucianism and China's Evolving Political Culture* (New York: Columbia University Press, 1977).

58. This is especially the concern of Tu Weiming; see his *Confucian Traditions in East Asian Modernity.*

59. See, e.g., Neville, *Boston Confucianism.*

60. See Wm. Theodore de Bary, "Introduction," in *Confucianism and Human Rights* (New York: Columbia University Press, 1998), 25, and his book *The Trouble With Confucianism.*

61. The debate regarding human rights in China and the role of Confucianism has been vigorously discussed in the last decade. See especially *Confucianism and Human Rights,* ed. Wm. Theodore de Bary and Tu Weiming (New York: Columbia University Press, 1998); *The East Asian Challenge for Human Rights,* ed. Joanne Bauer and Daniel Bell (New York: Cambridge University Press, 1999); and Daniel Bell, *East Meets West: Human Rights and Democracy in East Asia* (Princeton: Princeton University Press, 2000).

62. See *Confucianism and Ecology: The Interrelation of Heaven, Earth and Humans,* ed. Mary Evelyn Tucker and John Berthrong (Cambridge, Mass.: Harvard Center for the Study of World Religions and Harvard University Press, 1998).

63. See, e.g., the work of Peter Bol, Benjamin Elman, Lionel Jensen, and Hoyt Tillman noted in the bibliography.

64. This preoccupation with ideology has been especially strong in the field of postmodern deconstruction.

65. Kang advocated the preservation of Confucianism and even its reestablishment as an institutional religion. He was particularly adamant that Confucius was a reformer and that therefore his ideas could be used to back the reforms being recommended by the Self Strengthening movement in the late nineteenth century. This in turn would help to preserve China from Western exploitation. See James Pusey, "K'ang Yu-Wei and *Pao Chiao:* Confucian Reform and Reformation," *Papers on China* 20 (December 1966). Published by East Asian Research Center, Harvard University. See also Chen Hsi-yuan, "Confucianism Encounters Religion: The Formation of Religious Discourse and the Confucian Movement in Modern China" (Ph.D diss., Harvard University, 1999).

66. Wm. Theodore de Bary claims, however, that these schools were not as rigidly distinguished as later historians have delineated (*Neo-Confucian Orthodoxy*).

67. See Norman J. Girardot, *The Victorian Translation of China: James Legge's Oriental and Oxonian Pilgrimage* (Berkeley: University of California Press, 2001), 35.

68. For further studies on this, see *Discovering China: European Interpretations in the Enlightenment,* ed. Julia Ching and Willard Oxtoby (Rochester: University of Rochester Press, 1992); Julia Ching and Willard Oxtoby, *Moral Enlightenment: Leibniz and Wolff on China,* Monumenta serica monograph series 26 (Nettetal: Steyler Verlag, 1992); J. J. Clarke, *Oriental Enlightenment: The Encounter Between Asian and Western Thought* (London/New York: Routledge, 1997).

69. Herrlee Creel, "Was Confucius Agnostic?," *T'oung Pao* 39 (1932): 55–99.

70. John Chaffee, *The Thorny Gates of Learning in Sung China: A Social History of Examinations* (New York: Cambridge University Press, 1985).

71. C. K. Yang, "The Functional Relationship Between Confucian Thought and Chinese Religion" in *Chinese Thought and Institutions,* ed. by John Fairbank (Chicago: University of Chicago Press, 1957). Thomas Wilson, on the other hand, raises the question of how the separation arose in China between religion and rational philosophy: "Yet it is not clear whether this 'transition' occurred in Confucius' day or whether it is the effect of a much later modernist separation between ritual, religion, activities of the body on the one hand, and ethics, rational philosophy and thoughts of the mind on the other" (*Geneology of the Way: The Construction and Uses of the Confucian Tradiition in Late Imperial China,* ed. Thomas Wilson [Stanford: Stanford University Press, 1995], 10).

72. This was, in part, the assumption of the May Fourth movement of 1919 in China, which had such strong anti-Confucian tones. This critical tone continued with such writers as Lu Xun and others who wished to "Destroy the old curiosity shop of Confucianism." See James Pusey, *Lu Xun and Evolution* (Albany, N.Y.: State University of New York Press, 1998); and Lin Yu-sheng, *The Crisis of Chinese Consciousness: Radical Antitraditionalism in the May Fourth Era* (Madison: University of Wisconsin Press, 1979). The Maoists also wished to overthrow Confucianism as "feudalistic," especially during the Cultural Revolution in the 1970s. This was also part of the appeal of John Dewey's ideas during his two-year stay in China (1919–1921) and even down to the present. See David Hall and Roger Ames, *Democracy of the Dead: Dewey, Confucius and the Hope for Democracy in China* (LaSalle, Ill.: Open Court, 1999).

73. See de Bary, *Sources of Chinese Tradition,* 546–50.

74. See *The Limits to Change: Essays on Conservative Alternatives in Republican China,* ed. Charlotte Furth (Cambridge, Mass.; Harvard University Press, 1976).

75. For an abbreviated version of the Manifesto, see Wm. Theodore de Bary and Richard Lufrano, *Sources of Chinese Tradition* (New York: Columbia University Press, 2000), 2:550–58. For the full version, see Carsun Chang, *The Development of Neo-Confucian Thought* (New York: Bookman Associates, 1962), 2:455–83.

76. See Berthrong, *All Under Heaven,* 191.

77. Gilbert Rozman, ed., *The East Asian Region: Confucian Heritage and Its Modern Adaptation* (Princeton: Princeton University Press, 1991). These various categories are described on p. 161.

78. Kim Kyong-Dong, "Confucianism and Modernization in East Asia," in *The

Impact of Traditional Thought on Present-Day Japan, ed. Josef Kreiner (Munich: Iudicium-Verlag, 1996), 51–53.

79. Wm. Theodore de Bary and John Chaffee, *Neo-Confucian Education: The Formative Stage* (Berkeley: University of California Press, 1989).

80. See de Bary, *Learning for One's Self.*

81. See, e.g., the study by Tetsuo Najita, *Visions of Virtue in Tokugawa Japan: The Kaitokudo Merchant Academy of Osaka* (Chicago: University of Chicago Press, 1987).

82. See Tu Weiming, *Confucian Traditions in East Asian Modernity.* See also the articles on modernization and development by Ronald Dore, Tu Weiming, and Kim Kyong-Dong in *Impact of Traditional Thought on Present Day Japan*, ed. Kreiner.

83. Robert Neville, "Introduction," in Rodney Taylor, *Religious Dimensions of Confucianism*, ix, x.

84. Tu Weiming, *Confucian Thought*, 132.

85. See the *Mean* in *Sources of Chinese Tradition*, ed. de Bary and Bloom, 333–39.

86. Tu Weiming, "Neo-Confucian Religiosity and Human Relatedness," in *Confucian Thought*, 133.

87. Taylor, *Religious Dimensions of Confucianism;* Rodney Taylor, *The Cultivation of Sagehood as a Religious Goal in Neo-Confucianism: A Study of Selected Writings of Kao P'an-lung (1562-1626)* (Missoula, Mont.: Scholars Press, 1978).

88. *The Ways of Heaven*, ed. Rodney Taylor (Leiden: Brill, 1986); *Geneology of the Way: The Construction and Uses of the Confucian Tradition in Late Imperial China*, ed. Thomas Wilson (Stanford: Stanford University Press, 1995); Patricia Ebrey, *Confucianism and Family Rituals in Imperial China* (Princeton: Princeton University Press, 1991); and eadem, *Chu Hsi's Family Rituals* (Princeton: Princeton University Press, 1991).

89. As we noted earlier, part of the difficulty in describing Confucianism as a religion or as religious are the assumptions and agenda one brings to the topic. For many people the term "religion" has negative associations with antiquated ways of thinking that need to be superseded by more rational, humanist, and modern modes of thought. This was true for Westerners such as the Enlightenment *philosophes* of the eighteenth century and for Chinese reformers such as Hu Shi in the twentieth century. These thinkers applauded the move from so-called superstition and ritual to rationalism and ethics as being a mark of the progress or development of a culture. For others, religion has positive associations of bringing a culture into dialogue with other cultures or worldviews where religion is valued. Some examples of this are the attempts of the Jesuits in seventeenth century China and the Christian missionaries in the nineteenth century to identify monotheism in the Confucian tradition as present in the early cult of the Lord on High (*Shangdi*) and in the concept of Heaven (*tian*).

90. See his article with this title in *Reader in Comparative Religion: An Anthropological Approach*, ed. William A. Lessa and Evon Z. Vogt (New York: Harper & Row, 1972), 167–78.

91. Smith, *Meaning and End of Religion.*

92. Clifford Geertz, "Religion as a Cultural System," in *Reader in Comparative Religion: An Anthropological Approach,* ed. William Lessa and Evon Vogt (New York: Harper & Row, 1972), 167.

93. This is especially evident in Han Confucian thought but it continued to influence the later Neo-Confucian tradition as well.

94. Joseph Needham, *Civilization in China* (Cambridge: Cambridge University Press, 1956), 2:291–93.

95. See Tu Weiming, *Confucian Thought.*

96. This is a term used by Roger Ames and David Hall in *Thinking Through Confucius,* 12–17.

97. Translated by Wing-tsit Chan, *A Source Book in Chinese Philosophy* (Princeton: Princeton University Press, 1963), 109.

98. These include, among others, the *Book of Changes* (Third Appendix); the *Book of Ritual* (ch. 7); the *Mean* (ch. 22); Dong Zhongshu, *Luxuriant Gems of the Spring and Autumn Annals* (ch. 44); the *Diagram of the Great Ultimate* of Zhou Dunyi; the *Western Inscription* of Zhang Zai; the *Commentary on the Great Learning* by Wang Yangming. See these texts in *Sources of Chinese Tradition,* ed. de Bary and Bloom.

99. Tu Weiming, *Centrality and Commonality,* 102–7.

100. See chs. 22, 25, 26 of the *Mean* in *Sources of Chinese Tradition,* ed. de Bary and Bloom.

101. See Thomas Berry's article "Affectivity in Classical Confucian Tradition," ch. 5 in this volume.

102. *Book of Changes* Appendix HI 2:1/8. See also the chapter on "Creative Principle" in Hellmut Wilhelm, *Heaven, Earth and Man in the Book of Changes* (Seattle: University of Washington Press, 1977). The Neo-Confucians frequently refer to the productive and reproductive forces of the universe (ch. *sheng sheng,* Jp. *sei sei*).

103. See Berthrong, *All Under Heaven.*

104. See the *Mean,* ch. 1 in *Sources of Chinese Tradition,* ed. de Bary and Bloom.

105. Taylor, *Religious Dimensions of Confucianism.*

106. See Kidder Smith, Peter Bol, Joseph Adler, and Don Wyatt, *Sung Dynasty Uses of the I Ching* (Princeton: Princeton University Press, 1990).

107. See *Explorations in Early Chinese Cosmology,* ed. Henry Rosemont (Chico, Calif.: Scholars Press, 1984); Sarah Queen, *From Chronicle to Canon: The Hermeneutics of the Spring and Autumn According to Tung Chung-shu* (New York: Cambridge University Press, 1996); Robert Eno, *The Confucian Creation of Heaven* (Albany, N.Y.: State University of New York Press, 1990); Henderson, *Development and Decline of Chinese Cosmology.*

108. See Tu Weiming's use of the term co-creator in *Centrality and Commonality,* 70, 78, 98, 102, 106.

109. *Mencius* 2A:2.

Part One

SYNOPTIC OVERVIEW

1

Individualism and Holism in Chinese Tradition: The Religious Cultural Context

Thomas Berry

THE RELATION BETWEEN the individual human being and the social group within which the individual exists and functions has been a subject of thought and discussion in the various human traditions throughout the centuries, especially in the more complex societies of the Eurasian world. While the reciprocal dependence of the individual and the group is obvious, there are differences of emphasis and of perspective. Despite great varieties within Western and Chinese thought, it would appear that Western society in its commitment to individualism has adopted one perspective and that China in its commitment to holism has adopted another perspective. How to identify, or even to verify, these perspectives and how to evaluate them are not easy tasks. Yet there is a certain urgency, both academic and practical, that China and the West reflect more profoundly not only on their own proper experience in social structure and functioning but on the experience and teaching of each other.

We propose in this paper to deal first with the Western tradition and the manner in which its dominant doctrine of individualism has evolved over the centuries from its religious and ontological foundations as well as in its social expression. Then consideration will be given to the manner in which the Chinese tradition has dealt with the individual in oneself and in one's relations with the social order and with the natural world, the most comprehensive expression of social existence. Finally, we will make certain general observations about the differences between these two perspectives and how they might be seen in relation to each other. In all of these discussions there is an awareness of the historical complexity and philosophical variety of these traditions which need further explication.

I

On careful examination we find that individualism and the creative effects of this teaching have their sources deep in the very origins of Western civilization. Those isolating tendencies that culminate in modern individualism can be discovered in the very earliest manifestations of a Western religious identity. From the beginning we can observe attitudes that tend toward negation of the unity, mutual presence, and organic relationships in reality that establish the individual as a participatory being integral with a higher process rather than as a relatively self-sufficient being essentially complete in itself. While the extreme modern statement of individualism would certainly be unacceptable in the earlier phases of Western development, a matrix was being prepared in which individualism as we know it would become possible.

The early forms of this matrix can be found in the opening scriptures of the biblical tradition. There the integral presence of the divine, the natural, and the human to one another is significantly weakened by establishing a personal deity transcendent to the natural world with direct revelatory communion only with a special segment of the human community. Because of this emphasis on personal transcendence, the organic metaphor of universal reality was no longer applicable. Loss of the organic metaphor required establishment of a legal and covenantal relation between the divine and the human. The integral unity of the human community was also negated by this election of a single segment of the human community as a chosen sacred community separated out from the larger human context.

In the biblical world the feeling for organic relations in reality was further diminished by acceptance of an ontological as well as a historical conflict within reality itself. If the Persian sense of dual principles in reality, namely, of good and evil, was rejected in the biblical context, a profound sense of the conflict of forces within reality as the essential aspect and interpretation of the historical process moved the Western religious tradition away from a feeling for integral relationships in reality. The ultimate conflict was to be resolved not by reconciliation between these forces but by a conquest of the good over the evil, of light over darkness. The military and political symbolism of the biblical world was carried over into the Christian world. Even though evil as such is recognized as a negative rather than a positive aspect of reality, this deficiency established an enduring antagonistic relationship with the historical process, as is outlined in the *City of God* by St. Augustine. This is something quite different from a *yin-yang* type of opposition in Chinese thought, which is ultimately more complementary than contradictory.

Another break in the integral conception of reality can be found in the later Christian concept of the individual soul as so exalted in its nature that it could not be handed on by those generative processes whereby the physical aspect of the human individual was brought into being. It could only come into existence by immediate divine creation, not by any change or derivation from a preexisting reality.[1] While this may seem to be a splendid compliment to the individual, in reality it diminished in a profound manner the integral being of the individual in one's origin, structure, and destiny.

This mode of spiritual dealing with the individual either originated from or was further strengthened by the Hellenic conception of the psyche, the ordering principle of the soul. This led to discussion of the ontological concept of "person," the focus of extensive discussion in the early Christian world with special reference to the identity of the historical individual known as the Christ. Ultimately "person" came to be defined as that mode of being of the individual that cuts one's being off from all other beings in its incommunicable identity as "I" and "me," and which constitutes the ultimate principle of attribution of any action performed by the individual or any activity or influence terminating in the individual.[2] Thus, a clear statement on personality developed in Western civilization grounded in the Christian tradition and in Hellenic thought.

An additional phase of this development of individual self-assertion can be seen in the martyr experience of the early Christian community, where a heroic confrontation style of individual action was established and consecrated in the death experience of many individuals. The martyrs, canonized as the first saints, were established as the ultimate norm of authentic existence. Thus, the heroic archetype in its Christian form first shaped by a savior personality and further developed in the martyr tradition gave an extraordinary realism to the individual in confrontation with both the political regime and the prevailing social mores.

Although both Hellenic and Christian thought placed extended emphasis on the social aspect of human development, the foundations had been established for a later powerful assertion of the individual as having ultimate rights and ultimate values in oneself. If at a later time a secular form of the heroic individual would assert itself not only against the established political power but also against the religious tradition, this would still be derived from this earlier religious context and by exaltation of the value of the individual originally asserted within this religious tradition. It is impor tant to realize, however, that this doctrine of the individual is a doctrine carried not primarily by an individual but by a society that saw itself as expanded, strengthened, and enhanced by this attitude toward individual rights and values; the society still saw itself in a reciprocal relation with the individual as microphase and macrophase of the one integral mode of human existence.

While this assertion of the individual was held firmly within a social unity throughout the high medieval period, an entirely new situation evolved in the fourteenth-century work of William of Ockham, the English theologian and philosopher who set forth a doctrine of atomistic realism. Although this was not solely due to Ockham, his writings did coincide with a movement toward analytical divisive processes in the functioning of human understanding which became the pervasive doctrine in Western thought and life in succeeding centuries. The individual, the particular, was henceforth seen as the true reality. All else was contrived, derivative, mental, and imaginative rather than substantial in its being. The holistic tendencies in Western tradition were for a while maintained in the surviving Platonism, but in general the Western thought tradition under the powerful influence of the scientific endeavor began to consider the ultimate particles of the universe as true realities. The holistic tendencies in the Western tradition became subordinate to the divisive tendencies.

Soon the reforming religious traditions would no longer function within a doctrinal or disciplinary allegiance to any establishment but in opposition. A doctrine of individual self-determination of belief asserted itself as normative. A further step, of perhaps even greater significance, was the break in identifying the ultimate basis for any social cohesion in the human group. Belief that society and the individual were given together in a spontaneous manner based on biological relatedness, survival need, and mutual human attraction was rejected by Thomas Hobbes (1588–1679). He proposed instead that the original state of humans was one of ferocity, of war against all, and that society arose on an assumed contractual or covenant basis whereby this destructive warfare was mitigated and a social and humanizing process could take place. The ultimate natural reality remained the individual. The social reality was artificial.[3]

While this shift of primary reality and value from the more comprehensive to the more individual took place in these earlier modern centuries, it was not until the late nineteenth century that it was clearly named and identified. Later in that century it would be further strengthened by social darwinism derived from Thomas Huxley and Herbert Spencer. By that time it had been seriously challenged by the conservatism of several French writers but nowhere so effectively as by Edmund Burke in England with his powerful presentation of the social process in terms of the organic metaphor. Yet his influence was overwhelmed by the widespread commitment to the creativity of conflict as in the doctrine of Heraclitus *Fragment 53* that conflict is the father of all things.

II

After such extensive consideration of the religious and humanistic origins of individualism in Western development, it can easily be seen how different is the Chinese mode of consciousness of the reality and the value of the individual. As in the West, however, consciousness of the individual depends on consciousness of the reality and value of the larger universe. Here the difference is great indeed. The Chinese intelligence awakens to a universe integral with itself, totally present to itself, a universe in which the part and the whole interact as dimensions of each other. The consensus on this in the various divisions of Chinese thought and in the long sequence of developments in Chinese cultural history is striking. Differences do exist within the larger complex of Chinese traditions, but even such traditions as that of the Legalists, who were atomistic in their view of the individual and the forces leading to an integrated social mode of being, never exalted the individual as having ultimate value in oneself. Indeed, the individual value was considerably diminished.

If there is a doctrine of *Shangdi* (Lord on High), *tian* (Heaven), *taiji* (Supreme Ultimate), or Tao, these ultimate terms of reference are not to be understood as designating a reality separated from the integral functioning of the natural and human worlds. What is designated is a mysterious impenetrable depth of reality that is recognized in its effects but not encompassed in its being by human understanding. Among the most impressive moments of Chinese thought are those moments when this somewhat mystical and mysterious realm is implicitly or explicitly referred to. While translators frequently become uneasy, awkward, and even disconcerted by these passages, it is important to understand that the essential concern for personality development in China is to assist in the more effective manifestation of this ultimate mystery in the natural and human orders.

The one who most manifests this ultimate mystery in China is the sage personality. As archetypal personality, the sage in China is not a conquering hero but an integrating personality; in the sage all realms of being are harmonized. Nor is the sage a yogi seeking release from the limitations of the phenomenal world; the sage is rather a person entering into the deepest rhythms of all natural phenomena. Nor is the Chinese sage a saint caught up in a unifying love for a personal deity who is both intimate and transcendent; the sage is rather a functional co-creator of the universe together with Heaven and Earth.

In this context and in fulfillment of this ideal there can be no such conflict as is found in the dualism that appears so strongly in the opposed forces of reality as experienced in the traditions of the West. Nor is there such an effort to establish the independent value of the individual as is done in the Greek concept of the psyche or in the Christian concept of person. Nor was there in the Confucian tradition any consistent basis for development of the doctrine of the individual and the particular as the ultimate reality in itself such as was presented by William of Ockham, or for development of the doctrine of universal antagonism of human beings such as was proposed by Thomas Hobbes. Nor could any such theory as Hobbes's covenant theory provide a basis for social cohesion.

There did exist in China a sense of the integral structure of reality such that the activity of any part flowed throughout the entire structure. In Confucian terms, the true ruler only needed to sit on his throne facing south and all activities of the realm responded in a grand harmony. This activity was fundamentally a mystical, moral, and human activity, not simply a complex of physical or administrative activities.

What developed in China was a remarkable sense not of individualism but of humanity having both a microphase and a macrophase. The microphase is the limited particularity of the individual in oneself; the macrophase is the same individual as present to the entire order or reality. The "profound person" of the *Doctrine of the Mean* (*Zhongyong*) is clearly the individual who, through the virtue of authenticity, has activated to his or her highest expression both the microphase and the macrophase of one's own humanity. All five of the classics are centered on bringing together these two aspects of the individual person, but it is developed especially in the *Book of History*, the *Book of Ritual*, and the *Book of Changes*.

The *Book of History* opens with the activation of the human consciousness of presence to the four extreme points of the universe, then to heaven above and earth below. This continues with the awakening of personal presence throughout the human community. Then provision is made for the fulfillment of human presence to the temporal sequence of the seasons. Later the primary symbolizations are set forth: the sun, moon, stars, mountains, dragon, flowers, animal, water, plant, fire, peeled grain rice, the five colors, the five sounds. In all of this we see a presence of the emperor, a presence later fulfilled by the sage as archetypal figure and, in imitation of the archetype, by the individual human personalities. Only in this universal communion is the human being activated in any integral manner and enabled to fulfill one's functional role in the total order of the universe. The final validation of this role is that "Heaven's hearing and seeing work through our people's hearing and seeing."[4]

So, too, in the *Book of Ritual* (the *Liji*), the integration of the individual and society requires an intimate harmony with the seasonal sequence in the natural world. The individual is shaped inwardly by this context and in turn participates in the functioning of the cosmic-human order. The seasonal sequence is a kind of round dance performed by heaven, earth, and humans. Any of the three may take the lead, but each must be in step with the others. The key passage that might be selected from the *Book of Ritual* is the definition of the human as the "heart and mind of heaven and earth."[5] From this principle we can see how powerful the organic metaphor of the universe is in the Chinese tradition. The individual is established in this vast universal context as well as within the particular mode of one's own limited personal existence.

The *Book of Changes* (*Yijing*) is especially clear on this reading of the individual in terms of the larger complex of forces and situations that come to pass in the universal order of things. Each particular moment or situation must be interpreted by the larger context. To understand this context is to have a fathomless source of wisdom in dealing with all possible earthly situations. So in the *Great Appendix* of the *Book of Changes* we find that the sage is identified as the one who understands things from their beginnings to their endings.

> There is a similarity between him and heaven and earth, and hence there is no contrariety in him to them. . . . He comprehends as in a mold or enclosure the transformations of heaven and earth without any error; by an ever-varying adaptation he completes all things without exception. . . . It is thus that his operation is spirit-like unconditioned by place, while the changes which he produces are not restricted to any form.[6]

Thus, in the *Book of History,* the *Book of Ritual,* and the *Book of Changes,* there is constant reference to the full development of the microphase mode of the human in terms of one's ability to understand and commune with the larger dimensions of reality that constitute the macrophase of one's own personal existence.

The highest moments in the expression of this interaction are found, however, in the *Doctrine of the Mean* (*Zhongyong*) and the *Great Learning* (*Daxue*). These two chapters of the *Book of Ritual,* excerpted from their context and given independent status, express the quintessence of the entire

Chinese tradition. Canonized in the Neo-Confucian period, they have a simplicity, a power, and a comprehensiveness in establishing the contours of the Confucian tradition that is not likely to be surpassed. The opening section of the *Great Learning* harmonizes perfectly with the ending of the *Doctrine of the Mean*. The radiant virtues that fill the universe in a transforming splendor arise out of its depths in the individual. This originating source in the individual can be further seen in the metaphor of the tree, which dominates the entire treatise of the *Great Learning*. The ultimate wisdom is to know that the branches of the tree are nourished and sustained by a root system that in turn is nourished by the mysterious earth itself. This Chinese expression of the individual as the great tree of life provides the vital botanical metaphor so much needed in all efforts to understand the Chinese life experience.

Confucius, in the *Analects,* remains the archetypal realization of this union of microphase-macrophase dimensions of the individual; he also remains the one who first outlined the personal discipline needed in the individual person to activate this fullness of development. Only thus could satisfactory meaning be given to human existence. The ease and majesty that we witness in the bearing of Confucius provide an all-encompassing organic metaphor of the Cosmic Person. Although Confucius is dealing constantly with the microphase aspect of his disciples, he is outlining the larger dimensions of the human personality to be reached in terms of identity experiences rather than by aggressive attitudes.

Mencius, the first great Confucian essayist, expounded more fully the inner dynamics of nature out of which this expansive tendency of the individual originates. This is such a spontaneous process, so distinctively and universally human, that he could say of Confucius that he did nothing extraordinary.[7] He could also note that all things are complete in the individual person.[8]

The one who provided the enduring synthesis and functional application of these classics to the imperial regime after the Qin period is Dong Zhongshu. In his work the particular and the comprehensive dimensions of the individual are seen with exceptional clarity. As the transitional figure in the earlier Han period, he can be considered of major importance in selecting the Confucian expression of this basic Chinese tradition as the guiding vision of the empire and as the primary civilizing discipline of the Chinese people.

But here is perhaps the place to identify one of the principal aspects of the Confucian view of those virtues whereby individual capacities are activated in both their microphase and macrophase expression. Those virtues generally recognized as goodness, righteousness, decorum, and understanding constitute what might be considered the personal discipline whereby the full range of personal, social, and cosmic relations is carried out. Yet there is also a series of what might be called the *meta* or comprehensive virtues with a primary concern for the macrophase or cosmic dimensions of the individual. These may be listed as humaneness (*ren*), authenticity (*cheng*), reverence (*jing*), and filial piety (*xiao*). These four have a special status.

Humaneness is a particular virtue and also a comprehensive virtue. As a primary and comprehensive virtue it can be presented as identical with heaven itself: "The highest humanity rests with Heaven for Heaven is humaneness itself."[9] Because Heaven (*tian*) in some sense is *ren*, then *ren* is normative for all existence. In this comprehensive role *ren* enables a person to regard "Heaven and earth and all things as one body. There is nothing that is not part of his self."[10] A further clarification of this statement of the unity of the microphase and macrophase of the individual person involves the statement of Cheng Yi that if one does not activate this virtue in his own being "he will be thousands of miles away from heaven and earth and the myriad things."[11]

Cheng, translated as "authenticity," has a remarkable presentation in the *Doctrine of the Mean*. It is the virtue that reaches deep within the *Urgrund* of personal existence to an ultimate power capable of transforming the human community and the entire universe. This power is correlative with the heavenly and natural powers and, with these, originates, sustains, and transforms the universe itself.

Jing, meaning "reverence," is the special virtue manifested by Yu at the very origins of Chinese civilization. It radiates a sense of sacred awe with which the individual regards the universe in its lowest and most particular as well as in its highest and most universal aspects. This virtue of reverence was considered so ultimate in its origin that it was a prerequisite for later development not only of the particular virtues but even of that most powerful meta-virtue of authenticity. It is indicated by Cheng Yi that those who have not yet attained the virtue of authenticity must first establish in themselves this interior state of reverence. There is such richness in this term, and it is used in such varied nuances, that it is difficult to enunciate the more basic significance out of which the multiple meanings emerge. It seems to involve an attitude of awe at the mystery of things, even at the mystery of one's own being, that predisposes a person toward that modesty of deportment that enables particularity to integrate itself at the most profound level of human feeling with the universality of things. This disposition enables a mutual indwelling to take place between the particular individual and the magnificent and myriad world without. Through this virtue Yu disposed himself for his spatial presence to heaven above and earth below and to the four extreme points of the world. Then he proceeded to integrate human affairs temporally with the sequence of the seasons. His constant reiteration, especially to the ministers, was "Be reverent, be reverent!"[12]

Filial piety (*xiao*) is that special virtue associated with origins. Origin moments are sacred moments, for these give to beings their very existence. This capacity to stand forth magically out of a prior nonexistence into existence is always related to another existence. To this prior existence a unique and absolute reverence is due. This virtue is a metaphysical and ontological as well as a moral mode of being. Without filiality there would be nothing. The phenomenal universe exists in itself and in all its relations only by the power of this virtue. The *Classic of Filial Piety* (*Xiaojing*) says that filial piety "is the first principle of heaven, the ultimate standard of earth, the norm of conduct of the people."[13] The power of this encomium to filial piety was felt not only by the Chinese but also by the Japanese, especially by the Neo-Confucian Nakae Toju in the seventeenth century: "Filial piety is the root of humans. When it is lost, then one's life becomes like a rootless plant. . . . What brings life to heaven, life to earth, life to humans and life to all things, is filial piety."[14] Elsewhere he envisages filial piety as something like the world soul of Plato: "Filial piety dwells in the universe as the spirit dwells in humans. It has neither beginning nor end; without it is no time or any being; there is nothing in all the universe unendowed with filial piety."[15]

From all of this we can see that in China interrelatedness is grounded not in any religious covenant, nor in any social contract, but in the very origin, structure, and functioning of the universe. To think that human society comes together by some "contract" would be as foolish as to think that the sun and the moon or the wind and the waters established formal contracts with each other in some negotiated way.

Even though these virtues of interrelatedness are so natural and so instinctive, even though there is absolute continuity with the natural process itself and with what might be called the genetic coding of the individual, these virtues do not simply and inevitably emerge into being. They are, indeed, like the four limbs or like the various organs of the body, but their development is a human growth process that requires conscious care and cultivation, long years of discipline, of learning, and of practice. If they belong to the genetic coding, they also belong to the cultural coding of the society.

The relationship between genetic coding and cultural coding is among the most delicate of all issues in discussion of human thought modes and life disciplines. For the Chinese the cultural coding is ultimately contained within and guided by the genetic coding. Yet the emergent individual requires a lifelong cultivation for this total genetic-cultural coding to reach its full expression. This can be observed in the life of Confucius himself. There we find a sixfold sequence of development of an emergent individual. This is a sequence that begins in an instinctive awareness of the need for personal discipline and culminates in such intimate personal identity with the mysterious Heavenly Mandate (*tianming*) that one can move in perfect accord with those personal, social, and cosmic forces which one experiences as a great identity.

The art of arts in this context is in preserving the continuity of the cultivated, namely, the cultural coding, and the spontaneous, the genetic coding. This requires a sensitivity trained to those subtle tendencies so deep in human nature that they emerge naturally from that ultimate realm of existence known in the rich vocabulary of the Chinese as Heaven (*tian*), Heavenly Mandate (*tianming*), Great Tao, or Supreme Ultimate.

While cultivating the spontaneous, teaching the instinctive, disciplining the natural are all contradictory or paradoxical expressions, they all suppose an integral or organic relationship within the entire order of reality. No human mode of existence, of activity, or of value is possible except in a natural and social context. To awaken an individual to a consciousness of one's own being and to activate the full expansion of one's individual personality in this context are the primary obligation of society. The importance of this consciousness and this discipline can be seen when we consider how the entire order of the universe rests on the individual. Each individual becomes creator, sustainer, and fulfillment of the universe. If the Greeks in their generally objective way of knowing discovered in the subjective order of the psyche the source of order in the universe, the Chinese discovered a more integral and more intimate presence of the universe and the individual to each other along with the discipline that would provide the functional efficacy needed by the individual.

While this Chinese mode of consciousness does not provide a basis for a doctrine of individualism such as this has been known in the modern West, it does provide a basis for an expansive development of the human quality of life. As mentioned previously, this might be called a doctrine of humanity with a microphase and a macrophase rather than a doctrine of individualism. This richness of personal development and creativity in the Chinese tradition can be seen in the long list of persons who have given expression to the cultural ideals of that tradition. But perhaps even more significant is the human shaping of a people. The distinctiveness of the Chinese tradition can be observed in the general competence of the Chinese people in carrying out their survival program of growing food, building homes, engaging in commerce, and evolving appropriate technologies. It can be seen also in their vigor and refinement of thought, of artistic and literary expression, and in their capacity for community existence and for political administration of a vast complex society over several millennia.

When we examine the existential basis for development of this integral sense of the individual and the society, we may discover this in the turbulent history of the Chinese throughout their formative period. This experience seems to have evoked the insights and the energies needed to establish a tradition that may be identified in its full sublimity as a *mystical humanism*. Only some extraordinary experience of the affective aspects of the universe itself in its deepest origins could have given the Chinese such an exalted feeling for what it is to be human. To develop this experience into a cultural coding, to set it forth in clear and appropriate language, to evolve the intellectual tradition associated with this vision, to ritualize its expression in music and movement, to establish a way of communicating this vision, this discipline, and this lifestyle to subsequent generations—all this is the positive creation that both reveals the expansiveness of the Chinese personality and defines the Chinese alternative to chaos.

III

But even after we have indicated these differences between the individualism of the modern West and the doctrine of humanity with its microphase and macrophase in traditional China, we might inquire into the meaning these have for each other and also into the larger question of the meaning these have for historical processes in their more comprehensive dimensions.

The Western emphasis on excess rather than containment, on adversary relations, on the titanic conflict with deity as expressed in the Promethean story, on the principle of Heraclitus that "war is the father of all things," on the Christ–Anti-Christ conflict in the redemptive process, on the Faustian dissatisfaction with any achieved state, on the social darwinist "survival of the fittest"—all this has given to the West its aggressive and destructive qualities, but also much of its creativity. The Western world has been restless, has found difficulty in accepting limits, has been merciless in its own self-criticism as well as oppressive in its demands on others. Western history may be seen as a series of assaults against the limitations of the human condition. This has given to the West its tradition-destructive, society-destructive, and nature-destructive aspects. Much of this is associated with an extreme commitment to individualism. Yet there exist vast creative aspects of this process. The West lives marginally to the human in the hope of expanding the human by exceeding all existing boundaries, while the Chinese live centrally in the human seeking to activate those vast creative instincts that emerge from the fathomless depths of the Great Tao.

The main instruments of Western assault in recent centuries have been science as combined with technology. These have given to Western society an experience of the universe and a corresponding capacity to interact with the deepest forces of the universe such as could never have been attained except through the violent assault on all limits and all restraining obstacles to human inquiry into the nature and functioning of the world. The presuppositions of this inquiry have been creativity of conflict, the need for assault against the sacred, the primacy of analysis over synthesis, nonconformity as a basic requirement for personal growth, and ultimately nonconformity for the intellectual and cultural development of society. This is driven by a feeling that every possibility must be tried in searching toward a more expansive vision and experience of the universe. In this context we perceive the reversal of values. Reverence and irreverence change places— so too order and chaos, wisdom and folly, creativity and destruction, the primacy of the society and the primacy of the community.

It is an awesome and astounding adventure. This is a turbulent process, always present, if somewhat controlled, in earlier Western development, but in more recent times it is shaken loose from its former limitations to suddenly bring about undreamed-of changes in the entire human-earth situation. We still have no adequate assessment of these changes in terms of their ultimate creativity and destructiveness, yet the present period reveals itself as one of entrancement with quantitative modes of knowing, with mechanistic rather than organic processes, and with exploitive relations with the natural world. These exploitive relations concern not only the natural world but also the human world.

This exploitation began with the Western drive toward expansion in all its economic, political, social, and cultural dimensions of the last five hundred years. By the nineteenth and twentieth centuries the technologies of the West were sufficiently developed that neither the natural world nor human societies could adequately limit Western expansion. It is important, however, to understand the multivalent aspects of this tide of Western influence, especially in relation to individualism. This expansionist thought around the world was generally considered by Westerners not simply as exploitive, but as the liberation of other peoples from the confinements of cultural determinations and from conformity to tribal custom or cultural fixations. Traditional harmonies needed to be shattered; the traditional sense of the sacred needed to be abandoned. The value structure was to be changed. Briefly stated, the organic metaphor of reality, of society, and of the individual was to be replaced by a more atomistic sense of reality and a more legalistic metaphor of social relations based to a large extent on the ultimate value of the individual.

While China tried consistently throughout the nineteenth century to contain itself and its ancient ideals rooted in the integrity of its traditions, it found at the end of the century that it would need to enter a new period of turmoil. China would need to enter developmental history and to modify its dominant organic-person metaphor by the journey metaphor of the Western world.

The Chinese had possibly developed their doctrine of individuality as far as it could be developed within the context of this basic organic metaphor, which might be considered primarily a spatial metaphor. The tree symbolism referred to in the beginning of the *Great Learning* is a very significant symbol in Chinese tradition. This tree grows within a universal space. The individual in the macrophase of one's being experiences a certain radiant presence throughout this space and a certain biological and geological identity with all those beings, those ten thousand beings, that live and move and have their being in this space.

For the Western world the basic symbolism is more temporal than spatial. Journey, historical journey, requires movement, change, and transformation on a scale not compatible with established rituals or with fixed patterns. Yet it must be recognized here that we are speaking not of the journey through seasonal time or of a journey toward a fixed center in space such as the journey to the center in a mandala context. Nor are we speaking of the journey of Ulysses back to his prior home, or even of the journey of Rama, the journey into exile and return. We are speaking here of the more comprehensive journey of the emergent universe, a unique and irreversible journey of galactic systems, of earth formation, of living forms, of human community—a journey passing through a sequence of unpredictable discontinuities more extensive than is generally thought possible or even desirable in a more traditional context. In the West these transformations have been considered necessarily beneficial. The West in the past few centuries has been driven by a mythic sense of inevitable progress. This sense of progress and of journey originated in the biblical journey, especially in the exodus from Egypt to Palestine. It was historically interpreted further by Daniel, by John the Evangelist, by St. Augustine, and by Joachim of Flores as primarily a spiritual sequence of developments within a fixed universe. Later in the period of Francis Bacon and in the eighteenth-century French Enlightenment the journey was experienced as "progress," especially as progress of human understanding as in the ten stages of human intellectual development outlined by Condorcet; then as the journey of social improvement in the nineteenth century by Fourier, St. Simon, and Marx; as metaphysical journey by Hegel; as biological journey by Darwin, and finally as the immense journey of the universe by physicists and cosmologists of the twentieth century. This journey in recent times has been seen as activated by and terminating in individuals with a willingness to deviate from existing norms, even the most sacred norms of belief and of action.

The biological and even the geological structure and functioning of the planet were no longer normative as in the ancient ritual books of the Chinese. These as well as social bonds were seen as restrictive unless subordinated to human exploitive processes whereby the great journey was now being carried forward. The planet itself, swept up in a vortex of change, was being consumed for human individual advantage.

By the mid-twentieth century the ancient dialectic observed by the Chinese in the Great Tao had begun to assert itself. After intensive activity, quiet; after four centuries of particularity, wholeness; after a period of temporal discontinuity, a spatial expansion and continuity; after individualism, holism. So now the West experiences with a certain admiration the Chinese expression of relatedness, wholeness, inner cultivation, spontaneity, authenticity, universal reverence, communion with all the living and non-living components of the universe community.

These tendencies manifest themselves even from within the Western process itself. This we observe in the attraction of the West toward the organicism of Whitehead, toward the biological integrity of the planet presented by Lewis Thomas, toward the hologram metaphor of David Bohm, the synchronicity of Carl Jung, the integral dynamics of the post-industrial solar village of John and Nancy Todd, toward a sustainable economy grounded in the living cycle of renewable resources, and eventually toward a functional cosmology wherein the human personality experiences itself in both its microphase and macrophase of the universe itself. Now we can move toward understanding a macrophase that has both traditional spatial and historical temporal dimensions. Such a macrophase activates the society–individual relations in a greater tension than is generally the case on the principle that the most desirable state of an organism is not in its highest degree of harmony, but in the greatest tension between order and chaos that the organism can bear creatively. This includes a modified doctrine of individualism.

But if the West appears destined to express itself in a modified form of individualism, China, it seems, is destined to express itself in a modified form of its doctrine of humanity. China has not only a cosmos to commune with but a journey to take. So far China has kept in a single functional vision what in the West has been divided: the primordial integrity of the universe, the existential order of historical time, and the future order of harmonious presence of the heavenly, the earthly, and the human to each other. In China these three are overlays on each other. The Age of Yu and Shun is simultaneously primordial, present, and future; it is a memory to be kept, an ideal to guide the present, and a future to work toward.

History in the West originated in dividing these three stages in clear and definitive terms. So, too, with the individual and the society, the West differentiates these and places them in an extreme tension with each other. We might almost say that the West is activated more by fission processes while China is activated by fusion processes. As both fission and fusion in the nuclear world produce extraordinary energies, so those vast energies for sustaining and developing the great civilizations can be produced by either process. While such an analogy should not be mentioned in anything more than a passing and suggestive way, it does indicate in some slight manner the differences that can be taken in human affairs with special reference to the interaction between the individual and the society.

In some manner also these different approaches imply their opposites. The extensive commitment to tension and conflict in the West implies an extraordinary confidence in the capacity of the social structure to sustain this tension without disintegrating. So too the commitment to community on the part of the Chinese goes with an understanding that the support of the total community and even of the entire natural world is necessary to sustain the full development and expression of the individual.

We might conclude by observing that while these patterns of society–individual interactions will possibly remain identifying features of Chinese and Western traditions, these traditions may in the future find it helpful to take greater cognizance of each other.

Notes

1. Thomas Aquinas, *Summa Theologica*, trans. English Dominican Fathers, 3 vols. (New York: Benziger Brothers, 1946), pt. 1, q. 90, art. 4: "Since, therefore, the rational soul cannot be produced by a change in matter, it cannot be produced, save immediately by God."

2. The first formal definition of "person" comes from Boethius, *De duabus naturis* 3, where he says: "Person is an individual substance of a rational nature." This was further modified by St. Thomas with the term *incommunicabilis* (incom-

municable) in the *Summa Theologica*, pt. 1, q. 30, art. 4, ob. 2.: "But the very meaning of person is that it is incommunicable." Later in the *Summa contra Gentiles* he
added the term *subsistentia*, or subsistent being. Earlier Richard of St.-Victor in
1173 had given the definition of person as "intellectualis naturae incommunicabilis
existentia." (incommunicable existence of a rational nature) in his work *De Trini-
tate*, 4.22, 24. For further details concerning the definition of person in the earlier
Western tradition, see Max Muller and Alois Halder, "Person," in *Encyclopedia of
Theology*, ed. Karl Rahner (New York: Seabury Press, 1975). The consequence of
this definition of person as indicated by the authors of the article is the Western
commitment to the "absolute value and significance" of the individual human
being.

    3. Thomas Hobbes, "Leviathan," ch. 8. See Edwin A. Burtt, ed., *The English
Philosopher from Bacon to Mill* (New York: Modern Library, 1939), 161. "Hereby it
is manifest that during the time men live without a common power to keep them
all in awe, they are in a condition which is called war; and such a war as is of every
man against every man." See also Hobbes's introduction to "Leviathan," where the
state is described as an "artificial man" (p. 129).

    4. Bernhard Karlgren, *The Book of Documents* (Stockholm: Museum of Far East-
ern Antiquities, 1950), Bulletin 22, Kao yao mo 7., p. 5.

    5. James Legge, trans., *Sacred Books of the East*, vol. 27, *Li Ki*, bk. 7, sec. 3, ch. 7,
p. 382.

    6. Z. D. Sung, ed. and trans., *The Text of the Yi King* (New York: Paragon
Reprint Corp., 1969), sec. 1, ch. 5, p. 279.

    7. James Legge, trans., *The Works of Mencius* (Oxford University Press; reprint,
Shanghai, 1935), 4B:2, p. 321.

    8. Ibid., 7A:4, p. 450.

    9. Wm. Theodore de Bary et al., *Sources of Chinese Tradition* (New York:
Columbia University Press, 1960), quotation from Tung Chung-shu, p. 179.

    10. Ibid., 530.

    11. Ibid.

    12. Karlgren, *Documents*, Yao tien 22, p. 5.

    13. Mary Lelia Makra, ed. and trans., *The Hsiao Ching* (New York: St. John's
University Press, 1961), ch. 7.

    14. Wm. Theodore de Bary et al., *Sources of Japanese Tradition* (New York:
Columbia University Press, 1958), 383–84.

    15. Galen Fisher, "Nakae Toju: The Sage of Omi," *Transactions of the Asiatic
Society of Japan* (1908): 64.

2

The Ethical and the Meta-Ethical in Chinese High Cultural Thought

BENJAMIN I. SCHWARTZ

I
N THE FOLLOWING VERY PRELIMINARY REMARKS I shall focus on what seems to me to be a persistently recurring problematic or what some might even call an aporia in Chinese "high cultural" ethical thought. It is a problematic not peculiar to China and can be discerned within Indian thought and even in some strands of Western thought.

I shall not here dwell on the question of the applicability of the Western category "ethics" to Chinese thought. At this point I would simply baldly assert that I am satisfied that many of the themes discussed in modern Western discourses on ethics—such as the role of prescriptive normative rules, the role of individual "virtues" in human affairs, the Socratic concern with what is a "good life," the question of moral obligation, the nature of moral evil, and finally the question of how what we call the ethical relates to the entire nonhuman frame of things, whether this be called the universe, "nature," or cosmic reality—are to be found in Chinese thought. It is, of course, possible to discuss all of these themes without in any way denying the vast difference between the positive contents of varying ethical systems across cultures and across time.

What I would like to focus on particularly is the last theme—the relation of the ethical as a peculiarly human phenomenon to the "cosmic." Again, it is to be noted that this ethical theme has been problematic in all the higher civilizations, including the culture of the post-Cartesian West.

Many people who have few other associations with China think of Chinese culture as a culture particularly oriented to the ethical or moral. Here the role of what has been called "Confucianism" as the mainstream of the culture has no doubt played a decisive role. In the post-Cartesian and post-

Kantian secular Western world, where the ethical has come largely to be accepted as an eminently human and basically practical enterprise, the ethical orientation of Confucianism—particularly enhanced by the close linkage of the ethical to matters we call political—has reinforced the view of Confucian ethics as an essentially "humanistic" practical and "this-worldly" ethic. Here the words *humanist* and *practical* almost seem to presuppose the full weight of the modern antithesis of the cosmically based versus the human and the postmodern antithesis between the foundational and the practical.

It is quite true that the Confucius of the *Analects* has his attention firmly fixed on the sphere of human action in the human world and that his central vocation is the restoration of the pristine normative order, which had been actualized in the past yet had been lost. His task is thus not scientific or theoretical but pragmatic in a soteriological sense. In this, indeed, his profile resembles that of the Gautama Buddha as depicted in the early Theravada Sutras; he is equally pragmatic, albeit in a far less this-worldly mode. It is also quite clear that this Confucian pragmatism is an ethical pragmatism to the extent that Confucius is acutely aware of the enormous gap in his world between the empirical actualities of the way things are in his society and the way they ought to be ("The world, *tian xia,* is without the Way, *Dao*"). In neither Confucius nor the Buddha, however, is there any real evidence that they do not accept some of the prevailing assumptions in their culture concerning the nature of the larger nonhuman reality in which they found themselves or that they had the notion of a total disjuncture between the human realm and the nonhuman realm. Thus, if one considers all the references in the *Analects* to the word *Heaven* one may raise all sorts of questions about the ambiguous ways in which the term is used. Yet in all its uses it points to a transhuman reality that we can neither bracket nor dismiss as a "manner of speaking."

Thus, while the *Analects* is often presented as almost the key text of early Confucian ethical humanism and practicality, it is my view that it clearly relates to another vast discourse that both precedes and follows this text, which deals with matters we would—perhaps problematically—categorize as religious, mystical, cosmological, scientific, and metaphysical. The common element is that the discourse refers to a reality that lies beyond the human and in some sense embraces the human. There has also been a tendency to discern in this vast stream of thought certain pervasive and persistent dominant orientations that might be characterized in very loose terms almost as a kind of Chinese *philosophia perennis,* although like many others I would emphatically insist on the presence of pronounced counterorientations such as are to be found in Mohism and other modes of thought. It is also by no means clear that this orientation is in any sense "primordial" or stored up in the collective subconscious of the "Chinese mind." Most of the texts that point to this orientation do not appear before the second half of the first millennium B.C. It is an orientation that has often been described as holistic or organismic. The "whole," whether thought of as an all-embracing order or as a reality rooted in ineffable mystery, is—to use our language—immanently present in all the entities and relationships which it, as it were, engenders. It is also most often conceived of as embracing both the human and nonhuman worlds, and it is precisely in this area that the problem of the ethical arises.

It is often also called "naturalistic," although the question immediately arises whether the term naturalism refers to something closer to Aristotelian naturalism or to modern "scientific naturalism." The order of the world is not a "reductionist" order in which the world is built up out of particular parts but a plenum that engenders all the phenomenological diversity and plurality that we observe in our ordinary human experience of nature, and the nature of the parts is "spontaneously" governed by the whole. To the extent that we associate "non-naturalistic" action, with deliberate purposeful action, with reflection and even with the discursive rationality that we observe in the ordinary transactions of human life, it must be said that the behavior of this organismic world is governed by "non-action" (wuwei). It has been noted that this term as a way of describing the behavior of the universe is by no means exclusive to Daoism and appears in the very text of the Analects as a way of describing the ideal behavior of the sage king Shun. Indeed, the concepts of wuwei ("non-action") and ziran ("spontaneity"), which may be called "naturalistic," are closely associated with this Chinese philosophia perennis in all its permutations and transformations.

Finally, it should be noted that the atmosphere that pervades this holistic organismic vision tends on the whole to be affirmative and even celebratory. As in the creation account of Genesis, there is an overwhelming tendency to say that "it is good." It is not a world of indifferent neutral facticity as opposed to a world of value. On the contrary, it is the cosmic source of value, however value is conceived. To be sure, this "good" is not necessarily the good of human morality. It may, in the "philosophic" Daoist Laozi and Zhuangzi texts, be a good that lies beyond the "good and evil" of ethical discourse. It may be the good of mystic experience and/or of return to that "primitive" level of social life in which the human is no longer sundered from the unreflective spontaneous level of one's being. In the Zhuangzi the good seems to reside not only in the sense of oneness with the ineffable Dao but also in aesthetic contemplation of the inexhaustible diversity and wonder of the natural world.

To the extent that this apprehension of the holistic organismic and "good" cosmos can already be detected in the *Analects,* how does it relate to the Confucius who is profoundly distressed by the yawning gap between the moral good and evil with the human sphere? To the extent that the word *Dao,* or the Way, refers to both the order of nature and the human order, how do the two relate? Here we find a particularly pregnant passage attributed to Confucius in the *Analects.* "I would rather not speak," says the Master. When his disciples protest, he goes on to say, "Heaven does not speak, yet the four seasons run their course through it and the hundred creatures are engendered by it. Why should Heaven speak?"

As far as the organismic order of nature is concerned, it may be regarded as a perfect order in which an immanent Heaven realizes itself directly in all the diverse entities and patterns of nature. Even when we turn to the human sphere, it is clear from the *Analects* as a whole that there is the notion that the normative pattern of a good human order has been set forth, as it were, in the teachings of the "sage-kings," which derive from Heaven itself and even at times have been realized in the course of past history. Its pattern is present both in the normative rituals and ceremonial rules that govern the network of roles that maintain the harmony of family and society and in the realized virtues of sages and noble persons. The notion that these patterns of the good human order are all, as it were, "close at hand" may account for what may seem to be both the epistemological and moral optimism of Confucian ethics.

Yet the fact remains that Heaven has *not* guaranteed the immanent presence of its patterns within the human sphere. In the human being, Heaven has mysteriously engendered a creature that has the ominous capacity to obstruct Heaven's immanent presence and to create disorder. He or she is a creature who manages to create a fatal breach within the organismic whole. The gap that has thus been created makes possible the existence of moral evil. It has thus created a new reality in which the immanence of the whole is disrupted. By the same token, Heaven now finds itself in a relation of transcendence vis-à-vis this human reality.

To be sure, Heaven has also endowed some humans with extraordinary power to grasp the Heavenly pattern for the ordering both of their own individual lives and for the ordering of society. Indeed some of them—the mythic sages and superior persons—in particular seem to have the power to embody within themselves the holistic power of Heaven. Yet even they must communicate with other humans through language. When Confucius says that he would rather not speak, he seems to be projecting his persona as that of the sage who in a good society is able, like Heaven, to radiate his spirit over the society as a whole through his presence and his noble behavior without speech. Yet the fact remains that Confucius—who does not present himself as a sage—spends his life speaking. Language is, to be sure, a profoundly ambiguous gift. On the one hand, language ideally provides us with the ideal normative patterns of the good social order. The true definition of the term *father* embraces all the ideal qualities of a father. On the other hand, the misuse of the language can easily become the vehicle of deceit, treachery, and all other human vices. Confucius cannot emulate Heaven. He cannot seek ethical advance without language. Not only does he need language to influence others; he also needs the normative language—the language stored in sacred texts of the past—in order to cultivate himself. If language is indispensable, it must, however, also be conceded that the use of language in most of our discourse (poetry may offer exceptions) is a *yuwei* and not a *wuwei* language, of ordinary discursive rationality and the incremental accumulation of empirical knowledge. It may at moments reflect spontaneous expressivity, but it is mainly deliberate. There may be moments of epiphany, in which the "wholeness" of reality is grasped in a synoptic intuition. There are also moments of doubt and perplexity. While Confucius is quoted as saying that after the age of seventy he could follow his spontaneous desires without transgressing the norms of human order, the account of the process of "learning" or education is one of arduous, scrupulous, and cumulative study, reflection, and acquisition of empirical knowledge. Indeed, when one reads the texts of the *Analects* as a whole, one has the impression that the view of ethical life is of a lifelong arduous struggle most often marked by nonspontaneity. "Non-natural" deliberative action is accepted as a necessary and even positive aspect of the human condition.

I shall not dwell here on this age-long dialectic of the interplay between the organismic *philosophia perennis* and modes of thought that emphasize the nonspontaneous and the *yuwei* within the human sphere. The *philosophia perennis* is by no means all-embracing. Indeed, within that ancient mode of thought called Mohism, we even find a radical rejection of its major premises. In other streams of thought such as Confucianism and Legalism, what we find is a complex dialectic tension between strains of thought that lean to the holistic organismic direction and strains of thought that run in precisely the opposite direction.

Within the history of Confucianism the vision of a world of preexisting immanent harmony with which one "reconnects"—a world in which the ominous gap that emerges within the human ethical sphere can "easily" (*jian*) be bridged—exercises an enormous attraction over the centuries. Yet the duality of moral good versus moral evil remains a singularly recalcitrant duality. The *philosophia perennis* can easily accommodate many of the dyadic aspects of the world within the larger whole. Such dualities, however, are most often thought of as complementary or even as the opposite poles of a spectrum. Yet in the world of moral good versus moral evil we cannot escape duality as a mutually exclusive antithesis. Evil must be eliminated and the good must triumph. Thus, in interpreting the thought of the famed Confucian thinker Zhu Xi, of the Sung dynasty, there has been an ongoing interpretative battle between those who regard him as an ultimate adherent of the *philosophia perennis* and those who regard him as an out-and-out dualist. There can be no doubt that on one level of his thought he accepts the *philosophia perennis* and even posits the possibility of establishing connections with the whole through meditation. Yet, on another level, he devotes most of his energy to the elaboration of a philosophic anthropology that provides a solid "ontological" basis for the reality of the enormous gap between moral good and moral evil. On this level his language is not the Daoist language of spontaneity and non-action, but the language of reflection, purpose, and deliberate intent.

I shall not attempt in these preliminary remarks to elaborate the possible implications of the tension between the dominant *philosophia perennis* of China and the history of "high cultural" ethical thought as it related to the ethical and political history of China, to the "popular" culture of the masses, or to the cultural crisis of modern China. Its implications are, however, certainly no less profound than those of the "fact/value" antithesis in modern Western thought.

3

Between the Heavenly
and the Human

YING-SHIH YÜ

T HE IDEA OF THE "UNITY OF HEAVEN AND MAN" (*tianrenheyi*) has been generally regarded a feature uniquely characteristic of Chinese religious and philosophical imagination. The *tianren* polarity as a category of thinking was already essential to Chinese philosophical analysis in classical antiquity. Thus, in the *Zhuangzi* the question is often asked as to where the fine line is to be drawn between "the heavenly" and "the human." Zhuangzi's emphasis on the notion of *tian* was later sharply criticized by Xunzi (third century B.C.E.) as being blinded by the heavenly and insensitive to the human. However, on his own part Xunzi also insisted that true knowledge of the world must begin with a clear recognition of the distinction between the two realms.

By the second century B.C.E. at the latest, the *tianren* category had been firmly established as a basic way of thinking due, in no small measure, to the pervasive influence of the *yin-yang* cosmology in general and Dong Zhongshu (second century B.C.E.) in particular. Throughout the Han dynasty (206 B.C.E.–220 C.E.) belief in the mutual interaction between the Way of Heaven and human affairs in both elite and popular cultures was nearly universal. It was in such a climate of opinion that Sima Qian (145–90? B.C.E.), the Grand Historian of China, devoted his entire life to the writing of his monumental *History*, which was intended, in his own words, "to examine into all that concerns Heaven and man." Thus he set an example for historians of later centuries to follow. It is by no means a mere coincidence that Liu Zhiji (661–721), the great Tang official historiographer was praised by his contemporaries as a man "whose learning joined together the realms of Heaven and man." In the eighteenth century, Zhang Xuecheng (1738–1801), arguably the most philosophically minded of all historians in the Chinese tradition, also took great pride in the purpose he set for his work, which was "to show the interrelatedness of the heavenly to the human thereby throwing light on the Great Way." In both cases, the allusion to Sima Qian is unmistakable.

The *tianren* polarity also figured prominently in both Wei-Jin Neo-Taoism and Song-Ming Neo-Confucianism. He Yan (d. 249) and Wang Bi enjoyed each other's company because they could always discuss "matters concerning the interrelationships between Heaven and man" with perfect understanding. Needless to say, complex metaphysical issues arising from the basic distinction between "Heavenly principle" (*tianli*) and "human desires" (*renyü*) constituted the very core of Neo-Confucian discourse. The story is too familiar to require further elaboration here.

The notion of "unity of Heaven and man" proves to be so surprisingly resilient that it continues to haunt the Chinese mind in the twentieth century. In the early 1940s Chin Yueh-lin (1895–1984), a leading Chinese metaphysician thoroughly trained in Western philosophy, and Fung Yu-lan made a concerted philosophical effort to develop the idea of *tianrenheyi* each in his own way, with the explicit purpose of exploring the possibility of its relevance to the modern world. In a comparativist context Chin singled out *tianrenheyi* as the "most distinguishing characteristic" of Chinese philosophy. Fully aware of the comprehensiveness and complexity of the thesis, he nevertheless tended to interpret it in terms of the "unity of nature and man" and contrasted it to the dominant Western idea of "conquest of nature."[1] On the other hand, Fung applied this thesis to what he called "the transcendent sphere of living," the highest ideal in his philosophy of life. In his own words, "the highest achievement of the man living in this sphere is the identification of himself with the universe, and in this identification, he also transcends the intellect."[2]

Since the early 1990s a great controversy has flared up in the Chinese intellectual world around the notion of *tianrenheyi*. In this ongoing debate many questions have been raised regarding the exact meanings of this classic thesis. Some are continuous with Chin's interpretation but focus more sharply on the dilemma of how to achieve oneness with nature and simultaneously accommodate science and technology in Chinese culture. Others echo Fung's metaphysical, ethical, or religious concerns but go beyond him by drawing modern and even postmodern implications from this thesis for Chinese spirituality. The details of this current debate need not concern us here. I mention it only to show that *tianrenheyi* is by no means a fossilized idea of merely historical interest. Instead it remains a central component of the Chinese frame of mind to this very day. Indeed it may hold the key to one of the doors leading to the world of Chinese spirituality.

As a historian, however, I do not feel at ease with pure speculation. In what follows I proposed first to offer an account of the genesis and development of this idea and then to try to explain how it eventually evolved into one of the defining features of Chinese mentality. My approach is essentially historical.

To begin with, let me introduce the ancient myth of the "Separation of Heaven and Earth." Briefly, the myth runs as follows: In high antiquity humans and deities did not intermingle. Humans, for their part, held gods in reverence and kept themselves in the assigned places in the cosmic order. On the other hand, deities also descended among them from time to time through the intermediaries of the shamans (*wu*). As a consequence, the spheres of the divine and the profane were kept distinct. The deities sent down blessings on the people and accepted from them their offerings. There were no natural calamities. Then came the age of decay, in which humans and deities became intermingled, with each household indiscriminately performing for itself the religious observances that had hitherto been conducted by the shamans. As a result, the people lost their reverence for the deities, the gods violated the rules of the human world, and calamities arose. It was at this point that the sage-ruler Zhuanxu (traditionally dated to the twenty-fifth century B.C.E.) intervened, presumably with the approval of the God-on-High; he rearranged the cosmic order by cutting the communication of Heaven and earth.[3]

This myth is very rich with meanings and can be interpreted in a variety of ways. In the present context I wish to make only a simple historical observation: it may have served as a justification of the fact that in ancient China only the universal king had direct access to Heaven. According to tradition, under the Three Dynasties of Xia, Shang, and Zhou, making sacrificial offerings to Heaven was a prerogative exclusively reserved for the king. The local feudal lords were entitled to communicate with the earthly deities through sacrificial rites within their domains but not with the celestial ones. In other words, the "unity between the Heavenly and the human" was strictly confined to the Son of Heaven, who, as one modern interpretation suggests, was also the head shaman.

Here, however, a difficulty inevitably arises: the idea of the "unity between the heavenly and the human" mentioned in the beginning of this paper is built on an assumption diametrically opposed to the myth of the "Separation of Heaven and Earth." It presupposes that every individual person on earth is in principle communicable with heaven. Admittedly the exact meanings of the concept "heaven" are quite different in these two theses. Nevertheless, structurally speaking, the two must be viewed as each other's negation. The very notion that everyone can communicate with heaven without the assistance even of a shaman clearly implies that access to heaven is no longer a royal monopoly. Since, as we shall see, the beginning of an individualistic version of *tianrenheyi* can be traced to no earlier than the sixth century B.C.E., we may assume that it was developed, at least partly, as a conscious response to the ancient myth of "separation" which had dominated the Chinese mind for many centuries. It is to this important development of Chinese spirituality that I must now turn.

The author of the last chapter of the *Zhuangzi*, perhaps a latter-day follower of the Master, describes with a profound sense of sadness the "breakup" of the primeval oneness of *Dao*. He linked this "break-up" to the rise of the "Hundred Schools" of philosophy in China. Each of the schools, he said, comprehended but a singular aspect of the original whole. It is like the case of the ear, the eye, the nose, and the mouth, each having a particular sense, without being able to function interchangeably. As a result the purity of Heaven and Earth and the wholeness of *Dao* have been forever lost.[4] In this earliest account of the first philosophical movement in Chinese classical antiquity, our writer historicizes an original allegory suggested by Zhuangzi himself. It runs as follows:

> The God of the South Sea was called Shu [Swift], the God of the North Sea was called Hu [Sudden], and the God of the central region was called Hundun [Chaos]. Shu and Hu from time to time came together for a meeting in the territory of Hundun, and Hundun treated them very generously. Shu and Hu discussed how they could repay his kindness. "All men," they said, "have seven openings so they can see, hear, eat, and breathe. But Hundun alone doesn't have any. Let's try boring him some."
>
> Everyday they bored another hole, and on the seventh day Hundun died. (p. 97)

I am quite convinced that the latter-day follower's historical account is a truthful reading of the Master's original allegory. The analogy of sensory apertures in both cases makes it clear that Zhuangzi's Chaos (Hundun) is the symbol of the primordial wholeness of *Dao*. In making use of this famous allegory about the death of Chaos, Zhuangzi must have had in mind what historians today see as a "swift" (Shu) and "sudden" (Hu) beginning of spiritual enlightenment in ancient China. Laozi, Confucius, and Mo Di, to mention only three of the greatest names in the history of Chinese philosophy, all appeared in the sixth and fifth centuries B.C.E.

Now the question is, How are we to understand this sudden spiritual enlightenment and relate it to the distinction between the heavenly and the human? In this connection I would like to begin by placing the question in a comparative perspective, because China was not the only civilization in the ancient world that experienced this enlightenment. It took place in other civilizations as well. Some four decades ago Karl Jaspers called our attention to the most fascinating fact that in the first millennium B.C.E., which he called the Axial Period, a spiritual "breakthrough" occurred in several high cultures, including China, India, Persia, Israel, and Greece. It took the form of either philosophical reasoning, or post-mythical religious imagination or a mixed type of moral-philosophic-religious consciousness as in the case of China. Apparently, the breakthroughs in the Axial Period all took place independently of one another and no mutual influences can be established. The most we can say about them is probably that when civilizations or cultures developed to a certain stage they would undergo a common experience of spiritual awakening of some kind. Jaspers further suggested that the ultimate importance of this Axial breakthrough lies in the fact that it tended to exert a defining and formative influence on the character of the civilizations involved.[5] In the past decades much has been discussed about Jaspers's concept of "breakthrough," and there is a general consensus that the great transformation of the Chinese mind in the time of Confucius can be more sensibly understood as one of the major breakthroughs during the Axial Period. It is therefore all the more remarkable that Zhuangzi and his followers had already grasped the historical significance of the very intellectual movement which they themselves were promoting. "Death of Chaos" or "break-up of the primeval *Dao*" has indeed captured the essential meaning of the idea of "Axial breakthrough."

There are many ways of characterizing the Axial breakthrough. For the purpose of my discussion here I prefer to see it as China's first spiritual awakening involving centrally an original transcendence. It is "transcendence" in the sense of, as Benjamin I. Schwartz has suggested, "a kind of critical, reflective questioning of the actual and a new vision of what lies beyond."[6] The transcendence is "original" in the sense that it has ever since remained, by and large, a central defining feature of the Chinese mentality throughout the traditional period.

Scholars are also in basic agreement that the Axial breakthrough led directly to the emergence of the dichotomy between the actual world and the world beyond. This is essentially what transcendence is all about: The actual world is transcended but not negated. On the other hand, however, the exact shape, empirical content, and historical process of transcendence varied from civilization to civilization as each had taken place on a pre-breakthrough foundation uniquely its own. In what immediately follows I shall try to say something about the uniqueness of the Chinese transcendence. Some Western scholars have already noticed that in contrast to other Axial breakthroughs China's appears to have been a "least radical"[7] or "most conservative"[8] one. I think this judgment is well grounded and reasonable. There are many different ways to argue for the case. One would be the Chinese emphasis on historical continuity during and since the Axial Period. The "breakthrough" did occur, but it was not a complete break with the pre-breakthrough tradition. Another way is to look into the relationship between the actual world and the world beyond.

In the Chinese breakthrough, the two worlds, actual and transcendental, do not appear to have been sharply divided. There is nothing in the early Chinese philosophical visions that suggests Plato's conception of an unseen eternal world of which the actual world is only a pale copy. In the religious tradition the sharp dichotomy of a Christian type between the world of God and the world of humans is also absent. Nor do we find in classical Chinese thought in all its varieties anything that closely resembles the radical negativity of early Buddhism with its insistence on the unrealness and worthlessness of this world. In the case of China during the Axial Period, the idea of *Dao* emerged as a symbol of the transcendental world in contrast to the actual world of everyday life. This was equally true of the Confucians and the Daoists. But in either case *Dao* was never perceived as very far from everyday life. Confucius said: "The *Dao* is not far from man. When a man pursues the *Dao* and remains away from man, his course cannot be considered the *Dao*." The *Doctrine of the Mean* also stressed the point that the *Dao* functions everywhere and yet is hidden. Men and women of simple intelligence can share its knowledge or practice it; and yet in its utmost reaches there is something that even the sage does not know or is unable to put into practice. Both Laozi and Zhuangzi took *Dao* to be a "higher realm" of existence as opposed to the actual world. Generally speaking, the distinction between "this world" and "other world" is more sharply drawn in Daoism than in Confucianism. Nevertheless the Daoists' two worlds are not neatly separate either. Thus, when Zhuangzi was asked: "This thing called the *Dao*—where does it exist?" The Master's answer is, "There is no place it doesn't exist." As he further explained to the questioner, "You must not expect to find the *Dao* in any particular place— there is no thing that escapes its presence!" (pp. 240–41). Zhuangzi's admirer once described him in the following way:

> He came and went alone with the pure spirit of Heaven and earth, yet he did not view the ten thousand things with arrogant eyes. He did not scold over "right" and "wrong," but lived with the age and its vulgarity. . . . Above he wandered with the Creator, below he made friends with those who have gotten outside of life and death, who know nothing of beginning or end." (p. 373)

In other words, Zhuangzi lived in "this world" but at the same time his spirit wandered in the "other world."

Up to this point what I have been trying to show is that as a result of the Axial breakthrough China also developed its own duality of the transcendental and actual worlds. However, this Chinese duality differed from that in other civilizations by being not as sharply differentiated. The typical Chinese description of the relationship between these two worlds is "neither identical nor separate" (*buji buli*). This description may be hard to comprehend for those who are accustomed to dichotomist thinking, but it does constitute a central feature of the Chinese transcendence. The title of my paper, "Between the Heavenly and the Human," is also chosen to convey this unique Chinese imagination. To take a step further, I now propose to interpret the Chinese case as "inward transcendence."

The inwardness of Chinese transcendence cannot be understood without a brief discussion of the historical process of the Axial breakthrough in early China. It has been suggested that the Axial breakthrough took place in Greece against the background of the world of Homeric gods, in Israel against the background of the early books of the Bible and the story of Moses, and in India against the background of the long Vedic tradition. What then was the Chinese background against which the breakthrough occurred? My straightforward answer is: the long ritual tradition of the Three Dynasties (Xia-Shang-Zhou). By "ritual tradition" I refer to both *li* ("rites") and *yue* ("music"), which had been embodied in the way of life of the ruling elite since the Xia dynasty. Confucius's famous characterization of the Xia-Shang-Zhou ritual tradition as a continuous but ever-renovating system (*Analects* 2:23) seems to have been validated by every major advance in archaeology as far as the last two dynasties are concerned. However, by the time of Confucius this ritual order was already on the brink of total breakdown due largely to the widespread transgressions and violations of rites by the ruling elite. Here we have a classic example of breakdowns preceding breakthroughs in history.

Next we must try to establish the historical link between the Axial breakthrough and the ritual breakdown in terms of transcendence. In the interest of brevity it suffices to point out that the ritual tradition was indeed the point of departure of Chinese transcendence resulting directly from the Axial breakthrough. One of Confucius's central visions consisted in transcending the existing ritual practice by searching for the "basis of rites." His new search ended, as we all know, in the reinterpretation of *ren* (in this case, "human-heartedness") as the spiritual kernel of *li*. Thus he departed from the traditional view that *li* originated in human imitation of the divine models provided by Heaven and earth (*Zuozhuan*, Duke Zhao, twenty-fifth year). Instead of looking outwardly toward Heaven and Earth, he now turned inwardly toward the human heart for the "basis of rites." Similarly, both the Mohist and the Daoist breakthroughs, which came after Confucius's, also took the ritual tradition to serious task. Mozi not only viewed the ever-growing complexity and elaborateness of *li* through the ages as steadily but irreversibly falling into decay but also severely criticized Confucius's reform for its failure to eradicate all the existing ritual practices developed during Zhou period. Hence his advocacy of a return to the simplicity of the original Xia ritual system. As for the Daoists, theirs may be described as the most radical of all the breakthroughs among the pre-Qin schools of thought. This is the case because it alone drew a distinction between the actual world and the world beyond sharper than any other school. Zhuangzi, in particular, has been the main source of the strain of otherworldliness in the Chinese spiritual tradition. But it must be emphatically pointed out that the Daoists also took the ritual tradition as the starting point of their transcendence. As clearly stated in the *Daodejing* (ch. 38), "rites" are "the beginning of disorder," meaning that the spirit of original *Dao* has degenerated, step by step, to its lowest point. On the other hand, Zhuangzi tried to show us how to return to *Dao* by transcending the actual world, also step by step, beginning with the "rites" (p. 90).[9] Thus the process of "fall," so to speak, in the *Daodejing* is reversed to become the process of "salvation" in the *Zhuangzi*. Rejecting all the current ritual practices as artificial nonsense Zhuangzi nevertheless did not go so far as to propose discarding the very notion of *li* itself; he continued to speak of the "meaning of rites" (*liyi*). In his conception, obviously, "pounding on a tub and singing" in the presence of his wife's corpse is a more meaningful funeral rite than weeping (pp. 191–92). In the above three cases, it is significant that the founders of Confucianism, Mohism, and Daoism all "philosophically reinterpreted the existing religious practice rather than directly withdrawing themselves from it," a fact considered by Max Weber to be "of fundamental importance."[10] I would venture to suggest that reinterpretation instead of withdrawal may help explain to a large extent why, of all the Axial breakthroughs, China's turned out to be the "least radical" or "most conservative."

Lastly, let us examine inward transcendence in relation to the changing conception of the "unity of Heaven and man." It may be recalled that during the time when the myth of the "Separation of Heaven and Earth" was generally accepted, only the king could directly communicate with Heaven with the assistance of *wu*-shamans. As a result, the "unity of Heaven and man" became a prerogative exclusively reserved for the king, who, theoretically, was decreed by Heaven as the sole representative of all the humans on earth as a collectivity. In an important sense it was against this royal monopoly of the access to Heaven that the Chinese Axial breakthrough began as a spiritual revolt.

In his further characterizations of the Axial breakthrough, Jaspers particularly called our attention to two of its distinguishing features. First, the breakthrough is the spiritual awakening and liberation of humans as *individuals;* for the first time they "dared to rely on themselves as individuals" to embark on a spiritual journey beyond not only their own selves but the actual world as well. Second, with the breakthrough the spiritually awakened and liberated individual appears to have been in need of relating his or her own existence in this world meaningfully to "the whole of Being."

This general characterization, it seems to me, throws a comparativist light on the individualistic turn of the *tianrenheyi* thesis during China's Axial breakthrough. Take the idea of *tianming* ("Mandate or Decree of Heaven"), for example. Confucius said: "at fifty I understood the Decree of Heaven" (*Analects* 2:4) and the gentleman "is in awe of the Decree of Heaven" (16:8). As D. C. Lau rightly points out in his translator's "Introduction," "The only development by Confucius' time was that the Decree of Heaven was no longer confined to the Emperor. Every man was subject to the Decree of Heaven which enjoined him to be moral and it was his duty to live up to the demands of that Decree" (p. 28). Onozawa Seiichi also made a similar observation in 1978. By associating the concept of *tianming* with *xin* ("heart") and *de* ("virtue" also with a "heart" component) in a bronze inscription, he came to the conclusion that in the time of Confucius the idea of *tianming* underwent a subtle shift from something in support of dynastic politics to that which is to be conferred on the individuals and ultimately to be seated in their hearts.[11] Thus, with *tianming* being conferred on every individual, the direct line of communication between Heaven and individual humans was reestablished after a long period of "separation of Heaven and earth." As a result, Confucius often spoke as if he were constantly in personal contact with Heaven: "Heaven is author of the virtue that is in me" (7:23) or "If I am understood at all, it is, perhaps, by Heaven" (14:35). Statements like these clearly suggest that Confucius as an individual was capable of communicating with Heaven directly. It is also fascinating that Zhuangzi once put the following words into the mouth of Yan Hui, Confucius's most favorite disciple:

> By being inwardly straight, I can be the companion of Heaven. Being a companion of Heaven, I know that the Son of Heaven and I are equally the sons of Heaven." (p. 56)[12]

Here, in his unique way, Zhuangzi tried to convey the radical Daoist idea that every individual person, by being "inwardly straight"—a reference to "virtue" in the heart, could be a son of Heaven. With this twist Zhuangzi demolished the claim of the king that he alone is the Son of Heaven. Needless to say, as sons of Heaven all individual humans can directly communicate with Heaven so long as they are able to keep their hearts "straight."

Up to this point we have seen how the individual's turn of *tianrenheyi* led to the reopening of the direct line of communication between Heaven, on the one hand, and the spiritually awakened and liberated individual human, on the other. Moreover, as both Onozawa's study and the passage quoted from the *Zhuangzi* indicate, the center of communication seems to have been located in the heart. The time has now arrived for us to move on to the question of inward transcendence.

Communication was at the very center of the whole question of *tianren-heyi*. Therefore we must first ask: How did the universal king communicate with Heaven during the entire pre-Axial period? This question brings us to the communicative function of the ritual (*li*) practice. As already mentioned earlier, the king had all along relied on the assistance of *wu*-shamans to communicate with Heaven. As the king's trusted religious functionaries, *wu*-shamans claimed that they alone had access to Heaven: they either ascended to Heaven to seek instructions from the God-on-High, deities, and royal ancestral spirits on behalf of the reigning king or made celestial deities and spirits to descend to the human world. To do so, however, they had to perform certain rituals with the help of a great variety of ritual paraphernalia. To a considerable extent, the Axial breakthrough was directed against the shamanistic component of the ritual system. Confucius's reinterpretation of the ritual practice may well be understood in this light. As a spiritually awakened and liberated thinker, Confucius needed no *wu*-shamans to serve as intermediaries in his direct communication with Heaven. Thus, the enormous communicative power previously believed to be the monopoly of *wu*-shamans was now assigned to *ren*, the spiritual kernel of *li*, which could only be located in the human heart. This inward turn took a giant step forward in the fourth century B.C.E. with the emergence of the new cosmology of *qi*. According to this new theory, the *qi* permeates the entire cosmos. It is in constant movement and, when differentiated and individuated, all things in the world are formed. However, this *qi* is vastly varied in consistency, ranging from the most refined to the grossest. Generally speaking, two types may be distinguished: the pure *qi*, being light, is associated with Heaven, whereas the gross *qi*, being heavy, is associated with earth. The human person is a mixture of both, with his body being made up of the grosser *qi* and his heart being the seat of the refined *qi*.

With this cosmology of *qi*, the idea of *tianrenheyi* entered into a completely new age. As a consequence, thinkers of various persuasions began to develop their new versions of *tianrenheyi* with a view to displacing the earlier *wu*-shamanistic interpretation. When Mencius talked about his concept of *haoran zhi qi* ("floodlike *qi*"), he was actually presenting his individualist view of the "unity of Heaven and man." Only by turning inward to nourish the most refined *qi* in the heart can one hope to attain oneness with the cosmos (*Mencius* 2A:2). Elsewhere he also said, "A gentleman transforms where he passes, and works wonders where he abides. He is in the same stream as Heaven above and Earth below" (7A:13). In this new conception of *tianrenheyi* the communicative function was assumed, according to him, by the most refined *qi* seated in the innermost part—heart—of every individual human person.

A similar development may also be found in the *Zhuangzi*. In discussing the possibility of an individual person's attainment of oneness with the transcendent *Dao*, the Daoist philosopher offered his famous theory of "fasting of the heart" (*xin-zhai*). According to it, the heart must be, on the one hand, emptied of everything else and, on the other hand, filled with *qi* of the purest kind so that *Dao* may find it hospitable. Like Mencius, he also emphasized the utmost importance of cultivation of *qi*, which alone can sharpen one's sensitivity and ability to the highest degree in order to monitor the rhythm of the ever-ongoing cosmic transformation (pp. 57–58). Thus the cases of Confucius, Mencius, and Zhuangzi provide us with three concrete and vivid examples of what I propose to call "inward transcendence," which distinguishes the Chinese Axial breakthrough from the rest in a fundamental way.

The historical process reconstructed above is intended as an explanation of how the Chinese Axial breakthrough led to an inward transcendence and why. As shown in my brief discussion of the idea of *tianming*, Axial thinkers, as spiritually awakened and liberated individuals, made a subtle strategic move to break the royal monopoly of access to Heaven by transferring the center of communication from the ritual system dominated by *wu*-shamanism to the heart of every individual human. Here we have a concrete example illustrative of the breakthrough taking place right in the center of the Xia-Shang-Zhou ritual tradition. It also shows that the Heaven–human relationship took a decidedly new turn as China moved from the pre-Axial to the Axial period, which was individualist and inward in the same breath. Between the pre-Axial ritual tradition and the philosophic breakthrough, a qualitative leap in Chinese spirituality occurred. Having transcended the ritual tradition, the Chinese mind raised itself to a new level of articulation and conceptualization.

At this juncture, however, a further question calls for our critical attention. I have suggested above that all the three major schools of thought—Confucianism, Mohism, and Daoism—reinterpreted the idea of *li* each in its own way, and none arrived at a complete break with the ritual tradition. This less than complete break with the pre-Axial tradition seems to bear significantly, as I have hinted above, on the fact that the Chinese Axial breakthrough did not give rise to a transcendental world setting itself in explicit opposition to the actual. Such being the case, an account, however brief, of the continuity between tradition and breakthrough seems very much in order. Let me now return to the *tianrenheyi* thesis with special reference to the concept of Decree of Heaven.

To begin with, the whole notion of *tianrenheyi* itself was directly continuous from tradition to breakthrough, only differently interpreted. In the Shang-Zhou times the king and the ruling elite looked up to Heaven as the ultimate source of wisdom and power of the highest kind, to which the shaman-dominated ritual system alone provided the access. During the Axial period, spiritually awakened individuals also needed to keep themselves in daily contact with the sources of spiritual power. As shown in the cases of Mencius and Zhuangzi, they relied on the cultivation of the most refined *qi* in their hearts to accomplish this delicate task. Thus, the "heart" became the only medium through which the line of communication between the individual human and Heaven or *Dao* was kept open. The vast differences in terms of contents of thought aside, the continuity of the new version of *tianrenheyi* with its pre-Axial ritual archetype is clearly recognizable.

The concept of Decree of Heaven stood at the very center of the pre-Axial *tianrenheyi* thesis. The term *tianming* is generally believed to be of western Zhou origin, but it has also been suggested that a functional equivalent without this term may have already been available to the Shang king for legitimation of his political authority. At any rate it can be safely assumed that the necessity of renewing his *tianming* from time to time must have been among the most important reasons for the king to communicate with Heaven through performance of certain rituals aided by a wide range of paraphernalia. According to the Zhou theory, a reigning dynasty is qualified for *tianming* only when the king and the ruling elite are in possession of certain "brilliant virtues" (*mingde*) such as "fearful reverence of Heaven," "loving care for the people," "conscientious attention to administration," "practice of frugality," and so on.[13] Later, when Mencius summed up his discussion of this notion, he quoted a saying from a lost chapter of the *Classic of History* (*Shujing*) as follows:

> Heaven sees with the eyes of its people. Heaven hears with the ears of its people. (Mencius 5A:5)

This is clearly the Chinese version of *vox populi, vox Dei*. Modern classicists are well grounded when they suggest that the concept of Decree of Heaven, understood in this way, constituted the very essence of the *tianrenheyi* thesis in western Zhou times.[14]

Regarding the Decree of Heaven, I would like to suggest several lines of continuity between tradition and breakthrough. First, we have seen how Confucius used the term *tianming* to describe his personal relationship with Heaven. According to the *Zuozhuan* (Duke Zhao, seventh year), a nobleman of Lu made this remark about Confucius: "If a sagely man of brilliant virtue (*mingde*) does not get distinguished in his time, among his posterity there is sure to be someone of vast intelligence." It is important to note that the term *mingde*, which was the precondition for the king and his dynasty to receive the Decree of Heaven, also began to be applied to the individual, in this case the ancestor of Confucius. Thus we see that the whole notion of *tianming* continued well into the Axial Age despite its shift of emphasis from a collectivistic to an individualistic sense. Second, Confucius's famous "rule of virtue" (*Analects* 2:1) must also be understood as a continuation of the western Zhou conception of government based on "brilliant virtues," even though in the latter case the power of *de* may have been conceived of as associated with the ritual communication under shamanistic influences. For Confucius, however, the power of "virtue" was generated by the heart through "cultivation" (7:3). This line of political thinking later culminated in Mencius's idea of "benevolent government," with particular emphasis on the importance of "a heart sensitive to the suffering of others" on the part of the king (Mencius 2A:6). Indeed the thread of "rule of virtue" ran continuously from early Zhou through Confucius to Mencius, while turning ever-increasingly inward. Last but not least, the inward turn of the idea of *tianming* itself had its beginning earlier than the time of Confucius. The *Zuozhuan* reports a well-known event of 605 B.C.E., which may be summed up as follows. The Lord of Chu asked a court official of the eastern Zhou about the size and weight of the Nine Tripods, which were the ritual symbol of *tianming* for the Zhou. He meant to carry them back so that the Chu could replace the Zhou house as the new recipient of the Decree of Heaven. The Zhou official replied by saying: "The size and weight are not in the tripods but in virtue. . . . Though the virtue of Zhou is decayed, the Decree of Heaven is not yet changed" (Duke Xuan, third year). This is the earliest evidence, as far as I know, of the inward turn of *tianming* with specific reference to *de* as inner virtue or power vis-à-vis the Nine Tripods as sacred ritual symbol. This anecdote suggests that the Lord of Chu probably still subscribed to the traditional belief that whoever possessed the Nine Tripods also possessed the Decree of Heaven. However, the eastern Zhou official's reply clearly indicates that a new belief had come into being according to which the *tianming* was linked primarily to *de* as inner spiritual virtue, not the external ritual paraphernalia such as the Nine Tripods. In this connection I may briefly mention that the character *de* itself also underwent a similar change toward inwardness. Its earlier written form is composed of two parts, "action" and "straight." Then in some of the later Zhou bronze inscriptions, a third element, "heart," is added. It has been lately suggested that the meaning of *de* may have changed from something descriptive of external human behavior to that of inner human qualities. It may be significant that in the newly discovered Daoist and Confucian texts on bamboo slips from Guodian tentatively dated around 300 B.C.E., the character *de* is invariably written in the form of "straight" plus "heart." The inward turn of the *tianrenheyi* thesis may well have begun before the process of Axial breakthrough was fully activated.

With *tianrenheyi* as a central thread, I have outlined a historical account of the genesis and evolution of inward transcendence from the pre-Axial ritual tradition to Axial breakthrough. The continuity of the notion of *tianrenheyi*, in particular, strongly suggests that its earliest archetype may have been provided by the ritual communication between Heaven and human under the influence of *wu*-shamanism. As the "Separation" myth shows, *wu*-shamans played a pivotal role as intermediaries in this celestial communication. It is true that Axial thinkers beginning with Confucius eventually transcended the ritual tradition, which resulted in an epoch-making philosophic breakthrough. But they did this by way of "reinterpretation" of, not "complete withdrawal" from, the original ritual system. As a result, "Heaven" was reinterpreted in a variety of senses including Dao; the medium of communication changed from "*wu*-shaman" to "heart"; and ritual performance was also replaced by spiritual cultivation. Nevertheless, the archetypal structure remained intact: the spiritually awakened individual human continued to long for "unity" or "oneness" with the realm beyond, where the deepest sources of wisdom and power were supposedly to be found. However, since the center of communication is now located in the human heart (*xin*, also "mind"), the search for the realm beyond must of necessity begin by turning inward. This is beautifully expressed by D. C. Lau in his "introduction" to the *Mencius:*

> Acting in accordance with Heaven's Decree is something one can do joyfully by looking inwards and finding the roots of morality within one's own spiritual make-up. In this way, Mencius broke down the barrier between Heaven and Man and between Decree and human nature. There is a secret passage leading from the innermost part of a man's person to Heaven, and what per-

tains to Heaven, instead of being external to man, turns out to pertain to his truest nature.[15]

This is a perfect example of what I mean by inward transcendence.

Understood in this sense, the notion of *tianrenheyi* must not be misread as a "theory" with specific contents of thought. Instead it is only a mode of thinking manifesting itself in practically all aspects of Chinese culture such as art, literature, philosophy, religion, political thought, social relations, and so on, which cannot be pursued here. This also explains why inward transcendence has become a defining feature of Chinese mentality since the time of Confucius. In what follows let me indicate, in a highly sketchy manner, some of its expressions in post-Axial Chinese mentality.

I would like to begin with the negative side as a contrast to the external transcendence of the West. The Chinese transcendental world is not systematically externalized, formalized, or objectivized, especially when compared to its Western counterpart. After the Axial breakthrough, Chinese thinkers tended not to apply their imaginative powers to the nature, shape, characteristics, and so on of the world beyond, whether Heaven or *Dao,* even though they apparently had deep feelings about it. As best expressed by Zhuangzi, "As to what lies beyond the universe the sage admits its existence but does not theorize" (p. 44). This Chinese attitude contrasts sharply with the Western predilection to imagine, often vividly and profusely, about the world beyond with the aid of speculative reason.

As a matter of fact, the absence of theology in the Chinese tradition is something that no intellectual historian can possibly fail to notice. Chinese speculations on heaven or cosmos from the third century B.C.E. on led only to the rise of the *yin-yang* cosmology, not theology. Buddhism introduced to China not only a host of ever-compassionate deities in the form of bodhisattvas but also a hierarchy of heavens and hells. In imitation, religious Daoists brought forth a class of transcendent beings called *tianzun* ("venerable celestial deities"). These imported beliefs, though appealing to popular imagination, were never taken seriously by the thinking elite. Zhu Xi, for example, dismissed the Daoist *tianzun* as thoughtless imitations. Unlike in Plato or Kant neither the regular movement of heavenly bodies nor moral principles in the mind/heart could convince him of the existence of God.

By contrast, theology as a systematic knowledge of God began in the West with Plato's metaphysics and continued in Aristotle as one of the three "theoretical sciences." In medieval Europe, Christian theology prevailed over Greek thought. As Jaroslav Pelikan points out, however, "the victory of orthodox Christian doctrine over classical thought was to some extent a Pyrrhic victory, for the theology that triumphed over Greek philosophy has continued to be shaped ever since by the language and the thought of classical metaphysics."[16] Thus, the absence of theology in the Chinese tradition on the one hand and its full flowering in the West on the other may well be taken as an illustrative example of the contrast between inward transcendence and external transcendence. Hegel once criticized the sharp separation between the clergy and the laity in medieval Christianity as follows:

> Here arises *ipso facto* a separation between those who possess this blessing and those who have to receive it from others—between the *Clergy* and the *Laity*. The laity as such are alien to the Divine. This is the absolute schism in which the Church in the Middle Ages was involved; it arose from the recognition of the Holy as something external.[17]

Thus Hegel has confirmed my point about the externalization of Western transcendence in no uncertain terms.

Note further what the great Chan (Zen) Master Huineng had to say about the very same problem in the *Platform Sutra of the Sixth Patriarch* (section 36):

> Good friends, if you wish to practice, it is all right to do so as laymen; you don't have to be in a temple.

Again,

> From the outset the Dharma has been in the world;
> Being in the world, it transcends the world.
> Hence do not seek the transcendental world outside,
> By discarding the present world itself. (Trans. Philip B. Yampolsky)

Clearly, the two worlds, actual and transcendental, are linked together by the purified mind/heart in a way "neither identical nor separate." In this Chinese version of Buddhism we find a quintessential expression of inward transcendence.

Turning to the positive side, I would like to point out emphatically that the overwhelming concentration on the nature and function of the "mind/heart" (*xin*) in Confucian, Daoist, and Buddhist discourses has given rise to the unique Chinese "Learning of the Mind and Heart" (*xinxue*), which can be equated neither with "psychology" nor with philosophy of mind in the West. Thus we find in Mencius, "penetrating one's own mind and knowing one's own nature in order to know Heaven"; in Zhuangzi, "fasting of heart" for attainment of oneness with *Dao;* and in Chan Buddhism, "point directly to the human mind" and "see one's nature and become a Buddha." The greatest contribution to the Learning of the Mind and Heart comes, needless to say, from Neo-Confucianism. In spite of the central importance of "principle" (li) in his philosophical system, Zhu Xi nevertheless held that "principles," though obtained from Heaven, are ultimately embodied in the mind. In his own words, "Without the mind, principles would have nothing in which to inhere." But, after all, it was Wang Yangming who developed the *xinxue* to its full maturity. The following conversation between Wang and his friend will serve our purpose well. The friend pointed to flowering trees on a cliff and said:

> You say there is nothing under heaven external to the mind. These flowering trees on the high mountain blossom and drop their blossoms of themselves. What have they to do with my mind?

Wang replied:

> Before you look at these flowers, they and your mind are in a state of silent vacancy. As you come to look at them, their colors at once show up clearly. From this you can know that these flowers are not external to your mind.[18]

What Wang is saying is not that the "flowers" as a thing do not exist in the external world, but that what makes a flower "flower" to a human observer is the contribution of the mind. These include all its qualities, relations to other things, and the very fact that it is called a "flower." He identified this mind as *liangzhi*, "innate knowledge." Obviously, here Wang is talking about the sources and structure of values and meanings, not the external world and our objective knowledge of it. According to his way of thinking, we may say, values and meanings are provided by the mind or innate knowledge, which, being a unity of the Heavenly and the human, radiates a legislative power much broader than does Kant's practical reason. It may not be too much of an exaggeration to suggest that in Wang Yangming's philosophy the spirit of inward transcendence has found its fullest as well as highest expression.

To sum up, I have tried to establish the uniqueness of Chinese religious and philosophical imagination in a comparativist perspective by taking three interpretive steps. First, I used the idea of "inward transcendence" as an overall characterization of the Chinese mentality. Historically, it first took shape during the Axial breakthrough and then over the centuries has become deeply entrenched in Chinese spirituality, as shown in the three major traditions of Confucianism, Daoism, and Buddhism. Second, I further discussed inward transcendence in terms of relationship between the transcendental and actual worlds and suggested that it may best be described as "neither identical nor separate." Third, the recognition of the sacred as something internal led necessarily to a great deal of imagination about the wondrous function of the mind, in whose mediation alone lies the hope of a harmonious union of the Heavenly and the human.

In concluding, let me mention one specific point, namely, the possible relevance of inward transcendence to our modern world. In her penetrating analysis of the human condition in the modern age, Hannah Arendt made quite a point about the reversal of the hierarchical order between the *vita contemplativa* and the *vita activa.* As a result, action has dominated our modern life while contemplation has been reduced to nonexistence. But modern persons, according to Arendt, did not gain this world when they lost the other world.[19] More recently, Charles Taylor has also struggled with the same problem but from a different perspective and in different terms. As he sees it, the modern identity of the West consists very largely in what he calls the affirmation of ordinary life. However, not unlike Arendt, who is concerned about the "thoughtlessness" of modern persons, Taylor also shows considerable anxiety about a tendency in the Western culture "to stifle the spirit." In the end he only sees "a hope implicit in Judaeo-Christian theism and in its central promise of a divine affirmation of the human."[20] As far as I can see, this is a spiritual crisis rooted in the external transcendence of Western culture. Interestingly, we find a central element in the Chinese imagination which seems to be speaking precisely to this kind of crisis. There was a common saying among Chinese Chan Buddhists: "In carrying water and chopping firewood: therein lies the wonderful *Dao.*" Wang Yangming once described the *Dao* in this way: "It is not divorced from daily ordinary activities, yet it goes straight to what antedated Heaven." What both statements seem to suggest is that there is a possibility that contemplation and action or ordinary life and spiritual edification may be united without either being wholly abandoned. Above I used the words "speaking to" advisedly because I am not at all sure whether this line of Chinese thinking can really "provide solutions" to the modern crisis. Nevertheless, since the Chinese spiritual tradition has been centrally concerned with the question of how to live a life combining this-wordliness with otherworldliness, we have reason to believe that it may contain ideas worthy of reexamination. After all, this line of thinking is not wholly alien to the West. As is generally known, the idea of combining practical sense and cool utilitarianism with an otherworldly aim was developed by Calvinism long ago.

Notes

1. Yueh-lin Chin, "Chinese Philosophy," *Social Sciences in China* 1, no. 1 (March 1980): 83–93.

2. Fung Yu-lan, *A Short History of Chinese Philosophy* (New York: Macmillan, 1948), 339–40.

3. See Derk Bodde, "Myths of Ancient China," in his *Essays on Chinese Civi-*

lization (Princeton: Princeton University Press, 1981), 65–70. On *wu*-shamans, see K. C. Chang, "Shang Shamans," in *The Power of Culture: Studies in Chinese Cultural History,* ed. Willard J. Peterson, Andrew H. Plaks, and Ying-shih Yü (Hong Kong: Chinese University Press, 1994), 10–36.

4. *The Complete Works of Chuang Tzu,* trans. Burton Watson (New York: Columbia University Press, 1968), 364. I have translated the Chinese character *lie* as "breakup" instead of following Watson's "to be rent and torn apart." Hereafter all quotations from and references to the *Zhuangzi* are given by their page numbers in parenthesis in the text. Unless otherwise indicated, Watson's translation is followed.

5. Karl Jaspers, *The Origin and Goal of History,* trans. Michael Bullock (New Haven: Yale University Press, 1953), chapter 1, "The Axial Period" (pp. 1–21).

6. Benjamin I. Schwartz, "The Age of Transcendence," *Daedalus* (Spring 1975): 3.

7. Talcott Parsons, "'The Intellectual': A Social Role Category," in *On Intellectuals,* ed. Philip Rieff (Garden City, N.Y.: Doubleday Anchor, 1970), 7.

8. Benjamin I. Schwartz, "Transcendence in Ancient China," *Daedalus* (Spring 1975): 60.

9. I am following the text of the *Huainanzi,* where the transcending process begins with "rites and music" (*Sibucongkan soben* edition, ch. 12, p. 88). The textual problem is too technical to be discussed here.

10. Max Weber, *Economy and Society* (Berkeley: University of California Press, 1978), 502–3.

11. Onozawa Seiichi et al., eds., *Ki no shiso* (Tokyo: Tokyo University Press, 1978).

12. Here I have changed Watson's "inwardly direct" to "inwardly straight." The original term is *neizhi.* In this instance Zhuangzi is playing with the character *de* ("virtue"), which in his time was composed of two parts: "heart" (*xin*) and "straight" (*zhi*). "Straight" seems closer to the meaning of *zhi.* For the written form of *de,* see the most recently discovered texts in *Guodian Chumu zhujian* (Beijing: Wenwu Press, 1998).

13. Fu Sinian, *Xingming guxun bianzheng,* in *Fu Sinian quanji* (Taipei: Lianjing Press, 1980), 2:279–92.

14. Zeng Yunqian, *Shangshu zhengdu* (Beijing: Zhonghua, 1964), 35–36.

15. *Mencius,* trans. D. C. Lau (London: Penguin Books, 1970), 15.

16. Jaroslav Pelikan, *The Christian Tradition: A History of the Development of Doctrine,* vol. 1, *The Emergence of the Catholic Tradition (100–600)* (Chicago: University of Chicago Press, 1971), 44.

17. Georg Wilhelm Friedrich Hegel, *The Philosophy of History,* trans. J. Sibree (New York: Dover, 1956), 378.

18. Wang Yangming, *Instructions for Practical Living and Other Neo-Confucian Writings,* trans. Wing-tsit Chan (New York: Columbia University Press, 1963), 222.

19. Hannah Arendt, *The Human Condition* (Chicago: University of Chicago Press, 1958).

20. Charles Taylor, *Sources of the Self: The Making of the Modern Identity* (Cambridge, Mass.: Harvard University Press, 1989).

4

What Is Confucian Spirituality?

Julia Ching

IN THE INTRODUCTION to his *History of Chinese Philosophy,* Feng youlan discusses the relative absence of concern for philosophical methodology, on the one hand, and the presence, on the other, of much concern for practical "methods of self-cultivation" in the field of Chinese philosophy. To use his own words:

> Chinese philosophers for the most part have not regarded knowledge as something valuable in itself, and so have not sought knowledge for the sake of knowledge; and even in the sense of knowledge of a practical sort that might have a direct bearing upon human happiness, Chinese philosophers have preferred to apply this knowledge to actual conduct that would lead directly to this happiness, rather than to hold what they considered to be empty discussions about it.[1]

According to Feng, the Chinese philosophical ideal has been traditionally that of attaining "sageliness within and kingliness without." In other words, the ideal was to become a wise and humane person with a sagely disposition and, as well, with the ability to give order to the world—even if that means only the smaller world of the would-be sage's own human relationships. Feng writes:

> Because Chinese philosophers pay special attention to the way of becoming "sagely within," their methods of self-cultivation (*xiuyang*), that is, the so-called "methods of study" (*wenxue*) are very detailed and complete. Although these may not be called philosophy in the Western sense, China truly has a contribution to make in this respect.[2]

This chapter originally appeared in *Confucianism: The Dynamics of Tradition,* ed. Irene Eber (Jerusalem: The Hebrew University, 1986).

Such reflection on methods of self-cultivation which Chinese philosophy has to offer is also found in the Western tradition, but much more
often in its strictly religious development than in its philosophical treatises.
I refer here specifically to the *spirituality* of Western religious traditions,
which has not been adequately integrated into philosophy itself, even if
religious—and mystical—experience has served as the basis of much philosophical reflection. The English word "spirituality" is relatively little used
and often misunderstood, sometimes confused with the word "spiritual-
ism," which has to do with making contact with the spirits of the deceased.
"Spirituality" has usually been associated with theology, "spiritual theology" being sometimes used as another designation for what is also called
"ascetical and mystical theology," and that usually within the context of
Christianity. Here, the meaning has to do with the life of the *spirit*, including the ascetic and mystical life. More recently, the word is also being used
in the study of the spiritual teachings of non-Christian religions, including
not only Judaism and Islam, but also Hinduism and Buddhism. But what
about Confucianism and Neo-Confucianism?

Confucius the Model

Confucius was not only a philosopher; he was also a great spiritual personality, a paradigmatic individual. To a large extent, he personified his philosophical message: he *was* his message. Thus he remains the model and
inspiration even though his philosophy today no longer enjoys the protection of the state. His central doctrine is that of *ren*, translated variously as
goodness, benevolence, humanity, or human-heartedness. This was formerly a particular virtue, the kindness which distinguished the gentleman
in his behavior toward his inferiors. Confucius transforms it into a universal virtue, that which makes the perfect human being, the sage. He defines
it as loving others, as personal integrity, and as altruism. Confucius's philosophy is clearly grounded in religion—the inherited religion of the Lord
on High or Heaven, the supreme and personal deity. This is so even
though Confucius is largely silent regarding God and the afterlife (*Analects*
11:11). He makes it clear that it was Heaven which protected him and gave
him his message (*Analects* 7:23). He believes that human beings are accountable to a supreme being (*Analects* 3:13), even if he does show a certain skepticism regarding ghosts and spirits (*Analects* 6:20). Confucius's emphasis on
rituals is significant, as they govern human relationships, especially among
the aristocrats. The word for ritual, *li*, is related etymologically to the
words "worship" and "sacrificial vessel," both of which have definite religious overtones. The ancestral cult was surrounded with ritual; so was the

worship offered to Heaven as supreme lord (*Shangdi*, i.e., Lord on High). But the term *li* came to include all social, habitual practices, even to the extent of partaking of the nature of law as a means of training in virtue and of avoiding evil. It refers also to propriety, that is, to proper behavior. Propriety carries a risk of mere exterior conformity to social custom, just as a ritual might be performed only perfunctorily, without an inner attitude of reverence. But Confucius is careful to emphasize the importance of the correct inner disposition without which propriety becomes hypocrisy (*Analects* 15:17). In offering moral and spiritual perfection as the human ideal, Confucius has bequeathed a legacy that is perennial and universal, even if his cultural assumptions have their inherent limitations.

As a teacher of disciples, Confucius practiced the art of spiritual guidance, exhorting his followers to moderate the excesses of their temperaments by certain efforts of self-control, aided by the practice of self-examination. He gives this general advice: "When you meet someone better than yourself, think about emulating him. When you meet someone not as good as yourself, look inside and examine your own self" (*Analects* 4:17). His disciple Zengzi describes three counts of daily self-examination: "In my undertakings for others, have I done my best? In dealings with my friends, have I been faithful? And have I passed on to others what I have not personally practiced?" (*Analects* 1:4). Confucius said of his own spiritual evolution:

> At fifteen I set my heart on learning [to be a sage]; at thirty I became firm; at forty I had no more doubts; at fifty I understood Heaven's Will; at sixty my ear was attuned to truth; at seventy I could follow my heart's desires, without overstepping the line. (*Analects* 2:4)

This is the description of a man who consciously cultivated an interior life, who trained his mind to apprehend the truth and his heart to grasp the will of Heaven, until his instincts were also transformed, and who learned to appreciate the things of the spirit. Still, the mention of Heaven is discreet. Confucius's words do not vibrate with a passionate longing for union with Heaven, or God, as do the words of many Western mystics.

The Development of Confucian Spirituality

In the centuries immediately following Confucius and Mencius, Confucian spirituality is represented by the emphasis on *li* (ritual) and *yue* (music), while the religious belief in a supreme god as the Lord on High or Heaven continued to diminish in importance. During this period Xunzi interprets rites to mean such practices as the sacrifice to Heaven offered by the sovereign. He himself professes a disbelief in Heaven as a supernatural being or power. In speaking of the sacrifices to ancestors, of weddings and funerals, he pays some attention to the aesthetics of rituals, to details of rubrics as well as to a sense of balance and beauty:

> Rites trim what is long and stretch out what is too short, eliminate surplus and repair deficiency, extend the forms of love and reverence, and step by step bring to fulfillment the beauties of proper conduct. Beauty and ugliness, music and weeping, joy and sorrow are opposites, and yet rites make use of them all, bringing forth and employing each in its turn.[3]

For Xunzi, music serves the same functions as rituals, usually in conjunction with rituals. By music the ancient Chinese meant a union of instrumental and vocal music and rhythm with verse and dancing. The Confucian school was especially fond of the formal music performed at ancestral and other religious sacrifices.[4] In Xunzi's words, "Music (*yue*) is joy (*luo*; a variant pronunciation of the same character), an emotion which man cannot help but feel at times. Since man cannot help feeling joy, his joy must find an outlet in voice and an expression in movement."[5] In the *Book of Rites*, a text that manifests the undeniable influence of Xunzi, the chapter on music also extols it as a help in gaining inner equilibrium and tranquillity—the equilibrium is the reflection of the harmony of elegant music. According to this chapter, "it belongs to man's nature, as from Heaven, to be still at birth." In the process of growth, human beings are acted upon by external influences, and they respond by showing "likes and dislikes." Unless these are properly regulated by an interior principle, people run the risk of self-alienation, of becoming a stranger to one's original, deeper self, and thus of losing one's "Heavenly principle" (*tianli*). But music and rituals serve to maintain or restore this inner harmony, which is, or ought to be, a reflection of the harmony between Heaven and Earth.

> Harmony is the thing principally sought in music: it therein follows Heaven, and manifests the spirit-like expansive influence characteristic of it. Distinction is the thing principally sought in ceremonies: they therein follow Earth, and manifest the spirit-like retroactive influence characteristic of it. Hence the sages made music in response to Heaven, and framed ceremonies in correspondence with Earth. In the wisdom and completeness of their ceremonies and music, we see the directing power of Heaven and Earth.[6]

Doctrine of Equilibrium and Harmony

Emotional harmony and psychic equilibrium—the harmony of due proportion rather than the absence of passions—is to become in Song times the cornerstone of Confucian spirituality and the essence of Confucian meditation itself. Here, the *Zhongyong,* or *Doctrine of the Mean,* another chapter of the *Book of Rites,* is especially helpful. It speaks of two states of mind or heart, the "pre-stirred" state, before the rise of emotions, and the "post-stirred" state. According to this doctrine, the mean lies in the harmony of emotions which have arisen and which resembles the equilibrium of the earlier state. It goes on to say that this harmony puts a person in touch with the processes of life and creativity in the universe:

> While there are no stirrings of pleasure, anger, sorrow or joy, the mind may be said to be in the state of equilibrium (*zhong*). When these emotions have been stirred, and act in their due degree, there ensues what may be called the state of harmony (*he*). This equilibrium is the great root of all-under-Heaven, and this harmony is the universal path of all-under-Heaven. Let the states of equilibrium and harmony exist in perfection, and a happy order will prevail throughout Heaven and Earth, and all things will be nourished and will flourish.[7]

The philosophical assumption behind such speculation is the traditional correlation between the microcosm and the macrocosm, between the inner workings of the human mind and heart and the creative processes of the universe. The mystical dimension is obvious. And while the meaning of the word Heaven mentioned in the above passages is ambiguous, there is a clear expression of a belief that emotional harmony opens human beings to something greater than themselves. What this is, and how emotional harmony is to be acquired, remain unclear. But it is no surprise that such a text should provide impetus to the development of a form of meditation that may be called specifically Confucian.

The Neo-Confucian Contributions

A long time passed before Confucian spirituality became finally crystallized. This came about through the work of the Neo-Confucian philosophers of the Song and Ming dynasties. Their contributions were made partly as responses to the philosophy and spirituality of Buddhism. The responses themselves, however, were articulated in Confucian terms, even if the new worldview reflects Buddhist as well as Taoist influences. In place of the early belief in a supreme and personal deity, we tend to find a pantheistic, or should we say, panentheistic universe, with Heaven as an impersonal or transpersonal force.[8] We also find a mature doctrine of spiritual cultivation, oriented to the achievement of sagehood. The nature of the spirituality of the Neo-Confucian response is well revealed in the language of spirituality which was developed. Largely derived from Confucian texts, the words used by Neo-Confucians were now invested with technical meanings. Taken together, they form a language of specifically Confucian inspiration, even though some of the resonances may be Buddhistic. The dynamic quality of the language of spirituality makes it hard to analyze and classify, but we shall attempt to examine it under the two categories of "diminution" and "growth" in order to understand more clearly the specificity of Neo-Confucian spirituality. The distinction drawn is mainly heuristic, since, in spiritual terms, the two categories are paradoxically convergent, for spiritual growth is possible only when accompanied functionally by a certain degree of self-denial.

The Language of Diminution or Self-denial

In *Analects* 20:1, Confucius defines the virtue of *ren* in terms of "self-conquest" (*kiji*), undertaken for the sake of "restoring propriety" (*fuli*). This is an example of the language of diminution or "abnegation." It is what naturally follows self-examination—a purgative effort. In the same passage, when asked what are the steps of such self-mastery, Confucius gives the "guard or custody" over one's senses:

> Look not at what is contrary to propriety; listen not to what is contrary to propriety; speak not what is contrary to propriety; make no movement which is contrary to propriety.

The Neo-Confucians did not forget this lesson. They recognized the need of "preserving the Heavenly principle and eliminating human passions" (*cun tianli, qu renyu*). They also practiced the art of "self-examination" (*xingcha*), literally, of looking into, and of watching over, themselves, even frequently keeping a "spiritual account" of themselves. From biographies, we also know the discipline they followed, including in some instances such practices as keeping a detailed spiritual journal with precise accounts of faults detected and resolutions made.

Such developments brought with them a corollary: the practice of reading back into the classics a doctrine of asceticism, of attributing to the ancients the virtues of such asceticism. In Tang Shunqi's biography in the *Mingru xuean*, for example, Huang Zongxi refers to King Tang, the dynastic founder of Shang, who is said to have "sat up waiting for dawn,"[9] to Wuting, or King Gaozong, one of his successors, who "kept silence for three years," allegedly during a mourning period,[10] and to Confucius, who "did not know the taste of meat for three months" (*Analects* 7:13), as examples of reverence and self-discipline. Huang was, of course, following an interpretation established by a long line of exegetes. And yet, if we read the classical *Book of Documents* more carefully, we might not be so sure that these were such good historical examples of asceticism. The contexts seem to suggest that King Tang rose early in order to profit from the light of day, that Wuting's silence was remarked *after* the mourning period was over[11] and might even be the result of sickness, and, certainly, that Confucius lost his taste for meat because he was so enthralled with *shao* music while visiting the state of Qi, and so was hardly practicing any act of mortification.[12] The tradition, however, of reading the classics ascetically, and the language of diminution it produces, is witness to the importance of asceticism itself in the Confucian and, even more, the Neo-Confucian tradition.

We should nevertheless remember that Confucian—and Neo-Confucian —asceticism remained a discipline of moderation, which did not inspire any flight into deserts or produce any monastic movement. The Confucian teaching was to control one's passions, not to live as if one were without them. Besides, Confucian asceticism was always practiced for the sake of a higher goal, that of rendering the individual more humane for others, in the service of a larger group, namely, the family and the society.

The Language of Growth

The school of Confucius has always considered *becoming humane* (*ren*) as a process of spiritual growth. This view took on special significance when, under Buddhist influence, the word *ren* assumed the meaning of a "seed," with potential for growth and maturation.[13] With the Neo-Confucians, the word *ren* became interchangeable with the term "Heavenly principle" (*tianli*). To become humane—that is, a perfect human being—one must "preserve" (*cun*) and "nurture" (*yang*) the Heavenly principle within one's mind and heart. Its growth enables one to participate in the cosmic processes of life and growth—again the microcosm-macrocosm parallel. But how is this growth to be cultivated? On this point, the various philosophers do not always have the same answers. Zhu Xi, responsible for the synthesis of Song Neo-Confucian thought, offers the dual formula of *zhijing qiongli*, of abiding in a disposition to reverence and pursuing exhaustively the principles (*li*) of things. His is a formula which combines spiritual and intellectual cultivation.

The Doctrine of Reverence

The fact that scholars have translated the term *jing* in Zhu Xi's phrase as "reverence," "seriousness," or "composure" shows the difficulty of explaining its usage in general and Zhu's intended meaning in particular. The use of the word can be traced to various Confucian texts, including the *Book of Documents,* where the ancient sage kings are frequently described as being "reverentially obedient" to the Lord on High, while their descendants are exhorted to imitate such reverence. With Confucius, the word is used more with regard to oneself than to a higher being: "In retirement, to be sedately gracious, in doing this, to be reverently attentive (*jing*), in contact with others, to be very sincere" (*Analects* 12:19).[14] The *Book of Changes* continues in the same vein, when it says: "The gentleman practices reverence to maintain inner rectitude, and righteousness to assure exterior correctness."[15]

Zhu Xi, in speaking of "abiding in reverence," defines it in terms of single-mindedness and freedom from distraction (*chui wushi*), and compares it to the Buddhist practice of mindful alertness (*xingxing*). He also associates it specifically with the teaching of *shendu* ("vigilance in solitude" or being watchful over oneself when alone) in the *Doctrine of the Mean.* But he is careful to guard his disciples against a *dead* reverence which merely keeps the mind alert without also attending to moral practice. For Zhu Xi, "reverence" points to the process by which the original unity of mind is preserved and made manifest in one's activity. Thus he gives the meaning of the word a dimension of depth which transforms it from the earlier, occasional usage in Confucian thought to a doctrine of personal and spiritual cultivation. In his words:

> Reverence does not mean one has to sit stiffly in solitude, the ears hearing nothing, the eyes seeing nothing, and the mind thinking of nothing. . . . It means rather keeping a sense of caution and vigilance, and not daring to become permissive.[16]

The practice of reverence is very like that of "recollection" in Christian spirituality. The English word recollection is usually understood in terms of "remembrance." However, as a technical term in spirituality, it refers to the "collecting" or "gathering" of one's interior faculties, keeping them silent and "recollected" in an atmosphere of peace and calm, in preparation for formal prayer or in an effort to prolong the effects of such prayer. In a word on Christian spirituality, Canon Jacques Leclerq says:

> The word recollection has no meaning for many worldly people. . . . Yet recollection is the chief disposition required for the interior life. It is not itself interior life but it is so much a condition for it and prepares us for it to such an extent that it almost necessarily develops it. . . . It is simply the calm which is born into the soul through solitude and silence, interior calm. Man has need of it to find himself as well as to find God.[17]

The closest Chinese term to recollection is *shoulian* (literally, "collecting together"). While it also has a practical meaning ("gathering" a harvest), its usage in Neo-Confucian spirituality has made it too a technical term. Zhu Xi writes about the need for scholars to "keep always recollected (*shoulian*) without allowing oneself to become dispersed."[18]

Zhu Xi's predecessor, Zheng Yi (1033–1107), who articulated the doctrine of reverence before him, said that "Cultivation (*hangyang*) requires the practice of reverence." The term *hangyang* includes the meaning of nurturing. The aspirant to sagehood needs to nurture the seeds of goodness in his mind and heart, and reverence refers to this process of nurturing as well as to the goal of emotional harmony characteristic of the sage.

The Role of Meditation

The Confucian term for meditation is "quiet-sitting" (*jingzuo*). This term suggests strong Taoist and Buddhist influences, calling to mind Zhuangzi's "sitting and forgetting" (*zuowang*) and the Buddhist practice of *dhyāna* (meditation), from which the term *Chan* or Zen is derived. Zhu Xi had experience of both Taoist and Buddhist practices of meditation. But he also made a special effort to show the distinctiveness of Confucian meditation and its difference from Taoist and Buddhist meditation. For the Taoist or Buddhist, meditation is an exercise by which the mind concentrates on an object, including itself, to the exclusion of all distracting thoughts and for the sake of attaining inner unity. Especially in the case of the Taoist, the motive was to preserve health and prolong life. For the Confucian, unity and harmony are the goal, together with knowledge of the *moral* self, of one's own strengths and weaknesses. The Confucian sought through meditation to achieve self-improvement in the practice of virtues and elimination of vices.

Zhu Xi gives some importance to quiet-sitting, especially with the view of making possible a fuller manifestation of the Heavenly principle within. What is implied is a reversion: a return to one's original nature; a recapture of the springs of one's being; and the permeation of one's daily living by this state of psychic unity and harmony. Zhu Xi sees quiet-sitting as different from the Buddhist practice of "introspection," which has reference only to oneself and not to the larger world:

> According to the Buddhist teaching, one is to seek the mind with the mind, deploy the mind with the mind. This is like the mouth gnawing the mouth or the eye looking into the eye. Such a course of action is precarious and oppressive, such a path is dangerous and obstructive, such a practice is empty of

principle and frustrating. They may sound like us [Confucians]; they are in reality quite different.[19]

Confucian meditation as it developed assumes a character more and more different from Taoist and Buddhist meditation. It entails not just an examination of conscience, but is definitely oriented toward a higher consciousness through the emptying of the self and of desires. As a form of inner concentration, Confucian meditation stands somewhere between two other forms: the intellectual effort of discursive thought and the moral effort of assuring that there is no thought. Confucian meditation seeks peace without doing violence to human nature. It does not require the attainment of a state of intellectual and emotional impassivity. Thoughts may come and go; they need not become distractions except when one pays attention to them.

The Extension of Knowledge

A problem which frequently arises in the different spiritual traditions is the place assigned to intellectual cultivation. In Western Christian spirituality, it is formulated in terms of the primacy of the intellect or of the will in the soul's union with God, with the Dominican order, for example, preferring the intellect and the Franciscan order the will. Dominican spirituality is therefore more intellectually oriented, while Franciscan spirituality is more action-oriented, and can even be described as anti-intellectual.

The word *xue* (literally, learning) has a broader meaning than the solely intellectual in Confucianism, for it refers especially to "learning to become a sage." There is on the other hand an intellectual dimension to Confucian spirituality which is remarkable and distinctive. This is the tenet expressed in the *Great Learning*, that knowledge may be extended through the investigation of things (*gewu zhizhi*). It is a tenet especially fully developed in the philosophy of Zhu Xi, in which it is explained in terms of the "pursuit of principles" (*qiongli*). The focus is on the search for knowledge, especially for intellectual comprehension of the essences of all things, with the word "things" understood as including not only the objective world outside of the mind, but also the subjective world of the mind itself and the intersubjective world of human relationships and human affairs. As Zhu Xi writes:

> If we wish to extend our knowledge to the utmost, we must investigate the principles of all things with which we come into contact. For the mind and spirit of man are formed to know, and the things of the world all contain

principles. So long as principles are not exhausted, knowledge is not yet complete.[20]

According to Zhu Xi, the student is to proceed from the known to the unknown, moving from the knowledge one already possesses to the principles of things, and continuing one's investigation until the task is finished. The end is reached as a sudden breakthrough, an experience of inner enlightenment occurring at the end of a long and arduous process of search and exertion:

> After exerting himself in this way for a long time, he will suddenly find himself possessed of a wide and far-reaching penetration. The qualities of all things, both internal and external, subtle and coarse, will all then be apprehended, and the mind, in its entire substance (*ti*) and in its relation to things (*yong*), will become completely manifest. This is called the investigation of things; this is called the perfection of knowledge.[21]

If the mind is ordained to know the truth of principles, truth itself also modifies the mind, making it manifest and radiant. Here we observe a circular movement, from the mind to things and back to the mind, but note that it is not just a movement from the mind to the mind. This is because knowledge is desired not for its own sake, but in order to act properly, to know moral behavior.

A problem therefore arises in Neo-Confucian spirituality as to how important book learning or intellectual pursuits are to the quest for sagehood. Zhu Xi's contemporary and rival Lu Jiuyuan (1139–1193) and, in the Ming dynasty, Wang Yangming pointed out the problem inherent in any doctrine which gives too much priority to intellectual striving: that it necessarily makes intellectuals of all sages, rendering those deprived of the opportunities of study underprivileged in the quest for sagehood as well. Lu and Wang by contrast emphasize the moral and existential aspects of spirituality, regarding book learning almost as a distraction from the quest itself. While their influences have had an important impact, Confucian spirituality has still become mainly the spirituality of the intellectual, and the reading of the classics is itself interpreted as a spiritual exercise.

Mysticism

Spirituality is concerned with experiences of the inner person, and these may include mystical experiences. In Judaism, Islam, and Christianity, these are usually defined in terms of the soul's consciousness of its union with God, a union in which the two remain distinct, even if the experience of union is very intense and ineffable. The Confucian classics give evidence of a deep spirituality which suggests mysticism. Both the *Book of Poetry* and the *Book of Documents* represent the ancient sage-kings as partners in dialogue with the Lord on High or Heaven, indeed as reverential *sons* of Heaven, receiving from Heaven instructions and commandments, and asking of Heaven blessing and protection. This appears closer to the tradition of the Jewish kings and prophets than to that of mystical individuals lost in the contemplation of the divine. But the distinctively Confucian mystical tradition is better discovered in the *Mencius* and in those chapters in the ritual texts which speak less of the rites as such and more of the interior dispositions of the mind and heart.[22] Mencius alludes to the presence in the heart of an actuality greater than itself. According to him, knowledge and fulfillment of one's own mind and heart lead to knowledge and fulfillment of one's nature and to the service of Heaven:

> For a man to give full realization to his heart is for him to understand his own nature, and a man who understands his own nature understands Heaven. By preserving his heart and nurturing his nature he is serving Heaven. (7A:1)

Mencius's serene philosophy gave way to an intense quest for the ultimate on the part of various Neo-Confucians, probably under some influence from Buddhism. We possess one description of the experience of a mystical enlightenment (1593), by Gao Panlong during a journey to South China, first by boat and then on land. He wrote about his strict daily order, maintained even while on the boat, how he practiced meditation half of the day and read books the other half. He described how, for about two months,

> Whenever I felt ill at ease during meditation, I would just follow all the instructions of Zheng Yi and Zhu Xi—in all that concerns sincerity, reverence, concentrating on tranquility, observing joy, anger, sorrow and pleasure before they arise, sitting in silence to purify the mind, realizing in myself the heavenly principle. . . . Whether I was standing or sitting, eating or resting, I would not forget these thoughts. At night I did not undress, and only fell asleep when dead tired. Upon waking I returned to meditating, repeating and alternating these various practices. When the *qi* of the mind was clear and peaceful, it seemed to fill all Heaven and Earth. But such consciousness did not last.[23]

The ineffable experience of enlightenment came during his contemplation of nature, while he was staying in an inn, probably in Fujian.

[The inn] had a small loft which faced the mountains, with a rushing stream behind. I climbed up there and was very pleased. Quite by chance I saw a saying by Cheng Hao [1032–1085]. "Amid a hundred officials, myriad affairs and a hundred thousand weapons, with water as drink and a bent arm as pillow, I can still be joyful [*Analects* 7:15]. The myriad things are all man-made; in reality there is not a thing."[24] Suddenly I realized the sense of these words and said, "This is it. In reality there is not a thing!" And as this one thought lingered, all entanglements were broken off. It was suddenly as if a load of one hundred pounds had instantly dropped off, as if a flash of lightning had penetrated the body and pierced the intelligence, and I merged in harmony with the Great Transformation till there was no differentiation between Heaven and Humans, the outer and the inner.[25]

This is a testimonial of personal fulfillment, achieved not without earnest striving, but serenely simple as an experience. It is an experience of self-transcendence, of the consciousness of merging with nature. The inscription by Cheng Hao which became the occasion for this awakening is notable since it grounds the Confucian mystical experience in a life of full activity while expressing the central insight itself in a language of negation evocative of Buddhist philosophy. Confucian meditation developed in a tradition that did not know monastic life. It represents essentially a lay spirituality. And Confucian mysticism is the portion of the human that knows how to unite contemplation and action, the inner and the outer, for external activity is the expression of interior attitudes and of the fountain-head of one's intentions. Confucian mysticism enables the person to perceive the profoundly dynamic character of the Heavenly principle within, the principle by which birds fly, fish swim and human beings love virtue. One recognizes that this is the true meaning of human unity with Heaven and Earth and all things.

Confucian Spirituality

In conclusion, we return to the question posed at the outset: What is Confucian spirituality? The burden of this paper has been to offer an answer to this question by arguing that the quest for sagehood, which constitutes the heart of Confucianism, can only be understood with reference to the "interior life," to the life of the spirit, to personal discipline, and sometimes to mystical experience. This is tantamount to saying that Confucianism itself cannot be understood unless we have some sympathy for, and appreciation of, its doctrines and methods of spiritual cultivation. I have therefore attempted to show how the secular character of the Confucian tradition, which historically precluded the development of monastic movements usually associated with ascetic and mystical disciplines, has nevertheless permitted the development of a horizon of spirituality such as that found in the world's other great religious traditions. Indeed, I hope I have shown that this horizon is central to Confucianism, just as belief in God is central to Judaism and Christianity. Assuredly, it is a spirituality peculiarly Confucian, not dependent on belief in God, as is Christian or Jewish spirituality. And yet it does not deny God's existence. It is a spirituality that unites "inner sageliness and outer kingliness," a life of contemplation and a life of activity.

It would not be possible to say that Confucianism has an answer to every problem, or that Confucianism does not also have its own inherent limitations. On the contrary, I believe that Confucianism has all the limitations that human systems possess—even those constructed by the best of us. The limitations of Confucianism are, however, the subject for another study, while this one has sought merely to suggest the horizon of the spirituality we can discover in Confucianism, and the horizon of meaning this spirituality can help us find. Even for the most spiritual Confucian, life may continue to pose problems. In fact, Confucianism cannot resolve the problems of human existence; it can only help us find the wisdom and strength to cope with them, including those problems that we shall never understand. Yet the person who determines to follow the spiritual path that Confucianism outlines, a path committed to moral values and social responsibility, to culture and to life, may become a better human being; not necessarily a sage, but perhaps a more humane person. For that person will have discovered transcendence in immanence, the absolute in the relative, the constant in the transient, and meaning in every moment of time.

Notes

1. Feng Youlan, *Chung-kuo che-hsüeh shih* (Shanghai, 1935), introduction, pp. 8–9. English translation in Derk Bodde, *A History of Chinese Philosophy* (Princeton: Princeton University Press, 1952), introduction, p. 2.

2. Feng Youlan, *A History*, introduction, p. 10. The English translation is my own.

3. Ibid., 100.

4. Homer H. Dubs, *Hsün-tze: The Moulder of Ancient Confucianism* (London: Arthur Probsthain, 1927; reprint, Taipei, 1966), 162–63.

5. Ibid., 112.

6. James Legge, trans., *Li Ki*, vol. 28 of Sacred Books of the East series, ed. F. Max Muller (Oxford: Oxford University Press, 1885), 103.

7. James Legge, trans., *The Doctrine of the Mean*, vol. 1 of *The Chinese Classics*, 384–85.

8. There always were those who continued to believe in a supreme personal deity, as Huang Tsung-hsi (1610–1695). See his small tract, "P'o hsieh lun" (Against perverse theories), in *Li-chou yi-chu hui-k'an* (Shanghai ed., 1910).

9. James Legge, trans., *The Book of Documents*, vol. 3 of *The Chinese Classics*, 202.

10. Ibid., 466.

11. Ibid., 248. Hence Confucius's answer to Tzu-chang regarding the "universal" ancient practice of three years' mourning after the parents' death is not supported by the text as we have it today. Kuo Mo-jo proposes the possibility that Wuting was struck with illness and could not speak. See his *Ch'ing-t'ung shih-tai* (The Bronze Age) (Shanghai: Hsin wen-yi, 1951), 137–41.

12. It is even possible that Confucius was absorbed in *studying* this music. See Kuo Mo-jo, *Ch'ing-t'ung*, 200.

13. Wing-tsit Chan, "The Evolution of the Confucian Concept *Jen*," *Philosophy East and West* 4 (1955): 295–319.

14. Translation adapted from James Legge, *Analects*, vol. 1 of *The Chinese Classics*, 271.

15. Commentary on Hexagram No. 2. Translation adapted from James Legge, *Yi King*, vol. 16 of Sacred Books of the East series, 421.

16. *Chu-tzu yü-lei* (Recorded conversations of Chu Hsi) (reprint, Taipei, 1970), 12.10b. English translation adapted from Wing-tsit Chan, *A Source Book in Chinese Philosophy* (Princeton: Princeton University Press, 1964), 607.

17. *The Interior Life*, trans. F. Murphy (New York: P. J. Kenedy, 1961), 118. This meaning of the word "recollection" is, however, little known in today's English-speaking world.

18. *Chu-tzu yü-lei*, 12.2b.

19. "Kuan-hsin shuo" (On contemplating the mind), *Chu-tzu wen-chi* (Collected writings of Chu Hsi) (reprint, Taipei, 1972), 67.21b. Translation adapted from Wing-tsit Chan, *Source Book*, 604. It should not be surprising that Leclerq also says: "Reflection, recollection and prayer develop spiritual aspirations and are a source of enlightenment but a life solely devoted to contemplation places the soul in danger of turning in on itself and of succumbing to a very dangerous and refined type of egotism." See his *Interior Life*, 18.

20. This is taken from Chu's commentary on *The Great Learning*. Translation adapted from James Legge, vol. 1 of *The Chinese Classics*, 365.

21. Ibid., 365–66.

22. Julia Ching, *Confucianism and Christianity* (Tokyo: Kodansha International, 1977), 159–60.

23. Huang Tsung-hsi, *Ming-ju hsüeh-an*, ed. Ssu-pu pei-yao (SPPY), 58.17a. The translation is by Rodney Taylor, in *The Records of Ming Scholars*, ed. Julia Ching and Chaoying Fang (University of Hawaii Press).

24. *Erh-ch'eng ch'üan-shu*, ed. SPPY, 6.3a.

25. Huang Tsung-hsi, *Ming-ju*, 58.1

5

Affectivity in Classical Confucian Tradition

THOMAS BERRY

I N CONFUCIANISM WE PERCEIVE a consistent and all-pervading emphasis on the affective life of human beings. This emphasis on the feeling, emotional aspect of life was considered of primary importance in sustaining people in a human form of existence. Indeed, the awakening consciousness of the Chinese in the classical period consisted largely in a growing awareness of the intimate human relationships that bind persons to each other and the need for cultivating this aspect of human life. This became the very substance of the Chinese tradition, for while there were other cultural forces at work in Chinese society, Confucianism provided the dominant cultural form of the society, the basic human ideals, the political structure, the social discipline, the educational institutions—the comprehensive style of life. Thus from an early period Confucianism established itself as one of the dominant lifestyles governing human existence in the Eurasian world up until the present. Taoism and Buddhism offered no such integral life program or cultural form as Confucianism offered; they lived within the context provided by Confucian teaching. Legalism offered an alternative organizing program, but it sought to achieve its objective by imposition of external force rather than by human attraction. For this reason it was rejected by the Chinese shortly after it came to power.

According to Confucian teaching, a mutual attraction of things for each other functions at all levels of reality as the interior binding force of the cosmic, social, and personal life. More than most traditions, Confucianism saw the interplay of cosmic forces as a single set of intercommunicating and mutually interpenetrating realities. These forces, whether living or nonliving were so present to each other that they could be adequately seen and understood only within this larger complex. Not to appreciate this comprehensive vision of the world is to miss the numinous quality of Chinese life. Because of the intensity with which the Chinese experienced this interior, feeling communion with the real, they set themselves on perfecting humans themselves and the universe by increasing this sympathetic presence of things to each other within a personal and social discipline rather than by intellectual analysis and understanding. Indeed, the Confucian ideal of knowledge was that of an understanding heart rather than a thinking brain. Confucianism was less interested in the principles of physical causality than Greek philosophy, less oriented toward transcendental reality than Hinduism, and more willing to accept the temporal mode of human life than the Yogic and Buddhist traditions. The primary concern was for the manner in which people experience human existence by affectionate service to one another, by their sympathies in time of suffering, and by the sharing of community existence. There are many places in the corpus of Confucian writings where comprehensive statements are made concerning the creation of human community in its various forms: In the Great Plan in the *Book of History,* in the Seventh Chapter (*Li Yun*) of the *Book of Ritual,* in the Third Appendix of the *Book of Changes,* in chapters 22–31 in the *Doctrine of the Mean,* in the *Great Learning,* in chapter 44 of Dong Zhongshu's consideration of the *Spring and Autumn Annals,* in the *Explanation of the Diagram of the Great Ultimate* of Zhou Dunyi, in the *Western Inscription* of Zhang Zai, in the *Commentary on the Great Learning* by Wang Yangming. These are only a few of the many classical expressions of this profound intercommunion of Heaven, earth, and humanity. Almost every short essay on the interpretation of life in the Confucian traditions makes reference to this framework and derives its basic principles from these sources.

The cosmos is the macrophase of humans; humans are the microphase of the cosmos. The cosmos is encompassed in the human; the human in the cosmos. Each discovers itself in the other. But the final concern is with the common bond of the truly real, which is found in the mutual attraction that pervades the multiplicity of things and establishes this multiplicity as an order, as a cosmos. This highest ontological attraction of things to each other in the Confucian tradition can be indicated quite simply by the word "communion."

In this context, the role of the individual person becomes especially significant; for the cosmic is not simply the dimension of humankind—it is the larger dimension of the individual human person. In this enlarged experience of the individual are all those qualities of the universe itself. While this exalted ideal of personal–cosmic communion was thought of primarily as an experience of the sage-kings of ancient times and of a few later sages, it was so deeply enshrined in the tradition as the basic human ideal that it became the encompassing context within which humans saw most clearly the meaning of their existence and the cosmic function that they fulfilled. It is this macrophase of humans that makes of them a Third in the triad, together with Heaven and earth, a designation as ancient as the *Book of History,* but which is further developed in the teachings of classical Confucianism. Within this context we can identify several communities within which humans live their life: the supreme community of Heaven, earth, and humanity; the panhuman political community; the friendship community; the family community; and the personal community of individuals within themselves. Since all of these communities are founded on the bonds of affection that people bear to each other, discussion of the affective life of humans can best take place within this differentiation of communities and the corresponding differentiation of the human communication that takes place within this variety of life context.

I

First there is the community of Heaven, earth, and humanity. Heaven itself, the highest conception of Confucian tradition, is seen as a quiet Providence communicating itself to all beings, fostering and protecting them. The basic virtue of both Heaven and earth is not precisely any entitative attribute but "the bringing into existence."[1] In the writings of Dong Zhongshu we read: "The beauty of humaneness (*ren*) is found in Heaven. Heaven is humaneness (*ren*)."[2] Protecting, sustaining, transforming, and giving life to every creature, Heaven brings them to their fulfillment. Whoever beholds this heavenly presence must recognize that "Heaven's humaneness is inexhaustible and limitless."[3] In response to this affection, humans who received from Heaven their existence must also receive from Heaven its loving qualities and thus be loving. Because humans have received such inspiration from Heaven, they can then fulfill with proper affection all their duties to others, especially to their own parents and the other members of their family, for they have a heart that is loyal, trusting, compassionate, and kind. In another statement on this basic Confucian teaching, the *Book of Ritual* indicates that as a Third in the trinity, with Heaven and earth, humans attain a brilliance enabling them to enlighten all the earth. The highest insight of this phase of Confucianism is the awareness of humans as "the understanding heart of Heaven and earth."[4] Thus the function of humans is to provide that affectionate quality as well as the human mode of consciousness that perfects the trinitarian community achieved on this ultimate plane of being.

II

The second community is the panhuman community of earth, the community of all within the four seas, of all under Heaven. Confucian thinkers devoted a major part of their attention to cultivation of this public community. This community is the special object of affection from Heaven itself, which cares for the human community directly through the natural world, inwardly by identifying its voice with the voice of the people, and socially providing a ruler who is himself the Son of Heaven. In caring for the human community the ruler is to model his actions on the care that Heaven manifests for all things, on the affection of parents for their children, and on the concern the ruler has for his own being. The ruler, in a special manner, is to be father and mother of the people. Failure of the ruler to fulfill his function in a benign and loving manner invalidates his rule; he becomes subject to removal in favor of someone who will fulfill this role. Just as the ruler has a dominant part in the good order of society as the cosmic center in whom the planes of reality intersect in a special manner, so also he is the dominant cause of disorder in society.

The *Book of History* is an account of the dialectic of transition from one to the other, with all the attendant good and evil consequences. Thus the two central moments in the *Book of History* are the convulsive moments of transition from the Xia to the Shang and from the Shang to the Zhou. These equate with changes from a period of oppression of the people to a period of concern for the people. The establishment of the Zhou rule under the guidance of the Duke of Zhou represents the decisive moment of renewal and rebirth for the Chinese people, the introduction of all those ideals of the human quality of life that have marked the Chinese tradition ever since. As narrated in the *Book of History* this event transpired under the guidance of *Shangdi,* the Lord on High.[5] The great accusation directed against the Shang rulers was that they did not understand the suffering of the people; they turned to their own ease. The achievement of King Wen when he came to rule was that he esteemed and protected the lower classes of the people; he was gracious and good to widowers.[6] His praise is sung in *The Classic of Odes.*[7]

The dehumanization of the Xia and Shang dynasties has been the subject of reflection by the Chinese throughout the centuries. These events were the mirror in which the changing moods of historical existence could best be seen: the tragic tendency in all regimes to pass from high human ideals of community to a situation in which the rulers hardened their attitudes, gave in to their own satisfactions, and abandoned the people to their suffering. At such moments Heaven made its own judgment known in a direct fashion. Any injury to humans is an injury to Heaven, especially when the injury is to the community and when the ruler has indulged himself to the neglect of the people. There are not two orders of the real; there is only the one order, which encompasses the various modes of expression on the different levels of creaturely existence. Any break or corruption manifested in any phase of this universal order was a fault in the whole that could not be endured. For the Chinese it was not sufficient for this to be stated in abstract terms. It was necessary that the historical reality of earlier times be seen within this paradigmatic scheme and meditated on. Chinese history at this time is written within a pattern as much as biblical history was written within a pattern revealing that God himself is the guide of the people. The basic concern of God in Israel and of Heaven in China is that justice be done, that the community be fostered, that the lowly be protected, and that the suffering receive compassionate care. When the bond between ruler and people was broken, then the relationship between the ruler and Heaven was broken, divine judgment was executed, and a new and compassionate regime was installed.

The ideal of proper concern for the people was manifested by King Wen, who "treated the people as if he were tending invalids" (*Mencius* 4B:20, p. 131).[8] This compassionate awareness of the suffering nature of existence, this feeling for those on the lower levels of prestige with fewer resources and less talents—for the elderly without children, for children whose parents had died, for widows and widowers—is among the more striking features of the early Confucian tradition. The admonition of the emperor Shun to his ministers had been to be gentle with those far off and gracious to those nearby.[9] The ancient kings were held up by Mencius as rulers having "a compassionate heart" (*Mencius* 2A:6, p. 82). Unable to witness the suffering of others, they were moved to heal the affliction of the people whenever this was discovered. The emperor Yu considered "himself as responsible for anyone in the empire who drowned; Qi looked upon himself as responsible for anyone in the empire who starved" (*Mencius* 4B:29, pp. 134–35).

This ideal society of the classical period was evoked in the Confucian imagination during a period of social disorder and projected into the past as a reality that had existed in some primordial moment in the society. Later, during a period when the whole world seemed to be "drowning" (*Mencius*

4A:17, p. 124) so far as its human qualities were concerned, this ideal society was further elaborated by Mencius. Although this society was more dream than reality, it fulfilled for the Chinese a necessary function. It expressed what a truly human mode of social-political life should be; it judged the existing order with some depth of insight; it provided hope and guidance sufficient to sustain the Chinese civilizational effort over the centuries. There is no need to think that the Chinese ever expected to attain the full reality of the vision in any earthly historical regime. There was, however, a realization that, unless this vision was in some manner expressed in reality, the human quality of life was imperiled, not simply for the moment but, possibly, for the entire future. That the Confucian teachers stated the ideal so clearly, that they correctly identified the moral-spiritual means toward that end, that they evoked such effort from society; all this is evidence of the human depth of their thought. Mencius saw the issue with clarity when he pointed out the need for people in community to share in a common affective life, especially in the joy and the sorrow that pervade human existence: "The people will delight in the joy of him who delights in their joy, and will worry over the troubles of him who worries over their troubles. He who delights and worries on account of the Empire is certain to become a true king" (*Mencius* 1B:4, p. 63). There is only one alternative: decline in this community of human feeling, the diminishing of human capacity for communal sharing, with disastrous consequences: "When the path of morality is blocked, then we show animals the way to devour humans, and sooner or later it will come to humans devouring humans" (*Mencius* 3B:9, p. 114). The terror of chaos on the one hand and the inspiring vision of harmony on the other—both were needed to sustain the effort required to save the social order from disintegration and to foster development of those qualities of life which were within human capacities. If only rulers would appreciate the basic law of community existence, the sharing of joy and sorrow!

III

The friendship community, as a third group, is a community highly appreciated and wonderfully developed in the Confucian tradition. It is referred to in the first of the *Analects* with a simple exclamation of joy: "How delightful to be with friends who have come from afar!" Friendship is also the subject of a memorable passage of the *Book of Changes:* "People united, at first cry out, weeping; but afterwards they laugh. . . . Two persons inwardly united in their hearts are superior to any restraint of iron or of bronze; their words, responding to the intimate feelings of their hearts, are pleasing, like orchid-fragrance."[10] The conditions for true friendship are also enunciated in the passage of the *Analects* concerning youth who when at home should be devoted to their parents and when away from home should be respectful to their elders. Sincere and truthful, they should "love all extensively" (*Analects* 1:6)[11] and develop an intimate attachment to the good. As with the other phases of the Confucian life program, there was a need to ground friendship deeply in the moral life of humans, to make this one of the central features in the daily self-examination, as we see in the teacher Zang, who considered three main points: "faithfulness in dealing with others, sincerity in association with friends, fidelity in carrying out the teachings of the master" (*Analects* 1:4).

But while there are many instances of such observations and concern for friendship in the Confucian canon and in the writings of Confucian teachers, the friendship community is less mentioned in discussion of that weighty sequence of communities that passes from the universal cosmic order to the political order, to the state, the family, and the individual. This friendship community is, however, most important in fostering some of the deepest of all human experiences precisely because it is not ritualized, or politicized, or intellectualized, or subject to family obligation. It belongs to the order of the greatest freedom and creates a unique intimacy of its own. It is simply that attachment that individual persons and small groups of persons have for each other and the joy they have in their sharing of life and thought and feeling. So we have the fascinating episodes in the life of Confucius and his disciples. While this was not simply a community of equals but a fellowship under the guidance of a master, it was essentially a free association with a rare intimacy, generosity, and joy.

Where this friendship community comes to its fullest expression is in the poets, from the *Book of Poetry* throughout the entire course of Chinese literature. Even in the poetry of one so given to solitude and personal reflection as Tao Qian, there are passages of deepest feeling in relation to the friends and neighbors with whom he came into contact in such a casual way. Yet the warmth and intimacy, the human feeling for each other creates an atmosphere rich in the friendship quality of human relationships. So in his poem to the prefect Ding of Chai-sang, Tao Qian speaks of their outings together: "where we talked and we gazed, to give relief to our sorrows."[12] In his wandering with friends he never tired, and the day he saw a friend leave "the winecup held no joy."[13] With Tao Qian most often the theme was that of moments of joy tinged with poignant reflections on the evanescent character of human existence; all this was an intimate communion of thought. While there are endless expressions of sorrow at partings, there are also the joys of meeting and moments of unrestrained laughter while draining cups of wine. It is not easy to say which was more intoxicating, converse with friends or the cups of wine. But often enough it was simply the talk of friends late into the night. So with Du Fu in his poem for Vice Prefect Yen, with whom he had established an intimate friendship; "Nothing seemed to matter then, and my whole life seemed to be filled with never-ending bliss."[14]

Beyond this intimacy of friendship with others on a simple human, feeling basis, there is also the compassionate feeling for those who suffer. It would be too much to say that the Chinese were in fact more sensitive and helpful in this regard than other peoples, but what does come through in their essays and reflections of human life is a unique awareness of the interior movements of compassion in the human heart and the tendency to help those in need. While other peoples often searched for the indwelling divine presence within human, the Chinese sought in the human heart the most authentic mode of one's humaneness. This was found to be a way of feeling that was also a way of knowing. Yet it was the capacity for sympathy for others rather than any type of knowing that provided the specific identity and highest perfection of the human quality of life. Feeling and knowing, however, must not be opposed to each other, for in reality these were simply two forms of one thing, the communion of people with each other and the communion of humans with all the universe. Many are the writers on this subject and many the instances that can be quoted, especially in the later Neo-Confucian period. Zhou Dunyi was so sensitive that he would not permit the grass outside his window to be cut lest he be the cause of hurt to a living being. Wang Yangming explained how people experience pain whenever any living being is pained or even when the rocks or tiles are shattered. Zhang Zai, in his concern for human suffering, spoke of all those who are tired, weary, weak, crippled, or ill, all who are without family, without children or wives or husbands, as his brothers in a special way since they have no one to whom they can turn for help.

It was Mencius, in particular, who reflected on this sympathetic experience and clearly perceived in this compassion of the human heart an authentic revelation of the real in one of its most essential qualities. One of the reasons why Mencius is the supreme thinker in the classical Confucian tradition is because he, in all his writings, as King Wen in his rule treated the people "as if he were tending invalids" (*Mencius* 4B:20, p. 131). Inwardly sensitive to the hurt of others and perceiving that other people, even those without great moral qualities, were immediately moved at the sight of innocent suffering, Mencius attained an extraordinary intuition of the essential goodness of humans as manifested by this compassion, a goodness that parallels the instinctive goodness of parents and children for each other and also the goodness that Heaven shows for the human order of earth. Upon these three observations, Mencius founded his entire teaching concerning the goodness not only of human nature, but also of the entire existing order of things. If there was a destructive aspect of things, if there were wicked people and wicked rulers, this came not out of the order of things but out of a distortion and rejection of this order. The order of goodness, love, and compassion is immediate, easy, and mutually beneficial for humans; wickedness is secondary, deliberate, and mutually harmful. People tend toward goodness as water tends to flow downward. Yet in fact people often "have no respect for themselves" (*Mencius* 4A:10, p. 122); they have "no confidence in themselves" (ibid.); they have "strayed hearts" (6A:11, p. 167); they have abandoned "the heart of the new born babe" (4B:12, p. 130). "The Way lies at hand yet it is sought afar off, the thing lies in the easy yet it is sought in the difficult. If only everyone loved his parents and treated his elders with deference, the empire would be at peace" (4A:11, pp. 122–23). For indeed the sage is no different from anyone else (6A:7, p. 164). Confucius did nothing exceptional (4B:10, p. 129). The feeling of compassion is in all people in the very substance of their being for it is not infused into people from without (6A:6, pp. 162–63); it arises from the most basic tendencies of their nature. There is no lack of natural power or of the interior impulse: "There is no greater joy for me than to find, on self-examination, that I am true to myself" (7A:4, p. 182). The great need, then, is simply for a person to release oneself up to those sublime movements within one that produce the greatest human deeds and bring forth the full perfection of the human in oneself and in one's relations with others: "A great person need not keep his word nor does he necessarily see his action through to the end. He aims only at what is right" (4B:11, p. 130). All this is so marvelously easy because "A great person is one who retains the heart of a newborn babe" (4B:12, p. 131).

Perhaps the single greatest illustration of not losing the heart of a child can be found in the poet Du Fu. He illustrates to an extraordinary degree the fulfillment of those basic instincts for good and for compassion toward others. In his poem "Five Hundred Words from Zhang-An to Feng-xian," Du Fu presents the difficulties that he had experienced while away from home during years of warfare, and his sorrow on discovering that his little son had died of starvation while he was away. Yet he wrote at the end of the poem:

> I am one of the privileged, free from taxation,
> And exempt from draft.
> If my lot is so bitter,
> That of a common human must be worse.

When I think of those whose property has been seized,
And of those recruited to garrison the far frontiers,
My anxiety rises like a flood to innundate even the
    Southern Mountains,
With mad swells utterly impossible to abate.[15]

Again, on the occasion when an autumn gale had torn off the thatched roof of his house, he writes about how the cotton quilt of his bed was damp and torn inside because of the children moving about so restlessly. The roof leaking, there was no place in the house that was dry. But even in the midst of such discomfort he could think of building a huge house with numberless rooms to shelter others in a similar situation. He ends with the moving statement: "Oh, if I could only see this house suddenly appear before my eyes, let my hut be smashed, let me die alone in exposure and I shall die content."[16]

IV

The fourth community, the family, is the primordial community of human affection; without it nothing human would have either existence or significance. If we have mentioned these other communities first, it is to provide a setting in which the family community can be seen in its origin and meaning, for it is in the home and by the love manifested there that people learn "love for one another" (*Xiaojing*, 12). Neither the higher community of the ontological triad nor the political community exists separately. Each is the perfection of the other. Together they constitute the unique and harmonious fulfillment of people in the human quality of their lives: but of them all, the family, in the Confucian tradition, has a special place as the primary community in which the humanization process takes place. The two words that are of special significance here are *qin* and *xiao*. Both of these indicate the intimacy of family affection, but here we will consider especially *xiao*, or filial devotion, for special comment. As with the other expressions of affection in the cosmic community and in the pan-human earthly community, this family community, and the basic virtues that enabled it to fulfill its monumental role in Chinese life, attain what seems to be exaggerated expression. Filial devotion and service to parents are designated as the supreme dynamic of the universe: "Filial devotion is the interior pattern of Heaven itself, as well as the ultimate norm of earth and guide of the people. When people respond to this norm, then they also follow the design of Heaven and earth, which leads them by the brightness

of Heaven and the benefits of earth; then the whole world is at peace"
(*Xiaojing,* 3). Filial devotion, then, is the evocation within the human heart
of a quality found in the supreme reality of Heaven itself, for this reason it
becomes the "root" of all those human qualities of life which are designated
in the term *ren.*

The response of filial devotion, however, is evoked not so much by the
immediate presence of Heaven as by the warmth and affection bestowed
upon the infant by its parents. For this reason the father, representing both
parents, is exalted as "counterpart of Heaven" (*Xiaojing,* 9) even as the king
is exalted to that status in terms of the world community. But while this
heavenly model is used in reference to the family, the family model is used
in reference to Heaven. These reciprocally clarify each other, mirror each
other, and become a norm for each other. If the father is the counterpart of
Heaven, then Heaven is the counterpart of the father. Together these various communities establish that larger functioning community of communities, mutually identifying, mutually supporting, mutually humanizing,
and mutually present to each other throughout the entire extent of the real.

No virtue, even that of the sage, is considered greater then filial devotion; indeed, it is from the experience of love in childhood that the holy
sages were able first to experience, then to understand, and finally to teach
this virtue: "The sage, because of his love for his parents taught love" (*Xiaojing,* 9). This later developed into a capacity for establishing the proper relation with public authorities: "The father–son communication is derived
from the Heaven-given nature, also the prince-minister relation" (ibid.).
Finally, there is the fact that love is related to the bestowal of life. To
bestow life without love is not considered possible: "Parents originate life,
no relation is superior to this; they bestow care and affection, no concern is
greater" (ibid.).

Among the basic reasons for exalting the family community, and the
great virtue of filial devotion associated with this community, is that at the
sacred moment of birth, the first moment of existence, the instinctive
movement of the infant is to turn toward its parents with a total sense of
need and to receive from parents not only the first existence itself, nor simply the bodily nourishment, but also the affection that it needs for its continued existence. This intimacy, so essential to the very existence of the
child, must forever after remain the first and most absolute face of its being;
everything else is derivative. In speaking of filial devotion, then, it is no
wonder that the *Book of Ritual,* appreciating the full depth of this mystery
of the human, speaks of filial devotion simply as the authentic manifestation of an instinctive tendency. This "does not come down from Heaven, it

does not come forth from the earth; it is simply the expression of the human feelings."[17] It is little wonder, then, that the *Doctrine of the Mean* tells us that the greatest of virtues, *ren,* is to be identified with humans, and that its supreme manifestation is in loving parents (20:5),[18] or that the *Book of Ritual* says that humans should serve their parents as they serve Heaven, and that they should serve Heaven as they serve their parents.[19]

V

The fifth community is the community of the individual person with one-self, the harmonious indwelling of the phenomenal ego in the deeper interior self. Because the full development of an authentic self is a basic requirement for the development of the other communities, there is constant mention in Confucian thought of the need for turning inward and reflecting on a person's own thoughts, desires, and actions. There was need for daily renewal based on this interior examination. Thus the entire Confucian teaching can be considered as a tradition of personal self-cultivation, as the art of self-awareness, as a mode of self discipline. The purpose of all this was to become one who immediately and instinctively, without hesitation or reasoning, spontaneously manifests in his or her actions an authentic human personality. As we are told in the *Great Learning:* Only the good human is capable of rightly "liking what the people like and disliking what the people like" (10).[20] Only such a human can sustain the larger human order of society, for both cultural and political order rest on the individual person. The root of the empire is in the state; the root of the state is in the family; the root of the family is in the person (*Mencius* 4A:5, p. 120). Later, the short chapter from the *Book of Ritual* entitled the *Great Learning* was taken out of this classic and made into a separate work in its own right because it correctly identified the pattern of dependence throughout the entire human order, beginning with the universal human order and passing to the lower communities, until the final term of dependence was arrived at deep within the human personality. Everything in society, then, depended on the cultivation of this ultimate support. From the emperor down to the ordinary people, everyone in society must consider the cultivation of the person as the root of a humanly valid social order. It would be difficult to exaggerate the importance of this short essay in the course of East Asian intellectual, spiritual, cultural, and political history, an importance it still maintains for all who would understand the Confucian life program.

Although so much emphasis was given to the family community, the movement of Chinese reflection went down into this still deeper and more radical source in the determination of human affairs—the human heart and its most interior tendencies. There was an obvious need to cultivate the entire order of things there where the ultimate dynamic of human affairs has its origin, in the individual person. The strife and devastation in the political order and the suffering it had caused had already by the sixth century B.C.E. convinced thinking people that the supreme need was to develop people worthy of that designation. This is the entire significance of Confucius, who shifted the nobility title of *junzi* from a political to a moral/spiritual/human designation, and undertook the work of creating authentic human personalities in his followers. Confucius understood the interrelation of the various forms of community that have been here outlined. He saw that each depended on the others, that each had to be fulfilled in and through the other; but he also saw that the point of entry into this complex of interpenetrating communities must be the individual person. In a warring period when the surrounding world was going up in the flames of interstate conflict, when none of the rulers was willing to respond to his teaching, when a new barbarization threatened the world, Confucius committed himself to the shaping of the historical destinies of humankind by educating people capable of showing forth those rich and sublime human qualities latent in the depths of a person's being, qualities summed up in the single word, *ren*. Before he could carry out such a work, he had first to show forth in himself those qualities of which he was speaking. That he accomplished this is evident from the picture of Confucius that his disciples left for posterity, which became ever afterwards the model of what might be considered as a truly human mode of being. What is remarkable in the teaching of Confucius is its wonderful softness, gentility, and quietness; its modesty, restraint, and compassion, along with an inner firmness and resilience derived from personal discipline. It is a teaching that penetrates into the truth of things without iconoclasm or puritanism or excessive rigor. Rather, it maintained a benevolent quality of serenity and sureness. No fear, no anxiety; simply the teaching of an authentic human being capable of that affectionate attitude toward others indicated by the virtue of *ren*, which he once defined simply as loving others (*Analects* 12:22),[21] *ai ren*.

Confucius understood that the answer to barbarism was not some violent social effort, some external discipline, or even some intellectual insight. It lay rather in the human style of one's personal bearing, in a capacity for establishing a mutual presence with others, in fostering a tradition of service to the community. This had to begin where life began, in a home filled with family affection. This was primarily a school for the individual, the place wherein lay the security that would enable the finer human qualities to find their expression, where the capacity for responding to those profoundly human instincts could be developed. Everything in later life would depend on this sensitivity to the tendencies felt in the deep stillness at the center of one's being. Since Confucius himself could only indicate the broader outlines of his teaching, it was not until the time of Mencius that this sensitivity to the most secret wellsprings of human thought and feeling could be spoken of with any fullness. But when Mencius did arrive on the scene and began his teaching, he was able to present a vision and an experience of humans that remains a monument to this type of reflexive insight. He often spoke of the need of people to reflect on themselves and on their deeds, knowing that if this were done people would discover there a compassionate heart that could not bear to observe the suffering of others (*Mencius* 2A:6, p. 82). They would also discover there the seeds of goodness which only needed cultivation to produce a true human (ibid., 2A:6, p. 83). Once these instinctive tendencies were recognized as guides to the authentic way of human life, the distinguishing quality of humans, as that which identifies them over against the sub-human world, then a basis was established on which people could appeal to individuals and to rulers to exert their energies toward a social harmony wherein individuals, communities, and rulers share in common the joys and sorrows of earthly life. It was all a question of humanizing people from within, convincing them that their nature is good, that they have basic instincts emerging from nature that are infallible guides toward a fitting human existence, and that the way of life indicated by the very nature of things is a simple and easy way. If somehow people had lost their mind-and-heart, had distorted the human tendencies evident in childhood, this could be corrected. Until then, people would only do violence to themselves individually and to others, causing infinite damage to the community and unlimited suffering to the people.

VI

After presenting these various forms in which the affective life of humans is lived according to Confucian tradition, we might indicate one of the most distinctive aspects of this tradition—its concern for the development of the human quality of life in its infra-temporal, infra-human setting. Within this setting the most exciting experience available to humans is the discovery of the distinctive modality of one's own existence and the manner in which, precisely in virtue of this human mode of existence, one enters into communion with all that is and brings to the entire universe of existences one's own special transforming presence. Everything is complete within us (*Mencius* 7A:4, p. 182). The special transforming quality, the particular communion that humans establish with the real is identified by the word *ren*. This special way of feeling, of sympathetic communication, this mode of presence, is an experience in which all the world is expressed in its human meaning and in which humans discover the wonder of themselves in the vastness of the world. In the Confucian tradition, this experience is fulfilled in a kind of cosmic ritual, the enactment of a choreography participated in by the stars in the heavens, by the seasons of earth, by all living things, and finally by humans, in and through whom this mighty performance comes to conscious expression. This expression, which attains articulate form in the *Book of Ritual,* sought to strengthen the individual and the distinctive qualities of things while bringing each thing more intimately into communion with everything else. Thus there are two basic demands upon humans: first, their self-identity as humans; second, their communion with the larger society and, beyond that, with the universal order of things. Both of these are indicated by the term *ren,* for *ren* is *human* (*Doctrine of the Mean* 20:5),[22] and the basic fulfillment of *ren* is attained in communion with others on this extensive scale. These two functions, self-identity and presence to others, are eventually one, for communion is a process whereby persons discover their larger self not within the limits of their own individual being but in others, who establish with them a more complete self in which each attains fulfillment. This process of communion with others and the consequent fulfillment of humans has no limits other than the limits of the real itself. The supreme obstacle to this communion is found in the self-isolation of the individual, his or her inability to respond properly to others, his or her closing off from the family and social order in favor of a self-centered and self-limiting existence. This involves either a deliberate rejection of the tendencies of nature or neglect in cultivating these tendencies. The result is an alienation of a person from his or her own authentic self, a break in the family community, the political community, and the entire ontological order; the cosmic ritual is interrupted.

That this alienation of humans within themselves and the consequent disturbance of the universal community occurs on such an extensive scale that it causes so much suffering always remained a difficult problem within the Confucian tradition. The basic solution offered was to establish, first, a ritual order of life in which the basic virtues would be cultivated according to an established style of conduct, not simply by indicating in general terms how the cultivation should take place but by providing specific training in these disciplines of individual, family, and social living in a meaningful ceremonial context; second, to establish a humanistic tradition for education of the young that would center on the understanding of humans and the manner in which their special qualities are developed in an overall scheme of reality. In both instances, in the ritual participation as well as in the humanistic education, the principal attention was given to cultivating the feeling life of humans, the governing principles of their conduct.

If the critique is offered that both of these programs are utopian in their basic orientation, the Confucian answer is simply that humans themselves are utopian in the very structure of their being. The virtue of *ren* is utopian in its distinctive qualities. Heaven and earth are utopian in their most primordial functioning. Nature is utopian in the very dynamics of its functioning. Yet to the great Confucian teachers who had experienced deeply the chaos in human affairs and who saw people reject the most elementary human aspects of their existence, this utopian consciousness and the humanizing activities it evoked were the only satisfying things that could sustain humans in the authentic mode of their being. Not to be hardened by struggle, not to become cynical, not to engage in counterviolence of dehumanizing dimensions, this required the endurance shown by the long sequence of teachers from the days of Confucius himself. They were sustained in their position not simply by their valor in the face of opposition but by a conviction that the ultimate constructive forces at work in the world could not finally be overcome. The dynamics of Heaven and earth, the forces within human nature (*xing*), the dominant tendency emanating from this source, *ren*, were situated in an inviolable depth of the human. They had their own gravitation that could never be removed, the gravitation to an interior, mutual, subjective presence with others in a state of communion, the ultimate goal and fulfillment of the virtue known as *ren*. So long as one human being remained capable of response to another human being there was hope for a human order of life in the fullness of its meaning.

Notes

1. *Book of Changes,* trans. Sung, Appendix III, 2:1/8.

2. *Sources of Chinese Tradition,* ed. Wm. Theodore de Bary and Irene Bloom, (New York: Columbia University Press, 1999), 1:301.

3. Ibid.

4. *Li Chi, Book of Rites,* trans. James Legge (New Hyde Park, NY: University Books, 1967), 7:3, p. 382.

5. *Classic of Documents,* in *Sources of Chinese Tradition,* ed. de Bary and Bloom, 1:31–34.

6. *Classic of Documents* [*Shu Ching, Book of History*], trans. James Legge (Chicago: Henry Regnery, 1971), 180.

7. *Sources of Chinese Tradition*, ed. de Bary and Bloom, 1:37–38.

8. *Mencius*, trans. D. C. Lau (London: Penguin Books, 1970). References to the *Mencius* are to this translation.

9. *Classic of Documents* [*Shu Ching, Book of History*], trans. Legge, 15.

10. *Book of Changes*, trans. Sung, Appendix III, 1:8.

11. *Analects*, trans. Wing-tsit Chan, in *A Sourcebook in Chinese Philosophy*, 20.

12. *Poetry of T'ao Ch'ien*, trans. Hightower, 26.

13. Ibid., 2.

14. *Tu Fu: China's Greatest Poet*, trans. Hung, 1:1.

15. Ibid., 89.

16. Ibid., 172.

17. *Li Chi, Book of Rites*, trans. Legge, 32:10, p. 379.

18. See *A Sourcebook in Chinese Philosophy*, trans. Wing-tsit Chan, 104–5.

19. *Li Chi, Book of Rites*, trans. Legge, 24:18, p. 269.

20. See *A Sourcebook in Chinese Philosophy*, trans. Wing-tsit Chan, 92.

21. Ibid., 40.

22. Ibid., 104.

Sources

Book of Changes. Translated by Z. D. Sung. *The Text of Yi King*. New York: Paragon Reprint Corporation, 1960.

Book of History. Text from Bernhard Karlgren, *The Book of Ritual Documents*. Reprinted from the Museum of Far Eastern Antiquities, Bulletin 22. Stockholm, 1950.

Book of Ritual. Text from Seraphin Courvreur, *Memories sur les bienseances et les ceremonies*. Paris, 1950.

Chan, Wing-tsit. *Sourcebook in Chinese Philosophy*. Princeton: Princeton University Press, 1963.

de Bary, Wm. Theodore, Wing-tsit Chan, and Burton Watson, compilers. *Sources of Chinese Tradition*. New York: Columbia University Press, 1960.

Dong Zhongshu, Jun-shiu fan-lu, SPPY. *Chunqui Fanlu*.

The Great Learning, Doctrine of the Mean, Analects of Confucius, and *Mencius*. Text from James Legge's edition, *The Four Books*.

Hightower, James Robert, trans. *The Poetry of T'ao Ch'ien*. Oxford: Clarendon Press, 1970.

Hung, William. *Tu Fu: China's Greatest Poet*. New York: Russell & Russell, 1969.

Xiao jing, Xiao jing cheng-chu shu, SPPY.

6

Classical Chinese Views of Reality and Divinity

CHUNG-YING CHENG

REALITY AND DIVINITY ARE FUNDAMENTAL ISSUES for any philosophical tradition, because they embody fundamental human concerns for the human person. In fact, we cannot deny that the question of divinity arises as we ask how we could justify our life, settle our feeling, and decide on our action. For this reason we can hardly touch on any philosophical problem without raising questions of reality or questions of human origin and human destiny. Thus, in a certain sense all philosophical questions are disguised questions of reality, human destiny, or perfect existence. In dealing with the Confucian tradition, there is no exception. One may say that the whole development of the Confucian philosophy is premised on a fundamental understanding of the human being as a paradigm of reality and potential divinity. The crucial thing about this development is to realize the truth of being of the human person and to fulfill this truth by continuous practice of self-cultivation. Now from the vantage point of our time, as we look back to the very beginning of Confucianism and also look over the variegated evolution of the Confucian philosophy, we cannot but think of the problems of reality and divinity as the constant motivating power for both its beginning and its evolution. In this article I shall begin with the very beginning, namely, introducing the Yijing view of reality as embodied or developed in the *Yizhuan*. Then I shall discuss the Daoist view of reality not only with interest in itself but for its role in shaping and contributing to the formation of the Neo-Confucian spirit. Then I shall elaborate on the Chinese sense and explication of *shen*, or divinity, and introduce the Zhongyong notion of *cheng* as its pristine source.

113

The Yizhuan Theory of Reality

In the *Xici Commentary* of the *Zhouyi* we witness the emergence of the two basic concepts that characterize the ultimate reality that the human person has experienced. These two basic concepts are respectively that of the great ultimate (*taiji*) and that of the way (*dao*). Both concepts are derived from the human experience of the formations and transformations of things in nature that are referred as the *bianyi* or *bianhua* (change), but in a sense represent a general characterization of and a deeper insight into the general nature of change. In the first place it is said, "Thus the change has its Great Ultimate from which Two Norms (*liangyi*) are generated. The Two Norms generate Four Forms (*shixiang*), Four Forms generate Eight Trigrams (*bagua*)" (see the *Zhouyi, Xici-shang*, 11). We know that the sixty-four hexagrams are then generated from the doubling of the Eight Trigrams. This process of generation is remarkable in establishing a cosmogonical picture of the rise and development of reality as a world of things as well as in providing a cosmographical way of thinking to be symbolized in the systemic structures of trigrams and hexagrams. This process of generation we may also call the *dao*. The sustaining source of this process of generation is called the *taiji*. The *dao* is *taiji* in its process aspect, whereas the *taiji* is the *dao* under its origination aspect. Together they refer to the same thing, namely, the totality of reality of creativity, change, and transformation.

We may call this cosmogonic and cosmographical way of thinking and description of reality and world the "ontocosmology of the *taiji* and the *dao*." The "onto-" part of the term "ontocosmology" suggests the meaning of the *taiji*, and the "-cosmology" part of the term suggests the meaning of the *dao*. Since it is this theory of the *taiji* and the *dao* that forms the backbone and mainstream of the metaphysical thinking in the thirty-two-hundred-year history of Chinese philosophy,[1] we should regard it as the fundamental theory of reality in Chinese philosophy. Confucius in his late age has studied and commended the *Book of Changes*, which was since then regarded as one of the Confucian classics, even the leading one. There exist no doubt elements of Confucian reflections in the ontocosmological commentaries called the *Yizhuan* (commentaries on the *Zhouyi*, developed in the fifth to third centuries B.C.E.), but these could be seen as basically implicit in the contexts of the underlying philosophy or view of reality in the original *Zhouyi* texts and symbolism. This means that the ontocosmology of the *taiji* and the *dao* is not just Confucian but is an articulation of the ancient way of thinking, observation, and interpretation of reality in China. However, in order to distinguish it from the later Daoist approach to reality in the Daoist School of Laozi (around the middle of the sixth century B.C.E.; exact dates are uncertain) and Zhuangzi (ca. 370–300 B.C.E.) and its elaboration of the philosophy of the *dao,* we may refer to it as the "Yizhuan theory of reality," since this theory is suggested and implicitly formulated in the *Yizhuan,* particularly in the *Duan* and *Xici* portions of the commentaries.

In order to understand the "Yizhuan theory of reality" as the fundamental Chinese theory of reality, we should in fact take note of the following characterization of the metaphysical way of thinking with regard to our experience of change:

1. *Reality as inexhaustible origination.* We can trace the beginning of the presentation and development of the world reality to the beginning of a root source. This root source, called "the great ultimate" (*taiji*), is the absolute beginning of all things, but it is also the sustaining base for all things even at present because all changes of the world are based on it and contained in it. In this sense the *taiji* is in fact the primordial and inexhaustible source of the creative and transformative force of all changes and is conveyed by the notion of "creativity of creativity" or "generation of generation" (*shengsheng*) in the *Xici.* In this sense reality is not something stationary or static underneath a world of fleeting phenomena nor a world of forms or ideas reflected in a world of imitations or veiled from a screen of illusions or delusions. Neither is it something accessible only by abstraction of human thinking or revelation of a transcendent God, as in Christian theology. Reality is concrete, vivid, and holistic not only in the sense that all things are interrelated with a whole as originally defined by the oneness of the *taiji,* but also in the sense that changes and nonchanges underlying the changes are organically part and parcel of the same thing and there cannot be strict demarcation or bifurcation between appearance and reality. In this sense changes and the constant and continuous regeneration of things in reality are what reality is made of. Any scheme to divide or stratify reality will only serve a limited purpose and will be rendered inept by confrontation with reality. This means that all theories of reality share with reality the nature of change and must be subject to the continuous challenges of an ever-developing and becoming process of formation and transformation. Therefore we may understand the *taiji* as not just primary origination but constant or ceaseless origination. In a Whiteheadean spirit, we may say that the world is in the making and is constantly and forever in the making.

2. *Reality as polar-generative process.* When the *taiji* gives rise to things in the world, it does so by bringing in a whole of polarities, the positive and

the negative or the *yang* (the brightening/the moving/the firm) and the *yin* (the darkening/the restive/the soft). These polarities are subcontraries that exist simultaneously and are conspicuous on a specific level. They are also simultaneously contraries that are hidden on more concrete levels of things. In this latter sense they are identifiable with the *taiji* because the *taiji* as the source of all changes is always hidden under all things. The generation of new things occurs on the basis of the coexistence and interaction between polarities. Unlike Whitehead's postulation of the rise of novelty from pure ideas, novelties in this model derive from internal dynamics of the becoming of world, from which a division into the *yin* and the *yang* and a combination of the *yin* and the *yang* are the basic ways to give rise to new things. The novelty of things is inherent in the very source of the world itself, and it is also inherent in the creative potential of a thing which requires the interaction of forces to bring about.

  3. *Reality as multi-interactive harmony.* An individual thing or an individual class of things always has two sides: the *yin*, which pertains to its stationary state of existence and its receptivity to the outside world (it is its given nature), and the *yang*, which pertains to its dynamical state of developing its propensities in its interaction with the outside world. As the *yin-yang* polarities are definitive of individual things or individual classes of things, that a thing must interact with the outside world is in the nature of the thing itself. It is in this process of interaction that a thing fulfills its potentialities of nature and runs its course of bounded existence. It is in maintaining itself as a given nature that we can speak of the "centrality" of a thing, and in properly taking and giving with other things we can speak of "harmony" between or among things. There could be noncentrality and disharmony in the formation and transformation of things, which would be a problem and a crisis for its identity and its survival in the world of reality as things. Hence the natural dispositions of a thing to maintain its own centrality and to reach harmony with other things. But in the case of human persons these two aspects of existence must be cultivated in order to enhance and realize the fulfillment of the human propensity and potentiality.

  It is said: "One *yin* and one *yang* is thus called the *dao*. To follow it is goodness and to complete it is nature" (*Xici-shang*, no. 5). How do we understand this in reference to individual things? The *dao* is how things come into being and how they grow and develop in a process of time, and the process of one *yin* and one *yang* is made of the alternation, conjunction, and mutual interaction of the positive and negative forces and positive and negative activities of the individual things which result in formation and transformation of things.

4. *Reality as virtual hierarchization.* The world is made of many levels, each of which is a combination of the *yin* and the *yang* forces or activities of things. For the *taiji* and the *dao* model of cosmogony and cosmography (and hence ontocosmology) there are genuine general features of the *yin* and the *yang*, which are understood as rest/motion, darkness/brightness or invisibility/visibility and softness/firmness, closedness/openness, retrospective propensity/prospective propensities, and other such properties. Although these properties are basically described in phenomenal and experiential terms of human persons, there is no reason why they could not be described in a logical and scientific language of abstract and primary properties. Perhaps one could identify the *yin* and the *yang* elements or processes in the genetic code and the theory of subelementary particles, as many people have done. Similarly, there is no reason why the values and emotions and intentions could not also be described in the language of the *yin* and the *yang*. In this light, the *yin* and the *yang* should be regarded as neutral and variant functors or operators which act to generate relationships and changes. The important point is to remember that as there are levels of simplicity and complexity of structures and activities in a scheme of things in being and becoming, so there are levels of the *yin* and the *yang* in the world of reality. On the highest and most general level, there is the "great ultimate" (*taiji*). On the second level there are the *yin* and the *yang*. On the third level there are Four Forms. On the fourth level there are Eight Trigrams. This can go on forever and without limit. But individual things must be seen on an individual level of the *yin* and the *yang*, which represent a complex hierarchy of levels of the *yin* and the *yang* as well as a complex world of *yin/yang* interactions.

This means that the individual thing or person is only understood and acting in a context of field and web of forces; in this context one is still capable of making a creative impact on and a contribution to the formation and transformation of the world.

5. *Reality as recursive (not like a circle but like a spiral) but limitless regenerativity.* Although the commentaries of the *Zhouyi* have not mentioned the recursive and regenerative nature of the *yi*, the presentation of nature in eight trigrams and of the world in sixty-four hexagrams in the original symbolism (in hexagrams) of 1200 B.C.E. and appended judgments of divination clearly suggested that nature is a process of both collective and distributive balance and functions as a process of return and reversion, as

suggested by the rotation of seasons and celestial cycles. The interesting thing to note is that once we are able to represent the world in a collectively inclusive and individually exclusive enumeration of stages or facets, these stages and facets will have to recur as patterns or forms of understanding or existential characterizations on a special level. It is clear that we are able to limit our understanding and characterization to a special level or particular domain and then work out or design some definitive categorical system of description or projection. That is why we could use the eight trigrams and sixty-four hexagrams at the same time, because they belong to different levels of relevance and meaningful description. What is implied in this description of reality is that reality is both limited and limitless: It is limited on a specific level of description which serves a human purpose. It is limitless because any specific level of description could only serve a purpose in a limited way as it can be transcended or abandoned for a higher or more specific level of description. We may say that there are virtually unlimited numbers of levels of description, just as theoretically there could be an unlimited number of systems of scientific knowledge in the progression of scientific inquiry. On each level of description there is the recursion of the finite categorized reality. This is so because it is in the nature of change that the world of reality has to be regeneratively represented. This may be called regenerative recursion. It is this regenerative recursion that gives stability to the process and may be called structure of the process.

In the *taiji* and the *dao* model of reality, what is shown in the symbolism of the *yi* is a regenerative recursion by reversion; namely the stage of the *yin* has to revert to a stage of the *yang* in order to realize creative change and vice versa. It is the process of time that the *yin* and the *yang* are interacting by alternating. Because of this, one could expect that reaching the limit of the worst would mean a return to a better condition. Although in practice it is difficult to know whether one has reached the worst, or how long the getting better would last, it is nevertheless possible to conceive of reality as an alternation between good and bad on the same level as a natural process of change as in *Zhouyi*.

6. *Reality as organismic totality*. From the above description it is clear that the world of reality in the model of the *taiji* and the *dao* is totalistic in the sense that all things are included and there is nothing beyond it. It is said that "the book of the change is extensive and all-comprehensive. It contains the Way of Heaven, the way of man and the way of earth" (*Xicixia*, 10). For the early Chinese the world of reality was confined to Heaven, earth, and ten thousand things among which the human person stands out as the most intelligent and the one capable of forming a tri-partnership

with Heaven and earth. Everything in this reality comes from the *taiji* and follows or embodies the *dao*. Hence, there could not be anything outside this world of reality with the *taiji* and the *dao*. This implies that there is no transcendent being outside this world and in fact nothing is to be conceived beyond the world of the *taiji* and the *dao*. When we come to Laozi, we find that even when the notion of emptiness or void (*wu*) is introduced, what the term *wu* stands for is part and parcel of the universe of the *dao*. The *dao* in Laozi is simply enriched by something called the void or non-being (*wu*). Similarly, when Zhou Dunyi (1017–1073) speaks of the ultimateness (*wuji*) giving rise to the great ultimate, he is simply extending the *dao* to cover both void and non-void. There is no break between the void and the non-void, and hence one does not have a transcendent nothingness or emptiness apart from reality. In this non-transcendence we do not speak merely of immanence but also of totality. Immanence refers to values and powers inherent in the things themselves, but totality refers to all the inter-related parts of all things in reality. The reason why things belong or hang together is that in the ultimate reality all things are not simply contained but rather are all interrelated or even interpenetrating. It is the organismic nature of the totality that not only can there not be any object "outside," but all things exist together by way of mutual support or even mutual grounding. This is how immanence of Heaven in the nature of humanity leads to an interminable exchange between, as well as a unity of, humanity and Heaven.

The Daoist Theory of Reality

Although Yizhuan has developed the fundamental metaphysics of the *taiji* and the *dao* in Chinese philosophy, which inspires or perhaps grounds the Confucian view on the moral propensity of humans, it is in Laozi's *Daodejing* (Classic of Dao and De) that we find a better thematized theory of the *dao*. It might be said that a fuller but a more distinctive theory of reality was formulated in the *Daodejing*. We may call it the "Daoist theory of reality." It has been frequently argued that it is the "Daoist theory of reality" of the fourth century B.C.E. that has influenced the "Yizhuan theory of reality" of the third century B.C.E. It is even suggested that the "Yizhuan theory of reality" is basically Daoistic.[2] But this would seem not to be the case, the reason being that there exists a tight consistency and coherence of ideas in the *Yizhuan*'s notion of reality and creativity in reference to presuppositions that could be easily seen in the ancient texts of the *Zhouyi* and the even older practice of divination. On examining the basic methodology of thinking and the empirical beginning of the *Zhouyi*, I have pointed out that it is in the presupposed view and way of thinking in the *Zhouyi* symbolism and judgments that both the idea of the *taiji* as a root source of creative change and the notion of the *dao* as a polar-generative process of totalization were developed.[3] It is interesting to note that both of these ideas are also present in the *Daodejing* text as well as in the *Yizhuan*.

A better suggestion would be that both the *Daodejing* and the *Yizhuan* share the influence of the *Zhouyi* and that they develop as a result of this influence and an effort to understand the presupposed meaning of the *Zhouyi* symbolic texts. Hence, there is no denying that there are shared grounds of ontocosmology (as formulated above in the six points) between the two. But there should be also no denying that there is a difference between the Daoist approach to reality based on the presuppositions of *Zhouyi* and the Confucian approach to reality based on a creative understanding of *Zhouyi*. The high consistency of the *Zhouyi* and *Yizhuan* theory of reality reflects a Confucian emphasis on the moral and social relevance and importance of our understanding of reality. Understanding reality is essential for a moral person to become genuinely moral, for morality consists in practicing the comprehensive care for life in society and politics as derived from the way of Heaven, which is understood in the *Yizhuan* theory of reality. Insofar as the book of *Zhouyi* is infused with the spirit of pragmatism, a concern with rectitude, and an ethics of action, it is clear that the *Yizhuan* theory of reality is a continuation of the *Zhouyi* philosophy, which is further cultivated in the later stage of Confucius's life as a classical *ru* (cultured and learned) thinker who could also have embraced the Zhou values in terms of its cultural humanism and moral humanism.[4]

On the other hand, the *Daodejing* text, though to a great extent exhibiting the underlying spirit of *Zhouyi*'s understanding of reality as a process of change and of reversion and return, has its distinctive features, which can be perhaps interpreted as a creative response to, and a serious-minded critique of, its own times. For this reason the Daoist approach to reality must be treated independently as a new development of the theory of reality in Chinese philosophy.

There are four major distinctive features of the Daoist theory of reality that can be regarded as differentiating it from the Yizhuan theory of reality. In the first place, the *Daodejing* introduced a unique notion of the *dao* which is not embodied or conveyed by language. The first sentence of the *Daodejing* says: "The *dao* can be spoken, but it is not the constant *dao;* The name can be named, it is not the constant name" (ch. 1). What, then, is the *dao*? It is apparently the power or force underlying all changes and transformations of things in the world. The key here is that even though each thing has its way of change, they all share a common moving or motivating force for change. They also share in being in a common time and in a common space with one another. This oneness is further experienced in interrelatedness among all things in the world. But this power of change and this oneness are not separate from each other nor are they separate from the world or each individual thing of the world. It is difficult to express this beings-wide all-encompassing oneness, comprehensiveness, and moving/motivating power. When we choose the word "*dao*" to indicate or refer to this power, we cannot identify it with any of the things in the world because it is not one of the things our language describes. It is more or less like an inaccessible object such as the moon, to which we may point with the finger. Hence the *dao* is to be experienced, reflected upon, and intended in our speech; but it cannot be identified. Yet this is not to say that the *dao* is nonexistent, although it is invisible, inaudible, and intangible, nor is it to say that its existence is nonefficacious, although it is nonsubstantial. On the contrary, the *dao* is full of power and functions in all natural activities of things in the world. Specifically, one can even see that the *dao* is a power giving rise to all things without owning them, sustaining all things without dominating them, enabling things to act on their own without claiming its own work (*Daodejing*, chs. 10, 34, 51).

The *dao*, which we may call the "creative spirit of the world," therefore is real and profound and can be considered the absolute beginning and primordial source of all things. In this sense the *dao* can be said to exist before Heaven and earth and to be the forerunner of all things and the mother of all lives. It is also the naturally-of-its-accord spontaneity of things. Hence Laozi says: "While man follows earth, earth follows Heaven, Heaven has to follow the *dao* and the *dao* would act of its own accord" (*Daodejing*, ch. 25).

With all this said, the important thing to keep in mind is that although the *dao* is not the same as anything in the world, it is not separate from the world nor does it transcend the world. Moreover, although as the source of change and the basis of being for all things, it is not to be conceived as God in whatever sense a Western religion or theology may attribute to God. It is rather the very nature of things when they are considered as an interrelated whole and as a unity of multiplicity of being which exhibits its creativity and novelty through multifarious change and abundance of life. One sees in the *dao* a dialectical unity of transcendence and immanence, namely, the transcendence of immanence and the immanence of transcendence in the relationship of nature and individual lives in nature. This understanding would become even more intensified in the works of Zhuangzi, which would stress the *dao* as self-transformation (*zihua*) of things and the interpenetrating power of oneness (*daotong weiyi*).

We come to the second point about the Daoist theory of reality. Because the *dao* is indescribable and non-substantiable, it is conceived of as "void" or "empty" (*wu, xu*). It is said that "*Dao* is void and its function is infinite" (ch. 4). This voidness of the *dao* is also directly referred to as non-being (*wu*) by Laozi when he says, "*Wu* is to name the beginning of Heaven and earth, and *you* (being) is to name the mother of ten thousand things" (ch. 1). In fact, in order to appreciate how *wu* is a process of being's emergence from non-being, one might also see how *wu* is a process of non-being's emergence from being. To become non-being is to void existence of all determinate characteristics and to go back to a state when all determinations of characteristics are in the offing. Things come into being, in other words, from a nebulous and indeterminate state of non-being in which non-being could even be understood as indeterminacy of being. There are many passages, in fact, that would lead one to this view, for example, *Daodejing*, chs. 14 and 21. In this sense *wu* could be regarded as one aspect of the *dao*, the other aspect of which is simply *you*. *Wu* is no-thing or having-no-things (*wuwu*) and *you* is having-things (*yuwu*). As *dao* is a power creative of all things as well as the process of creative production, it has both the activity of *wu* and the activity of *you*, just as all things have both the *yin* (emptying) and *yang* (substantiating) functions. It is through the interaction of these two functions and their conjunction that things become what they are and reach a state of harmony. It is said that "all ten thousand things are holding *yin* in their back and embrace *yang* [in the front], and in an intimate and strong mixing [*chong*] of the two vital forces [*qi*] a harmony results" (*Daodejing*, ch. 42). It is also in this sense that Laozi speaks of the "mutual generation of *yu* and *wu*" (*youwu xiangsheng*, ibid., ch. 2), by which it is meant that *yu* and *wu* are mutually defining and conditioning as well as mutually forming and producing. One sees in this what the *Yizhuan* has described as the alternation of the *yin* and *yang* in the *dao*.

One way to reach the state of *wu* and hence the state of natural functioning of the *dao* is to have no desires (*wuyu*) and no actions (*wuwei*) on the part of a person. This is important for the Daoist theory of reality, for the theory is not a matter simply of abstract speculation; it is a matter of close embodiment of ontocosmological and life experience. In fact, without such an embodiment Laozi (the Old One) would not be able to describe so vividly the reality and creativity of the *dao*. From this one may very well think that for the Daoist any human being could come to an intimate knowledge and understanding of the *dao* if one is to reduce one's desires and knowledge and even actions to a state of oneness (*Daodejing*, ch. 39). This also means that at a minimum one should not let one's desires and knowledge block the open vision of the whole process of change and transformation in the *dao*. That one's vision could be blocked by one's desires and knowledge is no doubt a result of a close observation of reality. Hence, Laozi advises that one should keep oneself free from diversions of senses and the burdens of learning. For the *dao* reveals itself to those in a free state of mind or in an open state of nonfixation of belief. This point is also strongly stressed in Zhuangzi.

We come to a third point of the Daoist theory of reality. Reality in the name of the *dao* is always a matter of return (*fu*) and reversion (*fan*). It is said that "to reach for the ultimate of emptiness and to abide by the utmost of tranquility, ten thousand things will agitate at the same time. I would therefore be able to observe the process of return. There are many things and each would return to its root. To return to the root is called 'tranquility' and this is called 'return to destiny' [*fuming*]" (*Daodejing*, ch. 16).

It is interesting to note that whereas the *Yizhuan* approach to reality stresses the ceaselessness of the productive creativity (*shengsheng buyi*), the Daoist approach to reality stresses the constancy of return. In this sense the *Yizhuan* approach is dynamic and the Daoist approach is static. However, the Daoist note on return as a distinctive feature of reality was already implicit in the symbolism of trigrams and hexagrams. One can see that the relationship between the *yin* and the *yang* in the Qian and Kun trigrams and hexagrams demonstrate such a return when we see this relationship in a temporal process of alternation of one *yin* and one *yang*. If the *dao* begins with the *yin* and moves to a stage of the *yang*, then the only way it could go is to return to the *yin*. Similarly, from the *yin* it would return to *yang*. But if the root of being is non-being in the sense described above, one can see that the root is closer in nature to the *yin* than to the *yang*. This observation led later Neo-Confucianist Zhou Dunyi to speak of a state of the ultimateness as (*wuji*) logically if not temporally prior to the state of the great ultimate (*taiji*) in his famous work *Taiji Tushuo* (Discourse on the Diagram of the Great Ultimate). In this work the idea of return of the things to their root is also articulated, for according to Zhou, not only has the *wuji* given rise to the *taiji*, which produces all the things in the world, but the whole world is always a unity of the *taiji* and the *taiji* is no more than the beginning state of the *wuji*. From an ontological point of view one could regard *wuji* and *taiji* as two alternating states of the *dao* which exist at the same time and form a mutually defining unity. On this view, then, there need not be a temporal sense of return, and we can speak of the reversion of the *dao* from one state to another and vice versa. In fact, this is what is also observed by Laozi in the *Daodejing*.

It is said that "reversion is the motion of the *dao;* weakness is the function of the *dao*" (*Daodejing*, ch. 40). As return is a temporal reversion of the *dao*, reversion is a nontemporal return of the *dao*. They can be regarded as referring to the same action. On the other hand, it might be suggested that reversion is a more fundamental characteristic of the *dao,* as the *dao* always exists in opposites and reversion can be logically considered to be the exercise of opposition within a unity. But then we would have to consider return as a different function of the *dao* as well, namely, the function of going back to the unity of the *dao.* This would make return and reversion two different functions of the *dao.* But, although we can see *wu* and *you* as two opposite and yet mutually related processes of the *dao,* there is no good reason to see reversion and return as dualistic rather than as one process described under two forms, a process that has its opposite in the process of ceaseless productive creativity in the *Yizhuan.*

The fourth point should be a brief one. Given the pervasive nature of the *dao,* not only can one observe the *dao* both outside oneself and within one's own person and thus understand the *dao;* one can further cultivate the *dao* so that one can participate in the *dao* or imitate the *dao* to achieve or reach for a desirable and ideal state of life. For the Daoists, just as for the Confucianists, there are ample grounds for speaking of the unity of humanity and Heaven or the unity of the human person and the *dao.* This unity is important for both schools insofar as ethics, social action, and political life are all dependent on it.

We now have a composite picture of reality in classical philosophy by way of the *Yizhuan* approach and the Daoist approach. Their different points of emphasis should not overshadow their common roots and common vision of reality as a world of interrelated things in a creative process of change and transformation. At a later time there arose both the Neo-Daoistic and Chinese Buddhistic philosophy in which reality has been either presented and articulated on the basis of the Daoistic model of reality or presented and articulated on the basis of the Buddhistic theory of illusive consciousness and its emancipation in enlightenment. It is not until the rise of Neo-Confucianism in the Song period that the *Yizhuan* model would become the standard and norm. Yet the distinctive features of the Daoist model of reality together with some features of the Chinese Buddhist model of reality have been absorbed into the Neo-Confucian system. This leads to a theory of reality presented not only in terms of mutual production of *wu* and *you,* but in terms of new categories of *li* (principles) and *qi* (vital force).[5]

Divinity without Theology: Chinese Approach to Divinity

Any theory of divinity must be grounded on or must presuppose a theory of reality. Historically, a notion of divinity might appear on the scene first, but in time it must disclose the theory of reality presupposed by it. It may happen, of course, that when a theory of reality is first suggested, a theory of divinity could be founded on it. It must be also pointed out that a theory of divinity could attempt to give the ultimate grounding to a theory of reality and therefore would overrule the theory of reality as its consequence. Yet on the other hand, a theory of reality could also replace a given original notion of divinity and thus provide a new interpretation and new understanding of divinity in light of the theory of reality. We can see the development of Christian religion in the West as a classic example of the former case of the development from a theory of God to a theologically grounded theory of reality, whereas we can see the development of Confucian and Daoist metaphysics as an example of the latter case of development from a theory of *tian* (Heaven) or *di* (Lord on High) to an ontocosmology of reality which traces and reveals the activity of the divine in the creative productiveness and transformativeness of things.

In the Christian case, the ontologization of God makes God the foundation of all reality in a theology or *Ontotheologik* à la Heidegger. Hence, this is always the leading theme of theological interpretation of reality in the Western religious tradition. On the other hand, it is the "daoization" of the *tian* as God that replaced the *tian* with the *dao*, and therefore a theory of reality has subsumed a potential theology or "tianology" of divinity in the Chinese philosophical tradition. This tradition is therefore one in which we see processes of the depersonalization, the naturalization, and the humanization of the *tian*, without, however, giving up the spiritual meaningfulness of reality. Thus we have what may be said to be a notion of "divinity without theology." This "divinity without theology" is best expressed by the statement in *Xici* of the *Zhouyi* (Book of Changes): "Divinity has no form and change has no substance" (*shenwufang, yiwuti*).

As early as the beginning of the Xia era in 2000 B.C.E., there was already reference to the Lord on High (*di*) who would supervise and oversee human affairs and who controls human destiny from above. This notion of the *di* could be regarded as a spiritual projection of a powerful and venerated ancestor who has played the role of a ruler or a governor in his lifetime. The word "*di*" is also said to symbolize the bud of a flower and hence the source of life. It is clear, then, that the Lord on High as mentioned in the *Book of Documents* (*Shujing*) and the *Book of Poetry* (*Shijing*) is a supreme being who combines source of life and source of power in one person and who cares for the well-being of people (as his posterity) and the ordering of the state. He was thought of and worshiped as a personal god who could issue commands and mandates. In time, however, the notion of the *di* fused with the notion of the *tian* (heaven, sky, a term to be understood spatially rather than temporally). The *tian* too is to be conceived of as powerful and life-giving, and it is further conceived of as infinite. (In *Shijing* it is said: "The great heaven has no limit.") It is probable that a deeper and wider sense of reality made possible the transformation from the worship of the *di* to the worship of the *tian*, and that this took place as Zhou conquered the Shang people (who were known for their faith in ghosts and spirits and naturally *di*) around 1200 B.C.E.

This deeper and wider sense of reality diluted the personalistic character of *tian* as a supreme ruler on high and as a supreme creator of life. As this sense of reality focused increasingly on the unity of humanity and heaven, understood in terms of a common bond of creative activity, the *tian* eventually came to be regarded as the Way of Heaven (*tiandao*), which is manifested in nature and is to be realized as a moral command in man. We find this depersonization of the *tian* already in Confucius, although Confucius still occasionally spoke of the *tian* as if it was the Lord on High or a supreme moral being. The full naturalization and depersonalization of the *tian* occurs in Daoism, where the *tian* is seen as having arisen from the great *dao*, not the *dao* of something but the *dao* by itself as a creative process and reality that generates things in the world and imparts to them the power of self-autonomy and self-transformation with inherent dynamics of the *yin-yang* alternation and complementation.

The transformation of the *di* to the *tian* and then to the *dao* demonstrates a movement from a theory of personal divinity to a theory of depersonalized reality. Even though a personalistic notion of divinity is lost, which accounts for the fact that China, unlike the West, has not sustained a monotheistic religion, the sense of divinity is still preserved in the form of a profound understanding of reality as the process of creative change and as the inexhaustible source of novelty and life. This is what I have labeled the "divinity without theology."

What, then, is divinity in Chinese philosophy? The Chinese term *shen* is used to refer to all natural spirits, which may be conceived as personalized entities vested with life and special powers. In fact, *shen* is the living presence of power that may be said to exist in all of those living things of nature that can exert their influences upon other things. More specifically, the term *shen* applies to human persons in their possession of this living presence of powers to influence others. Thus, a person who accomplishes great deeds and achieves exemplary virtues, and who is consequently respected and wields great influence during life, leaves upon his death his *shen* (or influence, heretofore referred to as "spirit") to be worshiped or sought after. In this sense, the *shen* of a person is the natural extension of his life and the power of his influence projected into the present and the future even after the physical person is no longer present. When an unworthy person died, however, his spirit is not to be sought after but rather to be avoided, and he is known not as a *shen,* but as a *gui* or ghost—something belonging (one hopes) only to the past.

As *shen* is to be explained as the beneficial power of a person extending to the future from the present, *gui* is to be conceived of by contrast as the traces of a past human life. Even if the *gui* of a person may come back to affect the present, its coming back to the present would be a surprising and alarming event.

This conception of *shen* is well developed in both classical Confucian and classical Daoistic philosophy of the constitution of a human person. (This basic theory is found in the texts of Mencius, in the *Xici* of the *Zhouyi,* and in the texts of the four chapters of the *Guanzi,* in Laozi and Zhuangzi. This theory is developed into a basis for alchemy and the search for immortality by the Neo-Taoists in third century.) The human person is thus conceived of as formed of three or four levels of existence. On the first level, there is the physical reality which is the body (*shen*). On the second level, there is the essence of life (*jing*) or the essential elements of life as an organism. On the third level, there is energy and the circulating powers of life, which are referred to as vital breath (*qi*). Finally, there is the level of *shen,* which can be regarded as the quintessence of life and vital energy or the *ling* (efficacy) of *qi.* It is the freest element of life, but an element which also survives physical life in a free manner as it can be expressed in the arts and deeds, the work and the word of a person.

According to this conception, human existence is not a conjunction of mind and body, as Cartesian dualism would have it, but rather a holistic unity of interpenetrating life elements, each of which is to be conceived of holistically. The holistic conception of life differs from the atomistic conception of life in that there are no absolute, simple elements postulated, but rather nebulous wholes with basic organic parts interactively supporting each other. Thus, it is not simply that the higher level depends on the lower level but that the lower levels also depend on the higher levels. In this sense any lower level of existence could have a higher level which is its *shen.* Whether the *shen* stands out depends on the special influence or presence of power a thing has. Thus, for the ancient Chinese, all major mountains and rivers have their *shen* or spirits which are worthy of worship or respect. On the other hand, the *shen* of a human being who achieved great power of influence would be more vividly entertained in the minds of the relevant people and would thus become more an object of worship.

With respect to the last point, it is interesting to note the following saying of Confucius in the *Analects:* "[I] sacrifice to the spirits as if the spirits are present; if I am not engaging myself [*yu*] in the sacrifice, it is like not holding a sacrifice" (3-12). How does one feel that the spirits are present? One feels the presence of the spirits by using one's sincere feelings and vivid imagination in a projection of the known person or object. In the case of the unknown person or object it is to think deeply of the person or object in worship. It is a total engagement of one's person for the projected construction of the object, and as a consequence the object becomes the subject because it is infused with the best spirit and essence of life of the person engaged. A person who does not engage in sacrifice in such a manner is not considered to have genuinely performed a sacrifice.

When we enlarge on and extend the notion of *shen* as explained above, we shall see that the whole universe has its *shen*, particularly when we reflect and observe the life-generating and life-preserving power of the universe conceived of as an organic whole. The whole universe is then seen as a progenitor, maintainer, and preserver of life. As we have seen, it is in this way that the notion of the Way of Heaven was developed, in which heaven is both a concretion and an abstraction of the whole of nature focused upon in its influence and power of life generation and life maintenance. The *tian* is conceived of as both the whole of nature and the whole process of life production, in which both birth and death are regarded as part and parcel of the life-maintaining and life-generating process. In this sense, death is absorbed into the larger process and circulation of life and must be faced by a person with equanimity and peace of mind, a point which Confucianism and Neo-Confucianism has specifically stressed.

Zhongyong: Cheng as Source of *Shen* and *Sheng*

When we speak of the *shen* of the whole of nature or the universe, we speak of the divine. The divine, in this sense, is an elevation of the spiritual, because in becoming the divine, the spiritual is no longer confined to any projected or formerly existing person or thing, but pertains to the ever-present and ever-active life and vitality of the whole of nature. In essence it pertains to the ever-creative creativity of the source of life. Therefore, the power of influence of the spiritual becomes the power of generation and transformation of life. We find this sense of divinity presented in the writings of Mencius and the *Zhongyong* (*Doctrine of the Mean*). Mencius says:

> What is desirable is goodness. One holding to oneself [in self-knowledge] is integrity. To fulfill one's potentiality is beauty. To have self-fulfillment and shining out [and being influential] is greatness. Being great and capable of

transforming life is called sagely (*sheng*). When the sagely power is beyond the measure of knowledge, it is called the divine (*shen*—in the deeper sense of the spiritual or creative). (*Mencius, Jinxin-xia* or 7B:25)

It should be noticed that the spiritual creative power which is the divine is to be built up from the basic desires of life whose fulfillment is a form of goodness, according to Mencius. Only when one attains goodness based on one's genuine desire for goodness, will one achieve integrity in the sense that the self is not just a physical event but a value of importance. This integrity would then be the base or starting point for enlargement and extension of a transforming power that raises other beings and persons onto a higher level of existence. The key phrase for this transformation is "great and transforming," which is taken as the mark of the divine.

The divine is conveyed by the notion of sageliness (*sheng*), which culminates in the limitless influence and transformation it may entail, and one will thus have the full measure of divinity still known as *shen*. The combination of the "sageliness" and "divinity" in the term *shensheng* (divine and sagely) can be said to capture the meaning of the sacred or holy in the best spirit of the Western religious tradition without assuming its entrenched concomitant theology. Thus, there are two forms of divinity without theology: the Confucianist and the Daoist.

According to Mencius, the divine is rooted in human life and is continuous with human life, and hence there is no transcendent state of the divine outside of life. For this reason, Mencius even suggests that "a 'genuine person' [*junzi*] is capable of transforming people and preserving his spirit in such a way that he is in the same vein with heaven and earth [with regard to its creative and transforming powers]" (7A:13). The reference to heaven and earth is meant to underline the analogy between the creative and transforming power of the divine over things in nature and the power of a ruler over his people.

The Confucian has taken the political power of a ruler very seriously and sees in it the same creativity as in heaven and earth, because life and death and transformation of people's lives are vested in such power. Hence the analogy was suggested. But this analogy is also literally a reflection of the underlying cosmology of the unity of heaven and earth and the human person which comes to the fore at about the time of Mencius, namely, in the period of Warring States, when Confucianism has achieved a new stage of development based on the pristine insights and cosmic experiences of the second or third generation of the Confucian School. This is how we come to the positions of the *Doctrine of the Mean* (*Zhongyong*) and commentaries of the *Zhouyi* (*Yizhuan*).

In the *Doctrine of the Mean,* it is said:

A human person of utmostly sincerity is capable of fulfilling his own nature; capable of fulfilling his own nature he is capable of fulfilling the natures of others; capable of fulfilling the natures of others he is capable of fulfilling natures of things; capable of fulfilling the natures of things he is in a position to participate in the creative activities of heaven and earth. Being in a position to participate in the creative activities of heaven and earth, he is posed to form a tripartity with heaven and earth. (*Zhongyong* 21)

This important passage is again a testimony on the inner and virtual divinity of the human person in the sense of participating in the creative activities of heaven and earth. If we understand this to mean that a human person engaged in government could make decisions bearing on the life and well-being of people, it is quite clear how he could be creative and transformative just like heaven and earth, which bring forth things and regulate and preserve them. This means that there is a functional unity between humanity and heaven. But of course there is a deeper level of unity in the *Doctrine of the Mean,* namely, that the human person is endowed with human nature from heaven. (It is said that "what is endowed and mandated from Heaven is called the nature [of man].") This means that human creativity is derived from heaven, and thus the human person is capable of forming a unity with heaven and earth. Such is the vocation of humanity, and such is the ideal state of human existence in a political community and family of heavenly mandated order. This is not to equate humanity with heaven, for the human person is not to create things in nature like heaven, but can preserve them, just as modern ecologists would endorse; and in so doing the human person creates and preserves one's own life and well-being as far as the human community is concerned.

What the *Zhongyong* stresses is that when a human person exhibits the utmost sincerity, that person becomes creative and thus divine in the sense described above. But when the *Zhongyong* says that "the utmostly sincere is like the divine" (24), there is a special meaning attached to this use of "divine," namely, the ability to foretell the future or to have foreknowledge (*xianzhi*). This may refer to a diviner's act of divination using tortoise bones. But there is no doubt a sense of divinity which pertains to a power of knowing the future. One would know the future if one is able to grasp the totality of things and the direction of the whole process of change in addition to being able to participate in the change. This, then, defines the meaning of *zhicheng* (utmost sincerity). The utmost sincerity is real in the utmost, and this means to know the real and participate in the real as much as one can. This means, according to the *Zhongyong,* to devise the great principles of governing the world, to establish the great ground of right action, and to take part in the nourishing process of heaven and earth. In essence, it is to fulfill the heavenly virtue of creativity as a sage (32). Insofar as this creativity is interpreted as profound love (*ren*), it is directed toward and based on the Confucian ideal of human and self-cultivation of a human person. In this way, one sees as well how divinity in the sense described would result from cultivation of a person in *ren*.

We need to elaborate on the key concept of "sincerity" (*cheng*) in the *Zhongyong* in order to understand the creative and transformative power of humanity. We read in the *Zhongyong*:

> Next, to fulfil the hidden and subtle [desires of a man], one can be sincere in one's desires. Being sincere, there will be form of action; action being formed, it will become conspicuous; being conspicuous, it will be illustrious. Being illustrious, it will move. Moving it will change; changing it will transform. It is the utmost sincerity of the world which can transform. (23)

I would identify "the hidden and the subtle" with the genuine desire for change in a person. It follows that if one really desires change, one is able to effect the change because one will act on one's sincere desires, which will provide a base for the change. This process of transformation is how an inner motive leads to an outer result.

Sincerity as the motivating force is therefore a self-making and self-creating force. But *cheng* is not merely for self-making but also for the making of others, and is identified by the *Zhongyong* as the most fundamental force of origination and transformation in the world. In this sense, *cheng* is no more and no less than the root source of all beings, and the human experience of sincerity is only a manifestation or sign of the creativity of reality itself.

Based on its understanding of the divine, the *Zhongyong* maintains that when a person is able to achieve centrality and harmony, there will be a proper positioning of heaven and earth and nourishing ten thousand things. This centrality (*zhong*) and harmony (*he*) are derived from the divinity of heaven and earth, which perfects a person, a community, and the relationship between human community and natural environment. We need to see the centrality and harmony operating on two levels: the human and the cosmic. On the human level, centrality is described as the state of human emotion not yet issued in response to things outside, because things outside have not called for any response. When and if such a response is called for, because there is an unbalanced situation in need of being balanced, then the restoration of equilibrium would be the task of the emotions. The emotions lead to action and interaction between the subjective and the objective, which produces a new state of balance, and this is harmony. But this also means that there is a primordial state of harmony and balance of things derived from natures (or propensities) of things. In the primordial state everything follows its own nature, and thus this state can be described as the way of nature. Because not only the human being but all things have their natures, centrality is both the inner state of a thing and the totality of natures of things. This leads to the description of centrality on the cosmic level. Centrality is the state of nature in which natures of things are not engaged in response to outside situation. Cosmic harmony, on the other hand, is a matter of actions and interactions among things and events being balanced so as to allow their natures to function naturally. Here we can see, then, how in centrality and harmony there will be a proper ordering of heaven and earth as well as nourishing of all things therein. We might also suggest that centrality is a form of harmony, harmony in stasis; and harmony is a form of centrality, centrality in dynamism.

We may regard centrality and harmony as two aspects of the same thing along the lines of the ontocosmology of the *yin* and *yang*. Thus we can speak of the centrality as the nature (inward)-directed state of a thing, while we can speak of the harmony as the relation (outward)-directed state in which a thing is situated. A thing may at one and the same time exhibit two forces at work: it may centralize itself so that it maintains its given nature, and it may harmonize itself with other things in its development or growth. The former is inward- and self-oriented equilibrium and balance, whereas the latter is outward-and-relation-oriented equilibrium and balance. These two principles are opposite but yet are interdependent and complementary with regard to both the development of the individual and the development of a larger system in which the individual is situated. But when we ask how this centralization and harmonization (as two processes or two states) are possible, and how they are ontologically grounded, we have to go back to the texts of the commentaries of the *Zhouyi* for an answer. And in connection with this, we have also to take into consideration the Daoist views in Laozi and Zhuangzi, which have been expounded in the second section of this article.

Notes

1. The *Book of Changes,* or *Zhouyi,* was formulated as early as the beginning of the Zhou in 1200 B.C.E., although it was believed that the notion of change (*yi)* and method of divination (*pu*) based on a theory of change was developed much earlier, dating back to the very beginning of the Xia era in 2000 B.C.E. as evidenced in archaeological findings of oracle bone inscriptions.

2. Chen Kuying has argued for such a position in his book *Yizhuan yu daojia sixiang* (Taiwan Commercial Press, 1994). In a broad sense the idea of *dao* has pervaded the *Yizhuan* because the *Yizhuan* has contributed to defining and delineating what the *dao* is. The search for the *dao* was common among schools and scholars even at the time of Confucius. Hence the Daoist notion of the *dao* as we see it in Laozi and Zhuangzi is different in many ways from the *Yizhuan* notion of the *dao*, even though they could be said to share the same source or resources of understanding the *dao*, such as the texts of the *Zhouyi*.

3. See my article "Philosophical Significances of *Guan* (Contemplative Observation): On *Guan* as Onto Hermeneutical Unity of Methodology and Ontology," in *Guoji Yixue Yanjiu*, ed. Zhu Boqun, International Studies of I Ching Theory 1 (Beijing: Huaxia Press, 1995), 156–203.

4. The meaning and origin of *ru* have been discussed by many modern Chinese scholars, such as notably Zhang Taiyan, Hu Shih, Fu Sinian, Kuo Mouju, Yao Zongyi. In a recent article Zhu Gaozheng relates the notion and idea of *ru* to a few *Zhouyi* hexagrams to stress the meaning of the *ru* as a person of "relaxed airs" awaiting opportunities to put himself to public use ("*Lunru*," *Zhuantong wenhua yu xiandaihua* [Chinese Culture: Tradition and Modernization], no. 1 [1997]: 18–25). In the *Analects*, Confucius stresses ceaseless learning and self-cultivation as the main contents of being a *ru*.

5. For a basic understanding of reality in terms of *li* and *qi*, see my "Reality and Understanding in the Confucian Philosophy of Religion," in *International Philosophical Quarterly* 13, no. 1 (1973): 33–61.

7

Virtues and Religious Virtues in the Confucian Tradition

LEE H. YEARLEY

"VIRTUE (*DE*) NEVER DWELLS IN SOLITUDE; it will always bring neighbors." This quotation from Confucius's *Analects* (4:25) can strike both hope and fear into the heart of any reader or writer: hope because of its dramatic claim about how human excellence will never go unnoticed and about how true community will arise; fear because of its implied judgment on our failures to achieve community and overcome loneliness, whether as readers, writers, or people who try to live the best life they can. Most significantly here, this quotation (which comes from an early part of a very early Confucian text) underlines just how significant to Confucianism is the idea of virtue.

Indeed, I believe Confucian spirituality is best understood through ideas about virtues and those subjects that follow in their wake, most notably conceptions of the self. More controversially, I also believe the Confucian tradition speaks not only about ordinary virtues but also about religious virtues. That is, to understand Confucianism well we need to differentiate the sphere of virtues into two realms, realms that share some characteristics but also have others that sharply divide them.

My presentation of this subject will be comparative in that it approaches Confucian ideas of virtue in their relationship to three different things: (1) to those general ideas and categories that make comparison possible; (2) to the most significant virtue tradition in the West—the Aristotelian tradition in its Christian forms; (3) to all of us both as moderns and as people who are captured, or can be captured, by one or another facet of the Confucian tradition.[1]

The last relationship makes clear that a normative dimension is a feature of this comparative project, in fact must be especially prominent in any project that addresses spirituality. The Confucian tradition is not my tradition, nor, I presume, is it the tradition of most of us. Nevertheless, it not only has much to teach us, but it also even can present us with a "call" (*Ruf*), in the existentialist sense of a call to change our way of understanding and living. We must then study Confucian spirituality in a way that takes seriously its possible claim on our allegiances. I will discuss (in the last section) several reasons why that can happen, most notably features of its overall perspective and of the genres it uses. Let me note here, however, the most general reason why such a situation occurs and several implications that arise from it, notably one about the significance of multiple religious identities, as Robert Neville and John Berthrong's articles discuss it (see volume 2).[2]

Confucianism can call or teach us, I think, because it helps us to articulate something in our own understanding; it helps us to make explicit what is often or only implicit. Examining Confucian ideas of spirituality and virtue, that is, gathers up or focuses attention on discrete and valuable but heretofore inchoate features of our overall perspective. To move from an implicit affirmation of something to an explicit affirmation is to become more articulate about the important ideas and attitudes we possess but have no adequate vocabulary for expressing. This *articulation of the implicit,* this making explicit of what was inchoate, underlies what can occur in the study of Confucian spirituality and how it can inform our own spiritual quest and identity.

The normative dimension of my project does not mean we must accept what we discuss; we may even firmly reject it. Either the acceptance or the rejection, however, involves us in normative decisions. Think, for example, of what is involved in truly facing two texts: the quoted statement from Confucius that the virtuous always will have neighbors and Mencius's praise of the gamekeeper who faces death rather than respond to a ritually improper summons. We must, I think, reject Mencius's idea because we do not believe that a relatively inconsequential ritual should lead us to surrender our life. Confucius's statement, however, challenges us deeply because it forces us to think about the kind of power that is contained in being virtuous and to measure the effectiveness of our own virtue. In an inquiry such as this one, then, we are involved in a kind of spiritual exercise in which we try to place ourselves within a world that is much larger than the one we normally inhabit, a world the modern situation has, thankfully, forced upon us.

In pursuing this inquiry, this spiritual exercise, I will concentrate on the early Confucian tradition rather than on the Neo-Confucian tradition, and therefore when I say "Confucian" I refer only to one part of the tradition.

Practical reasons for doing this include the need to keep a focus and the limits of my own expertise, or at least zone of comfort. Theoretical reasons are, however, also involved. Most notable are my judgments (which are unshared by many contributors to this volume) that the earlier and later traditions differ substantially from each other and that the former contains ideas that are, for us, more illuminating, in significant part because they can fit within the web of beliefs that determine our contemporary understanding.[3]

Let us turn now to a discussion of the general notion of virtue. That discussion is necessary for an understanding of the notions I use and, most important, for a grasp of why I think we should approach Confucian spirituality through ideas about virtue.

The Character of Virtues

For many today the word "virtue" has an archaic ring. It often seems to be associated with problematic ideas like priggish scrupulosity; or to be restricted to narrow areas like sexual activity; or to reflect fixed unjust social hierarchies like those found in virtually all traditional societies. Moreover, a focus on virtues generates understandable suspicions in many contemporaries, whether in America or East Asia, because such a focus often seems to be a rhetorical adjunct to one or another dubious political agenda. (As the old saying puts it, "When they begin to talk about virtue it's time to emigrate.")[4]

Despite these understandable misgivings, I believe ideas of virtue provide us with a nuanced language that enables people to understand themselves in fuller and more subtle ways than they otherwise could, and therefore also to live better lives. This defense rests on the controversial but compelling idea that we often are strangers to ourselves and that we find it exceedingly difficult to think well, using ordinary language, about those things that matter most to us. The illumination that language about virtue can provide appears, I think, when we use the example of generosity to examine the concept of virtue.

One of my friends possesses or even exemplifies the virtue of generosity. If she sees a troubled person she is immediately inclined to give her time or money to that person. I, on the other hand, see a troubled person and often think of other things, for example, how much work I have to do or what helping the person will cost me psychologically and financially. I then probably also get tangled up in the question of whether being generous will, in the long term, be good for the troubled person. I might finally do generous things but I am not a generous person in the sense that my friend is. She possesses the virtue and I have at best a *semblance* of it.

The difference between semblances of virtue and virtue is important. Semblances generate activities that resemble the activities of real virtue but lack important elements in it. They characterize—to use an important Confucian notion—the village honest man (*xiang-yuan*). Such people are called the thief, not the epitome of virtue, because their apparently virtuous actions arise from an imperfectly virtuous character. Such people do a virtuous act not for itself but for consequences that nonvirtuous people would desire. Or they choose it not for their own reasons but because of some second-hand support such as custom, unexamined authority, or the inertia provided by accepted, routine reactions.

Virtues, then, display some characteristic pattern of desire and motivation, some disposition toward action. They are not simple thoughts that occur and pass: I do not manifest a virtue if I think how compassionate it would be to invite those lonely people to dinner as I walk on past them. Nor are virtues emotional states that pass quickly: I am not virtuous if I feel very strongly that I should at least talk to my troubled acquaintance but realize the movie is about to start and leave.

To speak more abstractly, a virtue is a human excellence or example of human flourishing. It is a permanent addition to the self, part of what makes people who they are, a feature of what we call character. Moreover, there must be some evidence of the presence of what we can call "thought and will" if a quality is to count as a virtue. A virtue, then, is a disposition to act, desire, and feel that involves the exercise of judgment.

The *judgments* may not be conscious—"to think a little and then act" is an absurd picture of human behavior even if we are talking just about academics. Nevertheless, judgment or "thinking" occurs, and what that means in this context is that, at minimum, I can explain (at some point, in some fashion) to myself or another person why I did something, why I was generous, for example. Confucians have, as we will see, a more subtle sense of thinking than appears in many modern Western ideas of "calculating rationality," but they still believe thinking is crucial. (To use terms drawn from Benjamin Schwartz's article, both *yuwei* and *wuwei* are necessary.)

Virtuous activity also involves choosing virtue for itself. I possess not the virtue of generosity but a semblance, or even counterfeit, of it if I act because of some ulterior motive such as that if I help specific people now they will think well of me, or help me later, or convince their rich relatives to give me money. Moreover, virtuous activity involves choosing specific virtues in light of some justifiable life plan. I believe, for example, that the best kind of human life involves generosity not selfishness, giving not just taking and possessing. I have a general view, and good reasons for it, that lead me to think that kind of life is better than one that lacks it.

One last theoretical comment about the concept of virtues needs to be made. Virtuous behavior has not only *acquisitive* but also *expressive* motives. That is, people choose a virtuous action not only because it contributes to goods they want to acquire but also because it expresses their conception of the good. (The latter motives, as we will see, underlie the ideas both of heroic virtue and of many forms of religious virtue.) The essential facet of the idea of expressive virtue, then, is the response it contains to one basic question: Why might, or even should, people embrace an ideal if they have severe doubts that it will have the kind of effects in the world that they hope it will? The answer is that the best kind of life simply demands such activity, and therefore no further questions about its contributions to the agent's or anyone else's happiness need to be raised. This does not mean such choices are made recklessly; indeed they must be well considered if they are to be fully expressive. Nevertheless, it is not the good benefits received or given but the good expressed that is the crucial motivating force.

Confucians do not explicitly employ this distinction. In fact, their formulations usually reflect the language of acquisitive virtue, and this can lead to some apparent confusions or at least murky formulations, as when Mencius criticizes forms of profit or utility (*li*) and yet also speaks about how beneficial Confucian ideas are. Confucians normally write, then, in terms of the goods that virtues can produce; they defend them in terms of their beneficial effects on both the world and the agent. Nevertheless, they continue to speak of how a person can choose an action or way of life because it expresses that person's conception of what is good and admirable. Indeed, one of the clearest examples of this to be found in any literature anywhere is Mencius's statement that although life is what he wants there is something he wants more than life and therefore he does not cling to life at all costs. Utilizing the distinction between acquisitive and expressive virtues helps us to clarify what is, I believe, one of the most cogent features, and defenses, of Confucian ideas.[5]

Central, then, to the appropriate motivation of truly virtuous action is the desire to manifest or express a valued state. In fact, it is the desire to express this state that makes slavishly prudential followers of virtue (village honest people at their best) doubt the sanity of those lovers of virtue who aim to express a virtue. This love and its apparent imprudence are, in fact, the critical defining mark of the heroic, the crucial feature, for Confucians, of all truly worthwhile people.

Confucians believe, that is, that ideas about virtue inevitably link with ideas about the *heroic*. They also recognize, however, that ideas about the heroic often travel in disreputable, even noxious company. This is especially true when the central trope for the heroic is military action. Confucians are well aware, then, that notions of heroism are liable to sentimental excess as well as raw corruption. They also believe, however, something perhaps best expressed by William James's statement that he "held the world to be essentially a theater for heroism. In heroism, we feel, life's supreme mystery is hidden."[6] That is, Confucians believe, as did James and Western tragedians like Sophocles, that heroes and heroism disclose to us realities understandable in no other way. Heroes disclose such things because they stand between the usually mysterious heavenly realm and the manifest but limited truths of normal life. The heroic, then, both uncovers features of higher realities and illuminates the pedestrian character of ordinary activity. This examination of heroic, or expressive, virtue, concludes our general treatment of the idea of virtue, and we may now turn to a more specific examination of Confucian ideas about virtues and religious virtues.

Four Central Confucian Virtues

My main concern is to examine specific Confucian virtues, but it is worth noting briefly the general conceptual model on which they rest. That model, which is a common one in many traditions, can be called a *developmental* model. That is, human nature has an innate constitution that manifests itself in processes of growth and culminates in specifiable forms. That fulfillment occurs, however, only if the organism is both uninjured and properly nurtured. The basic conceptual model is, then, relatively simple, and it draws on a biological framework. A basic set of capacities exists, and their unhindered, nurtured development generates qualities that lead to specifiable actions or characteristic forms. Those, in turn, provide the standard that allows observers to determine a being's nature and to judge whether any specific action represents its nature in normal, exemplary, or defective fashion.[7]

Those actualizations of nature that Confucians consider exemplary fit within, as is true in virtually all traditions, a list of virtues that is ordered in a hierarchical fashion. The list defines what qualities are virtues. The hierarchical rank helps determine in which situations one or another virtue should be manifested. That is, it allows a person to know, for example, that being patient rather than assertive, ironic rather than flamboyant, is the correct behavior when you are told your friend has been slandered.

Our concern here is not to inventory the hierarchical lists that appear in

Confucianism and decide what, if any, common features they have. Rather it is to focus on four virtues that appear prominently in Western and many other lists of virtue and then see what is distinctive and illuminating about the Confucian treatment of them. (Those four virtues will also provide the materials for our later examination of the ways in which religious virtues appear in Confucianism.)

Each of the four virtues identifies certain qualities that are necessary if humans are to manage well in the various areas in which they must operate. They illustrate well, then, how all virtues can productively be thought of as being *corrective*. Ideas of virtue rest, that is, on a picture of human weakness and need. Virtues correct some difficulty thought to be natural to human beings, some temptation that needs to be resisted or some motivation that needs to be made good. Industry, for example, can be said to correct a propensity to idleness; and perseverance, a tendency to give up before it is necessary to do so.[8]

Described briefly, the four virtues are as follows. One is a quality (or qualities) that allows people to overcome or control fear, especially those fears that impede people from doing what they wish to do or think they should do. (I will, in what follows, always speak of "a quality" for the sake of concision, but it can be either a quality or various qualities.) A second is a quality that enables people to control emotional reactions and, in some fashion, to modulate their normal desires for things that are attractive either for biological reasons (e.g., food) or cultural reasons (e.g., fame). A third is the quality that provides some kind of intelligent guidance of action. This quality makes action something other than mere reflex or inclination, and it involves some ability to give a verbal account of why one does what one does. A fourth is a quality that regulates one's interactions with other people, and perhaps with society as a whole. This quality, at minimum, adapts or controls one's inclinations simply to act in ways that will be beneficial, or apparently beneficial, only to one's own self.

It is unsurprising to find versions of these virtues in the lists of many cultures, given both that individuals need such qualities or virtues if they are to thrive, and probably even survive, and that societies need people to have them if they are to survive, much less thrive. What is distinctive about Confucianism is, first, the exact form these virtues take and, second, the other virtues that can accompany each virtue. Let us examine, then, the Confucian treatment, remembering as we do that the issues treated in examining them often provide the context for Confucianism's most significant debates. We will begin with the virtues treated in the least distinctive fashion and proceed to those where the Confucian treatment is most distinctive.[9]

The character of the first, "courage" or the overcoming of destructive fears, has distinctive marks, although it relates closely to some accounts in the West. The most primitive sense of this virtue, its military sense, continues to provide a central context for Confucian reflection. Nevertheless, even here we see a most distinctive emphasis on the role of an unnamed virtue, "yielding." (The phenomenon of "unnamed virtues" is found in almost all virtue traditions.) Yielding, that is, concerns the ways in which triumph may depend less on direct confrontation than either on apparent giving way or on a refocusing of the issue.[10]

Even more important, Confucians usually emphasize a set of fears that is far more subtle, and often far harder to identify easily and deal with well, than those that appear in contexts such as military ones. One example is the fear of not being honored by those around one, even those whose regard is usually thought to be of little value. Another, even more elusive, fear is the fear involved in undertaking the kind of self-cultivation that one ought to undertake. Still another, perhaps the most elusive of all, is the fear present in being committed to a perspective, the Confucian perspective, that seems to many people to be problematic, hopelessly out of date, or simply wrongheaded.

Our second quality, "moderation," is the one that enables people to modulate their normal desires for things that are attractive either for biological or cultural reasons. This arena is a central concern for Confucians, but the way in which it is a concern is, I believe, distinctive. The quality needed is unnamed, or at least not highlighted. Moreover, that part of the modulation which concerns biological drives is rarely highlighted, and it seems not to be seen as a central human problem. That is, the myriad variations of the erotic seem to have much less significance than in the West.

Most important to us, the modulation required is pictured not through the image of an ongoing battle but through the image of gradual formation and final success. The disruptive power of some movements of desire is surely recognized, and some thinkers even group them under the general category of obsession (*pi*). They are confident, however, that these movements can be dealt with through those various kinds of self-cultivation in which intelligence and other aspects of the spiritual life, such as the cultivation of *qi* or *shen*, operate. These movements, then, can be formed rather than simply controlled, and there is no notion that one must engage in a continuing battle with them. In this sense, then, truly virtuous people can behave "spontaneously," can manifest *wuwei*. Nevertheless, training produces such spontaneity and a form of intelligence is always operating— *yuwei* has a significant place.[11]

The character of the needed training and direction is the subject of the third virtue, the intelligent guidance of action. Disagreement about its exact form provides the context within which one of the major Confucian controversies is played out: that between Mencius and Xunzi. Especially striking for our purposes, however, are not the differences between these two thinkers but what they agree on, especially as it differs, often quite markedly, from treatments of this quality found in the West.

That is, both Mencius and Xunzi adopt a posture that focuses on the more delicate and subtle ways in which intelligence guides action. Both of them see the perception of, or attention to, salient characteristics as crucial to, perhaps even constitutive of, truly functioning intelligence. Both of them stress how proper inclination (whether it be the product mainly of training or of nature) can be relied on by intelligence. Both of them see intelligence as intimately conjoined with emotional reactions and think a key function of intelligence is the ability to inventory one's emotional reactions. Finally, both of them recognize the place for a conscious turning over of conceptual alternatives and long-term plans, but they rarely focus on that as the most significant feature of intelligence.[12]

The fourth arena concerns the quality that regulates one's interactions with other people or society at large. This arena is an especially complex one, and one that may contain the most exceptional of all Confucian treatments, and we need therefore a more extended treatment. Let us begin by noting that a distinctive feature of Confucian spirituality is simply how significant Confucians think this area is. Unlike some religious traditions, that is, an adequate response to the problems presented by personal relations and social organization is crucial to the overall spiritual vision. In this sense at least, Confucianism is a locative, not an open, religion. In *open* religions fulfillment occurs when people transcend any particular culture and reach a higher and different fulfillment either here or after death. In a *locative* religion such as Confucianism, however, fulfillment occurs when people locate themselves within a complex social order that is thought, potentially at least, to be sacred.[13]

The two most obvious master virtues which produce such location and its interactions are benevolence (*ren*) and righteousness (*yi*). Questions about their exact forms and, even more significantly, about which of them has precedence in which situations appear both in debates between Confucians and in the various formulations found in a single thinker. Mencius, for example, has two divergent cosmogonies, one that supports benevolence and one that supports righteousness. In the one, Heaven gives each person a nature, and therefore anyone can become a sage, a fully flourishing, benevolent person. In the other, past sages best understood Heaven's plans and provided highly differentiated social forms that need to be followed righteously.[14]

Debates like this (whether within a thinker or between thinkers) are important, but they are not most crucial here. More important to us is something that appears when we consider criticisms of the Confucian focus on these two virtues. Confucian benevolence can be called a virtue that is too limited in scope to meet fully the demands placed upon it. Confucian righteousness can be said to be but a limping form of what the Western tradition calls justice. These criticisms contain much that is worth pondering, but a response to them rests, I think, on realizing that Confucians frame the subject of relations with others in a most distinctive way, a way that extends considerably beyond these two virtues.

Benevolence and righteousness are not, that is, the only relevant virtues here. A variety of other "lesser" virtues are relevant; for instance, equanimity and the ability to respond to the animating power of models. Most important, however, are two other virtues. One is filial piety (*xaio*) and the other is "ritual" (*li*). Each casts a distinctive, and subtle, light on the question of how to relate well to other people.

Filial piety is a complex virtue that provides the locale for some of Confucianism's most significant debates. Most significant here, however, is that, to use Xunzi's formulation, filial piety deals with one of those three origins, the family, that make a full life possible. (The other two are culture's origin, e.g., teachers, and all life's origin, e.g., Heaven and earth.) People respond strongly to such origins because they recognize that with them unpayable debts have been incurred. That is, in most relationships, people receive and give in a fashion that allows for repayment; equity can be restored. In these relationships, however, people receive so much that there is no way for them to repay what has been given.

Our frailty, our fundamental dependence, is expressed then when we attend to any origin, but the origin that filial piety manifests is most intensely felt. Moreover, we must find ways properly to express the emotions that result if we are to flourish, given that failure to do so makes us fall prey to one or another human deformation. Filial piety allows us to make such a response because it embodies the notion that when we face debts that cannot be repaid, the only appropriate response is gratitude and those virtues, such as "respectful reverence" (*jing*), that manifest such responses. This, in turn, provides a foundation that enables other relationships to flourish. Without such a foundation those relationships will fall under the dark shadow cast by, among other things, the crippling attitudes of masochistic religion.[15]

The other relevant virtue is ritual (*li*). Ritual may be the most distinctive and complex of all the Confucian virtues, but put simply the single notion covers two activities that most contemporary Westerners think are quite different. One activity is solemn, explicit religious activities such as marital or death services. The other activity, however, is what we call etiquette or, more accurately, those reasonable and humane learned conventions that make up the ethos of a culture. Ritual covers, then, everything from the solemn performance of an elaborate ceremony to the "excuse me" after a sneeze. (There are, of course, differences: in specifically religious rituals, for example, the focus is on humans facing "thresholds," situations where people move to a new state or respond to what lies beyond their ordinary routine.)

Critics can claim that the Confucian combining of these two senses of ritual manifests an unsophisticated kind of thinking that does not differentiate what can and should be separated. Confucians think, however, that social rituals are more than just pedestrian social facts. Social and religious rituals resemble each other, that is, because both are sacred ceremonies that express and foster a spontaneous coordination that is rooted in reverence. Moreover, both exemplify learned, conventional behavior that manifests distinctly human rather than simply animal-like actions. Both therefore promote human qualities and respond to human needs. (A similar notion appears in, say, Dante's notion that "courtesy and human goodness are one and the same thing.")[16]

Combining the four virtues of benevolence, righteousness, filial piety, and ritual produces an account of how to relate to others that is, I believe, extremely powerful. It also, however, contains a dark side, and we do well to remember it. Put in a more charitable way, the account generates certain tensions, and their resolution is a crucial part of the enterprise of Confucian spirituality. For example, integrity of the nonmodern kind that Confucians prize can be lost through submersion in the community. Moreover, a crude, even mindless sort of respect for authority and tradition can thrive, and that can clog the wellsprings that nurture needed change and meaningful appropriation. Finally, the lack of a perspective that transcends the practices of a specific community can make people blind to the severe difficulties that beset some groups in the community, groups whose often wretched state helps preserve the privileges of those who are blind.

Difficulties, then, do haunt this area just as they appear, if in less virulent forms, in other areas. These difficulties point us to what is, I believe, the most problematic part of that facet of Confucian spirituality concerned with virtues: how and why failures to be virtuous occur and what can be done about them. Put in formal terms, the question concerns the theory of error needed to complete any theory of success. Put in terms more relevant to our enterprise, the question concerns the sensitivity to and explanation of failures to attain spiritual states. (Correlated to the latter, of course, is an understanding of the ways to correct those failures.) Any honest attempt to treat ideas of spirituality must examine this topic, but it is too complicated to do more than gesture at here. The gesture is important, however, and it also leads directly to our next subject, the significant role religious virtues play in Confucianism.

Confucianism shares with most religious traditions an understanding that spiritual failures are a "surd," something that ought not be and therefore is very difficult to explain adequately. Nevertheless, Confucians also seem to lack a way accurately to account for the most complex and often dangerous kinds of failures, failure manifested in the accounts in, say Christianity, of vices such as spiritual apathy, envy, and pride. That, in turn, may help explain why those energies which form into virtues in Christianity, such as forgiveness and repentance, are not, for good or ill, prominent in Confucian accounts.[17]

A superficial if venerable way to treat this apparent difficulty has been to talk of Confucian "optimism"—or, to use more theologically freighted language, of Confucian failures to understand "original sin" or the implications of the first of Buddhism's Four Noble Truths about the prominence of suffering. A more subtle way to treat this problem focuses on the Confucian lack of a perspective, and thus of those virtues which accompany it, that stands outside any specific, local viewpoint. Such a perspective and its accompanying virtues are important because they provide a viewpoint from which to evaluate and then to correct ordinary virtues and the normal perspective they represent.

This criticism at base rests on the idea that Confucianism lacks religious virtues and that such a lack is a significant shortcoming. I would agree with the criticism if in fact such virtues, and the perspective they manifest, were absent. I believe, however, that religious virtues are present in and important to Confucianism. Let me explain.

Religious Virtues in Confucianism: An Introduction

To distinguish between religious and ordinary virtues in Confucianism might seem to be very problematic or just wrongheaded. Confucians never, of course, make any formal distinction between normal and religious virtues. Moreover, their general conceptual framework does not lead them (and probably literally could not allow them) to distinguish between what in Christianity are called natural and supernatural virtues. They surely would, that is, reject any such distinction that rests on a clear-cut differentiation between what humans cause and what a deity, distinguished by the quality of aseity or being unmoved, causes.

Moreover, Confucians also surely lack the schematization of virtues that appears in, say, Catholic Christianity. The latter differentiates, for example, ordinary virtues from the theological virtues of faith, hope, and charity. Moreover, both kinds of virtue are differentiated from the seven gifts of the Holy Spirit; from specific gifts, such as prophecy, that only certain people have; and from those virtues that operate only in the life of spiritual adepts, virtues such as obedience, chastity, and poverty. We would search in vain (a blessing some might say) for anything in Confucianism that even remotely resembles this kind of scheme.

Nevertheless, Confucians do believe that some virtues (or unnamed features of some virtues) have a very special character. They produce actions and attitudes that both differ from normal virtues and change a range of normal actions in profoundly important ways. In fact, certain traditional Western ways of theoretically distinguishing religious virtues seem to be implied by Confucian accounts. Examples include sharp distinctions Confucians make among the kinds of objects pursued, among the goals of the intentions manifested, among the precise forms of behavior produced, and among the kinds of empowerment displayed.

Moreover, and even more striking, many Confucians think humans are susceptible to transformations so total as to make some people fundamentally different from what humans normally are. The most notable example is probably Mencius's depiction of the fully perfected sage, or even more dramatically of the daimonic (*shen*) who surpasses even the sage. But other examples are also present. They range from the state the human mind can reach to the effect ritual can have.[18]

Let us turn, then, to a more detailed examination of religious virtues in Confucianism. That examination has two parts. First, to provide a more textured account, we will analyze the four "ordinary" Confucian virtues treated earlier and focus on their religious features. We will, that is, look for forms of those virtues that satisfy the criteria for religious virtues. Second, we will examine in a more theoretical fashion the Confucian understanding of the relationship between ordinary and religious virtues. Our focus there will be both on the ontological character of that relationship and on the kind of thinking it involves.

The Religious Forms of
Four Central Confucian Virtues

The first of the four virtues treated earlier is the virtue that overcomes or reforms those fears that impede people from acting as they should, the virtue of courage. This virtue unquestionably contains forms that exceed what normally does occur, or even should occur if we use ordinary standards. Let me cite just three instances, beginning with one that relates closely to the operations of the ordinary virtue. In the first instance, a distinctive kind of courage pairs with hope whenever people undertake and follow through on real self-cultivation. Such courage is necessary because the process is extremely arduous. Under one influential view, for example, the process of teaching and learning that underlies self-cultivation never ends: the commitment to such an unending process must involve, then, facing continually a possibly debilitating set of fears.

Another distinctive and more mysterious instance involves possessing the distinctive kind of courage that can be adequately informed by *qi* or that can draw into itself what Mencius calls the floodlike *qi*. This form of courage seems to live in a symbiotic relationship with other high spiritual attainments, most notably an unmoved mind (*bu dong xin*) and a refined form of righteousness (*yi*). A last instance involves a form of courage that so transcends normal courage, with its continuing engagement with fear, that no fear at all is present. That is, the inclination to flee and the physiological reactions that normally accompany fear are absent; all that remains is a cognitive judgment about the presence of a fearful object. Courage of this sort is defined by a spontaneity that completely transcends the division, and even hesitancy, that defines even the best forms of ordinary courage.[19]

The second virtue, moderation, enables one to modulate one's normal desires for things that are attractive either for biological or cultural reasons. Many of the religious forms of this modulation appear prominently in other religions (and can be gathered under the rubric of "asceticism") but are absent in Confucianism. Indeed, Confucianism emphatically opposes many of the kinds of asceticism that in other traditions have characterized religious practice in this area, activities such as chastity or voluntary poverty. Moreover, Confucians oppose any notion of asceticism that involves placing special demands for ascetic surrender on a class of religious adepts who are separated from ordinary life.

Nevertheless, we do see a form of "moderation" that qualifies as a kind of religious asceticism. We find, for example, indications of a severe regulation of certain biological desires, although our lack of clear evidence makes problematic any firm conclusions. Most important, Confucian asceticism appears prominently in another area: in the surrender of normally desirable objects for the sake of higher goals such as learning, teaching, or service to the society. The surrenders demanded go much beyond what normal moderation would require, or even think beneficial. They involve both a commitment to the realization of these goals and a surrender of whatever might impede that realization, which far exceeds what the demands of a balanced life would suggest. Good clothes or positions appropriate to one's ability, for instance, are understood to be legitimate goals, but they are also seen as things that ought never be a central focus and may in fact need to be surrendered. Indeed, the defining characteristic of motivations in this area is that they are "expressive," not "acquisitive." One expresses a conception of the good through ascetic activity; one does not use it to acquire other goods.

The intelligent guidance of action, our third virtue, involves various features that underlie different, if related, religious virtues. Examples include how "timeliness" can operate or what is involved in having appropriate shame (*xiu*) effortlessly guide a person. I want here, however, to focus on just one such feature: belief. The intelligent guidance of action involves, of course, any number of beliefs. Moreover, one aspect of that guidance involves the evaluation of beliefs as to their plausibility, coherence, simplicity, and efficacy, to note the criteria that Xunzi uses.[20]

The Confucian perspective also contains, however, beliefs that go considerably beyond the evidence that would, and should, compel assent in normal affairs. These beliefs, which often play a prominent role in guiding action, seem to arise from a faculty or potential in the self that not all people have actualized. Examples include specific beliefs such as Confucius's and Mencius's belief not only in Heaven's general guidance but in their chosen role. They also include those more general beliefs that are, in fact, constitutive of a Confucian perspective. These include beliefs about the significance of certain books and historical figures or beliefs about the efficacy of some virtues.

These kinds of beliefs are often at the center of debates with those people who lack them because they find them either unintelligible or unjustified. The Confucian perspective, that is, is far from self-evident to everyone. It includes attitudes and confident judgments about many matters that seem problematic or even bizarre to many people. Moreover, Confucians themselves also entertain questions about their own beliefs; they are not inoculated against the queries and doubts that other people manifest, as Irene Bloom's article shows (see chapter 12 below). One crucial spiritual dynamic in the tradition, then, is to see obvious problems in the Confucian position, if one uses ordinary standards, and yet continually to reaffirm the beliefs that constitute the position.

When we turn to those virtues that regulate one's interactions with other people or with society at large, we are dealing with many separate subjects, and I will treat just two of them. The first concerns Confucian claims about what will occur if certain virtues are fully actualized. These claims are strong enough to signal a difference in kind between these virtues' ordinary forms and their fully actualized, religious forms. Perfected benevolence or righteousness, for instance, is said to generate effects not only on individual people but on all of society that truly are extraordinary. Mencius even claims that, were a ruler to manifest such perfected virtues, people from other states would inexorably be moved to participate in his state. The power unleashed by these consummated virtues truly exceeds, then, what any normal activity could produce.

This power may be most evident, if also most mysterious, when we turn to ritual, our second subject. Confucius claims, for example, that if he truly understood one specific ritual he could deal with everything in society as easily as he puts his finger into his palm (*Analects* 3:11). Even more important here, however, the Confucian understanding of ritual, as we discussed, combines kinds of actions and attitudes that by normal Western standards cover both ordinary and religious spheres. Ritual, that is, points to an arena of action in which religious qualities not only are evident but also actually transform more normal activity.

One major reason this occurs is that many formal rituals, including aspects of filial piety, deal with the reactions of human beings when they face "thresholds." Thresholds are those places where people either move from one to another state, from being a child to being a potential parent, or respond to events that radically differ from and challenge their ordinary routine, events such as the death of a family member. These transitional states usually concern origins or terminations. They manifest, that is, what makes possible or ends human life, and therefore they force people to encounter the sustaining and destroying boundaries of life. Such encounters inevitably foster the religious features of various virtues by turning those virtues from their ordinary sphere of activity to that which sustains and transcends the ordinary. They bring, for example, into ordinary social virtues a kind of reverence (*jing*) that deepens their forms and expands their range. Indeed, to connect together the four kinds of virtue we have discussed, ritual both manifests and deepens a new kind of belief and also draws from and helps generate a new kind of courage and moderation.

The differentiation of modes of virtues we see in the four spheres is, I

believe, significant enough to warrant calling some ordinary and some religious. Nevertheless, the differentiation is not as clear-cut as that found in
many religions, including Aristotelian Christianity. We can better understand why that is true by turning to the second part of our examination of
this subject and analyzing in a more theoretical way the relationship
between religious virtues and ordinary virtues.

Religious Virtues in Confucianism:
A More Theoretical Account

The conceptual framework underlying the relationship of religious virtues
to ordinary virtues in Confucianism is less fully spelled out than in the case
of ordinary virtues. Drawing out the implicit theory allows us, however, to
understand both one of the most distinctive features of the Confucian tradition and one of those areas most relevant to current understanding of
spirituality. That subject is best approached in two interrelated ways. One
way focuses on the ontology of the relationship of ordinary and religious
virtues; the other way focuses on the kind of thinking that is involved in
treating religious virtues.

Confucian ideas on religious virtues reflect an ontological perspective in
which the sacred realm and the ordinary realm are closely intertwined, in
which an "organismic," an interrelated and interdependent, cosmology
operates. Confucianism manifests, then, in its own fashion the ontological
principle that guides the analysis of this topic in Aristotelian Christianity:
the sacred does not destroy but presupposes and perfects the normal. The
ordinary is not, that is, obliterated by the religious and replaced by something fundamentally different. Rather, the ordinary provides the basis that
is developed into a more actualized form.

This general ontological principle divides off both traditions from those
many traditions in which thinkers argue that the sacred destroys and
replaces the ordinary. In fact, one can even argue that Confucians are able
to develop this principle more fully than could Aristotelian Christians
because they lack those theological ideas that "impede" a full development,
notably the notion of a natural order created by a God distinguished from
it by his aseity. Pursuing this argument would involve us, however, in an
inquiry that goes far beyond the boundaries of this paper. It is worth noting, nevertheless, that other papers in these volumes (e.g., Robert Neville's
in volume 2 on contemporary Confucian spirituality) do examine the question of whether Confucianism may contain a perspective that harmonizes
with, or even develops, those kinds of modern Western theologies that rest

on the acceptance of a more "integrated" cosmology and involve a concomitant "turn to the subject."[21]

The ontological point about the sacred presupposing and perfecting rather than destroying the ordinary does inform our second subject, but our focus with it is not on ontology but rather on the kind of balancing that is involved in thinking well about religious virtues. Treating religious virtues, that is, involves a kind of balancing of opposing demands. On the one hand, religious virtues are virtues where one cannot draw on too many normal presumptions and arguments to defend, or even to make plausible, the virtue, lest it cease to be a religious virtue. On the other hand, however, one cannot simply disregard normal presumptions and arguments, lest the virtue cease to be a plausible option for people who accept what seems sensible to them. This activity involves balancing on a tightrope and the specific kind of balancing involved is worth discussing. (As Wittgenstein said, an "honest religious thinker is like a tightrope walker . . . [who] almost looks as though he were walking on nothing but air . . . [because his] support is the slenderest imaginable . . . [and] yet it really is possible to walk on it."[22])

The balancing act that Confucians must perform in treating religious virtues involves their not falling into either of two dangerous alternatives. On the one hand, the religious virtue must not rely on notions that no reasonable person can really take seriously. The claim that only through sacrificial rituals can we appease a spirit's anger or a dead person's perturbation is an example of such a notion. (Xunzi's reinterpretation of the virtues involved in the death rituals exemplifies this point.) The virtues cannot rest, then, on what seem to sensible people to be implausible ideas. On the other hand, if the virtue is truly a religious one it must not rely on such common and sensible notions that most people would, with little thought, accept it. The idea that one should help others if the help causes neither pain nor dislocation to oneself would be an example. (Mencius's understanding of the village honest person exemplifies this point.) The virtue cannot, then, simply repeat the conventional wisdom of the day.

The need to balance that we see here is exemplified by but not restricted to thinking about ideas of religious virtue. Indeed, one of the most compelling, general features of Confucian presentations of spirituality, and one of their more significant contributions to a general understanding of spirituality, is their grasp of a crucial characteristic of religious reflection. Much thinking about the deepest religious matters, that is, is most fully aware of its distinctive subject matter when it sees itself faced with "irresolvable but revelatory and productive tensions," a subject Irene Bloom's essay in this

volume (chapter 12) treats admirably. These tensions arise from two different but related ideas that stand as the irreducible givens on which reflection
works. Both sides of the tension must be upheld and therefore any resolution that even diminishes either side must be rejected. In fact, a final resolution need not even be sought because seeing both sides is illuminating and
productive. That is, keeping the tension's irresolvability in mind can
enable people better to understand the character of religious reflection and
clarify their relationship to religious realities.[23]

This understanding is also, I believe, especially important to us today
because thinking constructively about the modern applicability of Confucian spirituality must deal constantly with two demands that initially may
appear to be incompatible or even only to generate conflict: what I will call
the demands of being both *credible* and *appropriate*. To meet the demand of
being credible is to formulate Confucian ideas about spirituality in a way
that is credible to, meets the conditions of plausibility found in, our common contemporary experience informed as it is by modern scientific explanations, historical consciousness, and ideas about the rights of all humans.
To meet the demands of appropriateness is to formulate Confucian ideas
about spirituality in a way that is appropriate to, shows appreciative
fidelity toward, its meaning as judged by the most basic norms found in the
tradition. Meeting both demands involves both a particular kind of balancing and a understanding of those irresolvable but revelatory and productive
tensions that inform true religious reflection.[24]

A grasp of the distinctive character of religious reflection characterizes
members of the Confucian tradition, and it leads them both to use the
genres they do and to do the kind of thinking about theoretical matters
they do. Some have seen this as a weakness. I believe, however, that it is not
only a strength but a strength that also illuminates the spiritual character of
the tradition and its possible contribution to modern understandings. This
observation leads us to our last subject: the general significance for us of
Confucians ideas about virtue.

The Significance of Virtues, Especially Religious Virtues, in Confucian Spirituality

The most important issue for us finally is not just whether or not, as a
descriptive fact, the Confucian tradition focuses on virtues or contains religious virtues. Nor is it how religious virtues may differ from and connect
with ordinary virtues. Rather it is, as we discussed in the introduction,
what of importance the Confucian understanding of virtues may teach us.
In my view, three subjects are especially important: the universal yet still

distinctive character of Confucian virtues; the genres Confucians employ to present virtues effectively; and several distinctive features of the general perspective that underlies Confucianism's understanding of religious virtues.

The first is both most simple and has been most extensively treated here, and I will just quickly review what was said earlier. Confucian treatments of ordinary virtues provide us with further evidence that there are spheres of human life, such as the four we discussed, that demand certain qualities or virtues. Moreover, we see a similar situation when we examine the religious forms of these four ordinary virtues. Even more important, however, Confucian treatments of all these virtues highlight significant features that differ from what appears in, say, Western treatments. These features enable us to clarify our understanding and improve our action in important ways by helping us to make explicit what is only implicit.

The second subject concerns "genres," the fashion in which Confucians present virtues in particular and spirituality in general. That fashion both is very effective and manifests well those distinctive characteristics of religious thinking we just discussed. This occurs because Confucians usually focus less on straightforward conceptual analysis than on presentations that both work with irresolvable but revelatory and productive tensions and aim to change people's understanding and action.

That kind of focus helps to explain their use of genres that are, to employ Western categories, more often literary than theoretical. Confucian presentations of virtues are not confined by (to use an especially striking example of a common phenomenon) the theoretical apparatus found in, say, medieval scholastic formulations of virtue. Such an apparatus often subverts sophisticated thinkers' desire to connect and refine their ideas of virtues; moreover, it is notorious for its inability to effect changes in people or even to engage their attention.

Confucian treatments, that is, exemplify in a way rarely seen elsewhere just how significant is the selection of genre when issues of virtue and spirituality are the subject. (This may help explain why Confucian classics, like the Four Books, could help sustain the spiritual exercise of reading, treated by Daniel Gardner in volume 2.) The choices about genre that Confucians make are, moreover, especially significant because at least some them (e.g., Mencius) were capable of, and well trained in, more theoretical forms of analysis. Their choice of genre leads us, then, to think about those dramatic cases in the West where something similar occurred: for example, Dante's abandonment of his philosophical work on ethics, written in a scholastic fashion, in order to write his last epic poem because of his judgments about how best to say what he wanted to say and persuade those he wanted to persuade. And it makes us ponder again Melville's statement about why he used the genres he did:

> For in this world of lies, Truth is forced to fly like a scared white doe in the woodlands, and only by cunning glimpses will she reveal herself as in Shakespeare and other masters of the great Art of Telling the Truth,—even though it be covertly, and by snatches.[25]

The genres Confucians use are often, I believe, uniquely suited for the subjects treated. That is true, in significant part, because they necessarily involve readers in an intensified spiritual version of the hermeneutical circle with all that implies about the articulation of the implicit. The hermeneutical circle, in its most basic form, refers to the way in which readers initially understand a text in terms of their own world but then have their world changed by the text, a process that continues on in a circle of changing understandings that remains as long as the work is really encountered. Any work (in fact almost any situation) can be part of such a hermeneutical circle, but some genres invite or even demand engagement in a way that others do not. Moreover, either the subject matter of some genres or the approach to them can be such that the issues involved in spirituality are paramount. We clearly have in Confucianism a paradigmatic example of such texts and processes.

Such genres also, of course, present a distinctive set of problems, notably finding the warrants for adjudicating differences; facing the virtual impossibility of truly moving the insensitive; and, as a result of that situation, accepting the apparently necessary role of the good-person criterion.[26] Confucianism provides, then, an especially rich field in which to discuss problems such as these, as well as the dramatic possibilities that are present in the use of genres that are often more literary than theoretical. That subject surely warrants more attention than I have given it here, but we need to proceed to our last subject, the general perspective implied by the Confucian understanding of specifically religious virtues.

The Confucian contribution here is both more dramatic and (unsurprisingly) also more controversial. Both qualities appear because, as we have seen, a Confucian understanding of religious virtues faces difficulties and produces corrections that go considerably beyond what occurs with normal virtues. The perspective on the human situation that results from this situation is a powerful one. Moreover, features of it connect closely to many contemporary people's views about, say, the fragility of many kinds of speculative inquiry, and the concomitant absence of the notion of a clearly defined, all-powerful deity.

At the core of this perspective is the following "irresolvable but revelatory and productive tension": Confucians are uncertain that perfected virtue will (as presented in the traditional picture of sagely virtue) transform all who meet it and therefore allow the virtuous to create and lead a harmonious society. Yet they continue both to praise virtue and to aim toward it. They believe that people should live from the hope that perfected virtue will join with other empowering forces and produce at least the beginnings of a humane society. The decision to live from this hope involves a "forced option," to use William James's terms, where not to decide is in fact to decide. The option is forced largely because the only other viable alternatives for most people are the worlds represented by forms of Legalism or Mohism, with their emphasis on the calculation of benefits to the person or to the state, and they will be accepted unless a person explicitly chooses against them.[27]

Confucians believe, then, that people either stand within, reaffirm, and make possible a world that destroys much of what is most precious or stands outside it. That option remains true, even if standing outside it will seem to many people simple-minded and surely can be dangerous. Moreover, a crucial feature of the "forced" aspect of the option is that Confucians believe that truly destructive people are active in the world. This evil is liable to be overlooked by, or to be imperfectly understood by, many decent people, but it can destroy much that is most valuable if not dealt with directly. Furthermore, the influence that either the sage or any virtuous person has is significant but difficult to specify, especially if we use only the criteria appropriate to the normal world. Certain of the powerful or the intellectually sophisticated may not, in fact, respond to the influence, but the belief and concomitant hope remain that it can deeply affect others.

Finally, this vision involves attuning or adapting oneself to "another" world. There is a vagueness about the character of this world and an unwillingness, for solid theoretical and religious reasons, to inquire too far into it. Certain features of it are, however, fairly clear. It is a world where the surrender of some evident pleasures and many kinds of aggression are paramount. It is a world where one participates in an ongoing reality that is larger, more benign, and finally more enduring and powerful than anything people clearly see around them.

This kind of adaptation to another world can only live, I think, from a hope that is religious and draws from virtue's expressive character. The special character of this hope arises largely from the fact that people cannot know the source of the hope with even the assurance a probabilistic judgment provides. The hope fits, then, between assurance and doubt, or normal confidence and despair, and it must draw on something other than the judgments that ordinary, seasoned reason makes.

Critics of religion, both at that time and now, have also identified such a hope, and the faith (or even love) on which it rests, as basic to religious attitudes. They see it, however, as infantile and dangerous.[28] Confucians, in contrast, believe that such perspectives not only contain conceptual difficulties but also allow for far too much that is truly horrible. Most important, they believe a real alternative is present. The alternative can appear, however, only if three things are recognized.

First, the character of the forced option must be seen. That involves, among other matters, a recognition of just how much suffering and evil occur and just how easy it is to justify them. Second, people must embrace a religious hope. That hope rests, in significant part, on a grasp of the perfected person's virtue, and the peculiar powers on which it draws, and what that implies about human capacities. Third, people must understand that virtues have an expressive aspect that not only can but also should motivate action. Moreover, it should inform a correct understanding of the forced option, as well as aid and be aided by religious hope.

In short, then, only through the actualization of religious virtues can the fundamental alternative be made present. Making something present and believing it true are, of course, different. And that remains so even if we accept Confucian arguments about how the two inform each other, about how belief and hope can help generate what they aim at or live from. Nevertheless, whatever our final evaluation of the continuing adequacy of the Confucian position, one thing is, I think, unquestionable: the significance, even the heroic character, of their inquiry and practice, and the account they produce. We must, I believe, grapple with that account, and we must do so in a way that reflects their own approach at its best. That is, we must combine sympathetic appropriation and critical evaluation. And we must emulate their insistence that we think about such matters to become better than we are, and to help others become better than they are.

Notes

1. The approach here draws on the comparative method or set of procedures I develop and use in *Mencius and Aquinas* (see especially 175–203; also note my essays "Bourgeois Relativism and the Comparative Study of the Self" and "New Religious Virtues and the Study of Religion"). That approach builds on the idea of similarities within differences and differences within similarities or, in fancy language, on the idea of analogical predication and of focal and secondary meanings.

Using "virtue" to translate *de* or other praiseworthy qualities presents its own set of comparative questions; for an analysis of them, see *Mencius and Aquinas,* 53–58.

References are few in the following notes except that I do (if with trepidation) refer extensively to my own work as it contains analyses that may be helpful to readers who want either to evaluate my more telegraphic comments or to see which scholars I rely on.

2. On the general issue of the normative in comparative studies and examinations of spirituality, see Hampshire, *Innocence and Experience;* and my "Taoist Wandering and the Adventure of Religious Ethics."

3. Neo-Confucian virtues are, I believe, deeply embedded in ontological ideas that differ substantially from earlier ones; that determine more completely the character of the virtues; and that are very difficult to defend, and therefore appropriate, today. All three of these claims are controversial, especially the last one, and this volume contains many essays that take a different approach. Of critical importance to my ideas about possible appropriation is the distinction between real and notional confrontations; see Williams, *Ethics and the Limits of Philosophy,* 160–67. I develop and criticize his notion, and also examine those places where "spiritual regret" is appropriate, in "Conflicts among Ideals of Human Flourishing" and "New Religious Virtues and the Study of Religion." On this general subject, see the comments in nn. 7 and 21.

4. For more detailed discussions of the idea of virtue, see my *Mencius and Aquinas,* especially 6–17, 53–58; also note my "Recent Work on Virtue" and "An Existentialist Reading of Book Four of the *Analects.*"

5. For a more extensive treatment of this distinction, see my *Mencius and Aquinas,* 20–23; that analysis draws on Irwin, *Plato's Moral Theory.* If this distinction is seen as simply descriptive, then any expressive motivation is acceptable, but in traditional accounts evaluative elements are always prominent; for examples, see my *Mencius and Aquinas,* 129–43, 154–68. More important, I understand that a muted version of this distinction will always inform ethical action given that we never know for sure that our actions will generate the results we desire. Nevertheless, the uncertainty is much greater if heroic or religious virtues are the subject, because the final outcome is, and even must be, very uncertain and a full knowledge of that uncertainty must inform a person's motivation.

6. James, *Varieties of Religions Experience,* 364; for a discussion of the implications of this, see my "The Ascetic Grounds for Goodness: William James's Case for the Virtue of Voluntary Poverty." On the idea of the heroic, see my "Heroic Virtue in America."

7. For a more extensive discussion of both the specific conceptual model and the general idea of lists of virtue, see my *Mencius and Aquinas,* 11, 58–60. Neo-Confucians have, I think, a different model, a discovery model; that is, human nature is characterized by a permanent set of dispositions that are obscured but that can be contacted or discovered. People do not, as in a developmental model, cultivate inchoate capacities; rather they discover a hidden ontological reality that defines them. For a discussion of this, see *Mencius and Aquinas,* 59–60.

8. For a further discussion of the ideas of virtues as corrective, and the related idea that virtues can be divided into inclinational and preservative categories, see my *Mencius and Aquinas,* 14–17.

9. For a treatment from an Aristotelian perspective of the idea that virtues concern areas of life or spheres of experience, see Nussbaum, "Comparing Virtues"; eadem, "Non-Relative Virtues" (p. 246 of the latter lists the relevant spheres in Aristotle). Another distinctive feature of Confucianism is that qualities we can call "skills" also accompany virtues and that they are not as sharply differentiated from virtues as they are in, say, the Western tradition. There are many implications of closely relating skills and virtues; see my "Zhuangzi's Understanding of Skillfulness and the Ultimate Spiritual State" for an analysis of some of those implications, if in the context provided by a Taoist thinker.

10. On yielding as an unnamed virtue, see my *Mencius and Aquinas,* 37; and "The Author Replies."

11. For a further discussion of the ideas of formation and control, see my *Mencius and Aquinas,* 102–6. I admit, incidentally, to finding mysterious the relative absence of the erotic, and remain uneasy with the most obvious explanations of it, explanations such as repression or displacement. It is also worth noting, however, that there are significant interpretative issues involved in understanding the Confucian position in this area because we know little about the specifics of the relevant cultural practices.

12. For further descriptions of these two thinkers on this subject, see my "Hsun Tzu on the Mind"; and *Mencius and Aquinas,* 96–102. When thinking about this issue in a comparative fashion it is worth noting that someone like Dante, the Aristotelian Christian, is usually much closer to the Confucian perspective on this virtue than he is to the Thomistic one; see my "Selves, Virtues, Odd Genres, and Alien Guides."

13. On this distinction, see my *Mencius and Aquinas,* 42.

14. For these two sides of Mencius's account, see my "A Confucian Crisis: Mencius' Two Cosmogonies and Their Ethics."

15. On this point, see my "Facing Our Frailty: Comparative Religious Ethics and the Confucian Death Rituals," 10–14; this article also contains a discussion of the idea of masochistic religion. Insofar as the basic character of filial piety and rituals of origin arise from an appropriate response to debts that cannot be repaid, they parallel exactly the classic Western definition, found in Aquinas, of religion.

16. For the quotation from Dante, see *Convivio* II.x.8; also note *Paradiso* III.43–45 and XII.142–45. Giuseppe Mazzotta examines the role of courtesy in Dante as well as various other topics that connect to this paper, although he makes no comparisons to Chinese materials (see *Dante's Vision and the Circle of Knowledge*). Given this, one might even be led to say that Legge, once again, was not so foolish when in the context of Confucius's discussion of the neighborhood in which to live he translated *ren* [benevolence] as "virtuous manners." *Analects* 4:1 contains the quotation from Confucius, a form of which also appears in Mencius 2A:7.

17. There is much worth considering in Legge's comments about Mencius, especially if we "read through" his overtly Christian language. He acknowledges that Mencius's "glance is searching and his penetration deep." But he also comments on an "absence of humility [that] is naturally accompanied with a lack of *sympathy*." Even more important, he links Mencius with those in the Western tradition, starting with Socrates, who argue that to know the good is to do the good. He says, that is, that Mencius shows "the radical defect of the orthodox moral school of China, that there only needs a knowledge of duty to insure its performance." For the full quotation, reference, and a discussion, see my *Mencius and Aquinas*, 86; pp. 84–95 discuss the general issue of failures to be virtuous.

18. For a discussion of Mencius's depiction, see my *Mencius and Aquinas*, 159. For descriptions of the mind's character and ritual's effects in Xunzi, see my "Hsun Tzu on the Mind" and "Facing our Frailty."

19. My *Mencius and Aquinas* deals with this last state in Mencius (pp. 156–59).

20. On this last point, see my "Facing our Frailty," 5–7.

21. For my analysis of how best to deal with the distinctions among and relationship between theories about ontology and about virtues, see my discussion of primary, practical, and secondary theories in *Mencius and Aquinas*, especially pp. 175–87; also note my "Teachers and Saviors" and especially "Theories, Virtues, and the Comparative Philosophy of Human Flourishings," which develops the three in new ways. For a treatment of why I think many or most secondary theories exhibit both deep theoretical and religious difficulties, see *Mencius and Aquinas*, 30–31, 182–87, although obviously these issues are too complex and significant for those brief treatments to deal with them adequately. Finally, for treatments of the relationship of nature and grace in Aristotelian Christian thought, see my "Karl Rahner on the Relation of Nature and Grace"; "The Nature-Grace Question in the Context of Fortitude."

22. Wittgenstein, *Culture and Value*, 73e. In thinking about this balancing act, extending other remarks Wittgenstein made are helpful. Wittgenstein said truly religious ideas manifest blunders that are too large to be simple mistakes. To use a mundane example: if I read that Clinton was first elected President in 1989 I assume the writer has made a mistake; if I read he was elected in the year 1228 I assume there must a different calendrical system involved. To believe a different system is operating does not, of course, end the inquiry because we must evaluate the possible truthfulness of the different system. Nevertheless, most important here is the notion that the oddness of religious ideas can arise not from mistakes but from the abnormality of the system they manifest. See Wittgenstein, *Lectures and Conversations*, 57–59, for remarks that point in this direction.

23. On the general idea that much religious thought deals with "irresolvable but revelatory and productive tensions," see my "Toward a Typology of Religious Thought," but also note "Mencius on Human Nature."

24. For an excellent treatment of the ideas of the credible and appropriate, see Ogden, *Point of Christology*, 4–6, 89–105.

25. Melville, "Hawthorne and His Mosses," 244. On the relationship between theoretical and literary genres, see my "Heroic Virtue in America."

26. See my "Conflicts among Ideals of Human Flourishing," for a discussion of the good-person criterion and related issues; my "Selves, Virtues, Odd Genres, and Alien Guides" treats the issue of genres at length.

27. On early Confucian ideas about virtue's power, see my *Mencius and Aquinas*, 54–56; for the example of Mencius's ideas see pp. 36–40, 58–72. Certain Taoist ideas also provide another alternative, and there are various permutations of the positions noted; see my "Facing Our Frailty," 9, 19.

28. These critics believe such attitudes represent a childlike inability to surrender unrealistic dreams and to come to terms productively with a world of unsatisfied longing and overt or hidden aggression. (Freud can be said to exemplify such criticisms; see my "Freud as Creator and Critic of Cosmogonies and their Ethics.") For them only the surrender of such a hope, and the faith it rests on, can allow people to find a modicum of social justice and personal satisfaction. For them, moreover, only that surrender can enable people to stop inflicting on themselves and others the pain that neurotic hope has generated and the aggression that unfulfilled hope has produced.

The general issues here are, of course, extremely significant ones, and I believe focusing on the idea of virtue in general and religious virtue in particular allows us to see well several powerful alternatives. For example, I think the Taoism of the *Zhuangzi* and the Confucianism of the *Xunzi*, as well as the religious philosophy of William James, contain a version of this kind of criticism, but each of these thinker couples it with a religious solution. Melville, in contrast, to all these figures, sees the force of the criticism and yet can accept neither the critic's solution nor a solution like the Confucian one; see my "Heroic Virtue in America," especially 82–85.

References

Hampshire, Stuart. *Innocence and Experience.* Cambridge: Harvard University Press, 1989.

Irwin, Terence. *Plato's Moral Theory: The Early and Middle Dialogues.* Oxford: Clarendon Press, 1977.

James, William. *The Varieties of Religious Experience: A Study in Human Nature.* New York: Penguin Books, 1985. [First published 1902]

Mazzotta, Giuseppe. *Dante's Vision and the Circle of Knowledge.* Princeton: Princeton University Press, 1993.

Melville, Herman. "Hawthorne and His Mosses." In *The Piazza Tales and Other Prose Pieces, 1839–1860*, 239–53. Evanston, Ill.: Northwestern University Press, 1987. [First published 1850]

Nussbaum, Martha. "Comparing Virtues: Book Discussion: *Mencius and Aquinas* by Lee H. Yearley." *Journal of Religious Ethics* 21, no. 2 (1993): 345–67.

———. "Non-Relative Virtues: An Aristotelian Approach." In *The Quality of Life*, edited by A. Sen and M. Nussbaum, 242–69. Oxford: Clarendon Press, 1993.

Ogden, Schubert M. *The Point of Christology.* San Francisco: Harper & Row, 1982.

Williams, Bernard. *Ethics and the Limits of Philosophy.* Cambridge, Mass.: Harvard University Press, 1985.

Wittgenstein, Ludwig. *Culture and Value.* Edited by G. H. Von Wright. Chicago: University of Chicago Press, 1984.

———. *Lectures and Conversations on Aesthetics, Psychology and Religious Belief.* Edited by C. Barrett. Berkeley: University of California Press, 1972.

Yearley, Lee H. "The Ascetic Grounds for Goodness: William James's Case for the Virtue of Voluntary Poverty." *Journal of Religious Ethics* 26, no. 1 (spring 1998): 105–35.

———. "The Author Replies: Book Discussion: *Mencius and Aquinas* by Lee H. Yearley." *Journal of Religious Ethics* 21, no. 2 (1993): 385–95.

———. "Bourgeois Relativism and the Comparative Study of the Self." In *Tracing Common Themes: Comparative Courses in the Study of Religion,* ed. J. Carman and S. Hopkins, 165–78. Atlanta: Scholars Press, 1991.

———. "Conflicts among Ideals of Human Flourishing." In *Prospects for a Common Morality,* edited by G. Outka and J. J. Reeder, 233–53. Princeton: Princeton University Press, 1993.

———. "A Confucian Crisis: Mencius' Two Cosmogonies and Their Ethics." In *Cosmogony and Ethical Order,* edited by R. Lovin and F. Reynolds, 310–27. Chicago: University of Chicago Press, 1985.

———. An Existentialist Reading of Book Four of the *Analects*." In *Confucius and the Analects: New Essays,* edited by Bryan Van Norden, 237–74. New York: Oxford University Press, 2002.

———. "Facing Our Frailty: Comparative Religious Ethics and the Confucian Death Rituals." *Gross Memorial Lecture, 1995, Valparaiso University.* Valparaiso, Ind.: Valparaiso University Press, 1996. [A publication sent in spring of 1996 to members of the CSR]

———. "Freud as Creator and Critic of Cosmogonies and Their Ethics." In *Cosmogony and Ethical Order,* edited by R. Lovin and F. Reynolds, 381–413. Chicago: University of Chicago Press, 1985.

———. "Heroic Virtue in America: Aristotle, Aquinas, and Melville's *Billy Budd.*" In *The Greeks and Us: Essays in Honor of Arthur W. H. Adkins,* edited by R. B. Louden and P. Schollmeier, 66–92. Chicago: University of Chicago Press, 1996.

———. "Hsun Tzu on the Mind: His Attempted Synthesis of Confucianism and Taoism." *Journal of Asian Studies* 39, no. 3 (1980): 465–80.

———. "Karl Rahner on the Relation of Nature and Grace." *Canadian Journal of Theology* 16, nos. 3 & 4 (1970): 219–31.

———. *Mencius and Aquinas: Theories of Virtue and Conceptions of Courage.* Albany: State University of New York Press, 1990.

———. "Mencius on Human Nature: The Forms of His Religious Thought." *Journal of the American Academy of Religion* 43, no. 2 (1975): 185–98.

———. "The Nature-Grace Question in the Context of Fortitude." *The Thomist* 35 (1971): 557–80.

——. "New Religious Virtues and the Study of Religion." *Fifteenth Annual University Lecture in Religion at Arizona State University.* Distributed by the Department of Religious Studies. Pp. 1–26. [A publication sent in autumn 1994 to members of the AAR]

——. "Recent Work on Virtue," *Religious Studies Review* 16, no. 1 (1990): 1–9.

——. "Selves, Virtues, Odd Genres, and Alien Guides: An Approach to Religious Ethics." *Journal of Religious Ethics* (25th Anniversary Supplement of the *Journal of Religious Ethics* on *The Study of Religious Ethics*) 25, no. 3 (1998): 127–55.

——. "Taoist Wandering and the Adventure of Religious Ethics." The William James Lecture, 1994. *Harvard Divinity Bulletin* 24, no. 2 (1995): 11–15.

——. "Teachers and Saviors." *Journal of Religion* 65, no. 2 (1985): 225–43.

——. "Theories, Virtues, and the Comparative Philosophy of Human Flourishings: A Response to Professor Allan." *Philosophy East and West* 44, no. 4 (1994): 711–20.

——. "Toward a Typology of Religious Thought: A Chinese Example." *Journal of Religion* 55, no. 4 (1975): 426–43.

——. "Zhuangzi's Understanding of the Skillfulness and the Ultimate Spiritual State." In *Essays on Skepticism, Relativism, and Ethics in the Zhuangzi,* edited by P. Kjellberg and P. J. Ivanhoe, 152–82. Albany: State University of New York Press, 1996.

1. Image of Confucius at the recently restored academy at Mount Ni, Shandong province. According to traditional accounts, Confucius was born near Mount Ni, which is located a few miles south of his hometown of Qufu. His face is veiled by rows of hanging diadems, indicative of the high rank he was granted posthumously. Images such as this were the focus of sacrificial offerings to the spirit of Confucius from at least the Tang dynasty until the sixteenth century, when such anthropomorphic images fell into disfavor in state-sponsored temples. Photo: Deborah Sommer, 2001.

2. Grave of Confucius, Kong family graveyard, Qufu, Shandong province. According to the *Mencius* (3A), Confucius was mourned at the grave by his favorite disciples, who resided at the site for three years. When the grave was desecrated in the Cultural Revolution, it was found to be empty. According to ritual texts, the physical body decays, but numinous energies survive death and can travel anywhere. Photo: Deborah Sommer, 2001.

3. Spirit tablet of Confucius, main hall, Confucian Temple, Zhanghua, Taiwan. Not only images but "spirit tablets," planks of wood or lengths of stone carved with the name and rank of the deceased, represent the presence of a spirit. According to ancient ritual texts, spirits abide in the hidden vastness of the skies but can be invoked to alight on spirit tablets during sacrificial offerings. This inscription reads "Supreme Sage and Premier Teacher, Confucius." Photo: Deborah Sommer, late 1980s.

4. Main hall of the Confucian Temple, Beijing. Within a few hundred years of his death, Confucius was revered not only by members of his own family but by the emperor himself. Commemorative offerings to him and other famous literati were institutionalized by the state government, and sacrifices were offered to them at temples across the land. Rites have been offered at this temple in Beijing since the fifteenth century, when the city became the capital of China.
Photo: Deborah Sommer, 2001.

5. Main hall of the Confucian Temple, Ilan, Taiwan. Small temples to Confucius and other literati were eventually constructed by regional governments in nearly every small town, such as the city of Ilan on the remote northeast coast of Taiwan. Such temples served as ritual, political, and civic centers for the local community.
Photo: Deborah Sommer, 1998.

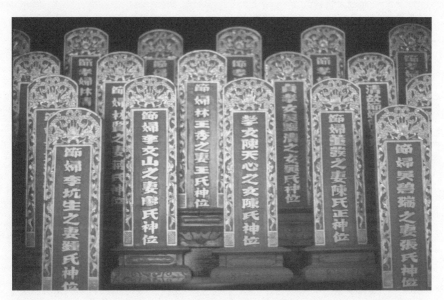

6. Spirit tablets of local female worthies, Ilan Confucian Temple, Taiwan. Ritual practices were by no means strictly men's affairs, as ancient texts such as the *Book of Rites* record the ritual participation of women on almost every page. This small side shrine in the Confucian Temple in Ilan is devoted to the spirits of local exemplary women.
Photo: Deborah Sommer, 1998.

7. Image of Confucius, Confucian academy, Ilan, Taiwan. At this small privately sponsored academy in Ilan, the ancient Confucian reverence for self-cultivation and education is put into practice by the many students who prepare there for the college entrance examinations. They pray before this statue of the Sage for assistance in their studies.
Photo: Deborah Sommer, 1998.

8. Shrine to the *Great Learning*, Confucian Temple, Tainan, Taiwan. Rites at Confucian temples invoke not only the spirits of those commemorated there but an entire body of classical literature. Reverence for this corpus is enshrined in the side chamber of the Tainan Confucian temple, where the text of the *Great Learning* is itself the main icon. Photo: Deborah Sommer, late 1980s.

9. Offerings at the autumn commemorative sacrifices to Confucius, Confucian Temple, Jiali, Taiwan. A presentation of an ox, pig, and sheep is traditionally one of the highest offerings presented to spirits. These meats and other foods are first offered to the spirits, who "consume" their aromas; the leftovers are then consumed by human participants. Gifts of food demonstrate the generosity of the sacrificers and recompense the spirit world for blessings received. Photo: Chu Ronguey, 1998.

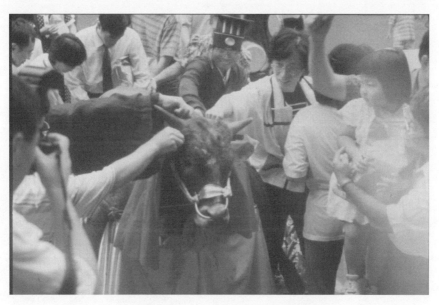

10. Ritual presentation of food offerings, Confucian Temple, Jiali, Taiwan. At the conclusion of the commemorative rites, food offerings are distributed to participants. According to folk tradition, the heads of sacrificial cattle used in the rites to Confucius are plucked for "wisdom hairs," souvenirs that are kept as talismans to insure academic success. Photo: Chu Ronguey, 1998.

11. Spirit tablets of famous literati, eastern gallery, Confucian Temple, Tainan, Taiwan. The historical depth of the ritual tradition is evoked by long galleries of spirit tablets that flank the east and west sides of the main hall of a temple to Confucius. These tablets, usually painted in the blood-red color that in Chinese religions signifies life energy, mark the identities of famous literati.
Photo: Deborah Sommer, late 1980s.

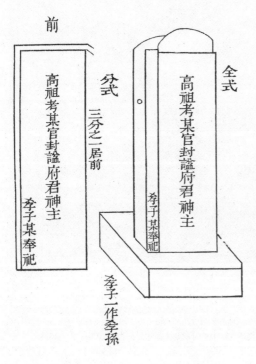

12. Diagram illustrating the proper construction of a spirit tablet. Dimensions of tablets follow ancient precedents, such as those outlined in this woodblock print from a nineteenth-century edition of the *Complete Works of the Cheng Brothers* (*Er Cheng quan shu*, Tu Zongying imprint, 1867, juan 10, p. 8b). This image instructs the viewer to record the generation, name, and title of the deceased ancestor and the name of the filial descendant who commissions the tablet. Collection Cheng Dexiang.

13. Offering the sacrificial eulogy, Confucian Temple, Tainan, Taiwan. The sacrificers' piety and sincerity are recorded in written prayers that are then transmitted to the spirit world by burning. Here a prayer is offered to Confucius's father, who has a shrine behind the main hall. In early medieval times, however, Confucius's mother, rather than his father, was revered in these shrines.
Photo: Chu Ronguey, 1998.

14. Musical instruments for commemorative rites to Confucius, Confucian Temple, Seoul. Music is an audial manifestation of larger harmonies in the cosmos; it guides human emotions and balances relationships. Attentiveness to music's inner structure facilitates the development of orderly governance; its metrical alignment and temporal regularity reflect the measured inner virtues valued in the Confucian tradition.
Photo: Chu Ronguey, 1995.

15. Statue of Mencius. Major figures of the Confucian tradition are commemorated at Confucian temples throughout Asia and are also honored in shrines in their hometowns. This image of Mencius (which sits next to that of his wife, father, and mother) is enshrined at a small temple that marks his birthplace south of Qufu in Shandong province.
Photo: Deborah Sommer, 2001.

16. Ancestral offerings, Cheng clan graveyard, Yichuan county, Henan. Commemorative rites are performed for spirits within one's own family. The descendants of the Song dynasty thinkers Cheng Hao (1032–1085) and Cheng Yi (1033–1107) present offerings to their forebears. Kneeling are the representatives of the descendants of Cheng Hao and Cheng Yi.
Photo: Cheng Dexiang, 1998 Qingming Festival.

17. Sacrificial food offerings, Cheng clan graveyard, Yichuan county, Henan. Filial descendants demonstrate thanksgiving to ancestral spirits with food offerings carefully selected to represent all forms of food preparation and agricultural labor. The contents of this box of sacrificial food for the Cheng brothers follows instructions recorded for generations in family genealogies. The box reads "Made for Cheng Sacrifices." Photo: Cheng Dexiang, 1998 Qingming Festival.

18. Calling for the return of the soul of the deceased, border of Yichuan and Song counties, Henan. At death one's numinous energies ascend to the skies and abide in the heavens above. The soul can be invoked, however, to return to a particular place. At the Qingming Festival, descendants of the Cheng brothers carry white banners to invoke the souls of the great-grandparents of the Chengs to descend in an open field that, before the Cultural Revolution, once contained their graves and family shrine. Photo: Cheng Dexiang, 1995.

19. Entrance to a Qing dynasty (1644–1911) imperial tomb, Western Qing tombs, Yi county, Hebei province. Entrances to shrines and temples are thresholds to spaces where descendants make offerings and spirits alight in sacrificial offerings. Entrances to tombs are analogous passages to the realm of the deceased, but the living may not readily cross them. Oversized altars are placed outside the gateway to the dead; they bear enormous stone vessels that offer their contents in perpetuity.
Photo: Deborah Sommer, 2001.

20. Rites commemorating visiting scholars and relatives, Cheng family graveyard, Yichuan county, Henan. Several branches of the Cheng clan participate in this ritual at the family graveyard in Henan, which commemorates a visit by Korean scholars who are descendants of the Cheng brothers. Transcending modern national boundaries, participants at once offer thanksgiving to common ancestors and renew academic and familial ties. Photo: Cheng Dexiang, late 1990s.

21. Ritual at a shrine in a local academy, central Korea. Local Confucian academies throughout East Asia were venues where children were first introduced to the values, practices, and ritual responsibilities of the Confucian tradition. Academies housed shrines containing the spirit tablets of famous Confucian figures. Here, Korean and Chinese descendants of the Cheng brothers offer incense to their common ancestors.
Photo: Cheng Dexiang, 2000.

22. Cheng family shrine, Korea. According to *Great Learning*, fulfilling family responsibilities is a stepping-stone toward fulfilling wider obligations within the state. Hence it is not unusual that larger clan shrines, such as this fifteenth-century shrine to the Cheng brothers in Korea, are venues of both family-sponsored and state-sponsored rites. Not only clan members but local government officials visit this site—the former, as filial descendants; the latter, as bearers of civic virtues. Photo: Cheng Dexiang, 2000.

23. Hall of Prayer for Good Harvests, Temple of Heaven, Beijing. Rites of thanksgiving and supplication were offered not only to deceased human beings but also to natural celestial and terrestrial forces: the sun, the moon, clouds, the forces of cold and heat, and the powers that generated crops from the soil. In this Qing dynasty (1644–1911) structure, rulers prayed for bountiful harvests. Photo: Deborah Sommer, 2001.

24. Mount Hua, Shaanxi province. According to the *Doctrine of the Mean*, the earth is a mysterious treasure house that supports all life. Since ancient times, rites of thanksgiving have been offered to the earth's mountains and rivers, which produce clouds that sustain human agriculture. One of the most sacred ranges is Mount Hua, whose central peaks resemble a gold ingot. Photo: Deborah Sommer, 2001.

Part Two

THE FORMATION
OF THE CONFUCIAN TRADITION:
SAGELY LEARNING,
RITUAL PRACTICE,
POLITICAL MORALITY

Li and the A-theistic Religiousness of Classical Confucianism

ROGER T. AMES

C LASSICAL CONFUCIANISM is at once a-theistic and profoundly religious. It is a religion without a God, a religion that affirms the cumulative human experience itself. Confucianism celebrates the way in which the process of human growth and extension both is shaped by and contributes to the meaning of the totality—what I will call human "co-creativity." In the classical literature the process of "co-creativity" has many related expressions (*ren, junzi, shengren, shen, he, zhongyong*), but in all cases it is, to use John Dewey's expression, "doing and undergoing" in the effort to get the most out of one's experiences.

There are several profound differences between this kind of religiousness and that of the Abrahamic traditions that have defined the meaning of religion in the Western cultural experience. In this essay, I will argue that, unlike the "worship" model, which defers to the ultimate meaning of some temporally prior, independent, external agency—what Friedrich Schleiermacher has called "absolute dependence"—Confucian religious experience is itself a *product* of the flourishing community, where the quality of the religious life is a direct consequence of the quality of communal living. Religion is not the root of the flourishing community, not the foundation on which it is built, but rather is its product, its flower.

A second important distinction is that Confucian religiousness is neither salvific nor eschatological. While it does entail a kind of transformation, this is specifically a transformation of the quality of one's life in the ordinary business of the day.

The definition of this "a-theistic," *li*-centered religiousness that I will attempt to elicit from the *Analects* and from its even more explicit statement in the *Zhongyong* will challenge both the familiar "Heaven (*tian*)"-

165

centered "christianized" interpretation of classical Confucianism and the default claim that Confucianism is merely a secular humanism. This discussion is particularly relevant to our contemporary world, I believe, because it provides us with a sophisticated example of a kind of nontheistic religious "humanism," or better, "naturalism," that was advanced with little success by an American movement that included Felix Adler, Curtis W. Reese, Charles Francis Potter, and John Dewey early in the twentieth century.[1] These philosophers believed that recent developments in human culture and in the sciences in particular, have placed humanity at a crossroads, making the supernatural dimensions of religious practices such as a theistic "God" not only obsolete but degrading, thus requiring a wholesale revisioning of religious sensibilities that celebrates the unqualified value of the human community. The failure of this religious humanism to win an audience was as much due to the vagaries that attended its articulation as it was to the inability of a population with allegiance to the supernaturalism of the dominant theistic religions to hear this new message. Perhaps the classical Chinese experience will enable us to understand better these religious reformers.

To bring classical Confucian religiousness into focus, I will begin by distinguishing the Confucian sense of "co-creativity" (*zhongyong*)—getting the most out of one's experience—from "creation-as-power" as it has been largely understood within the context of those religions that appeal to a transcendent, supernatural source of meaning. This fundamental distinction between "creativity" and "power" will enable us to generate an alternative vocabulary for Confucian religiousness and to understand better how ordinary human experience—ritualized living through the roles and relationships of family and community—can be the creative source of intense religious experience. I will explore the way in which the process of *li*, as a dynamic social grammar, not only locates but also creates meaningful human beings that are able to live profoundly religious lives. *Li*, I will claim, is quite literally the process of human "education" that "extends" otherwise inchoate persons into thriving centers of spiritual experience.

Creativity versus Power

David Hall appeals to the *wu*-form Daoist sensibilities (*wuwei, wuzhi,* and *wuyu*) in his attempt to bring the very recent Whiteheadian process notion of "creativity" into clearer focus:

> . . . "creativity" is a notion that can be characterized only in terms of self-actualization. Unlike power relationships that require that tensions among

component elements be resolved in favor of one of the components, in relations defined by creativity there is no otherness, no separation or distancing, nothing to be overcome.[2]

Such a definition of "creativity" cannot be reconciled with absolutist religious doctrines that appeal to determination by external agency. In fact, Hall worries over what he takes to be a persistent confusion that has attended all but the most recent thinking about religious experience within the *creatio ex nihilo* doctrines familiar to the Western religious culture: "*Creatio ex nihilo*, as it is normally understood, is in fact the paradigm of all power relationships since the 'creative' element of the relation is completely in control of its 'other,' which is in itself literally *nothing*."[3] It is this "power" relationship that introduces an ontological distinction between reality and appearance, the One and the many—a distinction that reduces "creativity" to "power" (in the sense of the power of one thing to determine another), and, in so doing, precludes the very possibility of "creativity" as self-actualization. As Zarathustra says: "What would it then mean to create, if there were—gods!"[4]

This "power/creativity" distinction is what for Steve Owen is at stake in his reluctance to use the English word "poem" to translate *shi:*

If we translate *shih* [*shi*] as "poem," it is merely for the sake of convenience. *Shih* is not a "poem"; *shih* is not a "thing made" like in the same way one makes a bed or a painting or a shoe. A *shih* can be worked on, polished, and crafted; but that has nothing to do with what a *shih* fundamentally "is." . . . *Shih* is not the "object" of its writer; it *is* the writer, the outside of an inside.[5]

Owen's point is that a poem is not artistic "power" creating something other than itself; it is a creative process of self-actualization. Owen would dissociate *shi* from Aristotle's "productive science (*poietikē technē*)"—the lowest of the sciences, actually, of which "poetics" is his example par excellence.

In the end, it is only a process of "co-creativity" in which ontological distinctions are abandoned in favor of cosmological parity among all things, and in which the unique particular and its environments are seen as mutually shaping, that can be meaningfully construed as "creativity." Said another way, "creativity" is always "co-creativity" since there can be no creativity that is not a transactional, processive, and cooperative endeavor. In fact, this process notion of creativity as a spontaneously emerging novelty is such a recent development in Western philosophical thinking that it is not until the 1971 "Dictionary Supplement" to the *Oxford English Dictionary* that this hallowed record of Western civilization includes this new

entry, with two of its three illustrations directing the curious reader explicitly to Whitehead's *Religion in the Making* (1926).

By contrast, in the noncosmogonic traditions of China—Confucianism
as well as Daoism—this notion of "co-creativity" is a familiar if not the
defining sensibility. In Daoism, it is captured in the notion of "non-coercive action (*wuwei*)," and in Confucianism it has many expressions. For
example, in the *Analects*:

> Authoritative persons establish others in seeking to establish themselves and
> promote others in seeking to get there themselves. Correlating one's conduct
> with those near at hand can be said to be the method of becoming an author-
> itative person (*ren*). (6:30)

The Co-creativity (*cheng*) of the Unique Narrative

Cheng—"co-creativity"—is most often translated as "sincerity" or "integrity."
The notion of integrity can have at least two very different meanings that
are corollary to the power/creativity distinction. The first belongs to
objects as integers in the creativity-as-power worldview. The second refers
to the persistence and continuity of changing events within the co-creativity
model as they shape and are shaped by their circumstances. As such, it is at
once integrity and "integration."

In the absence of the two-world reality/appearance distinction, the classical Chinese tradition does not generate the dualistic worldview necessary
to sponsor the notion of the real as the *objective*. Without this notion of
objectivity that provides a perspective outside of "objects" and thus creates
them as objects (they "object"), there can only be a stream of passing circumstances. Without *objectivity*, objects dissolve into the flux and flow, the
changefulness of our surroundings. They are not objects but events, and as
events they are continuous with other events, thus dissolving into the
transactional processes of our experience. A deobjectified, defactualized
discourse is the language of process, and to speak and hear that language is
to experience the flow of things.

In a world of objects defined as integers by their endowed essences,
integrity is the self-same identical characteristic shared by natural kinds
that makes each of them one-of-a-*kind*. They are thus meaningful in themselves.

Cheng, then, is the process analogue of this notion of essence defined by
the uniqueness and persistence of the constitutive relationships that define
a particular "event." "Event" is a more felicitous term than "object" or
"thing" because it suggests that such experiences are *one*-of-a-kind and that,

in this world, their meaning is something achieved in their relationships. The *Zhongyong* speaks to this question directly:

> Co-creativity [*cheng*] is self-realizing [*zicheng*], and its way [*dao*] is self-advancing [*zidao*]. Co-creativity is an event [*wu*] taken from its beginning to its end, and without this co-creativity, there are no events. It is thus that, for exemplary persons [*junzi*] it is co-creativity that is prized. But co-creativity is not simply the self-realization of one's own person; it is what realizes events. Realizing oneself is authoritative conduct [*ren*]; realizing events is wisdom [*zhi*].[6] This is the excellence [*de*] of one's natural tendencies and is the way of integrating what is more internal and what is more external. Thus, whenever one applies this excellence, it is fitting. (25)

There is no genetic fallacy entailed by *cheng*, in which there is assumed to be some essential and unchanging element that persists throughout the narrative of any particular. Co-creativity is the coherence of the narrative itself—its persistence and continuity—as it shapes and is shaped by its ever-changing context.

Translating this metaphysical distinction into more concrete terms, the tendency of philosophy to reify human nature and assume it to be ready-made is challenged by human nature as process, an aggregate of human experience. The basis of community is not a metaphysically identical, ready-made mind, but rather a "functional" or "instrumental" inchoate heart-mind (*xin*) expressed in the language of relations that, through communication, produces the aims, beliefs, aspirations, and knowledge necessary to establish the like-mindedness of effective community. Human realization is achieved not by wholehearted participation in communal life forms but by life in community that forms one wholeheartedly.

This idea of constructing the mind out of social transactions and effective communication suggests a further dimension of *cheng* that is not expressed fully by the translation "integrity," and is not made explicit in the translation "co-creativity." As we know, an alternative, perhaps more familiar rendering of *cheng* is "sincerity." The virtue of the term "sincerity" is that it describes a commitment to one's purposes, a quality of action, a solemn affirmation of one's process of self-actualization, a Confucian statement of *amor fati*.

Zhongyong as Staying Centered in Familiar Affairs

In addition to *ren*, another one of the early Confucian expressions for this "co-creativity" on which I have chosen to focus in this essay is *zhongyong*, which first appears in *Analects* 6:29:

The Master said, "The excellence born of staying centered in familiar[7] affairs is of the highest order. It is rare among the people to be able to[8] sustain it for long."[9]

Given the processional and aggregating nature of our narratives as human beings, it is incumbent upon the person who would flourish in the world that appropriate adjustments be made *mutatis mutandis* along the way. In fact, it is the sustained attention to achieving equilibrium by staying centered in the familiar affairs of one's life that leads ultimately to religious experience and pays off in religious dividends. Equilibrium (*zhong*)—the studied ability to remain centered within those natural, social, and cultural environments that both contextualize and constitute one—is productive of a thriving harmony (*he*) achieved through patterns of deference. And as one becomes increasingly extended in the world through these patterns of deference, this centeredness enables one ultimately to become a co-creator of cosmic proportions in the nurturing processes of the heavens and the earth:

> When equilibrium [*zhong*] and harmony [*he*] are fully realized, the heavens and earth maintain their proper places and all things flourish in the world. . . . Only those in the world of the utmost co-creativity are able to separate out and braid together the many threads on the great loom of the world. Only they set the great root of the world and realize the transforming and nourishing processes of heaven and earth.
>
> How could there be anything on which they depend?
> So earnest, they are authoritative [*ren*];
> So profound, they are a bottomless abyss [*yuan*];
> So pervasive, they are *tian* [*tian*]. (*Zhongyong* 2 and 32)

The Process of Education: *Educere* or *Educare?*

The growth and extension that occur within these patterns of deference are the product of education. The etymology of the English word "educate" provides us with a useful distinction that is again corollary to the power/creativity distinction. It can mean *educare*, "to cultivate, to rear, to bring up," suggesting growth in the sense of a process of discovery, the actualizing of a given potential, where the role of teacher, like Meno's Socrates, is only catalytic to something already there. However, "educate" can also mean *educere*, "to educe, elicit, evoke, lead forth, draw out," a collaborative effort on the part of *this* mentor and *this* student in which there is a focus on the particular conditions of the relationship, and their creative possibilities. While the first sense is perhaps more familiar in Western usage, appealing as it does to the articulation of ideal types, the second sense gives us "to educe" in the sense of assisting in "extending one's way" through a process of modeling and emulation that must be tailored to one's own specific conditions:

> In striving to be authoritative in your conduct, do not yield even to your teacher. (*Analects* 15:36)

Education so construed is a transactional process that entails both continuity and creativity—the growth of both *this* able teacher and *that* able student. It is this sense of education that is captured in the *Zhongyong*'s expression an "advancing pathway (*dadao*)" (*Zhongyong* 1 and 20).[10]

A classic statement that illustrates this second meaning of "leading forth" and "extending the way" is *Analects* 9:11, a wonderful passage in which Yan Hui recounts the process through which he is being led forward by Confucius one step at a time, creating his way in the very walking:

> Yan Hui, with a deep sigh, said, "The more I look up at it, the higher it soars; the more I penetrate into, the harder it becomes. I am looking at it in front of me, and suddenly it is behind me. The Master is good at drawing me forward a step at a time; he broadens me with culture (*wen*) and disciplines my behavior through the observance of ritual propriety (*li*). Even if I wanted to quit, I could not. And when I have exhausted my abilities, it is as though something rises up right in front of me, and even though I want to follow it, there is no road to take."

The Family as Governing Metaphor

The family as an institution, and the nexus of ritualized roles and relationships that define it (*li*), provides the model for this optimizing process of making one's way by both giving and getting the most out of the human experience.

> Exemplary persons (*junzi*) concentrate their efforts on the root, for the root having taken hold, the way (*dao*) will grow therefrom. As for filial and fraternal responsibility, it is, I suspect, the root of authoritative conduct (*ren*). (*Analects* 1.2)

The assumption is that persons are more likely to give themselves utterly and unconditionally to their families than to any other human institution. Promoting the centrality of family relations is an attempt to assure that entire persons without remainder are invested in each of their actions.

The power of the family to function as the radial locus for human growth is much enhanced when natural family and communal relations are not perceived as being in competition with, a distraction from, or dependent on some higher supernatural relations. It is from the family expanding outward that persons emerge as objects of profound communal, cultural, and ultimately religious deference. Beyond the achievement of an intense religious quality felt in the everyday experience of their lives, these exemplary persons emerge as ancestors for their families and communities, and as contributors to the ancestral legacy—*tian*—that defines Chinese culture more broadly construed.

The etymology of the Chinese term most often translated as "education" or "teaching" (*jiao*), is also suggestive, focusing the process of education squarely within the family context. According to the *Shuowen*, "education [*jiao*]" "is what the elders dispense and on which the juniors model," with the two elements of the character itself being explained as "those above providing culture [*wen*] with those below responding with filiality [*xiao*]." It should not go unnoticed that this same term *jiao* came to carry strong religious connotations early in the tradition, especially in its associations with both religious Daoism (*daojiao*) and Confucianism (*rujiao*) as a state ideology.[11]

Speaking generally, it is the patterns of deference that make up the family itself and the appropriate transactions among its members that give rise to, define, and authorize the specific ritualized roles and relationships (*li*) through which the process of refinement is pursued. As *Zhongyong* 20 explains:

> The degree of love due different kin and the graduated esteem due those who are qualitatively different in their character is what gives rise to the observance of ritual propriety (*li*).[12]

What makes these ritualized roles and relationships fundamentally different from rules or laws is the fact that not only must they be personalized, but the quality of the particular person invested in these *li* is the ultimate criterion of their efficacy.[13]

The Process and Content of Education

In our recent translation of the Dingzhou *Analects*, Henry Rosemont and I began our discussion of *li* with the following disclaimer:

> Perhaps the greatest obstacle to understanding what *li* means in the world of Confucius is thinking that "ritual" is a familiar dimension of our own world, and [that] . . . we [thus] fully understand what it entails. (52)

The *Shuowen* lexicon defines *li* paronomastically as *lu*, "to tread a path."[14] In reading the *Analects*, there is a tendency to give short shrift to the middle books 9–11, which are primarily a series of intimate snapshots depicting the historical person Confucius. Yet it is precisely these passages that are most revealing of the extent to which the appropriate behaviors of a scholar-official participating in the daily life of the court were choreographed: the slightest gesture, the cut of one's clothes, the cadence of one's stride, one's posture and facial expression, one's tone of voice, even the rhythm of one's breathing:

> On passing through the entrance way to the Duke's court, he would bow forward from the waist, as though the gateway were not high enough. While in attendance, he would not stand in the middle of the entranceway; on passing through, he would not step on the raised threshold. On passing by the empty throne, his countenance would change visibly, his legs would bend, and in his speech he would seem to be breathless. He would lift the hem of his skirts in ascending the hall, bow forward from the waist, and hold in his breath as though ceasing to breathe. On leaving and descending the first steps, he would relax his expression and regain his composure. He would glide briskly from the bottom of the steps, and returning to his place, he would resume a reverent posture. (*Analects* 10:4)

From this passage and many others like it, it should be clear that *li* do not reduce to generic, formally prescribed "rites" and "rituals," performed at stipulated times to announce status and to punctuate the seasons of one's life. The *li* are more, much more. The performance of *li* must be understood in light of the uniqueness of each participant and the profoundly aesthetic project of becoming a person. *Li* is a process of personal refinement—an achieved disposition, an attitude, a posture, a signature, an identity. Entailing the cognate notions of proper, appropriate, propriety, "a making one's own," *li* is a resolutely personal performance revealing one's worth to oneself and one's community. *Li* is both a personal and a public discourse through which one constitutes and reveals oneself qualitatively as a unique individual, a whole person. Importantly, there is no respite; *li* requires the utmost attention in every detail of what one does at every moment that one is doing it, from the drama of the high court to the posture one assumes in going to sleep, from the reception of different guests to the proper way to comport oneself when alone; from how one behaves in formal dining situations to appropriate one-off extemporaneous gestures. One expression of the intensity of this attention is *shen qi du:*

> It is for this reason that exemplary persons (*junzi*) are so cautious about what is not seen, and so anxious about what is not heard. It is because there is nothing more present than what is hidden, and nothing more manifest than what is inchoate that exemplary persons are ever circumspect in their uniqueness.[15]

Li is at once cognitive and aesthetic, moral and religious, physical and spiritual. It is singular as the narrative of this specific person, Confucius, and plural as the many consummate events that make up the business of the day. *Li* are learned patterns of deference performed individually and elegantly. They are value-revealing life forms that attract emulation and inspire religious devotion, fostering the like-mindedness necessary for a flourishing community. The cognate relationship between *li* and *ti*, from high religious performance to its physical embodiment, from *tian* to *di*, suggests the pervasiveness of *li* in the particular human experience. In the absence of a ready-made essence, a human being is ultimately an aggregate of experience, and *li* is a medium that ensures that this cumulative experience is refined and substantial.[16]

Growth and Extension

The life of *li* is a process of continuing growth and extension. One amplifies the scope and intensity of one's experience through sustaining a steady equilibrium in the process of advancing one's way on the journey of life, a life informed by and performed ceremoniously within the familiar bonds of *li*.

Most of the terms invoked to describe Confucian religious experience connote this process of growth and extension explicitly. For example, as we have seen, productive familial relations are the "root (*ben*)" whence one's way (*dao*) advances (*Analects* 1:2; see also *Zhongyong* 1.29, 32, and esp. 17). The repeated contrast between the exemplary person (*junzi*) and the petty person (*xiaoren*), the inclusiveness of appropriateness (*yi*) as opposed to the exclusiveness of personal benefit (*li*), and the emergence of the authoritative person (*ren*) from individuated persons (*ren*) and from the common masses (*min*)—all of these expressions entail growth and extension through patterns of deference. Even the term "spirituality" itself, *shen*, crosses the divide between "human spirituality" and "divinity," between "human clairvoyance" and the "mysteries."[17] *Shen* is itself cognate with the terms "to extend, to prolong (*shen*)."

The metaphors used to describe those ancestors and cultural heroes who have become "godlike" are frequently celestial—"the sun and moon," "the heavens," "the north star," and so on, expressing in a figurative way the familiar assumption that there is a "continuity between the human being and the ancestral realm (*tianren heyi*)." For example,

> Zhongni [Confucius] . . . is comparable to the heavens and the earth, sheltering and supporting everything that is. He is comparable to the progress of the four seasons, and the alternating brightness of the sun and moon. (*Zhongyong* 30; see also *Analects* 2:1; 19:21, 23, 24, 25)

The intensity of such religious experience is the measure of one's personal growth; it is the creative elaboration of oneself within one's narrative that is the source of one's religious experience.

Harmonized *qing* as a Confucian *amor fati*

The motive, self-affirming aspect in this process of self-actualization is often understated. The *Zhongyong* defines harmony itself as the achievement of proper measure in one's feelings so as to sustain equilibrium and advance one's way in the world:

> The feelings of joy and anger, of grief and pleasure, not yet having arisen is called nascent equilibrium (*zhong*); once the emotions have arisen, that they all achieve appropriate measure is called harmony (*he*). This notion of equilibrium (*zhong*) is the great root of the world; harmony then is the advancing way (*dadao*). When equilibrium and harmony are fully realized, the heavens and earth maintain their proper places and all things flourish in the world.

One term that has particular prominence in the Zisizi Confucian documents recently uncovered at Mawangdui and Guodian is *qing*. In fact, these recovered texts have not only reinstated the "emotions" as an important factor in self-actualization, but will help to resolve a long-standing dispute over the meaning of this recondite term itself.

A. C. Graham has defined *qing* as "how things and situation are in themselves, independently of how we name or describe them," as "fact," or "essentials," contending that it is Xunzi who first uses this term as "the passions."[18] In the early corpus, *qing* often appears with *xing*, "natural tendencies," and it is in this context that it seems to mean "how things are in themselves." The problem, however, has been, How can the same term mean both the facts of a situation and the emotions that attend it, both fact and value? Graham's answer, now demonstrably incorrect, is that chronologically it first meant "how things are" and only later came to mean "emotions."

A persistent feature of classical Confucianism corollary to the absence of "objectivity," is an unwillingness to separate description and prescription, reality and its interpretation. Everything is always experienced from one perspective or another, where both experiencer and experience are implicated in the event. And there is no design beyond how the sum of these particular perspectives construe their worlds. This prescriptive feature of the tradition is immediately apparent in the use of *shifei*, which means both "this/not-this" (fact), and "approve/disapprove" (value). *Qing* then is not simply "how things are in themselves" but entails the emotional character of the situation and one's role in it. Importantly, emotions are in the events themselves, not simply a response to something "other." And when these emotions are harmonious and one is fully co-creator, giving the most and getting the most out of experience, this achievement is attended by a Confucian version of *amor fati*: the unconditional affirmation of the facts of one's existence as they are.[19] Nietzsche calls *amor fati* "my innermost nature," "height and a bird's eye view in observation."[20] Co-creativity (*cheng*) as a transactional, processive, cooperative endeavor always has the element of affirming things as they are and participating in the process of *educere*. An individual does not bring novel things out of old situations— novelty is brought out cooperatively. And as with *ziran*, "none can tell how it is so" (*Zhuangzi* 5/2/37). It is this sensibility, then, that is the stuff of religious experience.

In comparison with the other Zisizi documents, the *Zhongyong* makes such infrequent reference to *qing* that it raises the question as to whether the *Zhongyong* belongs to the same lineage. I would suggest that the relative absence of explicit reference to *qing* is because, as noted above, *cheng* has an important emotional aspect which justifies its translation as "sincerity," and is thus doing the work of *qing*.

Rethinking the *Zhongyong*

It is the extended discussion of this notion, *zhongyong* "co-creativity," that serves as an illuminating commentary on the ambiguous opening passage of the *Zhongyong*, and which, by virtue of its signal importance as the method of becoming human, gives this text its title. And one despairs at those uncritical interpretations of key philosophical terms such as *tian, dao,* and *xing,* conventionally translated as "Heaven," "the Way," and "inborn nature," respectively, that would construe these ideas metaphysically as fixed and determinative principles, and in so doing, vitiate precisely that notion of co-creativity which is such a basic feature of classical Chinese philosophy.

The standard rendering of the opening passage of the *Zhongyong* is a case in point. It is the translation by James Legge which itself references the earlier Jesuit translations and which most subsequent translations, both in English and modern Chinese, follow rather closely:

> What Heaven has conferred is called THE NATURE; an accordance with this nature is called THE PATH *of duty;* the regulation of this path is called INSTRUCTION.

Legge counterbalances the high estimate that the tradition has lavished on the *Zhongyong* as one of the Four Books, with his own pious reservations about it:

It begins sufficiently well, but the author has hardly enunciated his preliminary apophthegms, when he conducts into an obscurity where we can hardly
grope our way, and when we emerge from that, it is to be bewildered by his
gorgeous but unsubstantial pictures of sagely perfection. He has eminently
contributed to nourish the pride of his countrymen. He has exalted their
sages above all that is called God or is worshipped, and taught the masses of
the people that with them they have need of nothing from without. In the
meantime it is antagonistic to Christianity. By-and-by, when Christianity has
prevailed in China, men will refer to it as a striking proof how their fathers
by their wisdom know neither God nor themselves.[21]

What is particularly telling about Legge's evaluation here is that in spite of
the overtly "Christian" interpretation he wants to give to this opening passage, he is entirely aware of the incongruency of this theistic interpretation
with the human-centered thrust of the ideas conveyed in the remainder of
the text. Legge's interpretation of the text, while wishing that it were otherwise, is not only that human beings have everything necessary to achieve
realization without reference to some transcendent deity, but further, that
the world itself is sufficiently served by human creativity that it need not
appeal beyond itself for divine intervention.

We have a choice. We can follow those commentators who, under the
influence of Neo-Confucianism and Christian doctrine, take this opening
passage to be confounded by the text that follows from it.[22] Or we can
attempt to understand this passage in a way consistent with the philosophical thrust of the document as a whole. A more nuanced reading of this
opening passage that would accommodate the commitment to co-creativity
without violating the tolerance of the language might be the following:

> What *tian* promotes[23] is called natural tendencies;[24] tutoring[25] these natural
> tendencies is called advancing the way;[26] improving[27] this roadway is called
> education.[28]

Co-creativity as Religiousness

For classical Confucianism, "religiousness" in its most fundamental sense
refers to a person's attainment of a focused appreciation of the complex
meaning and value of the total field of existing things through a reflexive
awakening to the awesomeness of one's own participatory role as co-
creator. It is only in discovering and investing in the connections among
things that one becomes aware of, and adds to, the meaning of things. This
"standing together" with all things is effected through an achieved and sustained equilibrium in the familiar experiences of our everyday lives that, in
the absence of any coercion that would detract from their possibilities,
allows for optimum creativity in every act. It is this quality of self-affirm-

ing religiousness that Confucius is referring to in reflecting on the progress of his own life:

> ... from fifty I realized the propensities of *tian* (*tianming*); from sixty my ear was attuned; from seventy I could give my heart-and-mind free rein without overstepping the boundaries. (*Analects* 2:4)

The vocabulary in this passage appeals to the pervasive "path (*dao*)" metaphor: striking out in a direction, taking one's place, knowing which way to go, realizing the terrain around one, following along (there has been speculation that "ear" here might be a corruption, but the Dingzhou text has this character), and then making one's way wherever one wants to go without going astray.

Notes

1. Although Dewey himself did on occasion use the term "humanism," his position with its "natural piety" is better described as a "naturalism" because he was not at all anthropocentric in his thinking. On the contrary, his contextualism locates the human being as radically embedded in the natural world, where the human community resonates with the rhythms and cadence of nature.

2. See David L. Hall, *Uncertain Phoenix*, 249. See a more recent discussion of these ideas in David L. Hall and Roger T. Ames, *Thinking from the Han*.

3. Hall, *Uncertain Phoenix*, 249.

4. *Thus Spake Zarathustra* II, 2, trans. Graham Parkes in Ken Nishitani, *The Self-Overcoming of Nihilism*, 49.

5. Stephen Owen, *Readings in Chinese Literary Thought*, 27. The only problem with Owen's reflection on *shi* is his seeming inclination to limit this insight to poetry alone as opposed to other art forms. As A. N. Whitehead suggests, "Art is the education of Nature." This is to be contrasted with art as the imitation of Nature's forms (Plato) or functions (Aristotle), as transformation of Nature (existentialists, romantics), or the sublimation of Nature (Freud).

6. This passage is reminiscent of *Analects* 6:23: "The Master said, "The wise [*zhi*] enjoy water; those authoritative in their conduct [*ren*] enjoy mountains. The wise are active; authoritative persons are still. The wise find enjoyment; authoritative persons are long-enduring." Wisdom entails appropriateness to context (see *Analects* 6:22). Thus, in realizing oneself, one is necessarily realizing one's situation.

7. "Familiar" is a felicitous translation of *yong* because it evokes the notion of "family," which, we will see, is at the center of the Confucian religious experience.

8. Assuming the *neng* found in the *Zhongyong* 3 version of this same passage.

9. This *Zhongyong* version is reminiscent of *Analects* 12:1: "If for the space of a day . . ."; 4:5: "Exemplary persons do not take leave of their authoritative conduct even for the space of a meal"; 4:6: "Are there people who, for the space of a single

day, have given their full strength to authoritative conduct?"; and 6:7: "With my disciple, Yan Hui, he could go for several months without departing from authoritative thoughts and feelings; as for the others, only every once in a long while might authoritative thoughts and feelings make an appearance."

10. The character *da* means to break through, like growing grain breaking through the ground.

11. The expression *rujiao* is attested as early as the *Shiji* (Sima Qian, *Records of the Historian,* 3184).

12. We have amended this passage on the basis of the *Kongzi jiayu* 17.1/34/14 passage, which has: "The teachings of loving kin and the graduated esteem due those with different quality of character are what has produced the observance of ritual propriety. The observance of ritual propriety is the root of proper governing." Confucius makes the point repeatedly that the observance of ritual propriety comes afterwards as an embellishment; see 3.8:

Zixia inquired: "What does the song mean when its says:
'Her smiling cheeks—so radiant,
Her dazzling eyes—so sharp and clear,
It is the unadorned that enhances color.'?"
The Master replied: "The application of color is to the unadorned."
"Does this mean that observing ritual propriety (*li*) itself comes after?" asked Zixia.
The Master replied: "Zixia, you have stimulated my thoughts. It is only with the likes of you then that one can discuss the *Songs*."
See also 3.4, 6.27, 12.15.

13. See *Analects* 3:3: "What has a person who is not authoritative got to do with observing ritual propriety? What has a person who is not authoritative got to do with the playing of music?"

14. According to Bernhard Karlgren, these two terms would be perfect homophones in the classical pronunciation (*Grammata Serica Recensa*).

15. One's own particularity should be understood relationally, entailing what one does for context and what context does for one, as well as the uniqueness of one's own particular relations. This passage recalls Whitehead, *Religion in the Making,* 16, "Religion is what one does with his own solitariness." *Shendu* occurs also in *Xunzi* 7/3/30:

This is because according with the force of circumstances one is ever circumspect in one's uniqueness. For persons effective in constructing the road to becoming human, if they are not authentic, they are not unique; if they are not unique, they will not take shape; if they do not take shape, although they initiate something in their hearts-and-minds, it is manifest in their countenance, and it is expressed in what they say, the common people will still not follow them, and even if they do follow them, they are certain to be distrustful.

This whole section of *Xunzi* uses the vocabulary of the *Zhongyong* and seems to be an elaboration on it.

The other example of this expression is in the *Daxue* (James Legge, *Chinese Classics*, 1:367) which uses a vocabulary reminiscent of *Xunzi*:

This is what is meant by the saying: "What is authentic within will shape one without." Thus, exemplary persons must be ever circumspect in their uniqueness.

In *Zhuangzi* 17/6/41 (see Graham, *Chuang-tzu*, 87; Watson, *Complete Works of Chuang Tzu*, 83) there is the passage:

. . . Having attained the brightness of dawn, he was then able to see his own uniqueness; seeing his own uniqueness he was then able to set aside past and present. . . .

The use of *du* is often glossed as "oneness" (*yi*), and is reminiscent of *Daodejing* 25 (following the Mawangdui text):

Standing uniquely, it is not improved upon; pervading everywhere, it does not pause.

Jeffrey Riegel ("The Four 'Tzu Ssu' Chapters," 209 n. 9) follows Henri Maspero (*La Chine Antique*, 456) in translating *shendu* as "guards his uniqueness."

16. Herb Fingarette underscores the way in which *li* becomes a medium of religious expression for Confucius (*Confucius*).

17. There are several definitions of *shen* proffered in classical corpus that preclude any severe distinction between humanity and divinity. For example, see the *Fayan;* the *Yijing* 41/5 says, "the sage is *shen*." *Huainanzi* 1/9/15 defines *shen* as "that which regulates life," 15/152/29 "that which knows what others do not," 2/16/8 "the abysmal source of wisdom."

18. See A. C. Graham, *Disputers of the Tao*, 97–100, 242–45.

19. For a compelling discussion of *amor fati*, see Nishitani, *Self-Overcoming of Nihilism*, 45–68.

20. Friedrich Nietzsche, *Will to Power*, 1004; and *Nietzsche contra Wagner*, trans. Graham Parkes, cited in Nishitani, *Self-Overcoming of Nihilism*, 50–51.

21. Legge, *Chinese Classics*, 1:55.

22. Riegel argues that such contradictions within the *Zhongyong* can be explained by the fact that it was originally the record of a Han court debate, with alternative sections seeking to refute each other ("The Four 'Tzu Ssu' Chapters," 102ff.). He suggests that this opening passage actually sets the topic for the debate, with passages 3–5 arguing for the impossibility of practicing such a philosophy (pp. 207–11).

23. Pang Pu defines *tian* as the "social environment," "social conditions," "social forces" that have a determining influence on human development ("Kong-Meng zhi jian," 92–93). Importantly, although these forces are human in their origins, Pang does see these same forces as being beyond the control of any particular human being. Pang Pu's reading stands in contrast to Tu Weiming's more familiar notion that this passage affirms "the ancient Chinese belief in a purposive and caring Heaven as the ultimate arbiter of human affairs" (*Centrality and Commonality*, 9). Riegel: "Because one's nature is fixed, *and fixed by Heaven*, one has an obligation to Heaven to cultivate it" ("The Four 'Tzu Ssu' Chapters," 208 n. 3).

24. This passage uses both *ming* and *xing*. *Mencius* 7B:24 uses these same terms

to establish a distinction in the foci of cultivation, where *ming* is more appetitive and *xing* is to be reserved for what is distinctively the content of human morality.

25. *Shuai* (GSR 498) is etymologically the same word as *shuai* (GSR 499), which means both "to lead (an army)," and "to follow the lead, to obey." That is, *shuai* means both "to follow" and "to lead," characterizing a situation of "leading and following" rather than the action of a particular agent. This is not unusual in classical Chinese, where *ming*, for example, means at once perspicacity on the part of the spectator and brilliance on the part of the object seen—a brilliant situation. For "tutoring," see the discussion of the distinction between *educere* and *educare* below.

26. There is a parallel passage in *Huainanzi* 11/93/20 that provides a very Daoistic and anti-Confucian commentary:

> Tutoring these natural tendencies and putting them in to advancing the way; realizing one's natural tendencies is called excellence. Authoritative conduct is prized only when these natural tendencies are lost; appropriateness is prized only when the way is lost. For this reason, authoritative conduct and appropriateness being established, the way and excellence have been dislodged; if the observance of ritual propriety and the playing of music adorn our lives, then pure simplicity has dissipated.

Riegel points out that when this *Huainanzi* passage is cited in the *Hou Hanshu*, it is introduced as "Zisizi says."

27. *Xiu* (GSR 1077) means "improve, adorn, arrange, repair, attend to" and "elaborate," as well as "cultivate." It would seem to refer to "cultivating" in the sense of human cultural activity rather than nurturing the growth of something already predetermined. The Han dynasty commentator Zheng Xuan glosses this character as "building and broadening it, the human being extends and beautifies it," perhaps alluding to the *Analects* 15:29 passage, "it is the person who is able to broaden the way." Importantly, there is an element of "trailblazing" here.

28. As Pang Pu points out ("Kong-Meng zhi jian," 95), it is significant that what closes the circle in the process of human realization is education—something over which human beings exercise a certain degree of control, and for which they have some real responsibility. In *Analects* 20:3, parallel structure requires that *ming, li,* and *yan* all be understood as requiring participation rather than being regarded as some determinative imposition on the human experience. Similarly, *xing, dao,* and *jiao* are parallel in this passage, challenging the assumed "givenness" of *xing*. The expectation that one must participate in the construction of the road to becoming human is clear from the parallel structure.

References

Chou-i. Peking: Harvard-Yenching Institute Sinological Index Series, Supplement 10, 1935.

Fingarette, Herbert. *Confucius: The Secular as Sacred*. New York: Harper Torchbooks, 1972.

Graham, A. C. *Disputers of the Tao: Philosophical Argument in Ancient China.* Lasalle, Ill.: Open Court, 1989.

——. trans. *Chuang-tzu: The Inner Chapters.* London: George Allen & Unwin, 1981.

Hall, David L. *The Uncertain Phoenix.* New York: Fordham University Press, 1982.

Hall, David L., and Roger T. Ames. *Thinking from the Han: Self, Truth, and Transcendence in Chinese and Western Culture.* Albany: State University of New York Press, 1998.

Karlgren, Bernhard. *Grammata Serica Recensa.* Stockholm: Museum of Far Eastern Antiquities, 1957.

Lau, D. C., and Chen Fong Ching, eds. *A Concordance to the Huainanzi.* ICS Ancient Chinese Text Concordance Series. Hong Kong: Commercial Press, 1992.

——. *A Concordance to the Kongzi jiayu.* ICS Ancient Chinese Text Concordance Series. Hong Kong: Commercial Press, 1992.

Legge, James. *The Chinese Classics,* Volume 1. Hong Kong: Hong Kong University Press, 1960.

Maspero, Henri. *La Chine Antique.* Paris: De Boccard, 1927. Translated by F. A. Kierman, Jr., as *China in Antiquity.* Amherst: University of Massachusetts Press, 1978.

Nishitani, Keiji. *The Self-Overcoming of Nihilism.* Translated by Graham Parkes with Setsuko Aihara. Albany: State University of New York Press, 1990.

Owen, Stephen. *Readings in Chinese Literary Thought.* Cambridge, Mass.: Council on East Asian Studies, Harvard University, 1992.

Pang Pu Ãe. "Kong-Meng zhi jian—Guodian Chu jian de sixiangshi diwei" [Between Confucius and Mencius—The Place in the History of Thought of the Chu Strips found at Guodian]. In *Zhongguo Shehui Kexue* [Social Sciences in China] 5 (1998): 88–95.

Riegel, Jeffrey. "The Four 'Tzu Ssu' Chapters of the *Li Chi*: An Analysis and Translation of the *Fang Chi, Chung Yung, Piao Chi* and *Tzu I*." Ph.D. dissertation, Stanford.

Sima Qian. *The Records of the Historian (Shiji).* Peking: Zhonghua shuju, 1959.

Takeuchi Yoshio. "*Yi* to *Chuyo* no kenkyu." In *Takeuchi Yoshio Zenshu,* Volume 3. 1979.

Tu Weiming. *Centrality and Commonality: An Essay on Confucian Religiousness.* Albany: State University of New York Press, 1989.

Watson, Burton, trans. *The Complete Works of Chuang Tzu.* New York: Columbia University Press, 1968.

Whitehead, A. N. *Religion in the Making.* New York: Meridian Books, 1960.

9

Is There a Universal Path
of Spiritual Progress in the Texts
# of Early Confucianism?

HENRY ROSEMONT JR.

I F THE WORLD IS INDEED becoming a "global village" —by no means a good thing if it is governed by transnational corporations—it would seem to be imperative for all of its citizens to learn about cultures different from their own. But merely learning *about* other cultures will not suffice, especially for members of the culture that dominates all others economically and militarily. Rather must we—of the West—come to entertain seriously the possibility that we might learn *from* other cultures, just as we expect their members to learn from us.

Current debates about "Asian values" (supposedly Confucian-inspired) demonstrate this point vividly. In the West the expression "Asian values" is almost always used pejoratively, denoting a closed, authoritarian system as opposed to the open and liberal system of "Western values." It is not surprising that the debates are just that: debates. But what is needed if the peoples of this world are going to live more peaceably with each other in the twenty-first century than they have done in the twentieth are *dialogues,* not debates, and in order for the dialogues to be genuine, all sides must assume that they have something to learn from the other(s).

The present paper is a very small effort in that direction.[1] My major claim is that if we read carefully the texts of classical Confucianism in general, and the *Analects* in particular, we can all gain insights into the problem of constructing meaningful lives in a postmodern, postindustrial society very different from that of the agrarian China that birthed these texts over two millennia ago.

I believe this is a highly worthwhile endeavor, for two reasons: one sociopolitical, and the other religious. In the first place, the grinding poverty afflicting so many of the world's peoples today is contributing significantly to the growth of fanaticism among adherents of the several religious traditions to which the poor belong, a fanaticism that is straining the capacity for tolerance of "the Other" among those who seek a peaceful world. It thus seems important now to go beyond tolerance to understanding, beyond the fanatics to the great majority of the faithful in each tradition, asking: How could an altogether decent and intelligent human being hold political and religious views so different from mine? Only in this way, I believe, can we get beyond debate, and mere tolerance, to dialogue based on mutual understanding and appreciation of those with whom we must converse.

The second reason I wish to advance the Confucian persuasion herein is religious. All religions provide guidelines for leading not merely moral, but spiritually meaningful lives as well. There is much in the sacred texts of each religion that can speak to everyone. But once we get away from our own creed, understanding becomes more difficult, because the spiritual instructions offered in other religious traditions are often closely intertwined with a cosmological and/or theological orientation that is remote from our own, and very probably is incompatible with a number of pronouncements of modern science. Of course, the adherents of this other creed face the same problem(s) understanding our texts.

It is for this reason that Confucianism can offer lessons for everyone without insisting on faith, or conversion; none of those lessons require acceptance of any beliefs that fly in the face of physics or biology. In this sense, even atheists may read the Confucian canon with profit, learning how to live more meaningfully and usefully in *this* world, here, now.[2]

To begin with the *Book of Rituals*[3] (*Liji*), one of its chapters—the *Great Learning* (*Daxue*) conveys a religious message that is unique in its overall thrust. To find peace and dwell in the highest good, as defined in the philosophic and religious traditions of the West, it is not only necessary, but usually sufficient, to understand fully who we really are. "Know thyself!" Socrates teaches us, because "the unexamined life is not worth living."[4] And in the three great Abrahamic religions, our basic task is to know ourselves in relation to the God who created us and the world. But the *Great Learning* proffers different instructions:

> The ancients who wished to manifest their clear character to the world would first bring order to their states. Those who wished to bring order to their states would first regulate their families. Those who wished to regulate their families would first cultivate their personal lives. Those who wished to cultivate their personal lives would first rectify their minds. Those who wished to rectify their minds would first make their wills sincere. Those who wished to make their wills sincere would first extend their knowledge. The

extension of knowledge consists in the investigation of things. When things are investigated, knowledge is extended; when knowledge is extended, the will becomes sincere; when the will is sincere, the mind is rectified; when the mind is rectified, the personal life is cultivated; when the personal life is cultivated, the family will be regulated; when the family is regulated, the state will be in order; and when the state is in order, there will be peace throughout the world. From the Son of Heaven down to the common people, all must regard cultivation of the personal life as the root or foundation. There is never a case when the root is in disorder and yet the branches are in order. There has never been a case when what is treated with great importance becomes a matter of slight importance or what is treated with slight importance becomes a matter of great importance.

Note that explaining the world is not emphasized here, and looking inward and coming to know ourselves is more of a means than the end toward which we should strive. The ultimate goal is to augment "All under Heaven" (*tianxia*), which even granting the monocultural orientation of the authors of the text, may be fairly translated as "the world." And we are to do this by first steadily shrinking our perspectives and activities through the state, the clan, the family, and down to our own heart-mind (*xin*). But then we must expand our perspectives and activities until we encompass the world: true spiritual depth comes not from within but through active engagement in struggling for a decent life for everyone.

Moreover, while this passage should be read as providing moral instruction, it is also providing much more. Persons to whom the passage is addressed are not, in the first instance, free, autonomous, self-interested individuals who are being exhorted to become more altruistic; those are the readers and followers of Western philosophers and theologians. Rather are the readers of the *Great Learning* much more the sum of the roles they live (not "play") in society. They are children of their parents, parents of their children; grandparents too, perhaps, as well as aunts and uncles, nephews and nieces; they are friends, neighbors, students, teachers, and much more. It is relational persons, not autonomous individuals, who do the extending and investigating. The relationships are all reciprocal, and are best described as holding between benefactors and beneficiaries. Over time each of us will often go from one aspect of the relation to the other. When young I was beneficiary of my parents; when they became old I became the benefactor. I am similarly benefactor to my friend when she needs my help, beneficiary when I need hers.

The roles of children, parents, friends, neighbors, and so on, are obviously not unique to the Chinese people. All of us have stood and continue to stand in these roles, and consequently these instructions can be read as applying to *everyone*; they are universalistic. This may seem unusual at first, because of the widespread view, in both contemporary China and the West, that Confucianism is a *particularistic* belief system, and therefore can make no real claim to being a true moral or political theory, nor can it have any religious purchase in a postmodern global community.[5]

Worse, particularism, by definition, implies a relativism that all too easily can lead either to a sense of the superiority of our own particularity, or to a mindless tolerance for virtually any beliefs or behaviors whatsoever; seldom do we think seriously that we may learn from those distant from us in time, space, language, and culture, and consequently we are inclined to read the Confucian texts only for their antiquarian interest, or for what they might tell us about the contemporary Chinese, which would be akin to "eating the menu instead of the dinner."[6]

To be more specific, let us turn from the *Book of Rituals* to the Confucian *Analects*, asking what are the characteristics of, and relations between, the *shi, junzi,* and the *shengren* as they are found in the text. I translate *shi* as "scholar-apprentices," *junzi* as "exemplary persons," and *shengren* as "sages."[7] Toward each of these three kinds of persons Confucius and his disciples make only approbationary remarks. To be sure, the Master also speaks approvingly of other categories of persons as well: "great persons" (*da ren*), "good persons" (*shan ren*), "authoritative persons" (*ren ren*), and yet others, hence it may be asked why the former three have been isolated for examination. In the first place, there is some linguistic license for distinguishing the *shi, junzi,* and *shengren* from the others. Expressions such as *da ren, shan ren,* and so on, are made up of terms which in English function syntactically as modifiers and nouns respectively. In each case the modifying terms can and often do stand alone in other sentences in ancient Chinese. They can also serve other syntactic functions, and with the possible rare exception of *ren*, these modifiers can be used descriptively of things and abstractions as well as of human beings. The expressions *shi, junzi,* and *sheng ren,* on the other hand, exhibit different syntactic and semantic properties. *Shi* and *junzi* function only as names, not modifiers, and their reference can only be to persons. There are some exceptions to the first half of this generalization with regard to *sheng*. In the *Shijing* (*Book of Poetry*) *sheng* has the meaning of "wise" ("Mother was wise and good"; Mao 32), and there are several usages of *shengwang* in the classical texts. But these exceptions granted, *sheng* and *shengren* too are basically nouns, and compound nouns, referring only to people. If this be so, then the *shi, junzi,* and *shengren* should not be seen as examples of a particular virtue, or excellence, but rather as *kinds* of persons, persons with a multiplicity of integrated qualities.

All three of these expressions were in use before the time of Confucius. In the *Book of Poetry*, for example, the term *shi* is used for a man of middle social status, at other times for a retainer, and yet again to designate a servant. It also appeared to be the term for a lower-level functionary of a lord, perhaps a man of arms, somewhat akin to the old English knight (and Arthur Waley so translates the term.)[8] A *junzi* was a lord's son, or perhaps, as Peter Boodberg has argued, the bastard son of a lord.[9] The origin of the graph *sheng*, like *shi*, is unknown; in the *Book of Poetry* and the *Book of History* it seems to have, as noted above, the meaning of "very wise person."

Confucius appropriated all of these terms for his own use, giving them all connotations that shifted their sense and reference away from position, rank, birth, or function toward what we (not he) would term aesthetic, moral, and spiritual characteristics. It must be noted that as his disciples, and their disciples in turn, recorded what he said in the text that has come down to us as the *Analects*, Confucius never juxtaposes all three categories of persons. Thus it might well be argued that he himself did not link the *shi*, *junzi*, and *sheng ren* together progressively as will be done in what follows, and consequently it might further be argued in turn that I am interpolating too much, that I am reading my own, rather than the Master's views, into the text. To this criticism several replies can be made.

First, throughout the text *junzi* and *sheng ren* are used to designate exemplars, not mere holders of a station, political or otherwise. And as we shall see, they are ranked exemplars. 18:11 is only a partial exception to this generalization with respect to *shi*, but every other reference to *shi* in the *Analects*—especially the five in Book 4, the chapter closest to the time of Confucius himself [10]—also treats them as models, as exemplars to be emulated when they fulfill their obligations properly.

Second, a central tradition of Confucian thought is the necessity for each succeeding generation to reauthorize the texts, and only in this way to maintain the authority thereof. While textual scholarship was essential to Confucianism, following the letter of it quite often gave way to imbibing its spirit: in reviving the tradition and arguing against Buddhism a millennium later, the Song Dynasty Neo-Confucians invoked a number of concepts that were not found (or at least not interpreted) in the classical texts; but the Song thinkers were, for all that, nevertheless thoroughgoing Confucians.[11]

Still a third reason for the present attempt to reread the *Analects* in a contemporary context lies in the nature of the discipline of philosophy, difficulties with its definition notwithstanding. Thus, with all due respect for my archaeologically, historically, and/or philologically oriented colleagues, it is the task of the philosopher to ask what claim the ancient texts might have on our allegiance. Might what they say be true? Are there lessons to be learned from these texts today even if their authors—so different from us in time and space—did not consciously intend to teach them?[12]

With these (minimal) scholarly warrants for the present endeavor then, let us address the *Analects,* again, asking the question: What are the relationships between the *shi,* the *junzi,* and the *shengren?*

Twelve passages make reference to the *shi.* One of these (18:11) merely says that during the early Zhou period, four pairs of twins were *shi.* (They were all distinguished men.) In two other passages, the disciples Zigong and Zilu respectively ask about the qualities of the *shi.* To the first, Confucius answers:

> Those who conduct themselves with a sense of shame and who, when sent to distant quarters, do not disgrace the commission of their lord, deserve to be called *shi.* (13:20)

And he tells Zilu:

> Persons who are critical and demanding yet amicable can be called *shi.* They need to be critical and demanding with their friends, and amicable with their brothers. (13:28)

In another passage, Zizhang, asks how scholar-apprentices (*shi*) become prominent, and Confucius tells him:

> Those who are prominent are true in their basic disposition, and seek after what is most appropriate. They examine what is said, are keen observers of demeanor, and are thoughtful in deferring to others. (12:20)

These remarks suggest that the *shi* are indeed apprentices of some kind. They are to be formal, precise, polite, deferential. They have already extended their ways of relating to others, for in no passage of the *Analects* is *xiao*—filial piety—linked to the *shi.*

This reading of the *shi* is reinforced by Zizhang's description of them in the opening chapter of Book 19:

> Those *shi* are quite acceptable who on seeing danger are ready to put their lives on the line, who on seeing an opportunity for gain concern themselves with what is appropriate, who in performing sacrifices concern themselves with proper respect, and who in participating in a funeral concern themselves with grief.

Moreover, while the syntax of these passages, when rendered into English declarative sentences, suggests that the *shi* are being described, I believe they should be read rather as imperatives, as instructions for what the *shi* should *do* to become true *shi*. They have set out on a path (*dao*), but they still have a long way to go, and there is much yet to be done. As the senior disciple Zengzi says,

> The *shi* cannot but be strong and resolved, for they bear a heavy charge and their way (*dao*) is long. Where they take authoritative conduct (*ren*) as their charge, is it not a heavy one? And where their way ends only in death is it not indeed long? (8:7)

By describing the *shi* as those who have assumed the burden of authoritative conduct, or authoritativeness (*ren*), we get a hint that it is not only a moral apprenticeship the *shi* are serving, but a spiritual one as well, for the *ren* of Confucius is the highest and most encompassing of excellences, not radically different from the Socratic good. In another passage we see that the *shi* can be teachers (18:6), and in still another the *shi* are placed in conjunction with authoritative persons:

> The Master said, "For the resolute scholar-apprentice (*shi*) and the authoritative person (*ren ren*), while they would not compromise their authoritative conduct to save their lives, they might well give up their lives in order to achieve it." (15:9)

Further evidence that it is a spiritual as well as moral path the *shi* are following is found in two additional passages in which negative instructions are given, the thrust of which is to not take material well-being as a major goal.

> The Master said, "The *shi* who cherishes material comforts is not worthy of the name." (14:2)

And:

> The Master said, "The *shi* who, having set their purposes on walking the way (*dao*) are ashamed of rude clothing and coarse food, are not worth engaging in discussion." (4:9)

There are, of course, numerous other, positive instructions the Master proffers not only for the *shi* but for others as well: become steeped in poetry, and in history; study and practice rituals; listen to, play, become absorbed in good music; perform public service when it is appropriate to do so; above all—by engaging in all of these efforts—extend one's human sympathies beyond one's family, clan, and village, learn to become benefactor and beneficiary within ever-enlarging circles. Again, the *shi* are never instructed in the proper behavior and demeanor due their parents; they have already learned that filial piety is not confined to parental, or merely material needs:

> Zixia asked about filial conduct. The Master replied, "It all lies in showing the proper countenance. As for the young contributing their energies when there is work to be done, and deferring to elders when there is wine and food to be had—how can merely doing this be considered being filial?" (2:8)

If my reading of these passages has merit, it will follow that the major goal toward which the *shi* are striving is to reach a higher stage in life. And that stage must be to become a *junzi*,[13] who is the paradigmatic human exemplar for Confucius, being mentioned sixty-eight times in the *Analects*. A few examples:

> The Master said, "*Junzi* cherish their excellence; petty persons cherish their land. Exemplary persons (*junzi*) cherish fairness; petty persons cherish the thought of gain." (4:11)

> The Master said, "In the niceties of culture I am perhaps like other people. But as far as personally succeeding in living the life of the exemplary person (*junzi*), I have accomplished little." (7:33)

If the *shi* does, the *junzi* more nearly is. In the text, *junzi* are almost always described, not instructed. They have traveled a goodly distance along the way and live a goodly number of roles (5:16). Benefactors to many, they are still beneficiaries of others like themselves. While still capable of anger in the presence of evildoing, they are in their person tranquil (12:4). They know many rituals and much music and perform all of their functions not only with skill, but with grace, dignity, and beauty, and they take delight in the performances (12:8). Still filial toward parents and elders, they now work on behalf of others (12:16), especially the needy (6:4). Always proper in the conduct of their roles, that conduct is not forced, but rather effortless, spontaneous, creative. There is, in sum, a very strong aesthetic and ethical dimension to the life of a *junzi*, and a sense of the religious as well; they are indeed exemplars:

> Confucius said, "Exemplary persons (*junzi*) always keep nine things in mind: in looking they think about clarity, in hearing they think about acuity, in countenance they think about cordiality, in hearing and attitude they think about deference, in speaking they think about doing their utmost (*zhong*), in conducting affairs they think about due respect, in entertaining doubts they think about the proper questions to ask, in anger they think about regret, in sight of gain they think about what is appropriate conduct (*yi*). (16:10)

For most of us, the goal of *junzi* is the highest to which we can aspire. There is, however, an even loftier human goal, to become a *sheng*; but in the *Analects* it is a distant goal indeed. There are eight references to *sheng ren* in the text. In one passage Confucius dared not rank himself a *sheng* (7:33); in another he lamented that he never had, and probably never would, see one (7:25); and in still another he gently chastises Zigong when the latter likens him to a *sheng* (9:6). And later, even though Mencius allows that the man in the street can become a Yao or Shun (i.e., a *sheng*), he, too suggests strongly that this goal is beyond the reach of most mortals (6B:2).[14]

Yet the goal is there, and it is attainable. There are *sheng*. They have risen beyond the level of *junzi*, because 16:8 describes the *junzi* as those who stand in awe of the words of the *sheng*. From 6:28 we learn that one who confers benefits on, and assists everyone, is a *sheng*. Clearly such persons have extended their human feelings and thoughts to embrace the entire human race.

And finally, in 19:12, Zixia says that not even the *junzi*, but the *shengren* alone, are capable of uniting in themselves with that which comes first and that which comes last:

> Ziyou said, "The disciples and young friends of Zixia are quite all right when it comes to housekeeping, taking care of guests, and standing in attendance, but these are just the tips of the branches. What do you do about the fact that they have no roots?"

> Zixia heard about this, and responded, "Ah! Ziyou is mistaken! On the path (*dao*) of the *junzi*, what is passed on first and what must wait until maturity, can be compared to plants which must be nurtured differently according to kind. How can he so misrepresent the path of the *junzi*? And it is the *sheng ren* alone who walks this path every step from start to finish."

To summarize this brief reading of the qualities of, and relations between, the *shi*, *junzi*, and *sheng*: all *sheng* are *junzi*, and all *junzi* were formerly *shi*, but the converse does not hold. These are, in other words, ranked types of persons, and the ranking is based on a progression from scholarly apprenticeship to sagehood: *shi* are, relatively speaking, fairly numerous; *junzi* are more scarce, and *sheng* are very few and very far between, owing to "the heaviness of the burden, and the distance of the journey."

The *shi* have willed (*zhi*) to follow the *dao* as it is embodied in the *li*—customs, rituals, traditions—that govern the interpersonal relations definitive of the *shi's* several roles. The *shi* know some of the *li*, and are engaged in the ongoing activity of learning and practicing more, concomitant with the interactions appropriate to their new and continuing stations. Much farther along this learning and doing continuum we have the *junzi*, who know the *li* thoroughly enough to follow its spirit even in the absence of precedent; they perform their roles masterfully, and derive a deep satisfaction from the grace, dignity, effortlessness, and creativity with which they have come to conduct themselves with others, acquaintances and strangers no less than kin and neighbors.

And at the upper end of this continuum are the *sheng*. In addition to possessing all of the qualities of the *junzi*, the *sheng* appear to see and feel customs, rituals, and tradition—the *li*—holistically, as defining and integrating the whole of human society, and as defining and integrating as well the human societies of the past and of the future. This seeing and feeling can only be described in our terms (not Confucius's) as transcendent understanding, [15] the capacity to go beyond the particular time and place in which one lives, coming to a union not only with our contemporaries, but with all those who have preceded us, and all those who will follow; a union, in other words of self and all others, at-one-ment.

This reading of the *Analects* is, I believe, consistent with the *Mencius*, [16] and surely is with the *Xunzi*. To take only one brief quote from the "Discussion of Ritual" chapter, Xunzi says:

> Only the *sheng* fully comprehend the rituals, customs, and traditions (the *li*). The *junzi* are at ease in their performance, and the *shi* are careful to maintain them. [17]

If this interpretation can be sustained, and is at all faithful to the texts, it must follow that the charge of mere particularism against early Confucianism is woefully misplaced. Even the novice *shi*, while remaining rooted in specific duties, must nevertheless begin their trek along the Way by broadening their social horizons and interactions with others, and in doing so they cultivate the aesthetic, moral, and spiritual dimensions of their lives. A unique feature of the classical Confucian persuasion, I believe, is that spiritual self-cultivation *requires* others; it is overwhelmingly not a solitary exercise, as is outlined in the classical texts. Herbert Fingarette has stated the matter cogently: "For Confucius, unless there are at least two human beings, there are no human beings." [18]

Much more, of course, needs to be said about all of these matters, but if the universalism inherent in the tradition is brought to the fore, much more *can* be said about them. I believe it is altogether wrongheaded to suggest that Confucius did not have a strong sense of empathy with, and concept of humanity writ large, and if so, then perhaps he has much to say to us today.

All of the specific human relations of which we are a part, interacting with the dead as well as the living, will be mediated by the *li*, that is, the courtesy, customs, and traditions we come to share as our inextricably linked histories unfold, and by fulfilling the obligations defined by these roles and relationships we are, for early Confucians, following the human way (*dao*). It is a comprehensive Way. By the manner in which we interact with others our lives will clearly have a moral dimension infusing *all*, not just some, of our conduct. By the ways in which this ethical interpersonal conduct is effected with reciprocity and governed by civility, respect, affection, custom, ritual, and tradition, our lives will also have an aesthetic dimension for ourselves and for others. And by specifically meeting our defining traditional obligations to our elders and ancestors on the one hand, and to our contemporaries and descendants on the other, the early Confucians offer, again, an uncommon, but nevertheless spiritually authentic form of transcendence, a human capacity to go beyond the specific spatiotemporal circumstances in which we exist, giving our personhood the sense of humanity shared in common, and thereby a sense of strong continuity with what has gone before and what will come later. There being no question for the early Confucians of the meaning *of* life, we may nevertheless see that their view of what it is to be a human being provided for everyone to find meaning *in* life. The burden is indeed heavy, the Way indeed long; but the prize is great. If we are truly social beings, and if this is the only life we have to live, then it seems clear that the early Confucian texts can have much to say today as we continue the philosophical and religious search for answers to the question of how we should live our all-too-human lives, and why.[19]

Notes

[1] In other papers I have attempted to show that the texts of classical Confucianism can also make contributions to needed dialogues on other issues: human rights, democracy, freedom, social justice, and morality generally. See *Radical Confucianism* (Chicago/LaSalle, Ill.: Open Court Publishing, forthcoming 2004).

[2] A fuller account of these themes is in my *Rationality and Religious Experience* (Chicago/LaSalle, Ill.: Open Court Publishing, 2001).

[3] For most of the classical citations I have used the Taiwan reprint of the five-volume *Chinese Classics* of James Legge, with the *Daxue* and *Zhongyong* passages

taken from the 1962 Hong Kong reprint of his *The Four Books*. I have also used the 1977 Hong Kong edition of the *Shuowen Jiezi*, aided by the *Shuowen Da Zidian* (Tianjin, 1993). Axel Schuessler's *A Dictionary of Zhou Chinese* (Honolulu: University of Hawaii Press, 1987) has been very helpful, as has the venerable *Grammata Serica* of Bernhard Karlgren (Taipei, reprint of 1961), and the Harvard-Yenching Concordance Series. For the quotation from the *Great Learning*, see Wing-tsit Chan, *A Source Book in Chinese Philosophy* (New York: Columbia University Press, 1963), 86.

⁴ In the first quotation, Socrates is citing an inscription at the Oracle of Delphi in the *Phaedrus* 230a. The second is from the *Apology* 38a. Both are taken from E. Hamilton and H. Cairns, *Plato: Collected Dialogues* (New York: Pantheon Books, 1961), 23 and 478 respectively.

⁵ Of the Chinese in general, and Confucians in particular, Immanuel Kant had this to say:

Confucius teaches in his writings nothing outside a moral doctrine designed for princes ... and offers examples of other princes. ... But a concept of virtue and morality never entered the heads of the Chinese.

In order to arrive at an idea . . . of the good [certain] studies would be required, of which [the Chinese] know nothing.

(Cited by Julia Ching in "Chinese Ethics and Kant," in *Philosophy East and West* 28/2 [April 1978]: 169.) The distinguished China historian Joseph Levenson consigned Confucianism to the "dustbin of history" in his major work, *Confucian China and Its Modern Fate*, 3 volumes (Berkeley: University of California Press, 1960–1966). And a great many Chinese themselves condemned Confucianism, from the May 4th movement of 1919 through the intensive anti-Confucian campaigns of the second half of the "Great Proletarian Cultural Revolution" of 1966-1976. These are only three examples of modern dismissals of the Confucian vision; hundreds more could be given.

⁶ Alan Watts, *The Way of Zen* (New York: Pantheon Books, 1957), xi, paraphrasing a line from William James ". . . offering a printed bill of fare as the equivalent of a solid meal" (*The Varieties of Religious Experience* [Mineola, N.Y.: Dover reprint, 2002], 500).

⁷ I should have used the nonroyal "we" here. All translations from the *Analects* are jointly those of Roger Ames and myself (*The Analects of Confucius* [New York: Ballantine, 1998]). For deepening my understanding of Confucius, my debt to him is incalculable.

⁸ Arthur Waley, trans., *The Analects of Confucius* (Vintage Modern Library, n.d.) pp. 33-34.

⁹ Peter Boodberg, "The Semasiology of Some Primary Confucian Concepts," reprinted in *Selected Works of Peter A. Boodberg*, compiled by Alvin P. Cohen (Berkeley: University of California Press, 1979).

¹⁰ The dating of the several strata of the books of the *Analects* was a major goal of the translation of it by Bruce and Taeko Brooks (New York: Columbia Uni-

versity Press, 1998). While a number of their interpretations of the text are controversial, the book is a superb example of close textual and historical scholarship and should be consulted by everyone who has a serious interest in classical Confucianism.

[11] While long aware of the evolutionary nature of the history of Confucianism, I didn't appreciate fully its philosophical significance until reading Philip J. Ivanhoe's review of Kwong-loi Shun's translation of the *Mencius* in the *Journal of Asian Studies* 57, no. 3 (August 1998).

[12] Of course philosophers must be attentive to context, history, and philological issues when reading older texts, which is why I am so clearly indebted to my sinological colleagues who focus their research in these areas; but we continue to read Plato for his philosophical acumen, not merely to learn about ancient Greece. And while Confucius regularly affirmed his affection for what was old, we must also remember his words in 2:11: "Reviewing the old as a means of realizing the new— such a person can be considered a teacher."

[13] In his translation of the *Analects* (Harmondsworth: Penguin, 1979), D. C. Lau says "The *shi* is only the *junzi* who has taken office" (p. 229). I disagree with Lau only with reluctance, but he nowhere argues in support of this claim, nor does the text—especially Book 13—support his claim, in my opinion.

[14] As with the *Analects*, the *Mencius* does not link the *shi*, *junzi*, and *shengren* closely together in any passage. Most references to the *shi* are in 5B, and while *junzi* and *sheng ren* are also found in this section of the work, the relations (if any) between them is at least ambiguous. Xunzi explicitly links the three, and in the same rank order that I am arguing for herein, as my quotation from him below shows clearly.

[15] The term "transcendent" is used only in the sense given here. No ontological commitment should be inferred, for I endorse fully the arguments against an idea of a transcendental realm of being in ancient China made by David Hall and Roger Ames in their seminal *Thinking Through Confucius* (Albany: State University of New York Press, 1987), especially 158ff. and 267ff.

[16] See n. 14.

[17] Translation modified from *Hsun Tzu: Basic Writings*, trans. Burton Watson (New York: Columbia University Press, 1967), 110.

[18] Herbert Fingarette, "The Music of Humanity in the Conversations of Confucius," *Journal of Chinese Philosophy* 10 (1983): 217.

[19] For much of what may be of worth in this essay—but for none of what isn't— I am, in addition to those already mentioned in these notes, deeply indebted to a number of colleagues and friends. In the first instance I am grateful to Mary Evelyn Tucker and Tu Weiming for inviting me to participate in the Workshop on Confucian Spirituality held at Harvard in the summer of 1997, which led to the present volume. I am equally grateful for the perceptive insights of my draft paper by my commentator at the Workshop, Irene Bloom, and to David Keightley for equally perceptive comments on an earlier first draft read at a Berkeley colloquium in

1995. And last but not least, I am greatly indebted and grateful to Rosemary O'Connor, philosophy secretary at Trinity University, for the efficiency, grace, and warmth with which she turned my wretchedly scrawled handwritten pages into an elegant typescript, and to Heather Mitchell for the notes; a Luddite could ask for no more.

10

Ritual and Sacrifice in Early Confucianism: Contacts with the Spirit World

DEBORAH SOMMER

I N THE ACADEMIC STUDY OF RELIGION, the term "spirituality" has been used to describe such a wide variety of beliefs and practices that defining it with any precision, let alone applying it to early Chinese materials, is quite problematic. Nevertheless, in the following exploration of early Confucian spirituality, I first briefly explain how I understand the term "spirituality" in its Western usages and then survey ancient Chinese sources to consider whether there might exist some parallels to the notion of spirituality in early Confucian writings. Although the scope of this short article does not allow me to consider such issues as regional variations in belief or temporal shifts in ideas or to explore new archaeological finds, it will nevertheless provide the general reader with some materials for comparing early Chinese traditions with those described elsewhere in this series.

First, I must describe how I understand the notion of spirituality itself as it has been used in the academic study of religion. Although the term has been conceived in many ways in Western encounters with the divine ever since the letters of Paul, in more recent times it seems most closely associated, as I understand it, with such notions as belief in a realm of the spirit or spirits, a sense of devotion and piety, an appreciation of the "mystical" and the unknowable, a tendency toward asceticism, and a focus on the interior life that nevertheless incorporates an ethical imperative for enacting inner values in daily life.[1] With these criteria in mind, I have reviewed early Chinese materials and looked for religious beliefs and practices that might in some ways parallel these concerns. Did the early Chinese believe in the existence of a spirit world, and if so, how did they conceive of it? How did they respond to the perceived presence of divine or numinous powers and maintain relationships with those powers? Did they respond to the spirit realm with feelings of piety and devotion or with other sentiments altogether? Did notions akin to mysticism or asceticism—frequent synonyms of spirituality in the West since at least the eighteenth century—figure importantly, if at all, in early Chinese religious literature? What criteria informed the interior life, and how was that vision of life expressed in daily existence?

Second, I must describe how I understand the term "early Confucian." By "early" I mean primarily the Zhou period (ca. 1045–256 B.C.E., an era that is further divided into the Western Zhou, from about 1045 to 771 B.C.E., and the Eastern Zhou, from about 771 to 256 B.C.E.), especially the Eastern Zhou era, when Confucius (551–479 B.C.E.) and his contemporaries lived. By the term "Confucian" I mean the tradition of scholars, ritualists, or scholiasts (*ru*, the term often translated as "Confucian") who saw themselves as heirs to a heritage of sacred history recorded in classical documents. Some of the more important of these texts were the *Book of Changes* (*Yijing*, a divination handbook that dates to perhaps the ninth century B.C.E.); the *Book of History* (or *Shangshu*, a collection of orations by semihistorical figures from the Zhou era); the *Book of Odes* (*Shijing*, a collection of Shang and Zhou songs, hymns, and eulogies); the *Spring and Autumn Annals* (*Chunqiu*) and its commentarial text, the *Zuo Commentary* (*Zuozhuan*), a calendrical register of historical events and an interpretive commentary, respectively, of events in the state of Lu, Confucius's home region, from about 722 to 481 B.C.E.; the *Rites of Zhou* (*Zhouli*, a text that purports to describe the Zhou system of governance); and the *Book of Rites* (*Liji*), a description of late Zhou ritual perhaps not compiled until the early Han dynasty (206 B.C.E.-220 C.E.).[2] In addition to these texts are the works of such scholars as Mencius (fl. ca. 320 B.C.E.), Xunzi (b. ca. 335 B.C.E. and d. ca. 238 B.C.E.), and Confucius himself. I use the term "Confucian," then, in a very general sense to refer not just to the thought of Confucius and his immediate disciples but to a broad tradition of classical thought in ancient China.

Early Traditions of the Shang People

Before turning to the religious beliefs of the Zhou era, one might first consider the earlier traditions of the Shang people, who held political sovereignty in northern China from about 1500 to 1045 B.C.E. Shang religious culture was to be continued in some measure by Zhou successors, a people with whom the Shang were nevertheless very closely allied by marriage. The life, death, and afterlife of the single Shang figure Fu Hao (fl. ca. 1200

B.C.E.), a noted military leader who was one of the royal consorts of the Shang king Wu Ding, can serve as a focus for a brief survey of such Shang religious practices as divination and sacrifice.[3]

In life, Fu Hao directed the performance of sacrificial observances to spirits, beings that could influence the course of human events for good or ill. These were primarily spirits of deceased male and female ancestors, particularly ancestors of the ruling families. Fu Hao's military strategies, deliveries of royal children, and even toothaches prompted communications with the spirit world. Shang spirits, even ancestral spirits, were by no means necessarily kindly disposed toward their human supplicants; they might well cause misfortune. Ancestral spirits, besides intervening directly in human events, could also intervene on behalf of their descendants with a chief divinity, Di, the Lord or high god, a shadowy celestial power who had jurisdiction over agriculture, war, meteorological conditions, and other phenomena. Ancestral spirits were joined in the Shang pantheon by the powers of natural phenomena such as major rivers and mountain ranges.

Fu Hao's communications with the spirit world are recorded in divinatory inscriptions incised on cattle bones and tortoise shells. The tens of thousands of such "oracle bones" still extant that were created by Fu Hao and other Shang rulers suggest that the spirit world was consulted to diagnose the source and prognosticate the direction and outcome of virtually all aspects of human life: toothache, illness, childbirth, sacrifices, agricultural activities, military and hunting expeditions, the relocation of capital cities, meteorological phenomena, and so on.[4] Divination was a complex process that consisted generally of setting forth a problem, applying heat to prepared bones and shells, and then interpreting the problem based on the patterning of the resulting cracks. The issue at hand was inscribed on the bones and shells themselves. Some divinations were primarily diagnostic: Which ancestor is causing Fu Hao's toothache? Others were prognostic: Will the birth of Fu Hao's child or the outcome of her military expeditions be auspicious?[5] Still others were supplicatory or expiatory and indicated a reciprocal system of exchanges between humans and spirits: Will the sacrificial offering of a dog and a sheep cause so-and-so's toothache to go away?

But who, precisely, provided the answers to such questions? Was it the spirits, was it the process of divination itself, or was it, more likely, a combination of the two? And what do such divinations and sacrifices reveal of Shang "spirituality"? They clearly indicate a belief in a spirit world that could aid or harm, approve or reprove, the course of human events; there is little evidence, however, of a sense of piety, devotion, or other emotional response to the spirit world on the part of human beings. There is little evidence that humans desired to invoke spirits to draw nigh and manifest themselves more intimately so they might apprehend them directly. The efficacy of divinations and sacrifices was influenced perhaps by the quantity of the votive offerings of the sacrifices—the number and type of sacrificial victims, the timing of the offering or divination—rather than the tenor of the human sentiment purveyed. The laconic declarations of oracle bone inscriptions demonstrate that Shang rulers continually plumbed the spirit realm for clues for conducting human affairs, but they do not reveal how the Shang might have experienced encounters with the spiritual realm, let alone how they might have interpreted such encounters reflexively.

In death, Fu Hao was provided with a twenty-foot-long rectangular tomb (discovered only in 1976 near modern-day Anyang, Henan province) that was heavily provisioned for the life hereafter. The tomb contained over two thousand artifacts, ranging from a collection of over five hundred women's hairpins to a collection of axes, knives, and bows that attest to Fu Hao's military prowess. Over a dozen people and almost five hundred inscribed ritual bronze vessels accompanied her to the grave. These vessels conveyed the food offerings presented to Shang ancestors in sacrificial rituals. As an ancestral spirit herself, Fu Hao would have been expected to assist her own descendants, who would have commissioned bronze vessels in her honor. Directly above Fu Hao's grave are the remains of a rectangular pillared building that might have been used for rites that allowed her descendants to communicate with her spirit. The elaborate furnishings of Fu Hao's grave suggest that she was going to an afterlife state made more pleasant with the material goods the human world offered.

Religious Beliefs in the Zhou Period

Besides the short inscriptions on bone, shell, and bronze mentioned above, few texts are extant that could reveal much of the interior life of Shang "spirituality." Much more is known, however, of all aspects of the religious life of the succeeding Zhou culture, which, like the Shang, devoted a large percentage of its energies to communicating with the spirit world.[6] In the Zhou, as in the Shang, divination was one method that allowed humans to communicate with the unseen and to determine the future course of events. Diviners employed ox scapula, tortoise plastrons, and milfoil stalks for this purpose and also relied on the analysis of dreams. Divination handbooks such as the *Book of Changes* offered interpretive and reflexive models for explicating the results of divination. Moreover, divination was associated with moral behavior. According to the *Doctrine of the Mean* (a chapter of the *Book of Rites* that was eventually elevated to the status of an independent text), it was inner qualities rather than the interpretation of external signs that allowed one to foresee the future: the perfection of integrity gave one foreknowledge of events, and perfecting integrity transformed one into a spirit (*Mean* 22–24). Zhou texts, unlike their Shang predecessors on oracle-bone inscriptions, describe the spirit world in great detail and relate the human emotional, ethical, and religious response to the spirit realm with much greater self-consciousness and reflection.

As can be expected for an era that lasted for over seven hundred years, religious beliefs of the Zhou period exhibit a great variety of expression, and they were not subject to a uniform systematization. Understanding Zhou religious beliefs is complicated by the fact that almost all early Chinese texts are composite collections of documents compiled and reedited over many centuries; a text purporting to describe Zhou usages, for example, might not have existed in its extant form until the Former Han dynasty (206 B.C.E.–9 C.E.) or even later. Unfortunately, the following discussion is too brief to allow me to distinguish earlier Western Zhou usages from those of the later Eastern Zhou; as I have relied heavily on texts such as the *Book of Rites,* a later text, the reader should assume that most of what follows is more applicable to the later, rather than earlier, centuries of the Zhou era.

These caveats notwithstanding, one can nevertheless say with certainty that for the Zhou people, belief in a spirit world was a given assumption; maintaining relationships with spiritual beings was normative, not extraordinary. Textual evidence from the later Zhou also indicates the importance of maintaining relationships with the spirit world: the "ten norms" or "ten relationships" outlined in the *Book of Rites* place the normative principles for serving spirits at the head of its list, followed only secondarily by the norms for the proper comportment of rulers and ministers, parents and children, husband and wife, and so on ("Ji tong"; 28.245).[7] At all levels of society, from the ruler in charge of the highest sacrifices to the common person performing ancestral rites, interacting with spirits maintained the state, at one level, and maintained the family line, on another.

What was the character of the spirit world in the Zhou? In one cosmological schema, the world had two aspects: a visible (*ming*) realm and an invisible (*you*) realm. The visible or bright realm was the realm of perceived objects and was inhabited by human beings. The invisible, hidden, or dark realm, on the other hand, was the world of spirits; a vast unknown, its exact location was unspecified—although the qualities of darkness and obscurity were often associated with the north. Moreover, the north was the direction the dead faced. The spirit world was usually understood as being located high above, in Heaven (*tian*), as spirits most often descended when they manifested themselves. But the spirit world might also be understood not as another *place* but as another *dimension* that existed within this world, "embodied within things," as will be discussed below. This dimension could be invoked by anyone with the appropriate moral and emotional perspectives. Another cosmological schema described a tripartite universe of Heaven and its spirits, the human realm and its ghosts, and the earth and its terrestrial powers. These latter powers (*chi*) abided in the earth as autochthonous forces that welled up from within it.

What was the nature of the spiritual beings and supranormal powers humans encountered? Such phenomena, elusive and vague by nature, can be described with no great precision in any religious tradition, and no unified pantheon or categorization of spiritual powers existed in China throughout antiquity. Nevertheless, one can note that some of the more important kinds of numina in early times were Heaven and earth (*di*), spirits (*shen*), ghosts (*gui*), and wraiths (*li*). Human beings themselves were possessed of numinous aspects that allowed them to communicate with spiritual beings and eventually become spirits after death: these aspects were spirit (*shen*) itself, the vital energy (*qi*), and refined essence (*jing*). Moreover, a person had a numinous aspect called the *hun*, or cloud "soul," another phenomenon called the *po*, or material "soul," an ethereal aspect of the physical frame. These various "types" of religious phenomena, which I describe further below, are the results of my attempts to summarize materials for the general reader, but they should not be understood as entities with discrete ontological distinctions. Such ephemeral creations of the religious imagination, by their very nature, defy description and classification, and they were understood imperfectly and described elusively. The worlds of humans and spirits, nonetheless, were contiguous and the boundaries between them permeable; the realms overlapped, and it is by virtue of their commonality that humans and spirits could communicate with one another.[8]

The most powerful numina for the Zhou was Heaven, which was often identified with the Lord on High (*Shangdi*) in the compound "August Heaven, the Lord on High" (*Hao tian Shangdi*). The exact relationship between Heaven and the Lord on High is unclear; just as the Christian God of the Old Testament comprised a number of characteristics of divinities from several Near Eastern traditions, the Zhou Heaven/Lord on High was also probably a composite figure. Heaven was sometimes a place or a dimension where spirits reside: references to "Heaven's spirits" were common in early literature. Heaven was also a supreme divine authority and is described in terms that range from the anthropomorphic to the highly abstract. Like the Di, or Lord, of the Shang dynasty, the Heaven of the

Zhou period purveyed military expeditions, agricultural productivity, and meteorological phenomena and intervened actively in human affairs. The Zhou Heaven was, moreover, possessed of moral judgment and usually responded favorably to human rulers in direct proportion to the latter's virtue (*de*) and integrity, or sincerity (*cheng*).

Nevertheless, Heaven's powers were viewed with no little ambiguity by its human subjects. On the one hand, Heaven's perceptions of human affairs mirrored the people's own: it saw as the people saw, heard as the people heard, and shared an empathetic correspondence with them. The people, for their part, responded to Heaven with feelings of reverence, piety, respect, and awe; Heaven bestowed such pious supplicants with blessings and good fortune. On the other hand, Heaven could also act arbitrarily, causing famine, death, and destruction. In the *Book of Odes,* for example, the verse "The Great Fields" relates how the king as liturgist laments that he has served the spirit world diligently with sacrificial offerings and tendered it all due reverence and respect, yet a great drought has nevertheless set upon the land and created severe famine. He appeals to Heaven, the Lord on High, Hou Ji (a culture hero who developed agriculture), the spirits of past officials, and all other powers above and below, but in the end he receives no assistance and awaits death (*Book of Odes,* ode no. 258). Hence it is no surprise that in earlier Zhou texts a common human attitude toward Heaven was one of fear in the face of its awesome powers. In some later Zhou philosophical texts, however, Heaven becomes less threatening and is understood as a more generative force.

Much has been said about early Confucian attitudes toward Heaven, but less has been said about earth (*di,* a character different from the Shang divinity Di); the earth-based aspects of Confucian spirituality, however, should not be undervalued. Heaven and earth were very frequently mentioned as a pair, but whereas Heaven could be willful in its disposition of famine and death, earth was almost always nurturing and sustaining. Earthly powers were revered at several levels. At the state level, earth received sacrifices second in importance only to those of Heaven. At state, regional, and local levels, regular ritual offerings were made to the *she,* or powers of the land, and the *ji,* the powers of growing crops. Matters of state importance were announced to the spirit world at the *she* altars of the land, and the life of a state was closely bound to the activity of the sacrificial offerings presented there; when sacrifices were no longer offered at the altars of the land, the state was considered virtually extinct. Besides the *chi* terrestrial powers mentioned above, the Zhou people perceived mountains peaks, ridges, hills, and other geologic formations as spirits and gave them offerings called Distant (*wang*) sacrifices.

The term spirit, or *shen,* refers to the numinous aspect of a human being or of some power of nature. For the purposes of discussion, spirits can be described in terms of several large categories: (1) spirits of natural powers that were never once human beings, and (2) spirits of once-living human beings. This second category can be further divided into two groups: (a) the spirits of culture heroes or other people who have made a contribution to humanity, and (b) ancestral spirits, which were given sacrificial offerings by blood descendants. This latter practice is sometimes called "ancestor worship" in Western literature.

Apart from the powers of the earth itself, the powers of natural phenomena that provided humans with useful material resources were revered as spirits and were presented with sacrificial offerings of votive gifts to express sentiments of thanksgiving. In addition to the mountains and hills noted above, the sun, moon, stars, planets, cold and heat, rain, forests, rivers, lakes, and other natural phenomena—even the spirits of cats who killed crop-eating vermin—received sacrifices. So many spirits were worthy of one's attentions that a rite called the Encompassing (*bian*) sacrifice was formulated to thank a whole host of miscellaneous minor spirits who might have otherwise escaped one's attentions.

In addition to revering natural powers, the early Chinese also revered the spirits of once-living human beings such as legendary culture heroes, virtuous rulers and officials, and teachers whose benefits to other people in their own lifetime extended beyond their own kin groups. These latter were in a sense "public" spirits who could be worshiped by people not related to them. These people were usually higher-ranking appointed officials whose authority, like that of the spirits, extended beyond their own kin. Spirits of this kind could intercede with higher powers on behalf of human supplicants. The *Book of Rites,* for example, recommended that each district conduct offerings to pray for rain to the spirits of past officials and ministers who benefited the people ("Yue ling"; 27.274).

Whereas only officials could communicate with these public spirits, anyone could communicate with the spirits of their own ancestors. The transformation from human being into ancestral spirit was not entirely clear in ancient times, and even Confucius's disciples were puzzled on this matter. One passage in the *Book of Rites,* here narrated as if spoken by Confucius, offers one explanation of the relationship between the spirit, the ghost, the cloud and material souls, the vital energy, and refined essence ("Ji yi"; 28.220). One disciple wanted to know what the terms "ghost" and "spirit" actually meant. Confucius granted that this was a difficult question. He explained that vital energy was a burgeoning of the spirit; the cloud soul, a burgeoning of the ghostly aspect. When things died, as they inevitably must, they returned to the soil, and what returned to the soil was the ghost. Flesh and bones rotted away and went back to the land, but vital energy, however, shot forth in a great whoosh, rising upward as a shining brightness, soughing sadly. This latter phenomena, Confucius stated, constituted the refined essences of things and was the manifestation of the spirit.

The material soul went downward, but the vital energy went upward. This latter was sometimes called the "intelligent vital energy" (zhiqi), so it was thought to have some kind of awareness (Rites, "Li yun"; 27.369).[9] The bones and flesh returned to the soil, and it was said that when people died, they were called ghosts (Rites, "Ji fa"; 28.203). But the cloud soul and vital energy, however, could go anywhere (Rites, "Tan gong xia"; 27.193). As soon as someone died, relatives and friends went to a high place to call the cloud soul back to its old "abode" (the physical body), waving or wearing articles of clothing once belonging to the deceased. This rite was performed by religious professionals called wu, who functioned as priests but who are often called shamans. The poem "Summoning the Cloud Soul" (Zhaohun) from about the third century B.C.E. describes in lyric imagery how Priest Yang performs a dream divination and tries to summon back the soul of a person on the verge of death. He implores the soul to avoid the dangers of the perilous regions to the north, south, east, west, zenith, and nadir and to return to the center, his old abode, where his descendants have prepared elaborate festivities in his honor.[10]

Not all people successfully completed the transformation into an ancestral spirit at death. Those who did not became wraiths, or li, the specters of persons who died premature or violent deaths and wandered dangerously about the human realm. According to one account in the Zuo Commentary, the cloud and material souls one was endowed with at birth interacted with things during one's lifetime such that their refined essences multiplied and became stronger. Over time, they became spirits and became numinous. When ordinary people died violently, they could travel wildly as wraiths liable to injure or murder others. If they were accorded a spirit place (shenwei) at which they could receive sacrifices, however, they would be given a sense of direction, have a home to which they could return, and would not become wraiths (Zuo Commentary, Duke Zhao 7). Powers that did not receive the proper respect from the human world could thus become malevolent forces, and hence altars for wraiths were established at the state, regional, and local levels.

Spirits of all kinds, under most circumstances, were invisible and could not be apprehended with ordinary senses; the affairs of high Heaven, where the spirits abided, had neither sound nor smell (Odes no. 235 and Mean 23.6). How, then, could one detect their presence? They were experienced as a mysterious floodlike wave that hovered just above and around the head of the sacrificer (*Mean* 16.3). The manifestation of spirits was frequently described as unfathomable (*Mean* 16.4 and *Odes* no. 256) or, one might say, ineffable, to employ a term from William James's discussion of the qualities of mystical experience. Directly experiencing the unfathomable through the invocation of spiritual beings was one of the desired goals of performing sacrificial offerings and constitutes one of the primary kinds of religious experience in early literati texts. This experience was not engaged in solely for the aesthetic, personal, or spiritual delectation of the sacrificer, however, but was a means to the larger ends of seeking blessings for the family, the region, or the state.

Confucius was noted for sacrificing to spirits as if they were actually present with him (*Analects* 3:12), and in the *Doctrine of the Mean* his response to the manifestation of spirits offers some insight into later Zhou religious experience:

> How ghosts and spirits are possessed of virtue is truly marvelous. One looks for them and they cannot be seen; one listens for them but they cannot be heard. They are embodied in things but leave no traces. They cause everyone in the world to observe vigils and purify themselves, dress in their richest attire, and present sacrificial offerings. Then the spirits seem to float just above the heads of the sacrificers, all around them. As it is said in the *Book of Odes*, "The approaches of the spirits are unfathomable. How could one be unmoved by this?" [ode no. 256]. So it is said that what can barely be detected becomes evident, and that integrity cannot be kept concealed. (*Mean* 16.1–5)

Communicating with these virtuous spirits, which were embodied in all things but could not be apprehended by the senses, was thus a profoundly moving experience. One term commonly used to describe the invocation of spirits was *gan*, which meant to feel favorably toward someone or something, to arouse emotively, or to bestir a response; and *gan'ge*, which meant to invoke something to draw near.

Anyone might communicate with their own ancestral spirits, but only humans of appropriately high rank might communicate with those higher powers with whom they had no blood relations. Human sacrificers were required to be of the same class and kind as the spirit to whom they offered sacrifice, for otherwise the spirits would not accept the votive gift (*Zuo Commentary*, Duke Xi 31). In the case of state sacrifices that were not ancestral rites, sacrificers had to be of the same hierarchical status as the spirit to whom they presented offerings. Only persons who held statewide authority could address spirits of the highest importance; persons who held regional authority could address spirits of similar rank. The Son of Heaven could sacrifice to Heaven and earth; his vassal lords could sacrifice to the spirits of mountains and rivers and to the spirits of the land and grain within their domains; the great officers sacrificed to the Five Sacrificials, which were sacred or powerful locations within the household compound (variously described as the roof or the eaves, the well, the corridors, the gates, the walkways, and the hearth). Ordinary people sacrificed to their own ancestors. Transgressing these rules and presenting votive offerings to spirits with whom one had no appropriate relationship would bring no blessings and was perceived as iniquitous toadying with the spirit world (*Analects* 2:24), which was morally reprehensible (*Analects* 3:6).

What was the ritual context for communicating with the spirit world? Although rites were formulated by sages, rituals were not arbitrary creations but were based on Heaven and earth itself; they were offered for ghosts and spirits (*Rites*, "Li yun"; 27.367). It was often said that in the visible world, there are rites and music; in the invisible world, there are ghosts and spirits (*Rites*, "Yue ji"; 28.99). Communication between the two worlds could be effected during the presentation of votive offerings, or sacrificial offerings, which were set forth as gifts to recompense the blessings received from spiritual powers. With sacrificial offerings, one could pray for future boons, give thanks for favors already received, or ward off potential baneful influences (*Rites*, "Jiao te sheng"; 27.448). Spirits could sometimes grant these boons on their own authority, although in other instances they appealed to higher powers, such as the Lord on High or Heaven.

Sacrificial offerings consisted of quantities of food and drink presented in precious bronze vessels that were themselves works of art and insignia of social and political power; they were inscribed with invocatory liturgies that created alliances between the human and spirit world.[11] Food offerings were often accompanied by dances and pantomimes and were always accompanied by music. It was such performance arts—which offered much to the senses of sight, smell, sound, taste, and touch in the visible world—that, almost paradoxically, were intended to invoke the presence of spiritual beings from the realm of the intangible. Spirits were attracted to the smell of the viands and came to partake of it. When their presence was invoked, they descended and perched like birds near the offerings at the spirit places set aside for them.

Several types of votive offerings were common in early times. One of the primary food offerings was the meat of domestic livestock.[12] A sacrifice of one ox, one hog, and one sheep was one of the greatest of votive gifts. The meat was sometimes given as a burnt offering, in which case it would disappear as smoke (so the spirits could consume the vital energy of the victim), but it was also commonly consumed after the ritual by the people in attendance. The participants enjoyed the cuts of meat appropriate to their social ranking; higher ranking people ate first and ate best. Sacrificial animals were often consumed as food, but others were drowned (as in sacrifices to the spirits of bodies of water) or buried (as were some offerings to terrestrial divinities). Human sacrifices were not prescribed in the Zhou ritual documents, but the archaeological record indicates that such sacrifices were performed at least until the third century B.C.E. Spirits were given precious objects of jade and silk as well as consumable foodstuffs. The votive gifts of sacrificial offerings sustained a wide net of reciprocal obligations and maintained a highly elaborate system of exchange between the hidden and visible worlds. It was incumbent on human sacrificers to set forth offerings that were timely and appropriate in size and quantity; moreover, they had to be presented with the proper attitudes of pious reverence, devotion, gratitude, and respect.

Votive or sacrificial offerings were performed to serve the spirits, much in the same way that a person of lesser social ranking served his or her superiors. Hence, in one sense spirits were superior to human beings, who owed them obligations and debts of gratitude. But in the human world, debts between superiors and inferiors worked both ways, and the same principle informed the relations between spirits and humans: spirits also were dependent on humans for their sustenance and relied upon them for their existence. Human beings hosted the spirits as invited guests and tried to please them with succulent food offerings in the hopes that the spirits would repay them with blessings.

A favorable response from a spiritual being always required that the sacrificer first adhere to a strict code of ethics, develop nearly heroic virtue, and be concerned for others. Confucius's statement above, "So it is said that what can barely be detected becomes evident, and that integrity cannot be concealed" draws a parallel between the manifestation of invisible spirits and the revealing of the intangible quality of integrity. This revealing, or "revelation," if it could be called that, was a manifestation both of numinous presences (in the spirit world) and of human virtues (in this world), for only when the sacrificer had the virtue of integrity would spirits appear.

In fact, some early texts described spirits as the perfection of human virtues. Mencius, who otherwise talked little of the spirit world, explained spirits as people who were sagelike beyond ordinary understanding; they were people who had developed goodness and trust and who could transform others (*Mencius* 7B:25.7–8). In the *Doctrine of the Mean*, spirits were described as people who perfected the moral virtue of integrity (*Mean* 22–24). Whether these people were still-living human beings or were lately deceased is unclear; the fact that such criteria are not mentioned suggests that it is perhaps irrelevant. Entering the spiritual dimension, either in life or through death, was a liminal state that allowed access to both the visible and invisible worlds.

Spirits were just and morally upright by nature, and humans who desired to communicate with them were required to be equally virtuous. Spirits were not duplicitous but always acted according to unified constant principles; moreover, they were possessed of intelligence (*Zuo Commentary*, Duke Zhuang 32). Humans who ventured to invoke spirits were required to be persons of complete integrity (*History*, "Counsels of the Great Yu"). Spirits were under no imperative to accept all sacrifices, and they accepted only those proffered by persons of great integrity (*History*, "Tai Jia," Part 2). Although spirits were given food offerings, some argued that it was the scent of virtue that attracted spirits, not merely the scent of the steamed millet (*Zuo Commentary*, Duke Xi 5).

Spirits hearkened only to people of upstanding character who understood how to relate to other human beings. They listened to the entreaties of people who knew how to make friends, and they granted such people harmony and peace (*Odes* no. 165). Spirits admired sacrificers who were careful, circumspect, and paid attention to detail, and they rewarded such people with longevity (*Odes* no. 209). Managing the responsibilities of one's official position and associating with upright and straightforward colleagues ensured that spirits would grant one favors (*Odes* no. 207). One of the most famous examples of human virtues was the culture hero and legendary ruler Shun, who was noted for his sagacity, modesty, sense of order and organization, righteousness, reverence, and extreme filial piety. No doubt it was such qualities that fitted him for his task of giving order to the ritual system for sacrificing to spirits (*History*, "Canon of Shun"). King Wen (reigned until 1050 B.C.E.), another sage ruler from high antiquity, impressed spirits by following the precedents set by his ancestors (*Odes* no. 240); descendants who modeled themselves after King Wen could then expect that he in turn would descend to accept their offerings (*Odes* no. 272).

Human responses to communication with spirits had emotional resonances. In an answer to his disciple about the meaning of the terms "ghost" and "spirit," Confucius noted that such encounters elicited sentiments of gratitude and harmony. The sages, he stated, formulated the rites of burnt offerings to offer thanksgiving to the vital energy. This, he said, taught people that they should ponder their own ancestral origins and feel gratitude for those who gave them life. The sages also presented offerings of sweetbreads and entrails to the material soul; this was to teach people to love one another and to show that superiors and inferiors should care for one another (*Rites,* "Ji yi"; 28.222). The ideal human response to encounters with spirits, then, was an attitude of thanksgiving, a sense of obligation, and a heightened feeling of compassion for others. Gratitude was expressed through presenting votive gifts of foodstuffs and precious commodities.

As votive offerings to spirits were almost always communal rites, they engendered religious experiences far different from those of the solitary spiritual journeys of some other traditions. Confucian interactions with the spirit world enhanced the awareness that one was part of a larger network of human beings, natural phenomena, and supernatural phenomena to whom one owed reciprocal obligations; distant indeed from the eremitic spiritual practices of some kinds of monasticism in other traditions, the votive rites of the Confucian tradition kept the world in motion and were one of the primary vehicles of governance. Confucian spirituality was not an experience of escape from the mundane world, but on the other hand was an experience of connection and communication with people and beneficent forces both seen and unseen. At the highest levels of state, maintaining this network of obligations was the responsibility of rulers and officials who must have spent vast amounts of time, energy, and resources communicating with spirits on behalf of the people. Classical texts noted that presenting votive offerings to spiritual beings was one of the most important methods of governance; how this was accomplished, however, was actually something of a mystery, even to Confucius himself, who once noted that for anyone who understood the meaning of the major sacrifices, running the world would be as easy as looking at the palm of one's hand (*Analects* 3:11).

Communicating with the invisible world in commemorative rites to deceased ancestors and other spirits was not a casual procedure but required adherence to strict observances. As Confucius noted above, humans prepared to stand in the presence of the invisible by transforming themselves internally with vigils of purification and by transforming themselves externally with elaborate costuming and ritual. Descendants performing ancestral sacrifices approached the preparation of sacrificial offerings with emotional hypervigilance and performed them with the expectations of heightened sentiments of filial piety, reverence, devotion, joy, equanimity, and attentiveness. Sacrificers first performed preparatory vigils that required withdrawing from the sensory world, maintaining taboos regarding inauspicious things, and focusing the attentions toward the development of a pure inner virtue. This might be said to be a temporary removal from the visible realm in preparation for access to the invisible realm. These vigils of ordering and stabilization lasted for up to ten days, after which one could then communicate with spirits and numinous powers (*Rites*, "Ji tong"; 28.240). Confucius himself was noted for being extremely circumspect about the conduct of presacrificial vigils. He observed them by wearing immaculately clean clothing, by altering his diet and eating only soup and vegetables, and by moving from the place where he commonly sat (*Analects* 7:12, 10:7, and 10:8, 10). He thus removed himself from everyday existence in preparation for access to another dimension.

After the preparatory vigils, the actual rites of the sacrifices to the ancestral spirits began. Preparing the great varieties of foodstuffs and paraphernalia employed in the rites involved focus, concentration, and organization. But within all the complexity of the elaborate preparations, sacrificers then focused themselves on carrying out the rites in a state of vacuity (*xu*), a mind empty of other concerns. They demonstrated their filial devotion with the gravity with which they performed the presentations of votive gifts. In a state of what might be called mystical apprehension, or *huanghu* (literally, of being tenuous and indistinct), they communicated with the spiritual and numinous (*Rites,* "Ji yi"; 28.214). This state has been variously glossed as a condition of deep thought and concentration; a state of destabilized agitation, apprehension, and confusion; a formless state; and a state midway between existence and nonexistence.

One might compare the expression I have translated as "mystical apprehension"—the state of experiencing the tenuous and indistinct—to the appearance of the same expression in the *Daodejing*, or *Classic of the Way and of Virtue*, where the terms "tenuous" and "indistinct" refer to the qualities of the Dao itself.

> As a thing, the Dao
> Is tenuous, indistinct.
> Tenuous and indistinct,
> Yet within it are images.
> Tenuous and indistinct,
> Yet within it are things.
> (*Daodejing* 21, following D.C. Lau's translation)

The liminality of the experience of the Dao, which moves between the indistinct tenuity and the imaged thing, here in the *Daodejing* shares the same vocabulary as the liminal experience of the spirit world in Confucian sacrificial offerings, where communication between the visible and hidden worlds takes place. One does not want to make too much of a few passages, but when much secondary literature characterizes so-called Daoism as mystical otherworldliness and Confucianism as pragmatic secular humanism, it is important to note that texts from purportedly different traditions share unexpected commonalities.

Just as the *Daodejing*'s tenuity and obscurity enveloped images within it, so did the hidden realm of the ancestral spirits reveal images to the descendant who presented sacrifices. In most cases, spirits were not visible, but sacrificers who prepared themselves properly in presacrificial vigils could see the ancestral spirit to whom they were presenting votive gifts. After first undergoing the reversal of ordinary states of perception by removing themselves from the sensible world, sacrificers could then enter the "reverse dimension" of spirits. Vigils entailed a cognitive exercise that involved thinking about the deceased and remembering what they looked and sounded like, how they sighed and how they laughed, and by recalling those things that pleased the departed. The sacrificer became very involved in the emotional life of the deceased, and the memory of those emotive states helped trigger the responsive invocation of the spirit. On the third day of such preparations, the sacrificer saw the deceased and heard his or her voice (*Rites,* "Ji yi"; 28.211). The aim of these preparations was primarily to enhance the sacrificer's reverent devotion and sentiments of filial love toward the departed ancestor; the practitioner sought no gnosis, no intellectual perfection, and no personal benefits from these meditative vigils.

This direct experience of spirits can perhaps be understood as openness to a transcendent dimension. Yet this transcendent dimension was none other than the realm of the spirits of one's own ancestors, people with whom one possessed a connection of flesh and blood. Such a transcendent dimension could never be "wholly other," Rudolf Otto's *ganz andere,* for in fact it was necessary for some semblance of commonality to exist between spirit and sacrificer for the communication between the worlds to take place, as will be discussed below.[13] The spiritual direction one took was to turn back to one's own beginnings and primal ancestral roots: votive offerings enjoined one to recompense the source of one's own origins and turn again toward the beginning (*bao ben fanshi*). Seen in light of Mircea Eliade's notion of sacred time, this original time was infinitely repeatable and infinitely recoverable in the commemorative sacrifices to ancestral spirits.[14] The human community (the clan or the state) shaped by the hierophany of this sacred time was joined more firmly together by the sentiments of unity, mutual reverence and respect, and filial devotion.

The spiritual direction followed in the communication with spiritual beings was not an upward ascent toward the heavens, or onward into a utopian future, but backward toward those people and natural phenomena that had supported one's own life, and inward into one's own memories of, and feelings for, the deceased. Such a direction encouraged a sense of humility and an awareness of one's own mortality. The spiritual goals of these communications with spirits were to develop the social and familial virtues of reverence, filiality, devotion, and a sense of responsibility. Such spirituality had meaning only within the context of the family and was performed for the future benefit of the clan. A lone spiritual journey would have been meaningless in this tradition; one would have had no spirits with whom one might communicate.

In funerary rites, one knew almost immediately whether the ancestral spirits were happy with the offering because it was announced by the personator (sometimes called the impersonator) of the deceased. The personator was ideally a grandchild of the deceased, who might be so young that he or she was carried in someone's arms during the rites; the personator temporarily assumed the identity of the departed. High ministers, however, sometimes acted as personators upon the deaths of their rulers. As part of the funerary sacrificial offerings, the personator was feasted and entertained and was treated as if he or she was, for all intents and purposes, the dead relative. Generational ranking was temporarily inverted and senior relatives now paid their respects to a junior member of the family. One of the desired goals of these rites was to encourage the personator/ spirit to enjoy the food and drink proffered by the pious descendants. Provided the spirit was happy, he or she would then bestow blessings of longevity, good wives (for this was a primarily male audience), and a line of descendants that would prosper for tens of thousands of years to come (*Odes* nos. 247 and 248). This blessing was announced by the personator as a benediction at the end of the feast.

It is unlikely that this usage could be described as a kind of spirit possession; no suggestion of trance is indicated by the texts, and one could hardly expect a toddler (in the event of a very young personator) to experience an altered state of consciousness. Personators did not enter an ecstatic or dionysian state, for they are most often described as models of decorous and sedate posture. It seemed enough that the descendants considered the personator actually to be the deceased and that they acted for a brief time as if that were so. The primary "religious experience" of the personator/spirit seems to have been one of pleasurable gustatory enjoyment and of happiness at seeing the filial devotion, careful cooperation, and pious awe of descendants who had taken such pains to present delicious food and drink. One might see this as a performative ritual in which, at a rupture in the descent line caused by death, the cardinal virtues of harmony and filial piety are reestablished in the dramaturgy of communal role playing—in a community that included both the living and the dead. Through the liminal character of the personator, the transition of one member of the visible realm into the invisible realm was temporarily made manifest.

Mourning practices for recently deceased ancestors entailed a period of ascetic withdrawal from daily life, and this period could last several years, depending on the closeness of the kin relationship between the newly departed and the descendant. Fasting practices were quite extreme: descendants would perhaps not drink water or other liquids for several days at a time, although people who might otherwise fast until their bones showed or their hearing and sight were impaired were warned not to do so (*Rites*, "Tan gong," 27.133; "Qu li," 27.87). Speaking as well as eating was restricted. The ruler Wu Ding, for example, was in mourning for three years, and even at the end of that period did not speak but looked for an administrator who could speak for him (*History*, "Charge to Yue," Part 1). Mourning customs, while severe, nevertheless had a transformative moral dimension, as is revealed by the case of a profligate and irresponsible young prince who was admonished to live near the physical remains of his late father; at the end of the mourning period, the prince emerged a man of virtue (*History*, "Tai Jia," Part 1).

In many cases, serving the spirits was a responsibility that befell one because of one's position in the government (performing sacrifices was one of the most important aspects of governance) or in the family; such rites were not necessarily performed by experts, such as members of a hereditary priesthood, for example. But many kinds of religious professionals did specialize in communicating with spirits. The *Rites of Zhou*, a text that purports to outline the ritual system of Zhou times, describes an elaborate system of specialists whose professional function was to commune with the spirit world—ministers and stewards of rites, male and female invocators, priests and priestesses (*wu*, often called shamans and shamanesses), healers, exorcists, and diviners of tortoise shells, milfoil stalks, and dreams.

This text does not, however, describe the religious experience or the "spirituality" of these professionals. Whereas one can learn that the priests, for example, were responsible for dancing at the prayers for rain, exorcising baneful influences with peach wands, healing victims of illness, and performing other rites, one cannot determine their emotional or spiritual state when they were conducting rituals. Priests were praised by Confucius and Mencius, as I note below, for their stability and concern for human welfare, but one has difficulty ascertaining just how the priests communicated with the spirit world. Did they enter ecstatic trances when they danced the rain sacrifice? One cannot say with certainty whether their dancing was any more ecstatic than that of descendants who performed pantomimed dances at ancestral rites. Did their souls temporarily leave their bodies and venture off into other realms? Even the "Summons of the Soul" mentioned above, for all its lyric descriptions of the cosmography of the dead, tells us virtually nothing of Priest Yang's spiritual experience or even of his religious techniques, other than his recitation of invocatory verses. One can much more readily ascertain the spiritual life of religious nonprofessionals—the ordinary descendant who experienced vacuity and mystical apprehension at ancestral sacrifices—than of professionals.[15]

Priest Yang's lyric invocations aside, most communication with spirits, whether performed by professionals or laity, commonly took the form of such oral and written communications as sacrificial announcements (gao) or prayers (qi). Just as ministers kept rulers informed of events in their own regions, so did rulers inform the spirits of major events in the human realm by making announcements to them of such occasions as a new accession to the throne, the establishment of a new city, the presentation of new enfeoffments to vassal lords, or the commencement of military maneuvers. Humans were accountable to the spirit world for their actions (History, "Announcement of Tang").

In sacrificial reports, usually no boon was asked of the spirits, but in prayers of supplication it was. One could ask for timely rain or for offspring, and one could request anything that was for the common good or the good of the family. Personal requests for purely selfish ends, however, were not acceptable. Any ranking official could present prayers, although religious professionals also came into play: the chief priest led prayers for rain; the priestess chanted cries of supplication if some calamity befell the state; the grand invocator composed liturgies and prayed for blessings for the state; and the female invocator presented supplications on behalf of the queen.

One could pray to the ancestral spirits that one be allowed to substitute for someone else in death, as did the Duke of Zhou (reigned 1042–1036 B.C.E.) when he requested of the spirits of the royal ancestors that he be allowed to die in lieu of his ill king (History, "Metal-bound Coffer"). Prayer could also release one from illness. One of Confucius's disciples asked to pray for him when he fell ill; Confucius asked if that were usually done, and the student replied that in such cases one prayed to the spirits above and the terrestrial divinities below. Confucius replied then if that were the case, then he had already been praying for a long time (Analects 7:34). One might conclude from this that he believed he had already served the spirits all his life and felt no need to do so specially now.

One could also ask spirits for assistance in warding off and exorcising baneful influences and pestilence. Exorcists, invocators, healers, and priests often supervised these rites. Confucius himself noted the priests' and healers' quality of constancy and stability (*Analects* 13:22), and Mencius noted priests' concern for human welfare (*Mencius* 2A:7.1). Exorcists of varying ranks also participated in communal expiatory rites. Confucius was a spectator at such rites and put on court dress for the occasion (*Analects* 10:2). The origins of baneful influences are not clear; they inhabited no realm of their own but could appear from any direction.

Phenomena in the realms of the visible and invisible worlds could communicate with one another, but whereas these communications elicited feelings of wonder and could generate sentiments of filiality and devotion, they could also elicit fear, primarily regarding spirits with whom one's connections and commonalities were unclear. Such ambiguity is characteristic of attitudes toward supranormal powers in many religious traditions. One passage from the *History* relates admiringly how two culture heroes cut off communications between Heaven and earth and caused the invocations and descents of spiritual beings to stop. The passage seems to describe the desirability of stopping random, unpredictable manifestations of spirits and replacing them with more normative, predictable manifestations that could be controlled through human conduct (*History,* "Punishments of Lü"). A similar ambiguity toward encountering spirits appears in Confucius's admonition to be reverent toward ghosts and spirits, yet keep them at a distance (*Analects* 6:20). On the one hand, he insisted on being fully engaged when presenting sacrifices, and, on the other, his disciples noted that he rarely spoke of spiritual beings (*Analects* 3:12 and 7:20). Out-and-out skepticism about the very existence of a spirit world, however, is not characteristic of Zhou texts. Even such a thinker as Xunzi, who emphasized human endeavor at the expense of the spirit world, never doubted the existence of Heaven.

This brief survey of religious beliefs and practices illustrates, I believe, some dimensions of early Confucian spirituality, at least as I have defined that term above. Human communications with the spirit world, a world one rarely saw but deeply felt, were thus sustained by this elaborate system of sacrificial offerings and ritual exchanges, as relationships between the visible and the hidden were maintained by the mutual fulfillment of expectations and obligations. Those who might characterize "Confucianism" as a kind of secular humanism (an old saw that still appears in much secondary literature) might keep in mind the extent to which communicating with the spiritual and the numinous was integrated into the fabric of state, family, and personal life.

Notes

1. For introductions to the history and significance of the term spirituality, see, e.g., *Dictionnaire de Spiritualité*, s.v. "spiritualité"; Principe, "Toward Defining Spirituality"; and Alexander, "What do Recent Writers Mean by *Spirituality*?"

2. For dates of early texts and sources for English translations, see *Early Chinese Texts*, ed. Loewe; for Asian-language texts, see Overmyer et al., "Chinese Religions." For English translations of the *History, Odes, Zuo Commentary*, and *Doctrine of the Mean*, see Legge's *Chinese Classics*, vols. 3, *Shoo King;* 4, *She King;* 5, *Ch'un Ts'ew;* and 1, *Confucian Analects*, respectively. See these texts, for example, for chapters of the *History* and the numbered verses of the *Odes* cited herein.

3. See Zheng, "The Royal Consort Fu Hao and Her Tomb"; Keightley, *Sources of Shang History;* and Institute of Archeology, *Yinxu Fu Hao mu.*

4. For an introduction to the study of oracle bones, see Keightley, *Sources of Shang History.*

5. Ibid., 41.

6. A historical overview of the Eastern Zhou is provided in Li Xueqin's *Eastern Zhou and Zin Civilizations;* of the Western Zhou, in Hsu and Linduff's *Western Chou Civilization.*

7. For citations from the *Book of Rites (Liji)*, I have provided the title of the relevant Chinese chapter of the text in romanization, followed by the volume and page number of a parallel translation in Legge's *Li Ki.* All translations are my own unless noted otherwise.

8. Interpretations of various kinds of supranormal phenomena in early China are offered in Brashier, "Han Thanatology"; and Yü, "'O Soul, Come Back!'"

9. This could alternatively be translated as "intelligence and vital energy."

10. For an English translation, see Hawkes, *The Songs of the South.*

11. The material culture of early Chinese ritual is described in Wu Hung's *Monumentality in Early Chinese Art* and Rawson's *Mysteries of Ancient China.*

12. The kinds of animals used in sacrifices are discussed in Sterckx's "An Ancient Chinese Horse Ritual."

13. Otto, *Idea of the Holy.*

14. Eliade, *Sacred and the Profane.*

15. On the religious practices of priests in early China, see also von Falkenhausen, "Reflections on the Political Role of Spirit Mediums."

Bibliography

Alexander, Jon. "What Do Recent Writers Mean by *Spirituality*?" *Spirituality Today* 32 (1980): 247–56.

Brashier, K. E. "Han Thanatology and the Division of 'Souls.'" *Early China* 21 (1996): 125–58.

Dictionnaire de spiritualité. Paris: Beauchesne, 1990.

Eliade, Mircea. *The Sacred and the Profane*. New York: Harcourt, Brace, & World, 1959.

Hawkes, David. *The Songs of the South: An Ancient Chinese Anthology of Poems by Qu Yuan*. Harmondsworth, Middlesex: Penguin Books, 1985.

Hsu, Cho-yun, and Katheryn M. Linduff. *Western Chou Civilization*. New Haven: Yale University Press, 1988.

Institute of Archeology, Chinese Academy of Social Sciences. *Yin xu Fu Hao mu* [Tomb of Lady Hao at Yinxu]. Beijing: Cultural Relics Publishing House, 1980.

Keightley, David N. *Sources of Shang History: The Oracle-Bone Inscriptions of Bronze Age China*. Berkeley: University of California Press, 1978.

Lau, D. C. *Tao Te Ching*. Hong Kong: Chinese University Press, 1982.

Legge, James, trans. *The Chinese Classics*. 5 vols. [1865–1893]. Reprint. Taipei: Southern Materials Center, 1985.

———. *Li Ki*. Sacred Books of the East, ed. Max Muller, vols. 27–28. [1885] Reprint. Delhi: Motilal Banarsidass, 1964.

Li, Xueqin. *Eastern Zhou and Qin Civilizations*. New Haven: Yale University Press, 1985.

Loewe, Michael, ed. *Early Chinese Texts: A Bibliographic Guide*. Berkeley: Institute of Asian Studies, 1993.

Otto, Rudolf. *The Idea of the Holy*. 2d ed. London: Oxford University Press, 1950.

Overmyer, Daniel L., with David N. Keightley et al. "Chinese Religions: The State of the Field, Part I." *Journal of Asian Studies* 54 (1995): 124–60.

Poo, Mu-chou. "Ideas Concerning Death and Burial in Pre-Han and Han China." *Asia Major* 3d ser. 3, no. 2 (1990): 25–62.

———. *Muzang yu shengsi: Zhongguo gudai zongjiao zhi xingsi* [Burial and death: Reflections on ancient Chinese religion]. Taipei: Lianjing, 1993.

Principe, Walter. "Toward Defining Spirituality." *Studies in Religion/Sciences Religieuses* 12, no. 2 (1983): 127–41.

Rawson, Jessica, ed. *Mysteries of Ancient China*. London: British Museum Press, 1996.

Shaughnessy, Edward L. *I Ching: The Classic of Changes*. New York: Ballantine Books, 1996.

———. *Before Confucius: Studies in the Creation of the Chinese Classics*. Albany: State University of New York Press, 1997.

Sterckx, Roel. "An Ancient Chinese Horse Ritual." *Early China* 21 (1996): 47–79.

Vandermeersch, Léon. *Wangdao, ou la voie royale*. Vol. 2, *Structures politiques, les rites*. Paris: École française d'Extrême-Orient, 1980.

von Falkenhausen, Lothar. "Reflections on the Political Role of Spirit Mediums in Early China: The *Wu* Officials in the *Zhou Li*." *Early China* 20 (1995): 279–300.

Wu, Hung. *Monumentality in Early Chinese Art and Architecture*. Stanford: Stanford University Press, 1996.

Yang, Rubin. *Rujia shenti guan* [Confucian perspectives on the body]. Taipei: Academia Sinica, 1996.

Yü, Ying-shih. "'O Soul, Come Back!' A Study in the Changing Conceptions of the Soul and Afterlife in Pre-Buddhist China." *Harvard Journal of Asiatic Studies* 47 (1987): 363–95.

Zhang, Jiefu. *Zhongguo sangzang shi* [History of Chinese burial practices]. Taipei: Wenjin, 1995.

Zheng, Zhenxiang. "The Royal Consort Fu Hao and Her Tomb." In *Mysteries of Ancient China,* ed. Jessica Rawson, 240–47. London: British Museum Press, 1996.

11

Death and Dying
in the *Analects*

PHILIP J. IVANHOE

Should we not confess that in our civilized attitude towards death we are once again living psychologically beyond our means, and should we not rather turn back and recognize the truth?

—Sigmund Freud[1]

H UMAN REACTIONS TO DEATH play a prominent, diverse, and complex role in motivating and guiding religious thought throughout the world's cultures. In several Western traditions, a belief in life after death has been of such singular importance that our mundane existence here on earth fades dramatically in comparative value. Such a sense of proportional dissonance may yet inform contemporary inheritors of these traditions, appearing now in the guise of various more "secular" beliefs, attitudes, and behaviors and a general yearning for that something more beyond the lives we live that somehow will explain and justify our existence.

Many religious traditions have regarded the phenomenon of death as an aberration, a profound anomaly crying out for explanation and resolution. Modern psychological accounts of death, however, tend to insist that it is *we* who are doing the crying while working mightily to deceive ourselves and banish awareness of death from consciousness.[2] In those cultures that regard death as a breach of cosmic order, we often find myths about how death came into the world. Such stories usually associate the arrival of death with some particular human failing or explain it as a manifestation of an irrevocable tension or dichotomy in the universe itself. On such accounts, life and death are understood as in some sense the shadows or reflections of good and bad.

The early Confucian tradition offers no account of how death came into the world nor for that matter how the world itself came into being. Early Confucians did not regard the nature or origin of death as a great conundrum in need of explanation. This is not to say that they did not see death as posing profound and vexing problems to human beings. However, the nature of these problems and the tensions that they felt were conceived of differently. These thinkers were primarily concerned with understanding what place death and our reactions to it play in a well-ordered life, rather than in the essence or origin of death and its related phenomena.

With these remarks before us let us turn to the specific case of the founder of the Confucian tradition. How did Confucius himself conceive of death? How did he think one should react to it? How, if at all, should our conception of and attitude toward death inform our lives? These are the questions I will address by exploring Confucius's views on death and dying as found in the text of the *Lunyu* (*Analects*).[3] After presenting my interpretation of Confucius's views on death, I will question whether his position suffers from a problem identified by a number of modern Western thinkers. These thinkers, many of whom are associated with the broad category "existentialism," argue that certain conceptions of the ideal human life amount to an evasion of the most basic fact of the human condition: our finite existence and imminent death. Such conceptions manage to do this by drawing one's attention away from the concrete facts of human life and focusing instead on the project of bringing something really meaningful into being. They call upon one to sacrifice one's life for some abstract cause or future utopia. In so doing they allow one to avoid the subjective reality of one's mortal existence. Hence they encourage a fundamentally inauthentic form of life. I will argue that while Confucius's allegiance to the Dao can appear to present such an evasion, in fact it does not.

Let me begin with a claim that some may find controversial: Confucius did not believe in any strong sense of personal survival after death.[4] If he did hold some form of such a belief, it was not part of a developed eschatology and played no role in shaping his views about how one should live one's life. That is to say, if he did believe in some form of postlife survival, this was not embedded in a greater web of beliefs about a final judgment, subsequent punishment and reward, or any notion of reincarnation. I find no passages that lead me to think that Confucius believed that one's individual personality survived in any form beyond death.[5] And so I will take Confucius as believing that, for all practical purposes, physical death is the end of an individual's personal consciousness.

A number of thinkers have argued that death, so understood, cannot be considered bad for the person who dies.[6] If one believes that death really is the complete end of personal consciousness, then it is just a mistake or a kind of lack of nerve to worry about *being* dead—whether it is the death of another or oneself. This much seems right. But if we accept this claim, it might appear to present problems for Confucius. For as we shall see, in several places in the *Lunyu,* Confucius clearly seems to be worried about death. What I mean by "being worried about death" is showing a heightened concern about it, not dreading death but having a healthy respect for it, disliking it, wanting to keep it at bay and finding it, in at least some cases, a source of sadness, regret, and even tragedy. So the first issue I would like to explore is whether in worrying about certain cases of death, Confucius was making a fundamental mistake or showing a lack of nerve. Let us begin with cases of the death of another and then move on to the special case of one's own death to see, first, what Confucius found disturbing about death and, second, whether we can discern in these examples any legitimate reasons one might have for such concern.

Confucius clearly was distressed at the death and the threat of death of several people. In *Lunyu* 6:10 he bemoans the terminal illness of Bo Niu:

> Bo Niu was ill and the master went to ask about him. Holding his hand through the window, the master said, "It is all over! Is it not simply a matter of fate? But that such a man should have such an illness! That such a man should have such an illness!"

This clearly is not the attitude of a Stoic. Confucius is disturbed by the impending death of Bo Niu and distraught over the nature of his malady (perhaps leprosy). This passage and others like it present a stark contrast to those in which Confucius advocates a calm and determined acceptance of death.

When Confucius had to confront the death of his favorite disciple Yan Hui we see his distress reaching the point of openly uncontrolled grief. With the loss of Yan Hui, Confucius wails, "EEE, Heaven has taken him from me! Heaven has taken him from me!" (*Lunyu* 11:9). This leads his disciples to question him, in the following passage, for allowing his mourning to reach such extremes, something he explicitly warns against on other occasions.[7] Confucius responds by saying, "Have I lost control of myself? If not for this man, for whom then should I lose control?" These and other passages make it clear that Confucius thought that at least some cases of death warrant or at least allow for excessive displays of grief.

The two cases I have cited have at least three things in common. First, they involve the death of young people. Second, these young people were good people, leading lives in accordance with the Dao. Third, they died of illness. Together these three factors offer us a way to understand Confucius's excessive grief, which in no way contradicts what he says elsewhere about the proper attitude toward mourning. For cases like Bo Niu and Yan Hui represent genuine tragedies. They were good people cut down early in life for no apparent reason and in the service of no greater cause. Their lives end tragically and are events that even a cultivated person finds unsettling and disturbing.

It seems fair to speculate that Confucius would not have been particularly distressed—if at all—by the deaths of Bo Niu and Yan Hui had they been bad people—young or old. In one passage (*Lunyu* 14:46) Confucius even implies that someone who does not engage in self-cultivation would be better off dead. Thus, appreciating the *goodness* of Bo Niu and Yan Hui is critical for understanding Confucius's reaction.

Confucius thinks that we should mourn but not be excessively distressed when a good person dies at a ripe old age. As we shall see when we discuss the case of Confucius's own death, losing those we love and respect is always sad, but if they have lived proper lives, that is, lives in accordance with the Dao, we should see this event as the final act in the greater narrative of their lives and respond with genuine, ritually appropriate mourning. In such cases, "Mourning should reach to grief and then stop" (see *Lunyu* 19:14). But when a young person dies for no higher purpose, this pattern is disrupted and the event is much more difficult to accept. So the *youthfulness* of Bo Niu and Yan Hui is also significant.

The fact that the deaths of these fine young men lacked any special ethical significance is also critical for understanding Confucius's reaction. All good people, young and old, must be prepared to risk and even sacrifice their lives for the Way (*Lunyu* 8:13).[8] And those ethical heroes, young or old, who pay the highest price should be mourned with special reverence and esteem. For example, in *Lunyu* 16:12, Confucius praises the moral exemplars Bo Yi and Shu Qi, who sacrificed themselves for the Way, and he points out that their self-sacrifice bestowed upon them a kind of worldly immortality.

> Duke Jing of Qi had a thousand teams of horses and yet the day he died, the people found no virtue in him to praise. Bo Yi and Shu Qi starved to death at the foot of Mount Shou Yang yet down to the present day, the people sing their praises. . . .

In light of these various observations, we can begin to construct a general understanding of Confucius's view about the death of another. As will become even more clear below, his view is predicated on a conception of what makes life worth living. A good human life—one that is in accordance with the Dao—is a life well lived. Such a life requires that one be willing to sacrifice oneself in pursuit of the Way should the need arise. If this leads to death, then this is a source of sadness, as every death is, but it does not warrant excessive grief. For like the death of a good person who has lived out a full span of years, such a life fulfills the most important part of the true destiny of human beings—that is, the ethical part—and is in this respect proper and fitting. However, a promising young person who dies as a result of some calamity such as disease presents a profoundly different case. That person is denied the chance to fulfill his or her true destiny as a human being. Such cases are true tragedies and warrant the excessive grief we see Confucius express for Bo Niu and Yan Hui.

Since Confucius has a clear idea of what constitutes a good human life, he can explain what is bad about the death of another, distinguish different kinds of cases, and advocate a range of appropriate responses. Those who are able to live out their years following the Dao completely realize their full destiny as human beings. We mourn them at death because, given the social, relational nature of the Dao, they are part of our lives as well. When they die, we lose their participation in our greater communal lives. Our loss is greater or lesser depending on the closeness between us, that is, whether they are parents, relatives, friends, or fellow humans.[9]

Those who are young in age who are called upon to sacrifice themselves for the Way—for example, people like Bo Yi and Shu Qi—fulfill their ethical duty to the Way but are not able to fulfill all of the Way. For to follow the Way is to live out a full human life and fulfill the various role-specific duties that life presents at its different stages.[10] So we mourn for such martyrs to the Way with special reverence and respect and pay tribute to them throughout the ages. Finally, those dedicated to the Way who are cut down in youth for no apparent reason and in pursuit of no greater cause present truly tragic cases. To see a young and good person die of disease is tragic and well warrants the profound distress Confucius displays. This in no way contradicts his other teachings, nor does it manifest philosophical confusion or any lack of nerve. In each of these cases, Confucius's actual or recommended response reflects the structure of his larger philosophical perspective on the proper form and end of human life.

This larger philosophical perspective also gives Confucius a way to answer other questions concerning death. Among the most vexing of these is, What makes death not only bad but seemingly bad in a unique and unequivocal way? As noted above, it cannot simply be the fact that we will not exist. For if we do not exist, nothing can be of any consequence to us. This should be clear from the fact that we do not (or at least most of us do not) regret not existing for all the time that passed before we were born. What is bad about dying is that we will lose what we now have and what we still reasonably might have. With death the prospect is that these things—all of them—will be gone and gone for good.

To understand death and what is bad about it is not to understand what the state of death itself is like, for death is not just *like* nothing, to be dead is to *be* nothing. Rather, to understand death and its significance for us is to understand what it will deprive us of. Most generally of course, death deprives us of life, and what makes life valuable is all the various things that make life worth living. And so to understand the significance of death we must understand the meaning of life. If we understand what life is really about, that itself will give us an understanding of the significance of death. This is precisely what Confucius seems to say in *Lunyu* 11:12. There the disciple Ji Lu asks Confucius about how to serve ghosts and spirits. Confucius replies, "While you are not yet able to serve human beings, how can you serve spirits?" When the disciple goes on to ask about death, Confucius replies, "While you do not yet understand life, how can you understand death?"

In his footnote to this section of the *Analects*, James Legge claims that it is another example where "Confucius avoids answering the important questions put to him."[11] However, Legge simply missed the point. Confucius answers the question, saying that if one truly understands the significance of human life one will have attained a full and satisfactory understanding of death.[12] One will know all that there is to know about it. Such a perspective will provide one with an answer to the general question of what is bad about death (that is, it deprives one of all those good things that we value in living), and it will help one to begin to answer more specific questions such as, What, if anything, is worth dying for? So without engaging in the over-wrought pronouncements of certain existentialist philosophers, we can see how a consciousness of death indeed is an important and arguably a necessary perspective for answering questions about the meaning of life. A sense of the general aims of human life and its normal course and culmination allows one to appreciate the value of those things in life worth seeking and defending.[13] Such an appreciation of life is what gives death its sting. It tells us why and in what senses death is indeed bad. Such a consciousness of death focuses the mind in particularly revealing ways. Turning this view around, it is not at all unreasonable to maintain that an adult who had never sat down and thought deeply about the meaning of death could not possibly have a mature, full, and lively appreciation of the meaning of human life.

These same insights apply when we turn to the case of one's own death. There are good reasons to worry about one's own death, just as there are good reasons to mourn the death of others and to do so differently in different cases. While it is true that what happens after I am dead will be meaningless to me then (for I will no longer exist), it is nevertheless true that my death will affect many people and states of affairs in the world and the future fate of these people and affairs is important to me now and in whatever time I have left between now and then. This kind of concern is particularly acute in the Confucian tradition, where relational roles and their attendant duties play a large part in one's conception of oneself and in the nature of what one values. Moreover *how* I die, both the manner in which I face death and what I become in the time between now and then, are also issues of great importance to me. How I conceive of these future states can and should deeply affect and shape the life I still have left to live: what goals I seek to attain and promote and how I go about working for their realization.

These ideas are evident in a remarkable passage that purports to record an occasion when Confucius himself was on the verge of death.[14] *Lunyu* 9:12 says:

> The Master was seriously ill. Zilu ordered the other disciples to act as retainers. During a period when his condition had improved, the Master said, You [i.e., Zilu] have long been practicing deception. In pretending to have retainers when I had none, who would we be deceiving? Would we be deceiving Heaven? Moreover, would I not rather die in your arms, my friends, than in the arms of retainers? Even if I am not given an elaborate funeral, it is not as if I will be dying by the wayside.[15]

In this remarkable and moving passage we see several distinctive features of Confucius's views about death. In his last moments he is, as always, teaching: living out his particular role in the great Dao. And the message he delivers is that the best life for human beings is one of genuine love among our fellow humans. The marks of social rank, in this case retainers, while important, are only so in terms of their ability to engender a harmonious social order held together with genuine love and respect for one another. Such outward signs are not to be pursued or presumed for personal glorification. We see here Confucius living out his beliefs in what appear to be his last moments of life. In so doing he displays both a profound understanding and a courageous acceptance of his own death.

A passage that is remarkably similar in structure though strikingly different in meaning and sensibility can be found in the *Zhuangzi*. It is worth citing and discussing for the contrast it offers.

> When Zhuangzi was dying, his disciples wanted to give him a lavish funeral. Said Zhuangzi, "I have heaven and earth for my outer and inner coffins, the

sun and moon for my pair of jade discs, the stars for my pearls, the myriad creatures for my farewell gifts. Is anything missing from my funeral paraphernalia? What would you add to these?"

"Master! We are afraid the crows and kites will eat you!" said one of his disciples. "Above ground I'll be eaten by the crows and kites; below ground I'll be eaten by the ants and mole-crickets. You rob from one to give to the other. How come you like them so much better?"[16]

In this passage we find a very different message. While both Confucius and Zhuangzi sought to end their lives by taking their proper place within the universal pattern of the Dao, for Confucius this place was in the arms of his disciples, his proper position within the human social order. For Zhuangzi, the proper place was anywhere within the broad bosom of Nature; his community is the wider realm of the natural. This leaves him at home everywhere in the wide world, but he is without Confucius's special sense of belonging within the deep and precious relationships of human community. This leaves him without a justification for distinguishing the different responses to death that we have noted are characteristic of Confucius's position. According to such a view, the death of anyone at any time is equally acceptable. The only kind of death that is improper is the one that one brings upon oneself by following the foolish goals of the scheming human mind, but such a death is more pitiful than it is sorrowful or tragic.

Zhuangzi too is teaching with his last breaths, but his lesson is one of a probing skepticism. He seeks to leave his disciples by once more poking holes in their complacent certainty about what is right and wrong. He tries to move them out of their familiar frames of reference to look at things from a grander perspective, one in which human beings and their concerns assume a more diminutive stature against the background of an expansive and comprehensive natural landscape. As always, the lesson is delivered as a humorous and open question. Zhuangzi ends his life as he has lived it, in practice, a happy skeptic.

As I mentioned at the outset, certain thinkers in the Western tradition have argued that many views of death represent a misguided and deforming evasion of the human condition. In a fascinating essay, Michael Slote explores a number of versions of this view, which he argues can be seen as originating with Kierkegaard. Slote explains:

> According to Kierkegaard, to have an objective attitude toward one's life is to have the kind of attitude toward one's life encouraged by an Hegelian view of the world. On such a view, one is part of a larger "world-historical" process of the self-realization of Reason or Spirit, and one's life takes on significance if one plays a role, however minor, in that world-historical process.[17]

This kind of attitude, in a sense deferring one's life in order to bring something *really* meaningful into being or sacrificing one's life for some abstract cause or future utopia, is not restricted to any particular tradition or time. As Slote goes on to note,

> One does not have to be an Hegelian to think in this kind of way. One can be thinking in a similar way if, as a scientist or philosopher, e.g. if one devotes oneself to one's field in the belief or hope that one's life gains significance through one's contribution to something "bigger."[18]

These remarks bring the problem close—perhaps too close—to home. Many of us, at least at times, talk in precisely this "Hegelian" fashion. In the case of my own profession, many scholars find their energies and attention completely absorbed in the task of finishing that next book, article, or presentation. The meaning of our lives seems to consist solely in the effort to "move the field forward." As a result, teaching and personal life often are ignored, suffer, or are sacrificed (or, perhaps worse, they are valued only for the contribution they make to our research and advancement). However, how can we allow such an ephemeral project as "moving the field forward" (whatever that means) to draw us so completely out of our interpersonal obligations and relationships and our more immediate life projects—our subjectivity? There is something particularly perverse about teachers of the humanities allowing and even advocating this ongoing sacrifice to some amorphous future state of affairs. This is not a problem afflicting only academics; people in every walk of life can be heard giving voice to the same attitude.

My present aim is to determine whether or not Confucius's view of death, as I have described it, entails such an evasion of subjectivity. In other words, is Confucius's notion of the Dao like Hegel's notion of *Geist*, a ghostly depository of our greatest hopes and values, something we look up to in order to avoid facing our all-too-human lives, something really grand that we hope will inflate the value of our existence? Is his call to follow the Dao a way of fleeing from our subjectivity and in particular the prospect of our own deaths?

My view is that Confucius does not display or advocate this kind of false consciousness. If we consider again the passage that describes him facing his own death, in his final moments he is not looking away from his imminent demise and toward some Dao that relieves his pain and promises him peace or some greater reward. On the contrary, he is focused on and pointing his students' attention toward his approaching death and saying that he is ready to die in their arms. Thus, while Confucius sees himself and his life in terms of greater patterns and processes, the Dao is not ideal in the way that Geist is for Hegel. Rather than describing a world-historical process, the Dao often can be understood as a symbol for our all-too-human struggle to realize the good.[19]

Through concerted and ongoing human effort, the Dao can be realized to varying degrees in the world, but there is no place to be except here in the world we know, with all its faults, its pains, and even its tragedies. That is part of why we need the humanizing influence of Confucian ritual: to acknowledge and seek to ameliorate the faults, relieve some of the pain, and offer each other solace and solidarity in the face of tragedy. On such a view of human life, one can understand, endorse, and empathize with Confucius's excessive grief for Bo Niu and Yan Hui. For one feels the senselessness in the deaths of these fine young men.

According to Confucius, even if one finds oneself living in a severely disordered age, one's work and attention are to be focused on the tasks at hand, not on some future utopia or reward. The Confucian Dao is precious only as it is fulfilled and realized in the course of actual human lives. This is how I understand *Lunyu* 15:29: "Human beings can fulfill [i.e., fill out] the Way. The Way cannot fulfill human beings." Like any path, the Way fulfills its function only when people make use of it.

Confucius does express a fervent hope for the future revival of a past golden age, one that will herald the return of a utopia here on earth. He is willing and encourages others to make significant sacrifices to realize this grand goal. In regard to our present concerns, much depends on how we understand such exhortations. However, even if we grant that on occasion he asks too much of us,[20] it is still clearly the case that this greater project can only be won by working to develop our individual characters in the daily course of our lives and that the realization of this ideal society, however worthy of sacrifice, is not the sole source of value in our lives. Quite the contrary, Confucius wants us to keep our attention focused on the challenges and the joys that lie before us, if not in each and every moment, at least in each and every day. This concern for the everyday wonder and pleasure to be found in a well-lived life is evident throughout the text. For example, when, in *Lunyu* 11:24, Confucius asks various disciples to express their greatest aspiration, the one he approves of most is Dian, who suggests:

> In the waning days of Spring, wearing the new clothes of the season, with five or six young men and six or seven boys, to bathe in the River Yi, dry ourselves in the gentle breezes to be found at the Altar of Rain and then together, to return home chanting.

Confucius's appreciation of such simple pleasures is a critical aspect of his larger philosophical view. While he hopes and works for a brighter future, this does not cause him to lose sight of the everyday. This ability to comprehend and balance opposing tensions and concerns, to understand the extremes and yet hold to the middle is part of the subtle power of his vision. And so we should not be at all surprised to find that his understanding of human life includes a recognition and an appreciation of its inevitable conclusion in death.

Notes

All references to the *Lunyu* (*Analects*) are chapter and section numbers according to the *Harvard-Yenching Institute Sinological Index Series Supplement No. 16, A Concordance to the Analects*. All translations are my own. I thank the participants in the Confucian Spirituality Conference held at Harvard University, June 30–August 3, 1997, and the students and faculty who participated in the lecture series "Death and Dying, Life and Afterlife: Chinese Spiritual Reflections on the Human Condition," sponsored by the Pacific School of Religion and the Institute for World Religions in spring of 1998. Comments and suggestions from both these groups improved this essay.

1. Sigmund Freud, "Thoughts for the Times on War and Death," in *The Standard Edition of the Complete Works of Sigmund Freud,* trans. and ed. James Strachey (London: Hogarth Press, Institute of Psychoanalysis, 1957), 14:299.

2. In addition to Freud, one of the most eloquent and compelling arguments to this effect is offered by Ernest Becker, *The Denial of Death* (New York: Free Press, 1973).

3. Excellent work has been done on the text of the *Lunyu* in terms of arguing for different strata, their different dates and possible origins. See in particular the work of Bruce E. Brooks and Taeko A. Brooks, *The Original Analects: Sayings of Confucius and His Successors* (New York: Columbia University Press, 1998). However, I am interested in the figure of Confucius as a character in the received text of the *Lunyu* and the views attributed to him. I believe these hang together in a consistent manner and offer an enlightening perspective on the nature and meaning of death.

4. A number of scholars have said that Confucius is an agnostic about spiritual beings, citing *Lunyu* 6:22 in support. However, when Confucius encourages us to "respect ghosts and spirits but keep them at a distance" he would seem to be expressing a belief in their existence along with an admonition that they should not be one's primary concern. The critical issue for my purposes is not whether he believed in the existence of ghosts and spirits but what exactly his belief in such beings entailed. My view is that it did not entail any strong sense of personal survival and that, whatever beliefs he held, they were not a significant part of his general philosophy.

5. He does seem to allow that "spirits" do survive, but their identities are not personal. Their identities appear to be role-specific. Scholarly consensus seems to

indicate that the early Chinese believed that the spirits of different classes of people survived different lengths of time but that all gradually lost their individual personalities and eventually faded away. For a good discussion of this topic, see Yü Ying-shih, "'O Soul, Come Back!' A Study in the Changing Conceptions of the Soul and Afterlife in Pre-Buddhist China," *Harvard Journal of Asiatic Studies* 47, no. 2 (1987): 363–95.

6. Classical examples are thinkers such as Epicurus in his *Letter to Menoeceus* and Stoics such as Seneca, Epictetus, and Marcus Aurelius. Among modern thinkers, Spinoza is famous for claiming, "A free man thinks of nothing less than of death, and his wisdom is not a meditation upon death but upon life" (*Ethics*, Prop. 67).

7. His remarks about Yan Hui seem to go against claims like, "I do not complain against Heaven nor do I blame men" (*Lunyu* 14:35). They also seem to contradict his teaching that "Mourning should reach to grief and then stop" (*Lunyu* 19:14). It is also interesting that Confucius's state of mind is described as *tong*, "to be moved or upset with grief," which graphically is a close relative of *dong*, "to be moved." Mencius, of course, was renowned for achieving and promoting the attainment of a *bu dong xin*, "unmoved heart and mind."

8. But Confucius has no admiration for recklessness; see, e.g., *Lunyu* 7:11. The Way has such importance for Confucius that in *Lunyu* 4:8 we find him declaring, "If in the morning I heard that the Way was being followed, I could die that evening contented." My translation follows the earliest extant commentary, which offers the most sensible reading of this passage. It takes the line as Confucius's lament that he was nearing the end of life and had yet to see the Dao being implemented in the world. See *Lunyu Heshi deng jijie* 4.2b (*SBBY*).

9. Confucius distinguished different duties and responses depending on the closeness of the relationship. The most elaborate duties were, of course, for one's parents. These included the prescribed three-year period of mourning (*Lunyu* 1:11; 4:20; 17:19; etc.). However, he also discussed the duty one has to bury a friend whose relatives do not provide for him (*Lunyu* 10:14) and a general imperative to show respect for anyone in mourning (*Lunyu* 10:15).

10. Consider the example of Confucius's own spiritual autobiography described in *Lunyu* 2:4. This can be seen as lending further support to the He Yan commentary's interpretation of *Lunyu* 4:8.

11. See James Legge, trans., *Confucian Analects in The Chinese Classics*, Vol. 1 (reprint, Hong Kong: Hong Kong University Press, 1970), 241 n. 11.

12. This is how Cheng Yi interprets this passage as well. He comments, "When you understand the Way of life you will understand the Way of death. When you have completely fulfilled your service to human beings you will have completely fulfilled your service to the spirits" (quoted by Zhu Xi in *Sishu jizhu* 6.3a [*SBBY*]).

13. Bernard Williams argues that we need a conception of the bounded nature of our existence in order to find any significance in life. Immortality is a recipe for meaninglessness ("The Makropulos Case: Reflections on the Tedium of Immortal-

ity," in *Language, Metaphysics, and Death,* ed. John Donnelly [New York: Fordham University Press, 1978], 228–42).

14. Compare this with *Lunyu* 8:4, where Zengzi is seriously ill and is led to comment that, "When a bird is about to die its song is mournful. When a man is about to die his words are good."

15. Compare this and the following passage from the *Zhuangzi* with *Lunyu* 11:11, where Confucius scolds his disciples for giving Yan Hui a lavish funeral and blames himself for have failed his favorite disciple.

16. *Harvard-Yenching Institute Sinological Index Series No. 20, A Concordance to Chuang Tzu:* 90/32/47-50. Compare Burton Watson, *The Complete Works of Chuang Tzu* (New York: Columbia University Press, 1968), 361.

17. Michael Slote, "Existentialism and the Fear of Dying," in *Language, Metaphysics, and Death,* ed. John Donnelly (New York: Fordham University Press, 1978), 69–87.

18. Ibid., 70.

19. As a symbol, the Dao possesses value above and beyond the various goods it promotes. It gives us a guiding and inspiring metaphor by means of which we can organize and carry out our lives. Robert M. Adams puts this well, "Symbolically I can be for the Good as such, and not just for the bits and pieces of it that I can concretely promote or embody" ("Symbolic Value," in *The Philosophy of Religion,* Midwest Studies in Philosophy 21 [Notre Dame, Ind.: University of Notre Dame Press, 1998], 1–15).

20. In *Analects* 14:38 Confucius is described as one who "knows it is no use yet keeps on trying." This leads to interesting questions concerning the degree to which he is committed to pursuing a lost cause and how much of what is valuable is found in such pursuits. However, "lost causes" need not absorb all of life's values; like the sense of symbols discussed above, they can serve as ideals around which deeply meaningful yet in many respects quite normal human lives are organized. Josiah Royce argues that most religions represent such "lost causes," and his description offers profound insights into how such ideals can function in a human life. He says, "One begins, when one serves the lost cause, to discover that, in some sense, one ought to devote one's highest loyalty to causes that are too good to be visibly realized at any one moment of this poor wretched fleeting time world. . . . Loyalty seeks, therefore, something essentially superhuman. . . . In its highest reaches it always is, therefore, the service of a cause that was just now lost—and lost because the mere now is too poor a vehicle for the presentation of that ideal unity of life of which every form of loyalty is in quest" (*The Philosophy of Loyalty* [New York: Macmillan, 1908], 284–85).

12

Practicality and Spirituality in the *Mencius*

IRENE BLOOM

THE *MENCIUS*, LIKE THE *ANALECTS*, is often delivered to Western readers with various labels attached, one of which contains the clear instruction that this is a "philosophical" rather than a "religious" work.[1] This instruction is often proffered as if it were simple fact, the very simplicity of the disclosure all but ensuring its firm adherence to the surface of the text.

The providers of such labels, when pressed, will generally oblige with reasons for regarding the *Mencius* as a work of "pure philosophy." One of the more imposing of these is that religion is understood to entail an element of transcendence, while it is not immediately clear that an impulse to transcendence can be found in the thought of Mencius, whose perspective is so practical, this-worldly, and human-centered. The nature of the authority that underlies Mencian values also presents a problem. On what authority, other than his own experience and his understanding of the records of the experience of others in the historical past, does Mencius draw? Can there be a religion without a priesthood or class of professional religious teachers and officiants? Perhaps most important of all is the question of faith. Can Mencius's relation to Heaven allow for faith when Heaven's plan evidently remains so inscrutable, when he has to acknowledge, as had Confucius before him, that Heaven does not speak? Can there be faith without some fuller comprehension of the way Heaven works in the world?

In what follows I will suggest that Mencius's spirituality can be found right within his practicality, rather than at a remove from it, and as a correlate of his this-worldliness. The authority on which Mencius draws *is* indeed his own experience and the cumulative experience of the past as he understood it, especially that of the sages of antiquity and Confucius, who, he believed, were most mindful of the Way of Heaven and its ordinance. The issue of a priesthood is, of course, extrinsic to the text, as is a distinction between sacred and secular realms, though it is tempting to think that if Mencius had been made aware of that distinction, and of the role of a priesthood or of religious teachers in other traditions, his response might have been that what was absent among the *ru*—the Confucians—was actually not a clergy but a laity. Finally, while it may be valid to argue that Mencius's mindfulness of Heaven is not aptly described as "faith," this will depend on the amplitude of our understanding of what faith really is.

Confidence and Doubt

Certainly at the opening of the *Mencius* there are few clues that would signal any discrepancy with the notion of the *Mencius* as a "purely philosophical" work. When Mencius shows up in book 1A engaged in discussion with Kings Hui of Liang and Xuan of Qi, debating their use of language, their ethical disclaimers, and their complicity in war and its attendant misery, he appears altogether this-worldly and practical. There is no overt resorting to religious authority and only scant reference to customs, ideas, or language that are distinctively religious[2]—no visions of Heaven's rewards, no warnings of the power of Heaven's wrath. Instead, a case is made in purely human terms that what matters in the conduct of human life is moral motivation.

In the opening exchange with King Hui of Liang, Mencius makes a forceful argument that a ruler must be concerned with humaneness (*ren*) and rightness (*yi*) rather than with profit (*li*). It is his personal motivation, rather than the outcome of his thought or action, that is important. We may suspect that Mencius has no doubt that *ren* and *yi*, when practiced by a ruler, can be counted on for their efficacy as well, though he doesn't actually say so in this opening exchange, which is more foreboding in tone, focusing on the looming perils of putting profit ahead of humaneness and rightness.

The same is true of the second exchange with King Hui in 1A:2, in which Mencius and King Hui discuss the ruler's sharing (or failing to share) his enjoyment with the people. Mencius holds out the ominous example of the alienation of the tyrant Jie from a people prepared "to die with him," not in solidarity but purely for the sake of seeing him die.

In the third exchange with King Hui, and later in an interview with King Xuan, Mencius stiffens the argument by insisting that the humane ruler must make appropriate provisions for agriculture, sericulture, aboriculture, ecology, animal husbandry, and education—that he must adopt a comprehensive package of life-sustaining measures designed to respond in a practical manner to a range of earth-bound, this-worldly needs of the common people for whose welfare he is responsible.

Though much of book 1A is decidedly dark in hue, with the pervading presence of the specter of regicide, the memory and prospect of war, and the grim realities of death and starvation among the people, the main agenda of the book is actually a positive matter. Mencius tries to convince his interlocutors that they do possess the capacity for humaneness and rightness, and that, if they act on it, desirable results will ensue: violence will be alleviated and suffering ameliorated, rendering both ruled and ruler more secure. Despite the darkness of the backdrop, Mencius shows a sublime moral confidence. Even if we are unable to suppress the thought that this confidence may have been misplaced when it came to rulers as morally compromised as King Hui of Liang or King Xuan of Qi,[3] it is difficult to deny that Mencius's program is practical, his psychology astute, his tone assured.

If we skip momentarily from the beginning to the end of the text, the final passage in book 7B, we discover that the sublime moral confidence of the Mencius of 1A—the visitor to Liang and Qi—is no longer in evidence. Here we find what appears to be an older Mencius, apparently alone, revealing some doubt about his own role as a vehicle for the transmission of the moral Way. Perhaps he feels intimations of mortality; by his life's close the efficacy of his teaching is no longer clear. He seems to brood over the possibility that if there should be no one in his own time capable of carrying on the mission of the sage, and recognized in that role, there could be a break in the transmission he believed had passed over the centuries from the ancient sage kings to the founder of the Shang dynasty and, from him, to the founders of the Zhou, and from those early Zhou rulers to Confucius. At the very end, the last words we hear from him are these: "From Confucius down to the present day there have intervened something more than a hundred years. We are so little removed from the time of the sage, and so close to the place where he dwelled. Is there then no one? Is there no one?" (7B:38).

At least in this closing moment the Mencian confidence appears to have faded. We may imagine that, at the end, the bleakness of the historical situation has become so apparent, and hope so faint, that the depth of Mencius's devotion to Confucius as an exemplar of sagehood now merely deepens the poignancy of his own frustrated aspiration to fill a sagely role. Mencius evidently yearns to be assured of his capacity for sagehood, yet he must resign himself to the possibility that he may not figure into the tradition as the sages of the past had done.

This is not to suggest that the pattern of the *Mencius* text is linear, its structure revealing a sustained shift from confidence to doubt, optimism to pessimism, but only that the opening dialogues and the closing monologue present this moving contrast. The optimism of the opening dialogues is more typical of the text as a whole; the final monologue is, in fact, rather unusual in the *Mencius*, suggesting that the compilers had some specific reason for placing it at the end. But there are also other points throughout the text at which we find an interplay of confidence and doubt, neither canceling out the other, both apparently expressions of Mencius's commitment to and anxiety over Confucian values. This spiritual position may not be most aptly conveyed in the language of faith[4] but seems to entail the sort of patient waiting expressed in the language of *Mencius* 7A:1, which subtly commends "cultivating oneself in an attitude of expectancy" (*xiu shen yi si*), suggesting openness and receptivity rather than assurance. In what must be considered a spiritual achievement of some consequence, Mencius appears, perhaps out of the practice of such an "attitude of expectancy," to have achieved a subtle blend of moral idealism and sober realism, which, over time, worked its way into the Confucian fiber until it came to seem quintessentially Confucian.

This-worldliness and Practicality

The opening of the text and its close, in their very different modes, illustrate two significant themes in Mencian political thought—first, how the kingly ruler should think and act, and what inner resources he possesses that allow him to effect the approved behavior; and, second, how, historically, the transmitters of the Way are connected with one another as participants in a common enterprise. In neither case does religion come up overtly—unless one recognizes that what is unspoken in both 1A and 7B:38 is the unseen yet ever-present power of Heaven as the source of the people's life and livelihood and the model and standard for the sages.

In mid-book, with the conversational contexts frequently shifting, different questions arise, many of which are challenging from a religious point of view, but not all of which are approached in obviously religious language or within an overtly religious frame of reference. Ritual is less obviously a concern for Mencius than it had been for Confucius or than it would be for Xunzi;[5] Heaven is invoked less frequently than one might perhaps expect, and then often through the medium of quotations from the *Classic of Odes* or the *Classic of Documents* (allusions that may appear to a modern reader to be ambiguous as expressions of Mencius's own beliefs or those of the text's compilers);[6] the word for spirit (*shen*) is found but rarely;[7] any hint of an eschatology is absent, as is any mention of the idea of a soul (*hun, po*).

Recalling Max Weber's arguments about Confucian this-worldliness,[8] we may note too how grounded Mencius seems to be in his own time and place and how implicated in the immediacies of the quotidian reality that surrounds him. Deeply involved in the intellectual interactions of the fourth century, Mencius appears to be arguing much of the time, and not just when simultaneously defending his argumentativeness and excoriating the Yangists and Mohists in 3B:9. Much of the time he is fighting the good fight for Confucian values in language that seems deliberately and sometimes even gratuitously combative. Some of the arguments that he rehearses involve debating strategies his disciples are meant to employ in encounters with opponents—here is Mencius, claiming to dislike disputation, yet confidently teaching the practical art of argument to others (e.g., 6A:5). He is critical of the state of the world but not otherworldly: the importance attached to life in this world and to one's potential to affect the well-being of other human beings in this lifetime is immense.

To the extent that the *Mencius* looks "beyond" the here-and-now, it is backward in historical time: "the ancients" remain available as a source of reassurance and inspiration, and his apparent success in "looking for friends in history" (5B:8) goes some way toward justifying an underlying confidence that this world is both worthwhile and redeemable.

Human biological needs are taken seriously by Mencius: there appears to be an understanding throughout that priority is assigned to attending to life's basic necessities—food, clothing, shelter, and education. Mencius is aware that ordinary people will find it impossible to have "a constant mind" without a "constant means of livelihood" (1A:7), which, of course, is the basis for the comprehensive welfare program outlined in 1A and reintroduced thereafter.

In terms of style and language, the images that Mencius favors are often taken from nature and seem consistently chosen to support and to illustrate his abiding confidence in life and renewal. Trees and plants, emergent shoots and harvestable grains, along with life-giving water recur in the *Mencius* text, as metaphors for—or, perhaps more aptly, as analogues of—the natural processes involved in human cultivation, growth, and maturation. Proper tending of plants is an analogue of the cultivation of human potential, the clear-cutting of a mountain an analogue of the destruction of human potential. The primary value of groundedness in an agrarian society is palpable, as is the recognition of the importance of both human effort and the environment in human life as well as in the agricultural activities associated with the earth.

These are a few examples of Mencian this-worldliness and practicality. Yet practicality, it seems, is often practical primarily within a particular cultural context and, often enough, is of no special concern of religion—at least, not of religion as it opens outward toward universality. Is Mencius, in his fourth-century Chinese practicality, necessarily distanced from us in the modern world? Does that very practicality—that groundedness—make him a case in point for Weber's characterization of the Confucian life orientation as being finally devoted to "bureaucratic reasons-of-state and social ethics—an ethic which never reached for the stars"[9]?

It is, of course, *not* the case that ultimate questions and concerns are absent from the *Mencius*. Nor does Mencius typically deflect such questions, as Confucius occasionally did, apparently with the intention of diverting the focus of attention from what is ultimately unknowable to the thoroughly knowable sphere of right conduct in the here-and-now (*Analects* 6:20; 11:11). It is true, however, that Mencius's statements on some large and significant questions are proffered without the slightest Socratic savoring of the abstract possibilities of an issue or the least inclination to theorize about fundamental religious questions—for example, about the nature of Heaven, the working of Heaven's Mandate, the relation of human beings to Heaven, or that most Mencian of concerns, human nature. In some cases Mencius's explanations, where they are provided, seem cryptic or incomplete, particularly when read in a Socratic spirit, with the object of analyzing the meaning of basic concepts and the relation between them.

Religious Practicality

In an innovative and insightful article on religious typology, Lee H. Yearley has argued that it is precisely this tendency that marks Mencian religious thought as an example of a type that may be characterized as "practical," one that "deals with religious questions in an unspeculative fashion because its orientation is to the transformation of human action."[10] After having studied nearly thirty references in the *Mencius* to Heaven's Mandate (*tian ming*) or, more often, "the mandate," ("ordinance," "decree," "destiny," *ming*), Yearley observes that Mencian religious thinking is of a type not given to working at abstract problems or to resolving intellectual tensions:

Rather this type is guided by a concern for the direct religious usefulness of whatever is brought about and the desire actually to maintain rather than probe, certain basic tensions. The aims of guiding action and of upholding apparently conflicting poles are the distinctive marks of this type of religious thought. . . . Religious thought may often be most religious—most fully aware of its distinctive subject matter—when it sees itself faced with what I shall call "irresolvable but revelatory and productive tensions." These tensions are constituted by two different but related ideas that stand as the irreducible givens on which reflection works, the undeniable poles that form the two sides of its vision of reality.

An example of such a tension is found in the Mencian view of a human potential that must be realized through each individual's effort and yet derives from and depends upon a Heaven that may either further or actually frustrate its completion.

Because both sides of the tension must be upheld, any resolution that even diminishes either side must be rejected. Moreover, because seeing both sides is revelatory and productive, a resolution need not even be sought. In fact, keeping the tension's irresolvability in mind, developing a tolerance for such perceptions may be of considerable religious significance in making clear one's relation to the sacred.[11]

These two observations—of the concern for the "religious usefulness" of "guiding action" and of the determination to embrace rather than to expunge "irresolvable tensions" within a complex reality—help to clarify some of the less transparent passages in the *Mencius* and to foster a more nuanced appreciation of the nature of Mencian spirituality.

Yearley notes that Heaven's Mandate (or simply, "the mandate") is variously depicted in three kinds of utterances in the *Mencius* text: (1) those pronouncements that acknowledge Heaven as the valid source of political authority, with a focus "on 'political' leadership and the validation of certain people or actions"; (2) those that represent Heaven as the source or cause of human nature, a notion seen to involve "the internalization of sacred power"; and (3) those that recognize Heaven (or the ordinance, decree, or destiny) as the source for happenings and events that are beyond human understanding or comprehension.[12]

The argument is that tensions abound in a Heaven so conceived, as is especially evident in those passages that record Mencius's response to the chaos and injustice of the fourth-century Chinese world and those that reflect on issues of political leadership in that world. As Mencius leaves the state of Qi, having failed to persuade King Xuan to endorse his views of how a true king should think and act, the obvious, yet unasked, question is,

Why does Heaven not intervene to arrest the chaos into which the Zhou has descended and to create a new order? *Mencius* 2B:13 records the following exchange:

> When Mencius was departing Qi, Chong Yu questioned him along the way, saying, "From the Master's expression it would seem that he is unhappy. Yet on a former occasion I heard the Master say, 'The noble person neither repines against Heaven nor reproaches men.'"[13] [Mencius] said, "That was one time; this is another. In five hundred years a true king should appear, and in the interval there should be men renowned in their generation. From the beginning of the Zhou it has been more than seven hundred years. Given that number, the time is past due, and, considering the circumstances, it is still possible. Heaven does not yet wish to bring peace to the world. If it wished to bring peace to the world, who is there in the present age besides myself? Why should I be unhappy?"

And in 4A:7:

> When the Way is present in the world those of modest virtue serve those of great virtue, those of modest worth serve those of great worth. But when the Way is absent in the world, the small serve the great, the weak serve the strong. Both of these are due to Heaven. Those who follow Heaven are preserved; those who oppose Heaven are destroyed.

In 2B:13, while Mencius denies being unhappy, we are entitled to suspect that his resignation must be tinged with the disappointment that almost inevitably accompanies a sense of frustrated potentiality. The statement seems to resonate with 7B:38, discussed above, except that here there is at least a semblance of an explanation for Mencius's political failure, something that is altogether lacking in 7B:38. That "Heaven does not yet wish to bring peace to the world" may be, if somewhat ironically, a mitigation of the affliction. Even though we do not know *why* this is true, the fact that it *can be believed to be true* offers at least the austere comfort that comes from specifying where the responsibility lies—not with Mencius himself but with Heaven.[14] There is no abstract theory here, no attempt to analyze Heaven's motives, just a kind of resigned acceptance: *Heaven does not yet wish to bring peace to the world.*

In 4A:7 the "problem" is posed in more encompassing terms: Heaven presides over the world when the Way is present and also when the Way is absent. In Lee Yearley's view, "The dilemma put starkly is that a Heaven that allows or causes men to suffer must then be a power that cannot or will not help. If the power cannot help, its power is limited; if it will not help, its goodness is limited."[15] In the West, Yearley observes, such a dilemma would very likely be taken to represent an instance of the problem of theodicy, evoking a series of abstract questions about the relation between the human and the divine, the issue of causation, the problem of knowledge, and the origin of evil. We may note, however, that Mencius does *not* present the operation of Heaven as a "problem," nor does he pose this "dilemma" starkly, nor does he explicitly raise any of these questions.

One may interpret this, along with the apparent diversity of the statements and quotations concerning Heaven found in the *Mencius*, as a sign that the concept of Heaven was of scant importance in Mencius's political thought.[16] Alternatively, along the lines of Yearley's argument, one may see it as an indication that Mencius was given to such a complex sense of Heaven that abstract analysis would be conducive neither to the understanding of Heaven's true design nor to the cultivation of one's relation with the sacred. It seems to me that, taken in the context of Mencius's thought as a whole, the latter approach is decidedly more promising. Given the alternatives framed in the final sentence of the passage quoted from 4A:7, and the authoritative voice in which Mencius articulates these alternatives, the net effect is to underscore the ultimate power of Heaven.

A similar question arises concerning the notion of Heaven as the source of human life and the cause of human nature: Why, if Heaven creates life and endows each human being with moral potentiality, should that potentiality be realized by some and remain inert in others? This question *is*, in fact, posed by Mencius's interlocutors and recognized by Mencius himself (e.g., in 6A:6 and 6A:7). Mencius acknowledges that there is inequality of development and repeatedly draws attention to the practical importance of environment for the nurturance of the potential endowed by Heaven. This is the import of the famous discussion in 6A:6. Mencius said:

> As far as the natural tendencies are concerned, it is possible for one to do good; this is what I mean by being good. If one does what is not good, that is not the fault of one's capacities. The mind of pity and commiseration is possessed by all human beings; the mind of shame and aversion is possessed by all human beings; the mind of respectfulness and reverence is possessed by all human beings; and the mind that knows right and wrong is possessed by all human beings. The mind of pity and commiseration is humaneness; the mind of shame and dislike is rightness; the mind of reverence and respect is propriety; and the mind that knows right and wrong is wisdom. Humaneness, rightness, propriety, and wisdom are not infused into us from without. We definitely possess them. It is just that we do not think about it, that is all. Therefore it is said, "Seek and you will get it; let go and you will lose it."[17] That some differ from others by as much as twice, or five times, or an incalculable order of magnitude, is because there are those who are unable fully to develop their capacities. The Ode says,

> Heaven in giving birth to humankind,
> Created for each thing its own rule.
> The people's common disposition
> Is to love this admirable virtue. (Ode 260)

Heaven has created human beings with a shared rule, a common disposition toward goodness, but *there are those who are unable fully to develop their capacities.* Such a simple acknowledgment! The case for the importance of environment in the development of individual capacities is furthered in 6A:7, along with a reaffirmation that the failure of some human beings to realize their potential is not a matter of differences in "the capacities sent down by Heaven" but, rather, a matter of the environment—*what overwhelms their minds.*

Mencius offers no more theoretical explanation for human differences. This is part of a Mencian pattern and also, perhaps, strategically natural. Since he is committed to the view that Heaven is the source of the capacities that are shared by *all* human beings, and likewise committed to the practical cause of encouraging every human being to develop these capacities as fully as possible, why would he want to dwell on differences? That they are real, he accepts, holding this reality in balance with the reality that human beings share a common endowment and potential. Neither reality escapes him, but he chooses not to belabor the reality of acquired differences.

Similarly, in the case of the idea of *ming* (the decree, destiny) or Heaven as the source of events that occur apart from human agency and are often beyond human comprehension, there is the obvious question of what accounts for the lack of coincidence between meritorious actions and rewards and reprehensible actions and punishments? Does a moral order of the kind generally believed to be sanctioned by Heaven not *require* some more reliable coincidence? Mencius does not raise this issue directly— again, it would not have been strategic for him to do so. However, the likelihood that he thought about it at some level is suggested by the fact that at several points he depicts suffering as a condition—a kind of Heaven-created training ground—for higher accomplishments among human beings. As he remarks in 6B:15:

> Shun arose from amid the ditches and fields; Fu Yue arose from among the planks and boards; Jiao Ge arose from amid the fish and salt; Guan Yiwu arose from the [custody of] the [prison] officer; Sunshu Ao arose from the sea and Boli Xi arose from the market. Thus Heaven, when it is about to confer a great responsibility on a person, first subjects his mind and will to suffering, his sinews and bones to toil, his body to hunger, and his person to abject poverty. It undermines his efforts in order to stimulate his mind, strengthen

his nature, and support him in those things he is unable to do. People usually make mistakes and then they are able to change. After being troubled of mind and perplexed in thought they are able to act.

And, in 7A:18, "those who possess virtue, wisdom, and skill in handling affairs will usually be found to have endured through sickness and adversity." The trials and travails of Shun, as depicted in 5A:1–3, may also be understood to have a similar initiatory value as Shun enters onto his sagely career and, following long service to Yao, succeeds Yao as ruler.

These observations about suffering as a preparation for the refinement of one's intelligence and the enhancement of one's capacities represent a constructive guide to action and a practical approach to suffering. Commonly the focus of attention is shifted by Mencius from doubts that a moral order can be reliably recognized in the context of an individual lifetime toward confidence that Heaven's larger and higher purposes do entail such an order.

Such a shift—especially as found in 6B:15, which emphasizes the active power of Heaven—affords another example of the Mencian emphasis on the behavioral consequences of ideas and the value of "guided action," but it also necessarily involves Mencius's underlying intuitions about the way human beings are related to Heaven. At various points in the text, Mencius represents Heaven as beneficent, awe-inspiring, creative, and life-giving. More specifically, in its life-giving function Heaven also endows human beings with a mind that can think, a nature that can be developed, and a body and appearance, creating a connection and a bond between Heaven and each human being.

From the perspective of comparative religion, it is also significant that the relation between human beings and Heaven, while not close in the sense of intimacy or direct in the sense of explicit communication, is remarkably free of spiritual crisis. Heaven's desires and motives may often be opaque, even to a devoted aspirant like Mencius, and this, for some persons, may create a tension that at times approaches despair. Heaven may "send down calamities,"[18] or so the *Classic of Documents* warned, but on the whole Heaven is depicted in the *Mencius* as benign and supportive of human welfare and human moral action. There is nothing to resemble the spiritual crises experienced by followers of God in the Hebrew Bible—no counterpart among all-under-Heaven to Abraham, Jeremiah, Jonah, or Job.

This is especially evident from the beginning of Mencius's account of the life of Shun—perhaps the classic Chinese example of one who suffers undeservedly. Shun is introduced at the beginning of Book 5A as he is working dutifully in the fields. Grieving deeply over the implacable and inexplicable hatred visited upon him by his parents, toward whom he nonetheless maintains the utmost filial devotion, Shun cries and weeps and "calls on pitying Heaven" (5A:1). Deprived as he is of a loving relationship with his parents, Shun is depicted as having experienced the most profound loss a human being can endure, a psychic and spiritual suffering comparable, we may suppose, to the terrible losses of Job and, in a sense, more focused. Shun eludes the repeated attempts of his relentlessly cruel parents and brother to kill him, though not the burden of responding to them, despite their depravity, with filial and fraternal devotion.

Unlike the God of the book of Job, who speaks to Job out of the whirl-wind, Heaven does *not* speak. Mencius confirms this Confucian convic-tion[19] in 5A:5 in the context of discussing Shun's eventual succession to Yao as ruler. But Heaven does, at times, intervene decisively in the human world, notably in validating the choice of Shun as ruler. It was not Yao but Heaven that gave the realm to Shun to rule, Mencius says. But "Heaven does not speak. This was manifested simply through his actions and his conduct of affairs." Despite the muteness of Heaven, and the fact that its ways too cannot always be readily or fully comprehended, human beings are not distanced from Heaven as Job was distanced from his God. In fact, the line between Heaven's instructions and Shun's actions is virtually indis-tinguishable. So close can a sagely human being come to Heaven.

Neither in the *Mencius* nor, so far as I am aware, in any other Confucian text, is there any such soul-searing search for an answer to the problem of suffering as is found in Job. In the case of Mencius the reason that suffering can be contained is perhaps that he has found a way to surmount the doubt created by a present reality of suffering through realizing that what is immediate and present is a part, but only a part, of Heaven's order. He rec-ognizes the order that prevails in the wider world to be *relevant* to an indi-vidual life even if this order is not always *manifest* within the brief span of an individual lifetime.

And while Heaven appears to be just that—an order, rather than a deity—it remains, despite all of the uncertainties, a beneficent order and a source of life, support, and a kind of austere comfort. That Heaven's order may not be apparent in the short run, and that this must be accepted, is a major Mencian motif. That it is reliably present and intelligible in the larger frame is the basis for Mencian confidence. In the Mencian context, the issue is not Heaven's power but the transparency of Heaven's design. "Heaven does *not yet* wish to bring peace and order to the world" (2B:13)—this is one part of the tension. "Those who follow Heaven are preserved" (4A:7)—this is the other.

To sum up, we have examined three circumstances in which human confidence in the way the world works and the way Heaven works in the world is directly challenged: (1) the thwarting of human aspirations to achieve some worthy goal (for example, reforming the world and restoring peace and order, as in 2B:13) owing to the force of adverse circumstances; (2) the dissonance created by the disparity between potential human equality (implied by Heaven's endowment of ethical potential in every person) and actual *in*equality (based on differences in human development and fulfillment); (3) the moral quandary entailed by undeserved suffering. Each of these challenges surfaces in the *Mencius*, yet it is quite remarkable how indirect and muted the statement of them is, how calm Mencius appears to be, even in moments of serious disappointment and doubt. In the face of what might in other religious contexts evoke intense spiritual crisis, he seems unfailingly to hold on to the "irreconcilable tension" and move with it toward practical solutions.

"An Ethic which Never Reached for the Stars"?

Exactly what Max Weber had in mind when he ruled "transcendental values and destinies" beyond the mundane limits of the Confucian tradition is less than fully clear.[20] By the "transcendent" he certainly meant the Judeo-Christian God, understood as a supramundane deity, and by "transcendental values," he meant attitudes and actions concentrated on fulfilling the intentions of God and based on a strong sense of tension between sacred and secular realms, religion and the "world." Though this was not specified, "transcendental destinies" perhaps involved the eschatological dimension, referring to a life beyond death. This would be consistent with his judgment that in Confucian China "all transcendental anchorage of ethics, all tension between the imperatives of a supramundane God and a creatural world, all orientation toward a goal in the beyond, and all conception of radical evil were absent."[21]

Weber also did not explain his comment that the Confucian social ethic was one "which never reached for the stars."[22] Perhaps an ethic that *did* "reach for the stars," would have derived from the belief that one's conduct in this life would have a bearing on the career of one's immortal soul in the beyond and that this constituted a compelling motive for ethical conduct. If this was the case, he was not mistaken in his understanding that Confucian ethical thought never fastened on such a motive. The concept of the soul occurs nowhere in the *Mencius*, or in any of the Four Books, and the focus of concern is consistently this life rather than a life to come. Or perhaps Weber considered behavior according to the Confucian social ethic to be so routinized in its ritualism and formalized in its established patterns of mutual expectation and interaction that all energy must be drained away into conventionality, with little left over for soaring ethical imagination and lofty ambition.

Consider, however, the Mencian concept of *qi*. From the famous passage on courage, "the unmoving mind," and *qi* in *Mencius* 2A:2, in which Mencius comes as close as he does anywhere to outlining a metaphysics of the person, we learn that in the process of moral development a person's vital resources are the mind, the will (which, for Mencius, is the directedness of the mind), and the *qi*—vital force or psychophysical energy. Mencius sees a necessary connection between maintaining a sense of moral balance and "nourishing one's *qi*"—that is, between "holding firm one's will" (*zhih qi zhih*) and "doing no violence to one's *qi*" (*wu bao qi qi*). The will functions to guide and channel the *qi* but must accomplish this without repressing or injuring the vital energy, the source of moral stamina and ambition. Mencius's sense of the relation between moral balance and psychophysical energy reflects both the perception of a holistic relation between mind and body and a conviction that there is a fundamental connection between the overall vitality and health of the individual and the individual's capacity to relate to others. Personal well-being is both the condition for and the consequence of harmonious interaction with a larger whole that ultimately includes everything "between Heaven and earth."

The functioning of this overwhelming energy is explained in the course of an exchange between Mencius and the disciple Gongsun Chou, who asks Mencius what edge he has over his adversary Gaozi. Mencius replies that the advantage lies in his understanding of words and his ability to nourish his "vast, flowing *qi*." When asked to describe this "vast, flowing *qi*," he cautions that it is "difficult to speak of it," but then follows immediately with a description at once brief and memorable in the literature of world religion:

> This is *qi*: it is consummately great and consummately strong. If one nourishes it with uprightness and does not injure it, it will fill the space between Heaven and Earth. This is *qi*: it is the companion of rightness and the Way, in the absence of which, it starves. It is born from an accumulation of rightness rather than appropriated through an isolated display. If one's actions cause the mind to be disquieted, it starves. I therefore said that Gaozi did not understand rightness because he regarded it as external.

This is *qi*: a psychophysical energy, tied to bodily health, yet also, in this nondualistic view, "the companion of rightness and the Way." Moral behavior both issues from it and enhances it; moral energy is, quite literally, dependent on and conducive to health. Nourished with uprightness (here, presumably, the will is doing its work), and protected from injury (the will not acting with counterproductive harshness or coerciveness) "it will fill the space between Heaven and Earth."

It is of considerable consequence for the metaphysics of the person in the *Mencius*, as sketchily adumbrated as it is there, and in the later Confucian tradition, where it is more fully elaborated, that *qi* is both part of an individual's endowment and also a transpersonal reality. It is when the individual endowment of *qi* is nourished that the continuity of the individual with a larger and more encompassing reality becomes evident; honoring this sense of continuity with all living things contributes in turn to the well-being of the person. Through the individual's complement of *qi* that person is both vital and one with other living beings. When this *qi* is constantly and carefully guided by the mind and will, it is nourished and strengthened. It should be clear that, far from being an ethical view embedded in ritualism or formalism, a "social ethic" given over to "external conduct" with its heavy burden of conventionality, the practice of "nourishing one's *qi*" makes *qi* a "companion" in a dynamic process of self-cultivation and spiritual expansiveness.

This is an example of self-transcendence—not a self-transcendence that issues from acceptance and resignation, but one that derives from and confirms self-fulfillment. When an individual's complement of *qi* is cultivated effectively the self is expanded, spiritually as well as morally. Accumulating rightness—that is, working to establish a sustained habit of moral behavior—one is enabled to go beyond the normal limits of the self in the direction of greater individual potentiality as well as fuller participation in a common life. Both as a conception of self-cultivation and as psychological insight, Mencius's "nourishing the vast, flowing *qi*" represents a remarkable confluence of practicality and spirituality. It is practical in the sense that, while it may be "difficult to speak of" the "vast, flowing *qi*," the phenomenon Mencius describes is immediately recognizable in psychological terms, and the notion of cultivation he recommends is obviously accessible in terms of practice. In that it envisions an enhanced sense of connectedness to and involvement in a larger life, it is also spiritually dynamic. "Filling the space between Heaven and Earth"—could there be a better situation from which to "reach for the stars"?

A similar pattern of self-fulfillment leading to self-transcendence is found in 7A:1, which quotes Mencius as saying:

> By fully developing one's mind one knows one's nature, and by knowing one's nature, one knows Heaven. It is through preserving one's mind and

nourishing one's nature that one may serve Heaven. It is through cultivating one's self in an attitude of expectancy, allowing neither the brevity nor the length of one's lifespan to cause any ambivalence, that one is able to establish one's destiny.

The important point in this often-quoted passage is not, I think, that the human person is, as an ontological given, coincidental with Heaven,[23] but that the person, whose being embodies Heaven's gifts, may *develop* in such a way as to come into more sustained contact with Heaven. Here the process of self-cultivation is understood to move from fully developing one's mind (which, as 6A:15 specifies, is a gift from Heaven), to knowing one's nature (which in 6A:6 is identified with capacities also endowed by Heaven), to knowing Heaven, and from there to "preserving one's mind and nourishing one's nature that one may serve Heaven." Despite the spareness and brevity of the statement, we sense that the effort involved in fully developing Heaven's gifts must be immense. Along with the effort, control is evidently required, and yet that control also has its limits. The process of self-cultivation should be carried on "in an attitude of expectancy," says Mencius, "allowing neither the brevity or length of one's lifetime to cause any ambivalence." One must overcome the natural tendency to be unsettled by anxiety over one's own mortality, which remains, finally, within the purview of Heaven. By controlling what one can control and relinquishing control in matters that are beyond one's competence, one entrusts oneself to Heaven and is able to establish one's spiritual destiny.

Something similar seems to emerge from the equally famous passage in 7A:4 where Mencius is quoted as saying:

> All the ten thousand things are complete in me. To turn within to examine oneself and find that one is sincere—there is no greater joy than this. To dedicate oneself in all earnestness to reciprocity—there can be no closer approach to humaneness.

This passage has sometimes been interpreted as revealing a mystical dimension in the *Mencius*,[24] but the statement is more than its first sentence. When the statement is taken in its full context, the sense of relatedness between the self and all living things becomes a spiritual achievement that has grown out of the moral effort of cultivating sincerity and practicing reciprocity.

Some of the most telling expressions of Mencian spirituality are discovered at points when Mencius, in speaking about Heaven, reveals a sense of connection between that part of Heaven that is within us and the vastness that is without. The presence of Heaven within us is found in the human mind, which can think and, being relational, establish connections. It is found also in those capacities that are associated with human moral potential—that is, with the complex of predispositions known as human nature. The vastness that is without is known, to whatever degree it *can* be known, through the exercise of resources that Heaven itself has endowed within us, the presence within expanding to come into contact with the vastness without.

And here we return at last to the issue of faith. Mencius speaks of "delighting in Heaven" and of "being in awe of Heaven," though never of "having faith in Heaven." It is not even clear how he could have said that in the language of his time. He seems at points to feel that he is capable of being in contact with Heaven's vastness (as in 2A:2, 7A:1, and 7A:4), but more often to feel that contact with Heaven is somehow impeded, at least temporarily (as in 2B:13 and 7B:38)—thus, the interplay of confidence and doubt. Some might contend that such an interplay of confidence and doubt is insufficient to qualify as "faith." On the understanding of Wilfred Cantwell Smith, however, as expressed in his classic study *Faith and Belief*, faith is a "self-commitment, a dedicating or consecrating of one's life to . . ."[25] which would surely make the Mencian self-commitment not only sufficient but exemplary. Never doubting the power or the beneficence of Heaven, but only his own capacity fully to understand its plan, Mencius is arguably the more faithful, the more religious, for having carried with him both a profound confidence in Heaven's purpose and his own consolation to sustain him, unembittered, when his personal participation in Heaven's plan seemed to be in doubt.

Notes

1. For example, D. C. Lau observes in the introduction to his translation of the *Mencius*, "One great difference between moral philosophers in the Chinese tradition and those in the Western tradition is that the latter do not look upon it as their concern to help people to become sages while the former assume that that is their main concern. Western philosophers deal only with the problem of what morality is. They leave the problem of how to make people better to religious teachers. In China, however, there has never been a strong tradition of religious teaching, and the problem has always fallen within the province of the philosopher" (*Mencius* [Harmondsworth: Penguin, 1970], 23–24).

2. The exceptions to this are the mention of King Wu's Sacred Terrace and Sacred Pond in Ode 242, quoted in 1A:2, and the reference to the consecration of a bell in 1A:7, though the former is a historical reference, and Mencius himself has no apparent involvement in the latter.

3. The compilers of the *Mencius* saw this as well and opened 2B:12: "After Men-

cius left Qi, Yin Shi said to someone, 'If he did not realize that the King [of Qi] could not become a Tang or a King Wu, he was blind, but if he came realizing it, he was simply after advancement'" (trans. Lau, *Mencius*, p. 93).

4. This is my suggestion, on the basis of the evidence of what I have called an "interplay of confidence and doubt," but, obviously, there are other views. D. C. Lau argues, for example, that, "Not only does he [Mencius] believe that a man can attain oneness with the universe by perfecting his own moral nature, but he has absolute faith in the moral purpose of the universe" (trans. Lau, *Mencius*, p. 46). Likewise, Philip J. Ivanhoe makes an argument for Mencius's faith in Heaven in "A Question of Faith: A New Interpretation of Mencius 2B:13," *Early China* 13 (1988): 153–65. Ivanhoe goes so far as to describe 2B:13 as a "testament of faith."

5. Robert Eno's interpretation of Mencius's attitude toward ritual is that, "Mencius' theory of *hsing* [human nature] incorporated Ruist predispositions toward ritual action as a universal quality of mind. By treating *li* as an innate tendency rather than a positive code, Mencius defended Ruist ritual practice against the criticism that it absurdly sought an absolute perfection of mind, Sagehood, through an arbitrary dynastic code. While avoiding the claim that Zhou *li* constituted the path to Sagehood, Mencius' theory of *hsing* preserved an essential theoretical linkage between *li* and the ideal of Sagehood" (Robert Eno, *The Confucian Creation of Heaven—Philosophy and the Defense of Ritual Mastery* [Albany: State University of New York Press, 1990], 129).

6. See, e.g., 1B:3, 2A:4, 4A:1, 4A:7, 4A:8, 5A:4, 5A:7, 6A:6.

7. The first occurrence is in 5A:5 and refers to Shun's being accepted by Heaven to rule: "He was put in charge of sacrifices, and the hundred spirits took pleasure in them." The second is in 7A:13, describing the influence of the noble person: "Where the noble person passes by, there is transformation; where he resides, there is spirituality (*shen*)." The third is in 7B:25, describing the "good man," the "beautiful man," the "great man," and the "sage": "Being great and exerting a transforming influence, one is called a sage. Being a sage and unknowable, one is called spiritual (*shen*)."

8. Max Weber, *The Religion of China—Confucianism and Taoism*, trans. Hans H. Gerth, Introduction by C. K. Yang (New York: Free Press, 1964).

9. Ibid., 146.

10. Lee H. Yearley, "Toward a Typology of Religious Thought: A Chinese Example," *Journal of Religion* 55, no. 4 (October 1975): 426–43; quotation from p. 426.

11. Ibid., 433–34.

12. Ibid., 429–30.

13. Chong Yu is here quoting Mencius, who in turn was quoting Confucius in *Analects* 14:37.

14. For a somewhat different interpretation, see Ivanhoe, "Question of Faith."

15. Yearley, "Typology," 431.

16. This is the opinion of Robert Eno in *Confucian Creation of Heaven*, 101–6. Eno argues: "The key to understanding the role of T'ien in Mencius' political doc-

trines is to bear in mind that its role was marginal and of little intrinsic importance to the doctrines themselves or to Mencius' concrete political goals. Because Mencius' attention was not focused on articulating a consistent theory of T'ien in this regard, the meaning of T'ien in relevant statements varies with particular fluidity according to the instrumental context in which T'ien was discussed" (p. 101).

17. See also the statement attributed to Confucius at the end of *Mencius* 6A:8 below.

18. *Mencius* 2A:4 and 4A:8, quoting the "T'ai-chia" chapter of the *Classic of Documents*.

19. *Analects* 17:19 (*Harvard Yenching Concordance*, 17:17).

20. Weber, *Religion of China*, 145.

21. Ibid., 228.

22. Ibid., 146. The reference may have been to Kant.

23. This is the claim of Roger Ames in "Religiousness in Classical Confucianism: A Comparative Analysis," *Asian Culture Quarterly* 12, no. 2 (Summer 1984): 14. Ames argues that the idea of transcendence is "a distinguishing presupposition in Western cosmogony" (p. 11) and "misattributed to classical Chinese philosophy" (p. 15).

24. See Lau, trans., *Mencius*, p. 46.

25. Wilfred Cantwell Smith, *Faith and Belief* (Princeton: Princeton University Press, 1979), 103.

13

The Ethical and the Religious Dimensions of *Li*

A. S. CUA

THIS ESSAY PRESENTS A CONFUCIAN perspective on *li*. My main concern is the question, How can a Confucian moral philosopher move from the ethical to the religious dimension of *li*? The first section provides an analysis of the scope, evolution, and functions of *li*. The second section deals with the inner aspect of the foundation of conduct, the motivational aspect of *li*-performance. The third section discusses the outer aspect of the foundation of *li*, focusing on Xunzi's vision of triad of *tian*, earth, and humanity (*can tianti*), an interpretation of his use of *tian*, *shen*, and *shenming* as expressing a respect for established linguistic, religious practice without an endorsement of associated popular religious beliefs. This interpretation leaves open the question of the validity of reasoned religious beliefs, while presuming the religious dimension of *li* as an extension of Confucian ethics.[1] The final section centers on the ethical significance of the *li* of mourning and sacrifice and concludes with some remarks on the transformative significance of the religious dimension of *li*.

An Analysis of *Li*

For more than two millennia, traditional Chinese moral life and thought have been much preoccupied with *li* as a means for the realization of the Confucian ideal of *dao* (Way) or human excellence (*shan*). Implicit in this notion of *li* is an idea of rule-governed conduct. A rough indication of its scope may be gathered from a list of possible translations. Depending on the context of Confucian discourse, *li* can be translated as "religious rites, ceremony, deportment, decorum, propriety, formality, politeness, courtesy, etiquette, good form, good behavior, [or] good manners."[2] For convenience of reference it is sometimes desirable to use such terms as "propriety," "rules of propriety," or "rules of proper conduct" (Legge, Dubs). For marking the pervasive feature of the members of this list, one might propose such terms as "rites/rituals," "ritual propriety," or "ritual rules," especially if we think of "rites" in the broad sense as inclusive of any established practice or set of action guides that stresses formal procedures for proper behavior. But without explicit explanation, this usage is likely to be misleading, particularly in view of the different connotations of the term. For this reason, I shall retain the transliteration *li* in my discussion and adopt Xunzi's distinction between generic (*gongming*) and specific terms (*bieming*). A generic term is a formal, general, abstract term amenable to specification by other terms in different contexts of discourse. These terms, used in practical or theoretical contexts, may be said to be specific terms in the sense that they specify the significance of the use of a generic term adapted to a current purpose of discourse. *Li* will be used as a generic notion subject to specification in context by such locutions as "the *li* of *x*," where *x* may mean "mourning," "sacrifices," "marriage," "manners," and so on.[3] In this sense, law, morality, religion, and other social institutions, insofar as they require compliance with formal procedures, may be said to be concerned with ritual propriety. However, as a term for compendious description of the scope of *li*, "ritual propriety" or the like presupposes some understanding of the connection of *li* with other cardinal notions of Confucian ethics. Although we occasionally refer to the dependence of the ethical significance of *li* on *ren* (benevolence, humanity), and *yi* (rightness, righteousness), for present purposes, we assume their conceptual connection without elaboration.[4]

Our explication of *li* is based mainly on the works of Xunzi and *Liji* (*Record of Li*).[5] The *Liji* is one of the three extant ancient texts on *li*: *Zhouli*, *Yili*, and *Liji*. *Zhouli* deals with Zhou organization and institutions, *Yili* with codes of social conduct. The *Liji* mainly "deals with the meaning and significance of organization and institutions as well as with rules of social life and certain related academic matters."[6] The extensive scope of *li* is indicated by the title of James Legge's translation: "Collection of Treatises on the Rules of Propriety or Ceremonial Usages."

The Scope and Evolution of Li

In the *Liji*, we find a wide scope of *li*, ranging from the *li* governing special occasions, such as mourning, sacrifices, marriage, and communal festivities, to the more ordinary occasions relating to conduct toward ruler, parents, elders, teachers, and guests. Different classifications are possible. Zhu Xi points to five different sorts of concerns exemplified in the *li*: family, communities, study, states, and dynasties. A more modern but misleading classification can be offered in terms of law, religion, military matters, politics, and ethics.[7]

For elucidating the concept *li*, let us briefly consider its conceptual evolution. Following Hu Shi (1891–1962), we may view the wide-ranging scope as exemplifying three different strata in the conceptual evolution of *li*.[8] The basic meaning of *li* lies in the idea of rule. (In this sense, Dubs's rendering of *li* as "rules of proper conduct" is perhaps the best.) The evolution of *li* refers to its increasing extension. The earliest use, as far as scholars are able to ascertain, pertains to religious rites. The etymology of *li* suggests its connection with sacrifices to spirits. *Shuowen*, an ancient dictionary, notes that *li* is "compliance [with rules] for serving spirits (*shen*) and obtaining blessings."[9]

In the second stage, *li* becomes a comprehensive notion embracing all social habits and customs acknowledged and accepted as a set of action-guiding rules. In this sense, the scope of *li* is coextensive with that of tradition comprising established conventions, that is, customs and usages deemed as a coherent set of precedents. "*Li* is what distinguishes human beings from animals" (*Quli*, Legge, 1:64–65).

The third stage in the evolution of *li* is connected with the notions of right (*yi*) and reason (*li**). In this sense, any rule that is right and reasonable can be accepted as an exemplary rule of conduct. Rules can be constructed or revised, and thus are not exclusively determined by old customs and usages.[10] As one writer remarked: "The *li* are [the prescriptions of] reason. . . . The superior man (*junzi*) makes no movement without [a ground of] reason" (*Zhongni yanqu*, Legge, 2:275). Another emphatic passage maintains that "[the rules of] *li* are the embodied expression of what is right (*yi*). If an observance stands the test of being judged by the standard of what is right (*yi*), although it may not have been among the usages of the ancient kings, it may be adopted on the ground of its being right" (*Liji*, Legge, 1:390). It is quite evident that the *Liji*, like *Xunzi*, was concerned with the problem of ethical justification. As Arthur Waley reminds us, "The task of the ritual theorists in the third century B.C. was to detrivialize ritual, to arrest its lapse into a domain of mere etiquette or good manners by reintegrating it into the current system of thought."[11] The task consists, in part, in defending specific rules of propriety and, in part, in offering reasoned justification for the existence of an established normative system. This concern of ancient Confucians is shown in their occasional tendency to associate *li* with its homophone *li** (reason or rationale) and *yi* (rightness or fittingness).[12] The notion of *yi*, in part, is an attempt to provide a rationale for the acceptance of *li*. *Yi* focuses principally on what is right or fitting. Since what is right and reasonable depends primarily on judgment, *yi* may be understood as reasoned judgment concerning the right thing to do, more especially in particular exigencies. In two respects, acceptability of *li* depends on *yi*: (1) *yi* determines whether specific rules of *li* are the right sort of rules to regulate different types of conduct, and (2) the application of *li* requires *yi*, in the sense of reasoned judgment for their application to particular cases. Thus, any established system of *li* is subject to an *yi*-evaluation, given the conceptual connection of *li* and *yi*.[13]

For explicating the rationale of *li* (*lizhili*), we attend to overlapping questions concerning its significance (*lizhiyi*) and foundation of *li* (*lizhiben*).[14]

The Significance of Li (lizhiyi)

In his essay on *li*, Xunzi points out that the rationale of *li** (*lizhili*) is truly profound (*Lilun*, L428, W93). One must not confuse questions concerning the plurality or numerousness of *li* (*lizhishu*) and their underlying significance (*lizhiyi*). The *li*, or rules of proper conduct, provide models without explanation (*Quanxue*, L14, W20). For a *junzi* (the paradigmatic individual), moral learning must culminate in the state of integrity or "completeness and purity" (*quancui*). And the achievement of integrity depends on efforts to attain *guantong*, that is, to gain a comprehensive understanding of the meaning and practical import of the texts (*Quanxue*, L19, W 22).[15] We find similar emphasis on the significance of *li* in the *Liji*. In the chapter on border sacrifices, the writer stated that "what is esteemed in the *li*-performance is its [underlying] significance. When this is missed, the number of things and observances may [still] be exhibited (*Jiaode xing*, Legge, 1:439*).

To appreciate the significance of *li* (*lizhiyi*), it is instructive to consider its principal functions by pondering Xunzi's remark on the origin of *li*.

> What is the origin of *li*? I answer that men are born with desires. If their desires are not satisfied, they cannot but seek means for satisfaction. If there are no limits or measures to govern their pursuit, contention will inevitably result. From contention comes disorder and from disorder comes poverty. The ancient Kings hated such disorder, and hence they established *li* (rules of proper conduct) and inculcated *yi* (sense of rightness) in order to make distinctions (*fen*) and boundaries of responsibility for regulating men's pursuit, to educate and nourish (*yang*) men's desires, to provide opportunity for their satisfaction (*keren zhi qiu*). They saw to it that desires did not overextend the means of satisfaction, and material goods did not fall short of what was

desired. Thus, both desires and goods mutually support each other. This is the origin of *li*. (*Lilun*, L417, Watson 1963, 88*)

Delimiting Function

The main objective of *li* or its primary function is to prevent social disorder, which for Xunzi, is an inevitable result of humans' conflicting pursuit of things to satisfy their desires. Elsewhere he reminds his readers that the scarcity of resources to satisfy everyone's desires would inevitably lead to contention (*zheng*) or conflict. Notably, as a set of rules for proper conduct, *li* has a delimiting function, that is, defining the limits of individual pursuit of self-interest as well as boundaries of ethical responsibility. In this respect, the rules of *li* are functionally analogous to those of negative moral injunctions against killing, lying, stealing, and so on. We must also note that for Xunzi, there is also a complementary positive objective in *li*-regulation, that is, the rules of *li* are necessary to human life in society and community. For this reason, cooperation through division of labor and observance of social or class distinctions (*fen*) are required for an orderly, harmonious social life.

For Xunzi, the most important social distinctions are the distinctions of eminent and mean, elder and younger, rich and poor, important and unimportant members of society. These distinctions represent different sorts of responsibilities. From the sociological point of view, the *li* are concerned with the maintenance of social structure as a harmonious pattern of roles and statuses.[16] Much in the spirit of Xunzi, one writer in the *Liji* remarks: "It is by the *li* that what is doubtful is displayed, and what is minute is distinguished, that they may serve as dykes for the people. Thus it is that there are grades of the noble and the mean, the distinctions of dress, the different places at court; and so the people [are taught to] give place to one another" (*fangji*, Legge, 2:285; also 1:63). Again, it is said that "it is by the universal application of the *li* that the lot and duty [of different classes] are fixed" (*Liyun*, Legge, 1:378). For the ruler, the *li* are an important instrument of social and political control, but notably, the social distinctions are valued not only because of their traditional backing but also because of their display of personal moral merits. The significance of *li* as a tradition thus lies in its implicit critical moral acceptance.

Supportive Function

The idea of *li* as dykes for conserving virtues provides a way to appreciate the supportive function. Recall Xunzi's remark on the origin of *li*; the rules of *li* also provide satisfaction of desires within the boundary of proper conduct. Within this boundary of proper conduct, expression of feelings and desires must be recognized. In Xunzi's words, the *li* must provide for opportunity for their satisfaction (*geiren zhi qiu*). Thus, in addition to the delimiting function, the *li* have a supportive function; that is, they provide conditions or opportunities for satisfaction of desires within the prescribed limits of action. The *junzi*, ethically paradigmatic individuals, are the same as the small-minded persons with respect to their nature (*xing*) and capacities (*cai*) for acquiring knowledge and action.

> When hungry, they desire food, when cold, they desire to be warm; when exhausted from toil, they desire rest; and they all desire benefit and hate harm. Such are the nature that men are born possessing. They do not have to await development before they become so. (*Rongru*, L64, K1:191)

In an important sense, the supportive function of *li* acknowledges the integrity of our natural desires. So long as they are satisfied within the bounds of propriety, we accept them for what they are whether reasonable or unreasonable, wise or foolish, good or bad. The main supportive function of *li* is the redirection of the course of individual self-seeking activities, not the suppression of motivating desires. This is the *sublimating* function of *li*. Just as the delimiting function of *li* is functionally analogous to that of negative moral injunctions or criminal law, their supportive function may be compared with that of procedural law, which contains rules that enable us to carry out our wishes and desires, for example, the law of wills and contracts. Like these procedural rules, the *li* contribute to the fulfillment of desires without pronouncing value judgments. More importantly, the *li* also have an educational and nourishing function (*yang*) in encouraging learning and cultivation of personal character, the subjects of the first two essays in the *Xunzi*. To be a human being, in the ethical rather than the biological sense, is to aspire to become an ethically responsible scholar or official (*shih*), a paradigmatic ethical person (*junzi*), or a sage (*sheng*).

More generally, in ordinary human intercourse, we can appreciate the supportive function of *li* by pondering the significance of the *li* of civility. Much of the *li* of civility facilitates human intercourse, especially among strangers. The *li* of civility are especially important in a discursive or argumentative context, for their supportive function reminds the parties in conflict that there must be agreeable procedures for resolving conflict before they deal with substantive matters at issue.[17] A Confucian philosopher, while aware of the possibility of mere observance of *li* without appropriate regard for *ren* and *yi*, will not altogether reject their ethical value, because conformity to the *li* of manners and civility is an example of regard for the necessity of *li* as having an *enabling* function in promoting easy, effortless, smooth conditions for human interaction.

The Ennobling Function

The focus on the ennobling function of *li* is a distinctive feature of Confucian ethics and traditional Chinese culture. The keynote of the ennobling function is "cultural refinement," the education and nourishment (*yang*) of emotions or their transformation in accord with the spirit of *ren* and *yi*. The characteristic concern with the form of proper behavior is still present. However, the form stressed is not just a matter of fitting into an established social structure or set of distinctions, nor is it a matter of methodical procedure that facilitates the satisfaction of the agent's desires and wishes; rather, it involves the elegant form (*wen*) for the expression of ethical character. A *li*-performance is not just an exhibition of an empty form, for the *junzi* complies with *li* in order "to give proper and elegant expression to his feelings" (Legge, 1:331). In other words, the ennobling function of *li* is directed primarily to the development of commendable or beautiful virtues (*meide*). The "beauty" (*mei*) of the expression of an ethical character lies in the balance between emotions and form. What is deemed admirable in the virtuous conduct of an ethically superior person (*junzi*) is the harmonious fusion of elegant form and feelings (*Lilun*, L430, Watson, 96). In the ideal case, a *li*-performance may be said to have an aesthetic dimension. In two different and related ways, a *li*-performance may be said to be an object of delight. In the first place, the elegant form is something that delights our senses. It can be contemplated with delight quite apart from the expressed emotional quality. In the second place, when we attend to the emotion or emotional quality expressed by the action, which we perceive as a sign of an ethical virtue or character, our mind is delighted and exalted, presuming of course that we are also agents interested in the promotion of ethical virtues in general.

Notably for Xunzi, the desired transformation of the original, problematic human nature (*xing*) is not just an outcome of a process of inculcation of moral virtues, principally directed to conflict resolution, but also a beautification of original human nature. As Xunzi put it:

> human nature (*xing*) provides raw material, and constructive human effort (*wei*) is responsible for the glorification and flourishing of elegant form and orderly expression. Without constructive human effort, human nature cannot beautify itself (*zimei*). Only when human nature and effort become one and the person who succeeds in unifying the world is entitled to the ascription of sagehood. (*Lilun*, L439, Watson, 102–3*)

In this light the *li*-performance culminates in the experience of joy. In Xunzi's words: "All rites (*li*) begin in simplicity, are brought to fulfillment in elegant form (*wen*), and end in joy" (*Lilun*, L427, W94).

With the ennobling function of *li* in mind, we can appreciate some scholars' preference for "noble person" as a translation of *junzi* (Giles, Fingarette, Schwartz). Divested of its aristocratic connotation, a noble person is an ethically superior person or paradigmatic individual whose life and conduct exemplify *meide*, or virtues, in a very high degree, embodying particularly the concern for *jen* and *yi*. As we shall see in the third section, respect for traditional *li*, or rites of mourning and sacrifices, is in part an expression for the concern with *ren* and *yi*, because such practices exemplify the Confucian *dao*, or ideal of humanity.

The Foundation of *Li* (*Lizhiben*): The Inner Aspect

For a contemporary Confucian moral philosopher, there are questions concerning the foundation of a person's commitment to the practice of *li*. Of course, lying in the background is an implicit commitment to the *li*'s ennobling function, that is, to *ren* and *yi*. Our question of foundation (*ben*) inquires, so to speak, into the supporting edifice that provides the actuating force to the commitment to the practice of *li*. We may approach this question by distinguishing the inner (*nei*) and outer (*wai*) aspects of the foundation of *li* deemed as the anchorage of the agent's serious commitment to the Confucian *dao* or ideal of human excellence (*shan*). In the language of *Daxue* (*The Great Learning*) such a person has attained *cheng* (sincerity) and is free from self-deception; that is, he or she has attained, in Zhu Xi's words, the state of "truthfulness, genuineness, and freedom from falsity" (*zhenshi wuwang*).[18] Whereas the inner aspect of the *li*-performance pertains to *cheng* (sincerity) embracing a variety of moral attitudes, dispositions, and emotions, the outer aspect pertains to the underlying Confucian vision of the unity and harmony of humanity and *tian* (Heaven, Nature) and its implication for concern for the well-being of all things in the universe.[19] Differently put, the inner aspect pertains to the psychology of *li*-performance, the outer aspect to the committed person's ultimate concern, to his/her understanding of the *dao* as a moral vision with cosmic significance. As we shall later see, the outer aspect of the foundation of *li* provides a transition to Confucian spirituality, or the religious dimension of *li*.

Let us first consider the inner aspect of a *li*-performance conformable, say, to a *li* of civility, manners, or deportment. The *li* of manners and deportment are those formal prescriptions governing ordinary incidents of life, for example, greetings, bowing, handshakes, smiling in appropriate occasions, decency in speech and appearance, and so on. In this context, respectfulness (*gong*) and reverence (*jing*) are essential to the *li*-performance. More generally, the person must express *cheng* (sincerity). In one striking passage in the *Xunzi*, much reminiscent of *Zhongyong* (*Doctrine of the Mean*), we find the following: "For nourishing (*yang*) the mind of *junzi* (paradigmatic individual), there is nothing better than sincerity (*cheng*). For attaining sincerity there is no other concern than to abide by *ren* and to practice *yi*" (*Bugou*, L47, cf. Knoblock 1:177). Recall Mencius's saying: "Benevolence (*ren*) is man's peaceful abode and rightness (*yi*) his proper path" (4A:10).

Thus, the *cheng* (sincerity) of a *li*-performance presupposes a concern with *ren* and *yi*. In the light of *ren*, the agent, apart from attention to *wen*, or cultural refinement, must also have an affectionate concern for the well-being of one's fellows. And this concern involves *zhong* and *shu*—doing one's best to realize one's ethical commitment to the practice of *ren* (*Analects* 4:15; Lau 1979) and consideration of others' desires and thought (ibid., 15:24), presupposing *yi* as the ethical standard for the evaluation of conduct in an appropriate context of action.[20] Confucius's idea of *shu*, that is, "Do not impose on others what you yourself do not desire" (*Analects* 15:24), may be construed as a counsel of *humility* and *modesty*. While humility is compatible with just pride, it is a desirable moral attitude, because one's claim to knowledge about what is good for oneself and another must be proportional to accessible information and experience. While such knowledge may provide grounds for a claim for its significance for future conduct, reasonable persons would avow their sense of fallibility or humility. Sagacious or judicious judgments will also be informed by a sense of timeliness (*shi*), that is, an adaptation to the current situation in order to achieve equilibrium and an adjustment to varying, changing circumstances through the exercise of one's sense of rightness (*yi*).

Further, for the *ren*-person, humility is a desirable ethical attribute, because no human possesses the knowledge of all possible, appropriate specifications of the significance of the good for individual human life. As a result, one's understanding and concrete specification of the ideal of the good human life will always be made from a limited and partial perspective. When *shu* is positively construed, while it is compatible with just pride in ethical attainment, it is best construed as a counsel of modesty, which stresses the importance of making reasonable or moderate claims on others. One ordinary sense of "reasonable" indicates that a reasonable person will refrain from making excessive or extravagant demands on others.[21]

More fundamentally, in the light of Confucian *dao* or *ren* as an ideal theme of the good (*shan*), one must be modest in imposing wishes and desires upon others. A person committed to *ren* and *yi*, actuated by modesty or moderation, will be concerned with the mean (*zhong*) between excess and deficiency. Such a concern, however, presupposes that the agent exercises moral discretion (*quan*). As Mencius reminds us,

> Holding on to the middle [*zhong*] is closer to being right, but to do this with-out moral discretion [*quan*] is no different from holding to one extreme. The reason for disliking those who hold to one extreme is that they cripple the Way. One thing is singled out to the neglect of a hundred others. (Lau 1970, 7A:26*)[22]

Expression of concern for *ren* and *yi* requires, to borrow Hume's words, a delicacy of taste, sensitivity not only to *wen*, the elegant form of conduct, but also to others' "prosperity and adversity, obligations and injuries."[23] Again, recall Mencius's notion of commiseration as a beginning or seed of *ren* and a *ren*-person as one who has a *xin* (heart/mind) that is sensitive to the suffering of others (*Mencius*, 2A:6) and a sense of shame as a seed of the virtue of *yi*. On the latter, Xunzi would add that just as it is important to distinguish between intrinsic honor or honor justly deserved (*yirong*) and extrinsic honor or honor derived from a person's circumstance (*shirong*), one must also distinguish shame justly deserved (*yiru*) and shame derived from a person's circumstance (*shiru*). The honor and shame justly deserved are conditions of character for which one is ethically responsible. The shame justly deserved is thus the agent's responsibility, because the person has deliberately engaged in ethically wrong conduct, for example, conduct that is wayward and abandoned, reckless, arrogant and cruel, oppressive and rapacious (*Zhenglun*, L410–11, Knoblock 3:46). There is no assurance that intrinsic and extrinsic honor will coincide in practice. Abiding by benevolence (*ren*), acting in accord with one's sense of what is right (*yi*), and doing virtuous acts (*de*) are ordinarily reliable ways of managing one's life; however, it is possible that they may bring about dangerous (or unwanted) consequences (*Rongru*, L60, Knoblock 1:189). Yet it cannot be doubted that the honor and shame one morally deserves are products of one's own intentional acts and thus properly reflect one's virtues and vices (*Quanxue*, L5, W17). Implicit in both Mencius's and Xunzi's conceptions of shame is something like the distinction between social and ethical stan-dards.[24] Like Aristotle, classical Confucians were concerned with the noble and the base in the light of moral virtues and vices. Xunzi, in particular, would exalt a man of *li*, not just because his outward appearance and actions conform to *li*, but also because such a display makes manifest and glorious (*long*) his moral attainment.[25]

Before turning to the outer aspect of the foundation of *li*, let us briefly note that the attitudes, dispositions, and emotions involved in the inner aspect are complex and often associated with the names of virtues. The *Analects* provides an ample vocabulary of ordinary ethical virtues amenable to interpretation and reinterpretation of their significance. One thinks of such generic terms designating particular virtues such as filiality, courage, loyalty, fidelity, yielding to elders or superiors, uprightness, circumspection, and accommodation.[26] A different time and circumstance of the Confucian agents would yield different interpretations. Moreover, these terms refer to dependent virtues, for their ethical significance depends on concern for the cardinal virtues such as *ren* and *yi*. Positive attitudes toward these cardinal and dependent virtues are considered praiseworthy, just as negative attitudes toward the same virtues are disapproved of by the Confucians. Expression of emotions such as joy and sorrow, anger and resentment, as well as desires and aversions must observe the relevant *li* with due regard to *ren* and *yi*. Ethical attitudes, dispositions, and emotions are for the most part the outcome of education. The *junzi*, or paradigmatic individuals, persons whose lives exemplify a high degree of ethical attainment, play an important role in ethical education.[27]

Perhaps a bit stringent for people today, a Confucian would agree with Xunzi that such learning ceases until death (*Quanxue*, L2). Nevertheless, while moral learning is a heavy burden (*Analects* 7:7), it is not a process devoid of joy. Confucius once said of himself that his life is "so full of joy that he forgets his worries" (*Analects* 7:19). On another occasion, perhaps in a lighthearted mood, Confucius said that a *ren*-person would find joy in mountains and have a long life. The *ren* person, inspired by the ideal of *ren*, delights in mountains because his or her life is distinguished by an inspiration derived from the commitment to *ren*, as the highest ideal of the good human life as a whole (*shan*). In this sense, symbolically we may compare *ren*'s value height to the height of the mountains. And a person's *ren*-achievement, because of unwavering commitment and integrity, may be said to be still and firm as the mountains. But the idea that the *ren*-person is long-lived cannot be literally construed; for Confucius a paradigmatic individual (*junzi*), if the situation demands, "would sacrifice his life for the sake of *ren*" (*Analects* 15.9). The "long life" should be construed as "life-long" commitment to the ethical vision and/or the enduring character of *ren*-achievement. Perhaps, for this reason, Qian Mu, an eminent Confucian scholar, points out that this dialogue implicitly appeals to the Confucian ideal of *tianren heyi* (the unity and harmony of humans and Heaven [*tian*]).[28] When we turn to the outer aspect of the foundation of *li*, the relevance of this Confucian vision will become manifest.

The Foundation of *Li* (*Lizhiben*):
The Outer Aspect

One way to approach the religious dimension of *li* is to discuss the outer aspect of the foundation of *li*, which is intrinsically connected with the inner aspect. Because of the intricate complexity in scholarship on the religious or spiritual aspect of classical Confucianism, it is difficult for a Confucian moral philosopher to present an indubitable interpretation of the outer aspect of the foundation of *li* (*lizhiben*). Perhaps the reason lies in the essentially contestable and vague concepts such as "religion"and "spirituality" in contemporary Confucian and comparative Chinese and Western philosophy. If we think of such terms as somewhat descriptive of a person's "ultimate commitment," then for a Confucian, particularly for a Neo-Confucian like Cheng Hao and Wang Yangming, commitment to *ren* may be so characterized, because the Confucian *ren*, by virtue of the indefinite and inexhaustible extension of affectionate concern for all things, envisages the attainment of an exalted state in which one would "form one body with all things without differentiation."[29] This Confucian vision is commonly called by Chinese scholars *tianren heyi*, the ideal of the unity and harmony of humanity and Heaven (*tian*). More commonly in the classical texts, we find the notion of *can tianti*, humans "forming a triad with Heaven and earth."

Because of this vision, Xunzi exalts (*long*) the *li* as "joining Heaven and Earth in harmony" (*Lilun*, L427, W94). He is emphatic, however, that the profound rationale of *li* (*lizhili*) cannot be captured by the practitioners of the School of Names (Mingjia), arguing over such topics as "hardness and whiteness," "similarity and difference," nor by "uncouth and inane theories of the system-makers," nor by "the violent and arrogant ways of those who despise customs and consider themselves to be above other men" (*lilun*, L429, W94–95). Xunzi continues:

> He who dwells in *li* and can ponder it well may be said to know how to think; he who dwells in li and does not change his ways may be said to be steadfast, and in addition has a true love for *li*—he is a sage. Heaven is the acme of loftiness, earth the acme of depth, the boundless the acme of breadth, and the sage the acme of the Way. Therefore, the scholar studies to become a sage; he does not study merely to become one of the people without direction. (*Lilun*, L429, W94–95*)

As a preliminary to understanding Xunzi's ideal of *can tianti*, let us mention the different conceptions of the relation of *tian* and *ren* (humanity). In ancient China we find three different conceptions embodying different ideals of the good human life. First, we find the idea of *tianren ganying*, the vision of mutual interplay of *tian* and humans exemplified in *Mozi*; second, the Taoist vision of *yinren ziran* embodied in *Lao Tzu* and *Zhuangzi*, the vision of humans' harmony with the natural order of events oblivious of human desires and ethical concerns; and third, the more influential Confucian (Mencian) vision of *tianren hede* in the *Mengzi*, the vision of achieving unity and harmony of *tian* and humans through the perfection of ethical character and virtues. The fourth vision is exemplified in Xunzi's vision of *tiansheng rencheng*, the vision that *tian* provides materials for humans to complete their proper tasks, through the exercise of their native capacities.[30]

Tian as Nature

At the outset of Xunzi's essay on *tian*, we find a sharp distinction between *tian* and humans (*tianren zhi fen*). *Tian* is the domain of *chang*, constancy or regularities of natural occurrences. For the most part, human fortune or misfortune depends on human efforts. As long as one follows the *dao* with single-mindedness, *tian* cannot bring misfortune. Says Xunzi:

> To bring completion without acting, to obtain without seeking—this is the work of *tian*. Thus, although the sage has deep understanding, he does not attempt to exercise it upon the work of *tian;* though he has great talent, he does not attempt to apply it to the work of *tian;* though he has keen perception, he does not attempt to use it on the work of *tian.* Hence, he does not compete against *tian*'s work. *Tian* has its seasons, earth has its riches, man has his government. Hence man may form a triad (*can*) with the other two. But if he set aside that which allows him to form a triad with the other two and longs for what they have, then he is deluded. (*Tianlun*, L362, W79–80*)

The above citation is Watson's translation except for substituting *tian* for "Heaven," a common rendering of *tian*. One may question the adequacy of this translation in the *Xunzi*, for, unlike in Confucius and Mencius, *tian* in most of Xunzi's uses, especially in our citation, is best rendered as "Nature" or "nature" in the sense of *tian* as "the objective, abstract operation of certain processes and principles of Nature" (Knoblock, 3:7). On the other hand, rendering *tian* as "Nature" or "nature" often leads to ascribing implausible interpretive theses to Xunzi.[31] While we cannot settle the interpretive issues here, "nature" seems a useful term for capturing Xunzi's conception of *tian*. For *tian*, like *dao*, in Chinese philosophy, is a generic term (*gongming*) adaptable to different uses by different schools of thought.[32] For rendering *tian* as "nature" or "natural," some explanatory addenda are in order.

First, *tian* as nature is *chang*, the domain of regularities, that is, our normal, usual, or customary experience of events or states of affairs. In practical planning and deliberation, we rely on such experience in expecting occurrence or recurrence of events and states of affairs. For Xunzi, this domain of natural phenomena must not be confused with that of *wei*, or the *artificial*, that is, events and phenomena that occur as a result of constructive human efforts. This distinction is explicit in Xunzi's essay on *xing* (human nature), where he maintains that it is a mistake to attribute goodness to native human nature (*xing*), for human goodness or excellence (*shan*) is a product of *wei*. Attainment of *shan* is an outcome of *wei*, or constructive human activity molding *xing*, the basic and problematic, motivational structure of humans, into an ethically acceptable and beautiful nature. Of course, when a cultivated person achieves goodness, his or her virtues of integrity (*quan*) and purity (*cui*) will become second nature. Human nature is a raw material much like a potter's clay or a carpenter's wood for making pots and utensils (Xing'e, L550, W164*).

Second, *tian* as the domain of *chang* or natural regularities, does not preclude apparent anomalies such as falling stars and eclipses, which are viewed by ordinary folks as terrifying events or phenomena (*kong*), as objects of fear and anxiety, because of people's superstitious belief that these occurrences portend misfortune. For Xunzi, these strange, abnormal, and uncanny occurrences are proper objects of wonder or awe rather than fear.

> The sun and moon are subject to eclipses, wind and rain do not always come at the proper season, and strange stars occasionally appear. There has never been an age that was without such occurrences. If the ruler is enlightened and his government just, then there is no harm done even if they occur at the same time. But if the ruler is benighted and his government ill-run, then it will be no benefit to him even if they never occur at all. (*Tianlun*, L373, W83–84)

The proper objects of fear are such human portents as poor harvest, evil government that loses the support of the people, neglect of the fields, and starvation of the people. These are calamities that result from human actions rather than from natural causes (ibid., 84–85).[33]

While Xunzi clearly rejects superstitious beliefs concerning apparent anomalies of *tian* as objects of fear, it is difficult to interpret with confidence his view that they are the proper objects of wonder or awe. Perhaps his view is that these are marvelous events that require no explanation, because they have no relevance to human well-being. It is also possible that Xunzi has a special regard for the belief that the anomalies exemplify "the uncanny and the supernatural" as awesome events, for he does not deny significance to all omens. "He makes a clear distinction between those who presage human misfortune, and hence are to be held in awe, and those which do not, and may only be deemed wield (*guai*)."[34]

Notably, some seemingly unusual or rare occurrences are often viewed by common people as *miraculous* and as having potential beneficial or harmful effects on human welfare. For people who believe in the efficacy of magical practices, certain humans possess magical power. While Xunzi considered the belief superstitious, on par with belief in physiognomy (*Feixiang*, L73-91, K1:196-211), he did not condemn these practices.

> When you perform sacrifice for rain and it rains. Why? For no particular reason, I say. It is just as though you had not prayed for rain and it rained anyway. When the sun or moon are eclipsed, your try to save them; a drought occurs and you pray for rain; you consult the art of divination before making a decision on some important matter. But it is not as though you could hope to accomplish anything by such ceremonies. They are done merely done for the sake of *wen*. The ethically superior person [*junzi*] regards them as matters of *wen*, but the common people regard them as matters of *shen*. He who considers them as matters of *wen* is fortunate; he who considers them as matters of *shen* is unfortunate. (*Tianlun*, L376, W85*)

Recall that *wen*, the beauty or elegant form of behavior, pertain to matters of cultural refinement. In this passage, the belief that *shen* is responsible for rain is considered to be unworthy of acceptance, yet Xunzi does not condemn the rain sacrifice. Why? Perhaps, when we turn to Xunzi's remark on the three bases (*ben*) for the practice of *li*, another expression of *can tianti*, a plausible explanation is available.

> The *Li* have three bases: *Tian* and earth are the basis of life, the ancestors are the basis of the family, and rulers and teachers are the basis of order. If there were no *tian* or earth, how could men be born? If there were no ancestors, how would the family come into being? If there were no rulers or teachers, how would order be brought about? If even one of these were lacking, there would be no peace and security for people (*an*). Hence, *li* serves Heaven (*tian*) above and earth below, honors the ancestors, and exalts (*long*) rulers and teachers. These are the three bases of *li*. (*Lilun*, L421–22, W91*)

This passage suggests that peace and security (*an*) are primary considerations in the enforcement of the *li*, regardless of their reasoned explanation and justification. This concern with people's peace and security reflects the commitment to *ren*, an affectionate concern for the well-being of one's fellows in the community. Says Xunzi, "a *ren* person loves others. He loves others and thus hates what injures others" (*Yibing*, L328, W69*). But a *ren* person must respect others regardless of their capabilities or his own desire for association (*Chentao*, L298, Knoblock, 2:202).[35] For securing peace and security, the ruler and the well-informed Confucian elites must not interfere with people's religious beliefs, regardless of their reasonableness. For Xunzi, *xin* (mind) has a volitional function that may counteract its intellectual function. Given its autonomy, *xin* can act on its own will without regard to reason. And without the guidance of reason, it is bound to lead to delusion.[36] Yet, regarding the efficacy of the *li*, the ruler or responsible authority cannot ignore or legislate against ordinary people's religious beliefs, even if they are deemed unreasonable. It is not the business of those in government or ethical persons of the community to ensure that ordinary people hold reasonable religious beliefs. To borrow William James's term, respect for people's "will to believe" is essential to the preservation of a harmonious social and political order. Perhaps this concern with the efficacy of the enforcement of the *li* is implied in this passage: "The [efficacy of] *li* relies on conformity to human *xin* (mind) as foundation. Hence, even if there were no *li* in the *Classic of Li*, so long as they accord with *xin*, they may be considered as part of *li*" (*Dalue*, L605; cf. Knoblock, 3:211).

Moreover, recall our earlier discussion of *shu* as embracing modesty and humility. Having no infallible knowledge of the good (*shan*), the *junzi*, or ethically superior persons, without compromising their intellectual integrity, would refrain from condemning religious beliefs that they consider ill-founded or superstitious. They would adhere to their conviction that the rain sacrifice is a matter of *wen*, a cultural embellishment. The associated popular belief in magic has no positive ethical significance, since it does not contribute to the realization of the Confucian vision of the unity of *tian*, earth, and humanity (*can tianti*). Unless the practice of superstitious beliefs is detrimental to preserving the ethical order of the community, such beliefs may be condoned without endorsement. Perhaps Xunzi's attitude may be characterized by George Berkeley's epigram: "We ought think with the learned, and speak with the vulgar."[37] Admittedly some of Xunzi's uses of *shen* indicate approval of some religious beliefs, though we cannot be certain of his definitive views. Let us consider a couple of passages using *shen* and binomial *shenming*.

Shen and Shenming

Xunzi gives two explanations of the meaning of *shen*. We find the first and primary definition in his essay on *tian*. For convenience of reference, let us call this definition D_1. This passage involving *shen* pertains to natural regularities of *tian*, the transformative process of *yin* and *yang*:

> Although we do not see the process, we can observe the results. All people understand that the process has reached completion, but none understands the formless or unobservable factors underlying the process. For this reason, it is properly called the accomplishment of *tian*. Only the sage does not seek to understand *tian*. (*Tianlun pian*, L65, W80*)[38]

In this passage, *shen* pertains to the unobservable and inexplicable thing that underlies the process. This use of *shen* recalls the succinct remark in the *Yijing*: "The unfathomable *yinyang* process is what is meant by *shen*."[39] This use of *shen* seems to imply the existence of a supernatural or transcendental entity at the base of natural processes. Thus, *shen* is often translated as "spirit" or "god," as this is a common use in ancient literature. This use is exemplified in our earlier citation of the passage on the rain sacrifice. Here our question concerns not the propriety of translation but the interpretation of *shen* as referring to a special superhuman being. For Xunzi, the question concerning the existence and nature of such a being has no special relevance to resolving human problems; thus, the sage-aspiring person will not seek knowledge of *tian*. Because of his pragmatic attitude toward metaphysical or ontological discourse, Xunzi discourages inquisitiveness into the inexplicable factors that underlie natural processes, though, as we have seen earlier, he appreciates wonder or awe as a fitting response to strange and uncanny phenomena.

A secondary definition of *shen* (D_2) pertains to ascription of ethical excellence or goodness to ideal persons. "To be wholly good and fully self-disciplined is called *shen*"(*Ruxiao pian*, L141). In both D_1 and D_2 Xunzi makes use of the quasi-definitional locution *zhiwei* in two different ways. D_1, where *zhiwei* is a component of *fushi zhiwei*, provides both the necessary and sufficient conditions for the proper use of *shen*. D_2, on the other hand, provides only the necessary condition.[40] Divested of ontological interpretation, anything that satisfies the definition D_1 must be considered something mysterious and incomprehensible. I suspect that Xunzi is offering a demythologized conception of *shen* that echoes the one given in the *Yi Jing*. D_2, however, seems to be an explanation of the use of *shen* as a metaphor, while conveying the sense of the mysterious and the inexplicable. The context in which *shen* occurs in D_2 is concerned with characterizing the sage as one whose Way of life and thought proceeds from Oneness, that is, the person who resolutely holds fast to *shen*. This use of *shen* is plausibly a metaphor implying an analogy with *shen* in the sense of D_1 as in the expression *rushen*, which occurs in three passages that deal with good and well-ordered government.

Let us look at one passage involving *rushen*. In this instance, the discussion pertains to how an enlightened ruler (*mingjun*) unifies and guides the people by the Way (*dao*) and makes clear the ethical teachings and the use of punishment to forbid evils. Thus, says Xunzi, "His people are transformed by the Way as though his actions were those of a *shen*."[41] Here *shen* can be properly rendered as "spirit" or "god." In effect, Xunzi is saying that what an enlightened ruler accomplishes through *dao* is much like (*ru*) a *shen*. Much like the *yinyang* process, there is something mysterious and inexplicable, as indicated by Xunzi's remark that precedes his discussion: "It is easy to unify the people by means of the Way, though the ruler could not make them understand all the reasons for things" (*Zhengming*, L520, D289*). This remark recalls Confucius: "The common people can be made to follow a path but not to understand it" (*Analects* 8:9; Lau 1979).

First, let us note that the use of *shen* according to D_2, implies a positive, normative judgment, expressing both approval and commendation. If we consider this use to be metaphorical, then as in the case of D_1 ontological interpretation is irrelevant. At the heart of this use is an analogy between one thing and another. For instance, the expression "He is a *shen*" is essentially a collapsed simile "He is like a *shen*." Here *shen* is a metaphor in that it is a term that applies to something to which it is not literally applicable in order to suggest a resemblance to *shen* in the primary sense of D_1, a metaphorical extension of D_1.

For dealing with Xunzi's conception of *shenming*, let us look at an interesting passage where we find a connection between *cheng* (sincerity), *ming* (insight, clarity), and *shen*.

> For nourishing (*yang*) the mind of *junzi* (paradigmatic individual), there is nothing better than sincerity (*cheng*). For attaining sincerity there is no other concern than to abide by *ren* and to practice *yi*. When his mind (*xin*) has attained *cheng* and abided by *ren*, his *cheng* will become manifest. In this way, he becomes a *shen* and is capable of transforming things (*hua*). When his mind is sincere (*cheng*) and he acts according to his sense of rightness (*yi*), he becomes reasonable (*li**). When his mind is reasonable, it is in the state of *ming*. Consequently, he [can adapt himself] to changing circumstances. (*Bugou pian*, L47; cf. K1:177-78)

In this passage, construing *shen* as a metaphor, an ellipsis of *rushen*, we can render it as "godlike." Remarkably the passage recalls a similar idea of the connection of *cheng* and *ming* and the vision of the triad of *tian*, earth, and humanity (*can tianti*) in the *Zhongyong*, where we find the view that truly sincere (*cheng*) persons who possess *ming* can develop themselves as well as others and "can then assist in the transforming and nourishing processes of Heaven (*tian*) and Earth, [and] can thus form a trinity with Heaven and Earth [*can tianti*]."[42] More importantly, as Xunzi goes on to point out, although the sages are wise, without *cheng* they cannot transform the multitude (*Bugou pian*, L47). Implicit is the notion of the sage (*shengren*) as one who embodies the confluence of *cheng* and *ming*.

Let us turn to a passage involving *shenming* in the context of Xunzi's claim that all ordinary persons are capable of becoming sages—a view shared by Mencius, and Song-Ming Confucians. According to Xunzi, all ordinary persons have a native capability to understand the rationales (*li**) of *ren, yi,* and rules and regulations. If they devote themselves with single-mindedness to moral learning and contemplate the significance of *ren, yi,* and rules and regulations, persevere over a long period of time, through unceasing effort to accumulate good deeds, "they can acquire a comprehensive *shenming* (*tong yu shenming*) into the inner significance of things and form a triad with *tian* and earth (*can tianti*). Thus the sage is one who has attained the highest state through the accumulation of good deeds" (*Xing'e*, L552, W167*). After we consider another use of the binomial "*shenming*," we will comment on this use.

In the essay on dispelling *bi* (obscuration, blindness of the mind), Xunzi maintains that unless the mind is in the state of *ming* (clarity), it is liable to suffer from *bi*. Earlier we referred to this passage for Xunzi's conception of the autonomy of human mind without considering the full context involving the use of *shenming*. The passage runs: "The mind [*xin*] is the ruler of the body and *shenming zhi zhu*" (*Jiebi pian*, L488). We find different English translations for "*shenming zhi zhu*," e.g., "the master of godlike intelligence" (W139), "the master of the daemonic-and-clear-seeing" (Graham), "the master of spiritual intelligence" (K3:105), and "the host to such a divine manifestation" (Machle).[43] It is difficult to resolve the issue here. I propose, as a minimal interpretation, perhaps acceptable to these translators, that we regard *shenming* here in the light of the connection between *shen* and *ming*. Interpreting *shen* as "godlike" and *ming* as "insight" gives us a reading of *shenming* as a special characteristic of the sage, an interpretation closer to Graham and Knoblock, with an additional appreciation of Machle's rendering of *chu* as "host."[44] Construing *shen* in *shenming* as "godlike," we have the sense of insight (*ming*) that befits a god or spirit (*shen*), a rare and extraordinary human achievement. In this light, it is also accept-able to render *shenming* as "spiritual insight," which suggests an affinity to Descartes' notion of *intuitus*,[45] although for Xunzi *shenming* is more a form of wisdom or perspicacity—a product of cultivation, accumulation of goodness, and evidential learning (*chengzhi*), rather than an a priori intu-ition or way of knowledge. In the essay on encouraging learning, Xunzi remarks that "if a *junzi* engages in extensive learning and daily examines himself, his wisdom will become clear [*ming*] and conduct be without fault" (*Quanxue*, L2, W15*).

However, more accomplished is the sage who possesses an understand-ing (*zhi*) of the holistic character of *dao*. A doctrine of the *dao* based on a limited perspective, raising for attention "one corner" of *dao*, is insufficient to capture its intrinsic holistic nature (*Jiebi*, L478, W126; *Tianlun*, L381, W87). Because of this understanding of "the thread of *dao* (*daoquan*)," with-out deliberation or planning, the sage can respond appropriately to changes as they come.[46] The understanding (*zhi*) is an insight into the interconnec-tion of things rather than factual knowledge. Unlike a truth claim, the sage's insight is akin to keen appreciation or perception of the significance of the interconnection of facts that sheds light on human problems.[47] Suc-cinctly put, a sage has "a keen insight which never fails" (*Xiushen*, L33, W30).

If the foregoing remarks on *shenming* are considered adequate for under-standing Xunzi's use of *shenming*, we can also appreciate Machle's transla-tion of *chu* as "the host," rather than the common translation "the master," thus rendering the phrase on the mind (*xin*) as "the host of *shenming*." For insight (*ming*) arrived at through a long process of learning and self-cultiva-tion, including constant self-examination, is something that one acquires not as a result of thinking or inference but as a consummation and reward of a lifelong effort in pursuing *daoquan* or a holistic understanding of *dao* and *liquan*, the "thread that runs through the rationales of things." The sage is a recipient of *shenming*. Something echoing this interpretation of *shenming* may be found in Zhu Xi's conception of *qiongli* (exhaustive investigation of the rationales (*li**) of things. Zhu Xi writes:

> The first step in the education of the adult is to instruct the learner, in regard to all things in the world, to proceed from what knowledge he has of their rationales [*li**], and investigate further until he reaches the limit. After exert-ing himself in this way for a long time, he will one day achieve a wide and far-reaching penetration [*quantong*].[48]

Understanding the living significance of classical texts is an occurrence, something that happens independently of one's efforts, though efforts are the prerequisite for this experience. Recall our earlier emphasis on effort to *quantong* as essential to the *junzi*'s attainment of moral integrity, that is, to gain a comprehensive understanding of the meaning and practical import of the classical texts.[49]

As regards Xunzi's uses of *shen* and *shenming*, whatever translation one adopts, for example, "spirit," "god," "godlike," "godliness"—in the absence of our knowledge of his view on the nature and existence of *shen* and *shenming*—I sometime wonder whether Xunzi's attitude of wonder or awe toward *shen* as the unfathomable that underlies the *yinyang* process reflects the attitude of a conservative, linguistic revisionist, as suggested in his essay on "rectifying terms or names" (*zhengming*). There he points out that it is the task of a sage king to preserve old terms and create new ones as they are needed. To do so he would have to consider the following questions: "Why terms are needed? What is the basis for distinguishing similarities and differences between things, and the essential standard in regulation" (*Zhengming*, L510, W141*). The essential standard governing the uses of terms lies in abiding by appropriate conventions, for "terms have no intrinsic appropriateness. It is agreement that determines their actuality or concrete application (*shi*)" (*Zhengming*, L616, W144*).[50]

Moreover, for Xunzi, respect for linguistic practices is an important criterion for successful communication. Would Xunzi similarly regard his own use of *shen* and *shenming* as an example of respect for the linguistic practice of his time? An affirmative answer to this question would ascribe to Xunzi the thesis that the established usages of *shen* and *shenming* are acceptable independent of their associated religious beliefs, superstitions, and doctrines concerning their metaphysical or ontological status. Of course, this established linguistic practice provides a language for honoring and glorifying *shen* and *shenming*, indirectly exemplifying our pivotal ethical concerns in the light of *dao*. This interpretation has a partial support in Xunzi's uses of *long* (magnifying, glorifying, exalting) in connection with *ren*, *li*, and *yi*.[51] In this regard we find an interesting analogue in Hobbes's view of the language of Christianity, namely, that the use of "the Spirit of God" does not imply an understanding of "*what he is*, but only that *he is*; and therefore the Attributes we give him, [that he is omnipotent, benevolent, and wise,] are not to tell one another, *what he is*, but only *that he is* nor to signifie our opinion of his Nature, but our desire to honour him with such names as we conceive most honorable amongst ourselves."[52] I also wonder whether Xunzi would also endorse Hobbes's saying: "Words are wise men's counters; they do reckon by them; but they are the money of fools."[53]

The Religious Dimension of *Li*

For Xunzi, the practice of religious rites of his times, the *li* of mourning and sacrifice, has a profound significance for a good human life, not because of its association with specific religious beliefs, say, concerning the existence of the spirits of the dead, but because of ordinary, human longing for a long life and reverence for the dead, especially the beloved. His attitude echoes Confucius's and an earlier view of immortality (*shi er buxiu*), that immortality pertains to "establishing virtues [*lide*], establishing accomplishments [*ligong*], and establishing words [*liyan*]."[54] However, the fact of human mortality is a proper concern of *li*. While the wish for continued existence after death cannot be fulfilled, the beginning and the end can be properly honored. All human beings encounter the beginning of life and death as boundary situations. The religious rites for mourning and sacrifice provide occasions for honoring our roots, a symbolic expression of our reverence for human life. These rites deal with our conception of our own boundary situations—birth, marriage, and death.

J. L. Austin once remarked that "a word never—well, hardly ever— shakes off from its etymology and its formation. In spite of all changes in and extensions of and additions to its meaning, and indeed rather pervading and governing these, there will persist the old idea."[55] As noted in the first section, the etymology of *li* suggests its connection with sacrifices to spirits. The common translation of *li* as "rites" or "ritual" thus recalls the early pre-Confucian use of *li* in religious context. In the preceding section, especially in connection with *shen* and *shenming*, we have occasionally noted the associated beliefs in the existence of gods and their influence in human life. This feature is also prominent in some essays in the *Liji*. Xunzi's view somewhat echoes that of Confucius. Confucius seems to have an insouciant attitude toward the existence of spirits and the relevance of belief in an afterlife, though sometimes he appealed to Heaven (*tian*) as a quasi-purposive, religious being. We find, for instance the following:

> The Master said, "There is no one who understands me." Tzu-kung said, "How is it that there is no one who understands you?" The Master said, "I do not complain against Heaven [*tian*], nor do I blame men. In my studies, I start from below and get through to what is up above. If I am understood at all, it is, perhaps, by Heaven [*tian*]." (*Analects* 14:3, Lau 1979)

But, at another time, when he was asked about wisdom (*zhi*), Confucius said that one must serve the people with a sense of what is right and appropriate (*yi*) and respect the ghosts and spirits (*guishen*), but keep them at a distance (*Analects* 6:22). Confucius approved of the *li* of mourning and sacrifices largely because of his adoption of the Zhou tradition as an ethical guide to communal intercourse, not because of the specific associated religious beliefs about the existence of ghosts and spirits.

Notably, Confucius seems to have an "as if" attitude toward the existence of the dead as objects of sacrifice (*Analects* 3:12) and stresses the importance of reverence in sacrifice and sorrow in mourning (19:1). In the *Liji*, it is said that King Wen "in sacrificing, served the dead as if he were serving the living" (*Jiyi* 2:608, Legge, 2:212). We find a similar attitude in Xunzi: "The funeral rites have no other purpose than to clarify the rationales [*li*] of life and death, to send the dead person away with grief and reverence, and to lay him at the ground" (*Lilun*, L441, W105*). In sacrificial rites, "one serves the dead as though they were living, the departed as though present, giving body to the bodiless and thus fulfill the proper form of *li*" (*Lilun*, L451, W111*). Moreover, appropriate expression of emotions is essential. Says Xunzi:

> The sacrificial rites originate in the emotions of remembrance and longing for the dead. Everyone is at times visited by sudden feelings of depression and melancholy longing. . . . [These rites] express the highest degree of loyalty, love and reverence, and embody what is finest in ritual conduct and formal bearing. (*Lilun*, L450–51, W109–11).

For Xunzi, it is especially important for participants in a *li*-performance to aim at the "middle state," that is, between excessive emphasis on formality and the inordinate expression of emotions (*Lilun*, L430, W96).

For Xunzi, the rites of mourning and sacrifices have a profound significance, not as a statement of religious beliefs but as a profound expression of our attitude toward human life as a whole. The beginning and the end of our life may be depicted as extreme points of a line. These rites are especially important in *li*-performance, for they bespeak the spirit of human life in the intermediate regions. When we think of a person's life along a succession of stages from childhood, adolescence, adulthood, to old age, the beginning and the end occasionally cry out for attention. We mark their importance as "rites of passage." The *li* of mourning is an acknowledgment of the *terminus* of a person's life and accomplishments and failures, fortunes and misfortunes. It is a life worthy of respect and reverence. Thus the rites are to be performed with sincere generosity and reverent formality. The dead have a significance for the living. We honor them in rites as if they were present in order to ornament our grief and make sacrifices to them to ornament our reverence. These rites are an expression of our reverence and reasonable concern for *wen*, cultural refinement. As Xunzi remarks, "cherishing our roots [*ben*] is called *wen*, and familiarity with practical usage [*chinyong*] is called *li** (reason, reasonableness)" (*Lilun*, L424, cf. W92). The rites have a purely symbolic meaning. They are performed for the sake of unifying and honoring the beginning and the end. In these ritual performances, we consciously engage in a pretense without self-deception, in order to express our moral emotions of respect and reverence in a proper setting.

Focusing on the *wen*, or "ornamenting,"of emotions of grief and melancholy longing for our loved ones, the religious rites represent more an extension of the moral and the aesthetic rather than an autonomous domain of *li*-experience. It is an extension of a horizon for viewing life as a whole in terms of *ren*, the ideal of humanity, and *yi*, the right and fitting concern for the dead. The *li* of mourning and sacrifice are important for appreciating the value of human life, because they are an articulation, in a concrete setting, of the practical and actuating force of a commitment to *dao* or *ren* as an ideal theme, a standard of inspiration for Confucian agents.[56] In this light, honoring the dead with reverence is a way of celebrating our humanity. Notably, our *li*-performances here attain their distinctive character transcending our animality. Our care for the dead is in effect a care for the living human as a being invested with an ideal import. The ideal of *ren*, or humanity, has in this way acquired a quasi-natural habitat. Whatever virtues unfolded in this habitat may thus be seen as a partial realization of the Confucian ideal of human excellence (*shan*).

If we consider the moral, aesthetic, and religious dimensions of *li* together, the notion of *li* has an amphibious character. On the one hand, it expresses what the living humans regard as morally and aesthetically valuable. On the other hand, it points to the world in which humans anchor on a form of life that must, for each person, come to an end. Between the beginning and the end, we live our lives. To be mindful of the significance of religious rites as another dimension of *li* is to place an additional, special regard for our past and future. The past, in light of *li*, is no longer something fossilized and gone; we recall it, and in doing so in religious rites of mourning and sacrifice, we may be said to experience its significance in memory. It lives in our thought and action, as our beginning is a long tradition incarnate—the tradition in which human life anchors. This feature of *li* is well brought out by Herbert Fingarette. The powerful image of sacrificial vessels of jade "in the *Analects* may in this way be viewed as the transformation of the secular into the sacred. It is sacred not because it is useful or handsome but because it is a constitutive element in the ceremony."[57]

And when the contemplation of the end of life is seen as having prospective as well as retrospective significance, to honor the dead is to be mindful also of the continuing responsibility of the living. While we cannot separate ourselves from the anchorage, we cannot ignore the recurrence of problems. It is the here-and-now that must occupy the living. When the rites are properly performed, we take our leave and go on with our usual occupation. The symbolic significance of these rites must be taken seriously for our own sake.[58] The instruments deployed—costumes and varying bodily motions—to a sensitive Confucian inspire awe and reverence just as they serve to express the emotions of the participants in the *li* of mourning. The sorrow and the depressing grief are not just painful emotions felt but can be experienced as emotions that express a gladness of being alive. When they are directed toward the cosmos, it may even commemorate the Confucian vision of *can tianti*, the vision of the grand harmony of man and his world. In one edifying passage, Xunzi exalts the *li*:

> Through *li*, Heaven and Earth are joined in harmony; the sun and the moon shine, the four seasons proceed in order, the stars and constellations march, the rivers and streams flow, and all things flourish. Through the *li*, men's likes and dislikes are regulated and their joy and anger are expressed in proper occasions. Those below are obedient, those above are enlightened [*ming*]. All things change without creating disorder. Only those who turn back against the *li* will be destroyed. Indeed, we have no greater expression of the perfection of the *li*! Establish and exalt [*long*] the *li* to its utmost, no one in the world can add or subtract [from their significance]. Through the *li*, the root and the branches are put in proper order; beginning and end are made consonant; the most elegant forms embody all distinctions; the most penetrating insight explains all things. (*Lilun*, L427, W94*)

Here we have an example of Xunzi's exaltation of *li*, echoing his vision of *can tianti* or *dao*, a vision of the good human life. In this exaltation of *li*, moral values occupy their preeminent place in social and personal intercourse, the aesthetic values mark their pervasive quality, and the religious values celebrate the grand unity or harmony of humanity and the natural order. One finds no independent normative ethics, nor normative aesthetics, nor a philosophy of religion. Rather, one finds with the moral alongside aesthetic and religious values, an interesting and challenging view in axiological ethics. If the foregoing discussion of this conception is deemed intelligible and plausible, it is owed to the inspiration of Xunzi in offering us a distinctive, complex notion of *li*, providing an occasion for reflecting on an important problem of the interconnection between different types of values.

Conclusion

For a contemporary Confucian philosopher, an appreciation of the religious dimension of *li*, the *li* of mourning and sacrifices, does not depend on inquiry into their metaphysical or ontological significance. Tang Junyi points out that the significance of sacrifices to spiritual beings (*guishen*) depends not on any ontological view of their independent and external existence but on our *ren*-capacity to *guantong*, that is, to permeate or penetrate through all existent things.[59] Spiritual beings may be said to exist only insofar as they are the objects of this penetrating process—they "exist" as objects of our emotions or thought, expressive of our moral attitudes. In the ontological sense, they need not exist, for we have no knowledge of their nature independent of our emotions or thought. In the spirit of Xunzi, we may regard these entities as our own creations (*wei*); they exist as supervenient qualities of our reflective ethical experience, the resultant attributes of the expression of our ethical emotions or thought in the context of religious observances.[60] In this sense, the religious dimension of *li*, like its aesthetic dimension is an extension of its primary ethical dimension, and may properly be considered a constitutive feature of the Confucian ethical life. Differently put, ideally, in the growth of the ethical experience of a committed Confucian agent, religious quality may become a salient feature of his or her life. Xunzi's endorsement of the uses of *shen* and *shenming* in his own thought, aside from his respect for established linguistic practices, possibly reflects his appreciation of the transformative character of religious beliefs, insofar as they are consistent with *ren*, *yi*, and *li*.

In light of the Confucian vision of the unity and harmony of *tian* and humanity, especially in Cheng Hao and Wang Yangming, this ideal of the good human life encompasses all living and nonliving things. Although this ideal is a wish rather than an object of reasoned deliberation, it may be considered a religious ideal, for a person seriously committed to *ren* will regard all things as "one body." In the words of Wang Yangming:

> The great man regards Heaven, Earth, and the myriad things as one body [*yi-t'i*]. He sees [*shi*] the world as one family and the country as one person. . . . Forming one body with Heaven, Earth, and the myriad things is true not only of the great man. Even the mind [*hsin*] of the small man is no different. Only he makes it small. Therefore, when he sees a child about to fall into a well, he cannot help a feeling of alarm and commiseration. This shows that his humanity [*jen*] forms one body with the child. Again, when he observes

the pitiful cries and frightened appearance of the birds and animals about to be slaughtered, he cannot help feeling an "inability to bear" their suffering. This shows that his humanity forms one body with birds and animals.[61]

Wang goes on to point out that a man of *jen* also forms "one body" with plants, stones, tiles, mountains, and rivers. In this version of the Confucian vision of *can tianti*, the unity and harmony of humanity and all things become an ethical ideal that provides a cosmic perspective. In Tu Wei-ming's words, it is an "anthropocosmic" vision, where the human "self" is the center of all human and nonhuman relationships.[62] If the primary function of language of religious beliefs is an expression of religious commitment or of the "will to belief," this Confucian vision may properly be regarded as a religious vision, presupposing the Confucian ethical ideal of the good human life as a whole, variously termed as *dao*, *ren*, *tianren heyi*, or *can tianti*. For a committed agent, this vision may provide a motivating force in self-transformation, since the vision answers to vital personal perplexities that resist problematic formulation.[63] In this way, we can have an open, ethical vista that embraces and preserves the integrity of religious beliefs without prejudging their reasoned justification, thus leaving open a serious inquiry into the possibility of Confucian philosophy of religion and comparative religion.

Notes

1. For an extensive discussion of Confucian ethics—its tradition orientation; basic conceptual framework focusing on *ren*, *yi*, and *li* as interdependent notions; and principles for intercultural adjudication—see A. S. Cua, *Moral Vision and Tradition*, essays 12–14. For an introduction to Confucian ethics, see Cua, *Two Lectures on Confucian Ethics*.

2. Homer H. Dubs, *Hsüntze: The Moulder of Ancient Confucianism*, 113n. Here I replace Dubs's "religion" by "religious rites." In this essay, "rites" and "rituals" are used interchangeably.

3. For further discussion, see Cua, *Ethical Argumentation*, 6 passim.

4. In this essay, parenthetical expressions of transcription function primarily as focal indicators of meanings of terms and for facility in distinguishing homophones. For the connection of *li*, *ren*, and *yi*, see Cua, *Moral Vision and Tradition*, essay 13.

5. The *Liji* is one of the five basic Confucian classics, compiled probably in the first century B.C.E. Many chapters reflect the influence and further development of Xunzi's ethics. References to *Liji* are to James Legge, *The Li Ki or Collection of Treatises on the Rules of Propriety or Ceremonial Usages*. The original Chinese edition I used is Wang 1977. Emendations of Legge's translations are indicated by asterisks; the same device is used for citations from the *Xunzi*. Transcriptions are

inserted in the translations to indicate my interpretive reading of Chinese characters and for subsequent comment. The Chinese *Xunzi* text I use is Disheng Li, *Xunzi zhishi* (1979). For easy access, whenever possible, I refer to Burton Watson, trans., *Hsün Tzu: Basic Writings* (1963). Advanced students must consult John Knoblock, *Xunzi: A Translation and Study of the Complete Works* (1988–94), a complete and updated scholarly translation of Xunzi's works. Knoblock's translation is sustained with impressive scholarship. The novice will also profit from his long introduction in the first volume and informative introduction to each of Xunzi's essays. For a critical appreciation of Knoblock's first volume, see Cua, "Feature Review: John Knoblock, *Xunzi.*" The form of the references to *Xunzi* is the name of the *pian*, followed by page number of the Li edition, e.g., L23, and W15, K1:131 for Watson's and Knoblock's translations. Occasionally I also refer to Dubs's translation, e.g., D289. Asterisks indicate emendations of translations.

6. Ming Gao, *Lixui xintan*, 313.

7. Joken Kato, "Meaning of *Li.*"

8. The following discussion of the conceptual evolution of *li* owes largely to Hu Shi, *Zhongkuo zhexue shi dakang*, 134–43. My use of Hu Shi is independent of his apparent claim to being a historical account, for as Kato points out, it is not plausible to regard the original meaning of *li* as pertaining exclusively to religious rites. "The religious rites go back to the oldest antiquity when they were not something different from [those of] everyday life." But Kato does not deny that the Confucians in the classics made a distinction between religious and ethical rules as suggested by Hu Shi. Kato is more interested in the anthropological than the philosophical significance of *li* ("Meaning of *Li*," 82).

9. Yucai Duan, *Shuowen jiezi zhu.*

10. Hu Shi, *Zhongkuo zhexue shi dakang*, 137–38.

11. Arthur Waley, *Analects of Confucius*, 59.

12. Mao, *Lunyu xinzhu jinyi*, 185–87. For an explication of *li** (reason, principle), see Cua, "Reason and Principle in Chinese Philosophy." For the uses of *li* (reason, principle, pattern) in Xunzi and Wang Yangming, see Cua, *Ethical Argumentation;* idem, *The Unity of Knowledge and Action.*

13. Cua, *Moral Vision and Tradition*, 277–87.

14. This scheme of analysis is partially indebted to Chen Daqi (*Mingli luncong*). In his essay "*Li zhi fenshi*" (An Analysis of *Li*), Chen distinguishes three layers of *li*, ranging from the superficial to the profound: (1) the outer layer or the numerousness of *li* (*lizhishu*), (2) the middle layer or significance of *li* (*lizhiyi*), and (3) the inner layer or foundation of *li* (*lizhiben*), which stresses the appropriate attitude in human intercourse. We leave aside the complex question of justification of *li* (*li zhi lizheng*) (see Cua, *Moral Vision and Tradition*, essay 13, 296–302). An additional, more practical question may be raised on the efficacy or application of *li* (*li zhi gongxiao*). The present explication of *li* is an abbreviated and modified scheme given in Cua, "The Concept of *Li* in Confucian Moral Theory," elaborated in *Moral Vision and Tradition.* For two decades, often during preoccupation with other projects, I pondered on the rationale of *li* and published four studies. The

present essay represents no more than a compendious reconstruction of the Confucian notion of *li*. I hope scholars in cultural anthropology, comparative religious ethics, and philosophy of religion will find some useful materials for further study of this core concept of Confucian ethics.

15. For an interpretive study of *quantong*, see Cua, "The Possibility of Ethical Knowledge."

16. In sociological terms, *li* may be regarded as a structure in Robert Merton's sense: "the pattern arrangements of role-sets, status-sets, and status-sequences." See Victor Turner, *Dramas, Fields, and Metaphors*, 237, 284.

17. Cua, *Ethical Argumentation*, ch. 1.

18. Zhu Xi, *Sishu jichu*, 19. For a different translation of *chengyi* as "making the will sincere" instead of "making one's thought sincere," see Wing-tsit Chan, *A Source Book in Chinese Philosophy*, 89. For more discussion of *cheng*, see Cua, *Moral Vision and Tradition*, essay 11. Note that the inner aspect of the foundation of *li* may also be elaborated along the line suggested in the notion of *cheng* (sincerity) in the *Doctrine of the Mean*.

19. Cua, *Moral Vision and Tradition*, essays 2 and 7.

20. Cua, "Confucian Vision and the Human Community."

21. Cua, *Unity of Knowledge and Action*.

22. For further discussion of *shu* and the Golden Rule, see Cua, "Confucian Vision and the Human Community"; idem, "Reasonable Persons and the Good"; and Robert E. Allinson, "The Confucian Golden Rule." For an insightful, yet brief, discussion of the role of *yi* in evaluating three different versions of the "Golden Rule" (Confucius, Mencius, and Western versions), see Chen Daqi, *Chen Bainian xiansheng wenji*, 164–72).

23. David Hume, "Of the Delicacy of Taste and Passion," 4.

24. Here I use the generic term "shame," which has a number of specific terms in Classical Chinese—*xiu*, *ru*, and *chi*. Mencius often used the first, and Xunzi the second term. While these terms differ somewhat in meaning, Shun justly points out that their ethical significance lies in the distinction between ethical and social standards. I suppose Shun would agree that the distinction is not an exclusive disjunction, since social standards may also be accepted as part of ethical standards, so long as they share the same rationale. See Shun Kwong-loi, *Mencius and Early Chinese Thought*, 58–63. For further discussion of Xunzi's view, see Cua, "Ethical Significance of Shame."

25. For the extensive occurrence of *long* in connection with *li* or *li* and *yi*, see *A Concordance to Hsün Tzu*, 5/82270.

26. Chen, *Kongzi xueshuo*.

27. Cua, *Moral Vision and Tradition*, essay 8.

28. Qian Mu, *Sisho duben*, 2:165.

29. Cua, *Moral Vision and Tradition*, essay 7.

30. For a good, informative account of the topic of the relation of *tian* and humans, see Yang Huijie, *Tianren guanxi lun*. For my supplementary efforts, see Cua, *Moral Virtue and Tradition*, essays 2–5 and 9.

31. Edward J. Machle, *Nature and Heaven in the Xunzi*.

32. *Tian* may be said to be a "plurisign," or term suggesting varieties of uses and interpretations (Philip Wheelwright, *The Burning Fountain*) or a systematically ambiguous expression (Gilbert Ryle, "Systematically Misleading Expressions"). Clarification depends on the context of use. For this reason, unless clear explanations are provided, it is best to retain the transliteration *tian*. The explanatory remarks are partially indebted to Hume. In Appendix III, entitled "Further Considerations Regarding Justice" to the Second Inquiry, Hume complains about the "looseness" of the term "natural" in speaking of "natural justice." In a note, he points out that there are three uses of "natural": "Natural may be opposed, either to what is *unusual, miraculous,* or *artificial* (David Hume, *An Inquiry Concerning the Principles of Morals,* 124). For Xunzi, as we shall see shortly, *tian* may also comprise unusual and strange events.

33. While insisting that scarcity of goods to satisfy all human desires renders problematic cooperative social life (an argument for his thesis that "Man's nature is bad"), Xunzi also thinks that the problem of economic scarcity is often a result of mismanagement of existing natural resources. Thus Mozi's advocacy of economy of expenditure and attack on the Confucian stress on the importance of *li* and music are misfired and misguided. See *Fuguo*, L195, K2:126-29; and Cua, "The Quasi-Empirical Aspect of Hsün Tzu's Philosophy of Human Nature." For a more general discussion on the ethical significance of scarcity, see Vivian Charles Walsh, *Scarcity and Evil*.

34. Machle, *Nature and Heaven in the Xunzi*, 117.

35. For a *ren* person's love of others, see also *Analects* 14:42. Xunzi has the same notion that a *ren* person loves others, and would add that the person who practices *li* must also respect others (4B:28).

36. Cua, *Ethical Argumentation*, ch. 4.

37. A remark, according to Jessop, quoted from the sixteenth-century Italian Augustinus Niphus. See George Berkeley, *A Treatise Concerning the Principles of Human Knowledge*, §51.

38. See Machle, *Nature and Heaven in the Xunzi*, 93.

39. Nan Huaijin and Xu Qinting, *Zhouyi jinchu jinyi*, 372.

40. For a study of Xunzi's definitional locutions such as *zhiwei* and *weizhi*, see Cua, *Ethical Argumentation*, ch. 3.

41. Alternative translations somewhat differ from mine, though the import is similar. For example, Watson renders *rushen* as "as though by supernatural power" (W146); Knoblock as "as if by magic" (K3:132); and Dubs "as by magic" (D288). For two other examples involving *rushen*, see *A Concordance to Hsün Tzu*, 84/22/35 and 91/24/12.

42. Chan, *A Source Book in Chinese Philosophy*, 107–8.

43. See A. C. Graham, *Disputers of the Tao*, 252; Machle, "The Mind and the 'Shen-ming' in Xunzi," 383. Knoblock gives an informative account of the uses of *shen* and *shenming* in Xunzi's times. "The most common and ancient meaning of *shen* is spirits who dwell in the mountains and streams. In the *Guanzi*, 39 . . . , the

power of water to nurture plants and animals and to be stored up in all things is described as *shen*, 'the mysterious and magical.' In Xunzi, *shen* generally means the 'mysterious and magical' when applied to things that happen without apparent cause and 'godlike' or 'divine' when applied to abilities that transcend those of ordinary people." And "the idea of *shenming* intelligence seems to have been more connected with perspicacity and balance of judgment than with mere ratiocination" (Knoblock, 1:252–55). Knoblock's view is partly reflected in translating the phrase *tong yu shenming* as "penetrate as far as spiritual intelligence" (3:149). Graham's translation of *shenming* in Xunzi is "daemonic and clear-seeing," and more generally remarks: "The sense of mystery at the heart of things is seldom altogether missing in early Chinese thinkers, except in the Legalists and perhaps the Mohists. The definitive statement of it in the Confucian Classic is in the 'Great Appendix' of the *Yi*: 'It is the unfathomable in the Yin and Yang which is called daemonic' [the passage we cited earlier on *shen*]. For Hsün Tzu legitimate curiosity is limited to the human and to the directly useful to man, and when speaking of excess knowledge he can sound like a Taoist" (Graham, *Disputers of the Tao*, 253, 241). The contrary view is extensively presented by Machle's article on *shenming*. Machle's more literary translation of the phrase *tong yu shenming* is "to be in communication with the gods" (Machle, "The Mind and the '*Shen-ming*' in Xunzi," 373). My own interpretive translation given in the text, which reflects influence of Xiong and Li, is closer to that of Knoblock and Graham. The basis of the translation in part rests on interpreting *tong* in terms of *quantong*, thorough or comprehensive understanding—an idea implicit in Xunzi's use of *daoquan* (the thread or systemic core of *dao*) and *liquan* (the thread or coherence of rationales). For more discussion, see Cua, *Ethical Argumentation*, 62–65. However, *tong* can also mean "penetrate" (Knoblock) or "communicate" (Machle). While my interpretation is closer to Knoblock and Graham, it does not reject Machle's claim that Xunzi's uses of *shenming* convey a numinous or spiritual quality; for, given that *shenming* is the quality of the sage's insight or enlightenment, it may be said to have a spiritual quality, "spiritual" in the sense of "the sacred," of something that is worthy of veneration or reverence. As we have indicated earlier in connection with the inner aspect of the foundation of *li*, reverence is a required attitude for *li*-performance. When we turn to another passage on *shenming*, we will bring out Machle's alternative reading and its value. My own interpretation differs from Machle's in that I propose a minimal interpretation based on Xunzi's appropriation of Zhuangzi's use of *ming*, without Machle's confident attribution to Xunzi's belief about the existence and nature of the *shen* or *shenming* when these terms are construed as referring to ontological entities. In the next section, we will say something more about the Confucian perspective on this issue.

44. Machle also objected to the translation of *er* as "and" presumably because these writers regard "and" as a coordinating conjunction. But "and" can also be used with the force of a consequence or conditional result, for example, "He felt tired and decided to stay home." It is possible that Machle is right that *er* conveys this special sense of "and," though I find that the use of "and" in translation is perfectly acceptable if proper explanation is given.

45. See Harold H. Joachim, *Descartes's Rules for the Direction of the Mind*, 25ff.

46. Cua, *Ethical Argumentation*, 31–35, 61–65.

47. Cua, *Moral Vision and Tradition*, 95–99.

48. Chan, *A Source Book in Chinese Philosophy*, 89*.

49. Ibid., 22.

50. Cua, *Ethical Argumentation*, ch. 3.

51. See n. 25 above. A significant number of occurrences of *long* involve *li* alone, *li* and *yi*, and *ren*. For example, see *A Concordance to Hsün Tzu*, 3/1/36, 3/1/39, 20/8/11, 24/8/91, 43/11/136, 46/12/57, 54/15/22, 58/16/4, 64/17/43, and 72/19/39.

52. Thomas Hobbes, *Leviathan*, 304.

53. Ibid., 29; Colin Murray Turbayne, *The Myth of Metaphor*, 101.

54. Chan, *A Source Book in Chinese Philosophy*, 13.

55. J. L. Austin, "A Plea for Excuses," 149.

56. Cua, *Dimensions of Moral Creativity*, ch. 8.

57. Herbert Fingarette, *Confucius*, 75.

58. It is interesting to note that the anthropologist A. R. Radcliffe-Brown acknowledges Xunzi's conception of rituals as a precursor of his own view that rituals have a social and symbolic function, independently of magical beliefs ("Taboo," 119).

59. Tang Junyi, *Zhongguo zhexue yuanlun*, 141.

60. W. D. Ross, *The Right and the Good*, ch. 2.

61. Wang Yangming, *Instructions of Practical Living*, 273.

62. Tu Weiming, *Centrality and Commonality*.

63. Cua, *Dimensions of Moral Creativity*, ch. 8.

Bibliography

Allinson, Robert E. "The Confucian Golden Rule: A Negative Formulation." *Journal of Chinese Philosophy* 12, no. 3 (1985): 305–15.

Austin, J. L. "A Plea for Excuses." In *Philosophical Papers*. Oxford: Clarendon Press, 1961.

Berkeley, George. *A Treatise Concerning the Principles of Human Knowledge*. In *The Works of George Berkeley*, vol. 2. Edited by T. E. Jessop. London: Thomas Nelson and Sons, 1949.

Chan, Wing-tsit, trans. *A Source Book in Chinese Philosophy*. Princeton: Princeton University Press, 1963.

———, ed. *Chu Hsi and Neo-Confucianism*. Honolulu: University of Hawaii Press, 1986.

Chen, Daqi. *Chen Bainian xiansheng wenji*, vol. 3. Taipei: Shangwu, 1994.

———. *Kongzi xueshuo*. Taipei: Cheng-chung, 1977.

———. *Mingli luncong*. Taipei: Cheng-chung, 1957.

———. *Xunzi xueshuo*. Taipei: Zhonghua wenhua publication Committee, 1954.

Cua, A. S. "The Concept of *Li* in Confucian Moral Theory." In *Understanding the*

Chinese Mind: The Philosophical Roots, ed. Robert E. Allinson. Hong Kong: Oxford University Press, 1989.

———. "Confucian Vision and the Human Community." *Journal of Chinese Philosophy* 11, no. 3 (1984): 226–38.

———. "Dimensions of *Li* (Propriety): Reflections on an Aspect of Hsün Tzu's Ethics." *Philosophy East and West* 29, no. 4 (1979): 373–94.

———. *Dimensions of Moral Creativity: Paradigms, Principles, and Ideals*. University Park: Pennsylvania State University Press, 1978.

———. *Ethical Argumentation: A Study in Hsün Tzu's Moral Epistemology*. Honolulu: University of Hawaii Press, 1985.

———. "Ethical Significance of Shame: Insights of Aristotle and Xunzi." *Philosophy East and West* 53 (2003).

———. "Ethical Uses of History in Early Confucianism: The Case of Hsün Tzu." *Philosophy East and West* 35, no. 2 (1985): 133–56.

———. "Feature Review: John Knoblock, *Xunzi: A Translation and Study of the Complete Works*, Volume I, Books 1-6." *Philosophy East and West* 41, no. 2 (1991): 215–27.

———. *Moral Vision and Tradition: Essays on Confucian Ethics*. Washington, D.C.: Catholic University of America Press, 1998.

———. "The Possibility of Ethical Knowledge: Reflections on a Theme in the *Hsün Tzu*." In *Epistemological Issues in Ancient Chinese Philosophy*, ed. Hans Lenk and Gregor Paul, 159–83. Albany: State University of New York Press, 1993.

———. "The Quasi-Empirical Aspect of Hsün Tzu's Philosophy of Human Nature." *Philosophy East and West* 28, no. 1 (1978): 3–19.

———. "Reasonable Persons and the Good: Reflections on an Aspect of Weiss' Ethical Thought." In *Philosophy of Paul Weiss*, ed. Lewis E. Hahn, 495–514. Library of Living Philosophers. La Salle, Ill.: Open Court, 1995.

———. "Reason and Principle in Chinese Philosophy." In *A Companion to World Philosophies*, ed. Eliot Deutsch and Ron Bontekoe, 201–13. Oxford: Blackwell, 1997.

———. "Reflections on the Structure of Confucian Ethics." *Philosophy East and West* 21, no. 2 (1971): 125–40. See Cua, *Dimensions of Moral Creativity*, ch. 4.

———. *Two Lectures on Confucian Ethics: Tradition and Conceptual Framework* [with Chinese Translation]. Hsin Chu, Taiwan: Program for Research of Intellectual-Cultural History, College of Humanities and Social Science, National Tsing Hua University, 1998.

———. *The Unity of Knowledge and Action: A Study in Wang Yang-ming's Moral Psychology*. Honolulu: University Press of Hawaii, 1982.

Duan, Yucai. *Shuowen jiezi zhu*. Shanghai: Shanghai guji publisher, 1980.

Dubs, Homer H. *Hsüntze: The Moulder of Ancient Confucianism*. London: Arthur Probsthain, 1927.

———, trans. *The Works of Hsüntze*. Taipei: Ch'eng-wen, 1966.

Fingarette, Herbert. *Confucius: The Secular as Sacred*. New York: Harper & Row, 1972.

———. "Following the 'One Thread' of the *Analects*." *Journal of the American Academy of Religion, Thematic Issue* 47, no. 3S (1979): 373–406.

Fogelin, Robert J. *Understanding Arguments: An Introduction to Informal Logic.* New York: Harcourt Brace Jovanovich, 1978.

Gao, Ming (Kao Ming). *Lixue xintan.* Taipei: Xuesheng, 1980.

Giles, Lionel. *The Sayings of Confucius.* London: John Murray, 1907. Reprint, Charles Tuttle, 1993.

Graham, A. C. *Disputers of the Tao: Philosophical Argument in Ancient China.* La Salle, Ill.: Open Court, 1989.

Hobbes, Thomas. *Leviathan.* Oxford: Clarendon Press, 1952.

Hu, Shi. *Zhongkuo zhexue shi dagang,* Part I. Taipei: Commercial Press, 1947. Reprint of 1918 edition.

Hume, David. *An Inquiry Concerning the Principles of Morals.* Indianapolis: Bobbs-Merrill, 1957.

———. "Of the Delicacy of Taste and Passion." In *Essays: Moral, Political and Literary.* Oxford: Oxford University Press, 1963.

Joachim, Harold H. *Descartes's Rules for the Direction of the Mind.* London: George Allen & Unwin, 1957.

Kao, Ming (Gao Ming). "Chu Hsi and the Discipline of Propriety." In *Chu Hsi and Neo-Confucianism*, ed. Wing-tsit Chan. Honolulu: University of Hawaii Press, 1986.

———. *Sanli yanjiu.* Daibei: Liming, 1981.

Kato, Joken. "The Meaning of *Li*." *Philosophical Studies of Japan* 4 (1963).

Knoblock, John. *Xunzi: A Translation and Study of the Complete Works.* 3 volumes. Stanford: Stanford University Press, 1988–94.

Lau, D. C., 1979. *Confucius: The Analects (Lun yü), Translated with an Introduction.* London: Penguin Books, 1979.

———, trans. *Mencius.* London: Penguin Books, 1970.

Legge, James, trans. *Chinese Classics*, vol. 1. Oxford: Clarendon Press, 1893.

———. *The Li Ki or Collection of Treatises on the Rules of Propriety or Ceremonial Usages [1885]*, 2 vols. The Sacred Books of the East, ed. Max Müller. Delhi: Motilal Banarsidass, 1966.

Li, Disheng. *Xunzi zhishi.* Taipei: Xuesheng, 1979.

Machle, Edward J. "Hsün Tzu as a Religious Philosopher." *Philosophy East and West* 16 (1976): 443–61.

———. "The Mind and the '*Shen-ming*' in Xunzi." *Journal of Chinese Philosophy* 19 (1992): 361–86.

———. *Nature and Heaven in the Xunzi: A Study of the Tian Lun.* Albany: State University of New York Press, 1993.

Mao, Zishui. *Lunyu jinzhu jinyi.* Taipei: Commercial Press, 1977.

Mou, Zhongsan. *Mingjia yu Xunzi.* Taipei: Xuesheng, 1979.

Munro, Donald J. *The Concept of Man in Ancient China.* Stanford: Stanford University Press, 1969.

Nan, Huaijin, and Xu Qinting. *Zhouyi jinzhu jinyi.* Taipei: Shangwu, 1978.

Nivison, David. "Chung and Shu." In *Encyclopedia of Chinese Philosophy*, ed. A. S. Cua. New York: Routledge, 2002.

Qian, Mu. *Sishu duben*. 2 volumes. Taipei: Liming, 1992.

Radcliffe-Brown, A. R. "Taboo." In *A Reader in Comparative Religion*, ed. W. A. Lassa and E. Z. Vogt. New York: Harper & Row, 1965.

Ross, W. D. *The Right and the Good*. Oxford: Oxford University Press, 1930.

Ryle, Gilbert. "Systematically Misleading Expressions." In *Logic and Language*, First Series, ed. A. G. N. Flew. Oxford: Blackwell, 1951.

Schwartz, Benjamin. *The World of Thought in Ancient China*. Cambridge, Mass.: Harvard University Press, 1985.

Shun, Kwong-loi. *Mencius and Early Chinese Thought*. Stanford: Stanford University Press, 1997.

Tang, Junyi. *Zhongguo zhexue yuanlun: yuandao pian*, vol. 1. Taipei: Xuesheng, 1978.

Tu, Wei-ming. *Centrality and Commonality: An Essay on Confucian Religiosity*. Albany: State University of New York Press, 1989.

Turbayne, Colin Murray. *The Myth of Metaphor*. New Haven: Yale University Press, 1962.

Turner, Victor. *Dramas, Fields, and Metaphors*. Ithaca, N.Y.: Cornell University Press, 1974.

Urmson, J. O. *The Emotive Theory of Ethics*. London: Hutchinson University Library, 1968.

Waley, Arthur. *The Analects of Confucius*. New York: Random House, 1938.

Walsh, Vivian Charles. *Scarcity and Evil*. Englewood Cliffs, N.J.: Prentice Hall,1961.

Wang, Meng'ou. *Liji jinzhu jinyi*. Taipei: Commercial Press, 1977.

Wang, Yangming. *Instructions of Practical Living and Other Neo-Confucian Writings*. Trans. and ed. Wing-tsit Chan. New York: Columbia University Press, 1963.

Watson, Burton, trans. *Hsün Tzu: Basic Writings*. New York: Columbia University Press, 1963.

——, trans. *Mo Tzu: Basic Writings*. New York: Columbia University Press, 1963.

Wheelwright, Philip. *The Burning Fountain: A Study of Language and Symbolism*. New and rev. ed. Bloomington: Indiana University Press, 1968.

Wittgenstein, Ludwig. *Philosophical Investigations*. Oxford and New York: Macmillan, 1968.

Xiong, Gongzhe. *Xunzi jinzhu jinyi*. Taipei: Shangwu, 1975.

Yang, Huijie. *Tianren guanxi lun*. Taipei: Ta-lin, 1981.

Zhu, Xi. *Sishu jizhu* (An Annotated edition of the Four Books). Hong Kong: Daiping, 1980.

14

Xunzi's Piety

PAUL RAKITA GOLDIN

NE OF THE MOST INFLUENTIAL texts in discussions of piety in Western theology is Plato's *Euthyphro*. Socrates has come to the court on account of his recent indictment on the charge of corrupting the youth of Athens, and there he meets an acquaintance named Euthyphro, a young man who is suing his father for having murdered a serf. Euthyphro asserts that, however disagreeable or unusual his action may seem, he is bound to carry out his suit on grounds of piety. In a fairly complex argument that has not convinced all readers, Socrates seeks to undermine Euthyphro's overweening self-confidence by reducing the issue to the following dilemma: "Is what is holy loved by the gods because it is holy, or holy because it is loved by the gods?" (*Euthyphro* 10a). That is to say, must we follow the precepts of moral behavior dictated by the gods merely because the gods dictated them—or are the gods' laws just in their own right, in which case we ought to obey them even if it were *not* the gods who instituted them.

Each horn of the dilemma presents a serious problem. If we decide that what is holy is loved by the gods because it is holy, we must thereby postulate a concept of holiness that is independent of, and indeed *anterior to*, the gods. This amounts to a diminution of the gods' status and authority: it means that we recognize them as holy only insofar as they live up to the principles that *we* determine as holy—and, consequently, that we cease to revere them as soon as they depart from that standard. On the other hand, if we decide that what is holy is so because it is loved by the gods, then we must envision the possibility that we may venerate as "holy" something that we find utterly repugnant, because we derive no other motivation for holiness than that it is godly. What if we do not love what the gods love?

Are we required to obey when the gods utter a commandment that we find abhorrent?

At first glance, it may appear as though a parallel problem applies to the Confucian tradition. After all, the sages (*shengren*) laid down a system of rituals (*li*) that is accepted in its entirety as holy. Are the rituals holy because the sages devised them, or did the sages devise them because they are holy? One noteworthy feature of early Confucian philosophy is that it did not confront the so-called "Euthyphro problem," because that dilemma did not pose the same challenge in the Confucian context. The thinker who best exemplifies this dimension of Confucianism—and who comes nearest to formulating his own version of the "Euthyphro problem"—is Xunzi (ca. 310–210 B.C.E.).[1]

*   *   *

For centuries after his death, the one philosophical issue with which Xunzi was most closely identified was his attempted refutation of Mencius (371–289 B.C.E.?) on the issue of *xing*. (The usual translation of *xing* as "human nature" is inadequate, as we shall see.) One of the cornerstones of Mencian ethics is the conviction that *xing* is good. Humans are different from animals in that we possess a mind (*xin*) capable of moral deliberation. Furthermore, all humans possess what Mencius calls the "Four Beginnings" (*siduan*) of goodness, namely, the beginnings of humanity (*ren*), righteousness (*yi*), ritual (*li*), and wisdom (*zhi*). Mencius demonstrates his theory with the famous parable of the child and the well:

> Suppose a person suddenly saw a child about to fall into a well. Everyone [in such a situation] would have a frightened, compassionate mind, not in order to ingratiate himself with the child's parents, not because they want praise from their neighbors and friends, and not because they hate the sound.[2] From this we see: Who does not have a commiserating heart is not a human. Who does not have a heart of shame is not a human. Who does not have a heart of deference is not a human. Who does not have a heart of right and wrong is not a human. The heart of commiseration is the beginning of humanity. The heart of shame is the beginning of righteousness. The heart of deference is the beginning of ritual. The heart of right and wrong is the beginning of wisdom. Humans have these Four Beginnings as we have our four limbs. (*Mencius* 2A:6)[3]

Mencius's point is that the roots of morality are as innate as the four limbs of our body. Every human being has the potentiality of each of the four cardinal virtues. Anyone who sees a child about to fall into a well will instinctively feel fright and compassion; that is the response motivated by the "heart of compassion" lodged at the very core of our being. Mencius takes a similar stance in a discussion with King Xuan of Qi (r. 319–301 B.C.E.):

> [Mencius said:] "I heard Hu He say: 'The King was sitting at the top of the hall. There was someone with a sacrificial ox passing by the bottom of the hall. The King saw him, and said: What ox is that? The man answered: We are going to use it for a blood-sacrifice with a bell. The King said: Leave it; I cannot bear its fearful expression. It is like that of an innocent person approaching the execution-ground. The man answered: Then will you do away with the blood-sacrifice and bell? The King said: How can I do away with that? Change it for a sheep.' I am not aware whether that happened."
>
> The King said: "It happened."
>
> Mencius said: "This type of mind is sufficient for a [true] king. The common folk all thought that you grudged [the expense of the animal], but I know surely that it was because you could not bear the sight. . . . This is a manifestation of your humanity." (*Mencius* 1A:7)

Elsewhere, Mencius repeatedly rebukes King Xuan of Qi for his short-sighted and unenlightened rule, but here he points out that even this imperfect ruler has not lost the basic spark of humanity. As the philosopher goes on to show, the king's intentions may have been laudable, but the mere "beginning of humanity" hardly satisfies the moral responsibilities of kingship. The Four Beginnings must be cultivated continuously, or else they will wither and die, as the parable of Ox Mountain makes clear (*Mencius* 6A:8). Mencius holds that man's *xing* is good, but this is not the same as saying in English, "Human nature is good." "Human nature *has the potential* to be good" would be closer to Mencius's position. For by *xing*, Mencius means the state of being that humans can be expected to attain given the proper nurturing conditions.[4]

This was the philosophical view that Xunzi intended to discredit. "Man's *xing* is evil," he writes; "what is good is his artifice [*wei*]." He continues:

> Now man's *xing* is as follows. At birth, there is fondness for profit in it. Following this, contention and robbery arise, and deference and courtesy are destroyed. At birth there is envy and hatred in it. Following this, violence and banditry arise, and loyalty and trust are destroyed. . . . Thus obeying man's *xing*, following man's essence, must result in contention and robbery. This is in accordance with the violation of [social] division and disruption of the natural order, and a return to turmoil. (*X* 17.23.289; K 23.1a)[5]

Xunzi means to say that man does *not* possess any instinctive motivation to do good; on the contrary, the most basic human emotions are "fondness for profit" and "envy." It was precisely the evil in man that compelled the sage-kings to set down the rituals:

> In ancient times, the sage-kings took man's *xing* to be evil, and thought man to be partial, malicious, and not upright; shiftless, chaotic, and not governed. For this reason they established for us ritual and morality. They instituted laws and norms in order to reform and adorn man's essential *xing* and guide it. Only then did order ensue, in accordance with what is the Way. (X 17.23.289f.; K 23.1b)

And similarly:

> Whence did rituals arise? I say: Humans are born with desires. If they desire and do not obtain [the object of their desires], then they cannot but seek it. If, in seeking, humans have no measure or limits, then there cannot but be contention. Contention makes chaos, and chaos privation. The Former Kings hated such chaos, and established ritual and morality in order to divide [mankind], in order to nourish humans' desires and grant what humans seek. They brought it about that desires need not be deprived of objects, that objects need not be depleted by desires; the two support each other and grow. This is where rituals arise. (X 13.19.231; K 19.1a)

To the extent that Xunzi acknowledges the possibility that humans might become good, he actually agrees with Mencius. If we follow the rituals and curb our natural desires, we may become paragons of virtue, but without the rituals, the only prospect for humanity is iniquity and violence. The "gentleman" (*junzi*) is merely a "small man" (*xiaoren*) who has made himself into a gentleman through diligent effort (cf., e.g., X 17.23.296; K 23.5b). This process of continual self-cultivation is what Xunzi means by *wei*, "artifice."

In this respect, the difference between Xunzi and Mencius is not so great. The latter, too, asserts that wickedness is the only outcome for those who neglect their Four Beginnings. The real difference between the two thinkers lies in their understanding of the term *xing*. For Mencius, as we have seen, the *xing* is an organic component of humanity that must continually grow. By contrast, Xunzi makes his own definition of *xing* clear: "What is so from birth is called *xing*" (X 16.22.274; K 22.1b). *Xing* is what we are born with; if we must work at acquiring morality, then it cannot be in our *xing*. So when Mencius says that the *xing* is good, and Xunzi objects that the *xing* is evil, we must recognize that the two are not even talking about the same thing. While Xunzi uses *xing* to refer to what all members of a species hold in common, Mencius emphasizes that *xing* in his parlance indicates what distinguishes the members of a certain species from all other species (see, e.g., *Mencius* 6A:3).[6]

Consequently, most scholars are now inclined to see the rhetorical duel with Mencius as a peripheral issue in the study of Xunzi's philosophy. Xunzi himself would agree that the more central concern is not whether humans are originally good or bad but *how we become good*. And he is unambiguous on that matter: we become good by following the rituals.

> Through following ritual, there is order and success; through not following ritual, there is shiftlessness and chaos, sloth and neglect. When food and drink, clothing, residence, movement and quietude follow ritual, there is harmony and measure; when they do not follow ritual, they are offensive and lowly and beget disease. When appearance, attitude, entrance and exit, and rapid walking follow ritual, there will be elegance; when they do not follow ritual, there will be indolence, depravity and perversion, vulgarity and wildness. Thus man without ritual cannot live; affairs without ritual cannot be completed; the state and its families without ritual cannot be at peace. (X 1.2.13f.; K 2.2)

What does Xunzi mean by these "rituals," in concrete terms? The question is difficult to answer. We know from several passages that Xunzi has specific rituals in mind. At one point, for example, he analyzes the village wine-drinking ritual stage by stage, pointing out how it succeeds in "correcting the self and pacifying the country" (X 14.20.256; K 20.5). But with the exception of these rare instances, Xunzi's writings usually presuppose a basic familiarity on the part of the reader with the rituals that he has in mind. Perhaps we may infer that they are similar to the rituals preserved in such compendia as the *Liji* (*Record of Rites*) and *Yili* (*Ceremonies and Rites*), which cover such topics as salutation, sacrifice, courtship, and mourning.

Usually, Xunzi takes the rituals as a complete set of moral prescriptions, and he is absolutely convinced of their efficacy. In a debate on military strategy, he makes a startling claim: the more powerful army is not the one with the better weaponry or tactics, but the one whose ruler has been more assiduous at cultivating the rituals.

> Ritual is the ridgepole of order and discrimination, the basis of strengthening the state, the Way of awesome success, the sum of achievement and reputation. When kings and dukes follow it, that is how they obtain all under Heaven; when they do not follow it, that is how they ruin the altars of soil and grain. Thus strong armor and keen arms are not enough to be victorious; high walls and deep moats are not enough to be secure; strict commands and manifold punishments are not enough to inspire awe. Following the Way brings about success; not following it brings about downfall. (X 10.15.186f.; K 15.4)

The arms of the ancients were only lances, spears, bows, and arrows, but enemy states recoiled without a test. Walls and battlements were not managed, pits and moats not dug, strongholds and fortresses not planted, [war] machinery and changes [i.e., surprise tactics] not set up; however, that the state, in peace, did not fear foreigners, but was secure—there was no other reason for this, but that it was enlightened with respect to the Way and divided the people [i.e., their responsibilities] equitably, employed them in a timely fashion and sincerely loved the people; inferiors were in harmony with their superiors, like a shadow or an echo. (X 10.15.188; K 15.4)

The ruler's use of ritual is more important than the might of his army; for a massive military force, however well-armed, cannot achieve victory without conforming to the proper rituals, whereas an appropriately ordered state will inspire such awe in its enemies that they will not even dare to fight.[7]

One of the reasons why the rituals work is that they provide a framework of mutual understanding that allows human beings to coexist in peace.

Now the Way of the Former Kings, the principle of humanity and righteousness, are they not that by which societies live together, by which we support and nourish each other, by which we screen and adorn each other, by which we are peaceful and secure with each other? (X 2.4.41; K 4.10)

Thus, in one respect, Xunzi is a contractarian like Hobbes or Rousseau: *li* is merely a name for the nexus of regulations that allow human beings to enjoy nature's bounty harmoniously. With rituals in place, "desires need not be deprived of objects [and] objects need not be depleted by desires," as he puts it. People have desires, and were they each to go about satisfying them in *anomia*, the consequence would be *unrequited* desire. But chaos is resolved through ritual: with the establishment of a few ground rules, the roving egoists can fulfill their desires happily, and be sure that they will not be impeded by others in their midst. Everyone has his or her place, like the hairs in the famous figure of the fur collar (X 1.1.9; K 1.11).[8]

To be honored as the Son of Heaven [i.e., the ruler on earth], and to possess richly all under Heaven—this is the common desire of man's essence. But if people follow their desires, then boundaries cannot contain [them] and objects cannot satisfy them. Thus the Former Kings restrained them and established for them ritual and morality in order to divide them. (X 2.4.44; K 4.12)

One important difference between Xunzi and most Western contractarians, however, lies in Xunzi's conviction that one cannot simply invent *li* in the same way that a sovereign decrees his own laws. This is the impetus behind his criticism of a more liberal opponent: "Master Shen was blinded by laws and did not know [the value of] worthy men" (*X* 15.21.262; K 21.4). "Master Shen" is Shen Dao (fl. 310 B.C.E.). Elsewhere Xunzi elaborates:

> [Some] place laws at the top but have no laws; they place continuity at the bottom and like to be creative. Above, they obtain audience from the lofty; below, they obtain followers from the common folk. All day their speech is perfected, patterned, and documented, but if examined closely back and forth, then [it appears to be] unrestrained and have no place to which it returns. They cannot regulate the state or establish [social] distinctions. . . . These are Shen Dao and Tian Pian. (*X* 3.6.58–59; K 6.5)

The bone that Xunzi has to pick with Shen Dao involves the provenance of law. As we know from his surviving works, Shen Dao believes that sovereigns create laws in order to rule their states and avoid anarchy.[9] But this arrangement is unacceptable to Xunzi, because it permits the possibility of bad laws. Xunzi's response echoes an argument that harks back to Confucius (551–479 B.C.E.):

> The Master said: If you lead them with government and make them uniform with punishments, the people will avoid [the punishments] but have no shame. If you lead them with virtue and make them uniform with ritual, then they will have shame and be correct. (*Analects* 2:3)

According to Confucius, people governed by laws and punishments do not receive any moral instruction. They must be shown the proper rituals; then they will know how to behave both as moral and as social beings. From Xunzi's point of view, Shen Dao's laws have no authority because they are implemented by fallible rulers or ministers, and do not necessarily accord with the rituals.

For there are rituals that are right, and pretender rituals that are wrong. The proper rituals were established by the sage-kings and are proper because they conform to *human nature*. Xunzi is speaking here not of man's *xing*, but of the characteristic in humans that makes us unique:

> What is it that makes humans human? I say: their making of distinctions. Desiring food when hungry, desiring warmth when cold, desiring rest when toiling, liking profit and hating injury—these are all possessed by humans from birth. They are not things such that they must wait for them to be so. This is the similarity between Yu and Jie [a sage-king and a prodigal last ruler, respectively]. This being the case, what makes humans human is not specifically that they have two feet and no pelt [or plumage—i.e., that they are featherless bipeds]. It is their making of distinctions. Now the shengsheng-ape resembles [man], and also has two feet and no pelt. But the gentleman sips

his soup and eats his cutlet [i.e. eats his food cooked]. Thus what makes humans human is not specifically that they have two feet and no pelt. It is their making of distinctions. The birds and beasts have parents and children but no affection between parents and children. They have males and females but no separation between man and woman. Thus the way of man is nothing other than to make distinctions. (X 3.5.50; K 5.4)

Xunzi's argument here is that humans, by virtue of their nature, make certain distinctions that all other animals do not. Male is distinguished from female, old from young, etc. Xunzi continues:

There are no greater distinctions than social distinctions. There are no greater social distinctions than the rituals. There are no greater rituals than [those of] the holy kings. (X 3.5.50; K 5.4)

And similarly:

The gentleman having attained his nourishment, he will also be fond of separation. What is separation? I say: Noble and base have their ranks; old and young have their disparate [status]; poor and rich, light and heavy, all have what is fitting to them. (X 13.19.231; K 19.1c)

Put succinctly, ritual is the "ridgepole of the Way of man" (X 13.19.237; K 19.2d).

Xunzi cannot accept Shen Dao's flippant approach to laws because of his own commitment to the idea that humans have a certain *essence*, a peculiar characteristic which no other species shares and which we obtain from nature. This characteristic is our penchant for discrimination. Man distinguishes male from female, old from young, and so on, and it is *altogether natural that we do so*. That is the Way (*dao*). The rituals of the sage-kings conform to the natural order, and augment it, by confirming the distinctions that man is bound to make by nature. This is why there is only one set of legitimate rituals. There is only one Way. The sage-kings apprehended it, and their rituals embody it. There is no other Way, and no other constellation of rituals that conforms to the Way.

It is through the Way, moreover, that Heaven plays a role in the lives of human beings. Though without bias or caprice, and with no involvement whatsoever in the daily progression of human history, Heaven has nevertheless decreed the Way, and this Way functions as the fundamental mold of human existence. This is Xunzi's conception of Heaven's Mandate (*tian-ming*). Despite his famous rejection of the notion that Heaven is a willful and unpredictable power whose vagaries can be deduced from events transpiring on earth, Xunzi reserves a critical place for Heaven in human life. Heaven is not a personage, like a ruler, whose moods and predilections a minister must learn to recognize. Heaven is a constant presence with a constant *ethic* by which one must learn to live. Every being has its particular virtue, its part in the plan. Heaven's Mandate is that human beings be social creatures.

It would therefore be misleading to characterize Xunzi as a conventionalist. While it is true that Xunzi recognizes the value of convention in the process of harmonizing society, he does not tolerate the "Legalist" idea that these cultural conventions can be arbitrarily chosen and yet retain their efficacy. For the rituals have a *double* function: they facilitate peaceful society by establishing conventions of interaction, and they ensure at the same time that these conventions are appropriate to the human situation—and to the Way. The rituals embody everything that distinguishes humanity from the rest of the animal kingdom, and in keeping with the rest of Xunzi's philosophy, it is always up to us to make our move. Those who follow the rituals are able to live in harmony not only with their fellow human beings but also with the cosmos enveloping all. Those who do not are wicked and pitiable. The choice is ours.

*   *   *

An important consequence of Xunzi's refutation of Shen Dao is that the rituals are right not because the sage-kings established them, but because they conform to what he calls the "Way of Man." Even if there had never been any sage-kings, even if there had never been any rituals, there would still be a standard of morality for us to aspire to. After repeating over and over the importance of the rituals both for the welfare of the state and for one's personal moral development, Xunzi finally concedes that there is actually more to sagehood than the rituals alone:

> When the gentleman has dwelt in humanity by means of righteousness, then he is humane. When he has practiced righteousness by means of [conforming to] ritual, he is righteous. When he has formulated ritual by returning to the root and perfecting the branch,[10] he [has attained] ritual. When he has mastered these three, he is *dao*. (*X* 19.27.325; K 27.21)

We may come to understand the workings of the Way by performing the rituals, but the task of self-cultivation does not end there; for the rituals are but one manifestation of the multivalent Way. To practice the rituals and ignore all else would be to act as blindly as any number of other thinkers who knew one thing and could not integrate the rest.

> Mozi [i.e., Mo Di, d. ca. 390 B.C.E.] was blinded by utility and did not know refinement. Songzi [i.e., Song Keng, fl. late fourth cent. B.C.E.] was blinded by

desire and did not know attainment. Shenzi [i.e., Shen Dao] was blinded by laws and did not know [the value of] worthy men. Shenzi [i.e., Shen Buhai, d. 337 B.C.E.] was blinded by [administrative] skill and did not know knowledge. Huizi [i.e., Hui Shi, fl. fourth cent. B.C.E.] was blinded by propositions and did not know reality. Zhuangzi [i.e., Hui Shi's friend Zhuang Zhou] was blinded by Heaven and did not know man. . . . All of these several [ideas] are but one corner of the Way. The Way is constant in body and exhaustively changing. One corner is not enough to extrapolate the rest. People with parochial knowledge look upon one corner of the Way, and are never able to recognize it [as such]. Thus they think it sufficient and adorn it. . . . One school obtained the universal Way. They deduced from it and applied it, and were not blinded by their accomplishments. (X 15.21.261–62; K 21.4)

The "one school," of course, is the Confucians. The only real Daoists, in a manner of speaking, are the Confucians, since they constitute the only school that does not overemphasize one aspect of the Way to the exclusion of the others. The Confucians alone comprehend the Way in all its manifestations, and hence to be Confucian is to know the Way.

Thus the sages knew the Way and left behind a ritual code for future generations to follow:

Those who ford waters mark the deep spots; if the markers are not clear, then [those who come after] will drown. Those who govern people mark the Way; if the markers are not clear, then there is chaos. Ritual is the marker; to abolish ritual is to confuse the world. (X 11.17.212; K 17.11)

Though Xunzi impresses upon us repeatedly the difficulties associated with attaining the path to goodness, he hastens to point out that there is hope: the sages were successful and left behind a map to help us ford the river. These are the rituals, and the *junzi* cultivates them religiously.

Still, we must keep everything in its proper place. Though the rituals are invaluable as a map to the realm of the Way, they are, in the end, but a chart of the waters, a compass, or pole-star. Xunzi's *junzi* must recognize the function of ritual rather than be enslaved by it. However great a boon expertise in the rituals represents, it is still not one's final destination. Heaven has an enduring Way (*changdao*), a set of laws and forces that transcend the human will. Our project is to apprehend that Way and apply it to the advantage of humanity. But precisely because the Way is so complex and multifaceted, that project requires the dedication of one's entire life.

In the language of the "Euthyphro problem," then, Xunzi asserts that the sages set up the rituals because they are holy, and not *vice versa*. The ultimate standard of morality is not the sages at all: it is the Way, and the sages are sages only because they knew the Way and fashioned their rituals after it. As we concluded above, making this choice entails the inevitable diminution of the sages' godliness—and that is exactly as Xunzi intended. After all, the sages were not gods; they were human beings just like us who reached the highest levels of self-perfection through a lifetime of effort and virtue. If we try hard enough, we might one day be able to match them. "A man in the street can become Yu" (*X* 17.23.296; K 23.5b).

Xunzi's piety is therefore inextricably bound up with his idea of the Way. Both Confucius and Mencius had referred to the *dao*—indeed, it may well have been Confucius who first injected a moral dimension to the term—but Xunzi was the first thinker in the tradition to articulate the concept so clearly as a single and universal ontology. The Way is the principle of the universe, the "plan and pattern of order" (*X* 16.22.281; K 22.3). In his argument for a unified and ordered cosmos, we must see Xunzi as a child of the third century and a crucial—if unwitting—forefather of the philosophical system that would come to dominate the intellectual world soon after his death.

❊   ❊   ❊

Scholars often wonder how it could be that Xunzi's most famous student was the outspoken anti-Confucian Han Fei (d. 233 B.C.E.). Most of his other students do not turn on their former master so strikingly. It is easy to see, for example, how much Mao Heng and his son Mao Chang, the transmitters of the only surviving edition of the *Canon of Poetry* (*Shijing*), must have learned from Xunzi. Xunzi consistently interprets the *Poetry* along lines that are clearly related to the later Mao school of exegesis and quotes the poems according to a textual tradition that could not have diverged significantly from that of his students. Moreover, Li Si (d. 208 B.C.E.)—the future prime minister of the state of Qin who was responsible for Han Fei's suicide—was an opportunist by his own admission who probably studied with Xunzi only because he was at that time the most famous teacher in the Chinese world.[11]

But Han Fei represents a more difficult case, because he explicitly rejects some of the most central ideas in Xunzi's philosophy. Han Fei argues that the bedrock of humanity is not, as Xunzi would have it, "making distinctions," but "having likes and dislikes":

> Anyone who governs the world must accord with what is essential in man. What is essential in man is having likes and dislikes. Therefore rewards and punishments can be effective. Since rewards and punishments can be effective, prohibitions and commandments can be established and the Way of governing made complete. The ruler grasps the handles [the "two handles" are

rewards and punishments] in order to occupy the power-base; therefore what he commands is carried out and what he prohibits is stopped. (H 18.48.996)[12]

The consequences of this view are considerable. First, it means Han Fei must deny that there is a fundamental distinction between humans and animals. Dogs have "likes and dislikes" too, and indeed the ruler's method of controlling his populace—"rewards and punishments"—is hardly different from the kennel master's approach to his hounds. Han Fei's worldview entails a complete rejection of all Confucian moral philosophy. He does not believe that the common person possesses a mind in the philosophical sense; his Everyman does not have the capability—let alone the obligation—of self-cultivation. For the people are no wiser in old age than at birth:

> Those people today who do not know how to govern always say: "Apprehend the mind of the people." . . . The wisdom of the people is as useless as the mind of a baby. If you do not shave a baby's head, then its belly will hurt;[13] if you do not lance its boil, then it will gradually grow. In order to shave its head or lance its boil, one person must hold it while the compassionate mother cures it. But it still cries and calls out without ceasing. The baby does not know that suffering a small hardship will bring about a great benefit. (H 19.50.1103)

The ruler must simply keep his hands firmly on the "two handles" and ignore the objections of his subjects. He cannot let their opinions influence his policies. But is the ruler free to disregard the *dao* as well? That is to say, does Han Fei, like Shen Dao, grant the ruler the right to devise his own laws, however wicked or shortsighted they might be—or, like Xunzi, does he postulate a transcendent natural order with which the ruler's laws ought to comply? At different times Han Fei seems to give different answers.

On the one hand, he derides those who attempt to solve today's problems by yesterday's means.

> If people extol the ways of Yao, Shun, Yu, Tang, and Wu [four sage-kings] for the present generation, they will certainly be ridiculed by the new sages. Therefore the sage does not make a goal of cultivating antiquity and does not believe that standards are eternally applicable. He discusses the affairs of the age and makes the appropriate preparations. (H 19.49.1040)

Elsewhere, however, Han Fei seems to contradict his own view that standards (*fa*) are not eternally applicable:

> The Way is the beginning of the myriad things, the skein of right and wrong. Therefore the enlightened ruler maintains the beginning in order to know

the origin of the myriad things; he takes control of the skein in order to know the end-points of success and failure. (*H* 1.5.67)

Moreover, in spite of what we have just read about the fallacy of "cultivating antiquity," Han Fei avers that the "enlightened ruler" who bases himself on the Way is actually imitating the ancients: "The Former Kings took the Way as their constant and standards as the basis [of government]" (*H* 5.19.310). This is the reason, Han Fei explains, why the ruler should govern his country as though he were frying small fish:

> When frying small fish, if you poke them frequently, you will ruin them; and when governing a great state, if you change standards frequently, the people will take it as a hardship. Therefore the ruler who possesses the Way values tranquility and does not change his standards over and over. (*H* 6.20.355)

Is the Way eternal or not? Han Fei never resolves this evident contradiction in his writings, and it may well be that his premature death prevented him from organizing his ideas into a coherent whole. In all of his work, Han Fei is characteristically suspicious of any philosophy that claims to be universally applicable. He *deliberately* argues for different points of view under different circumstances. If, for example, his intended audience is the ruler, he may warn against the conspiratorial tendencies of ministers; but when advising those ministers in a different essay, he actually recommends the same duplicitous behavior that he elsewhere condemns (see, e.g., *H* 4.12.222 and 4.14.245). Han Fei is far more interested in rhetoric than in philosophy. When it is rhetorically convenient to resort to the trope that "standards are not eternally applicable," he will do so, but when the occasion calls for a trope like "the Way and its standards are constant," he will not hesitate to apply it. The former contention—that the ways of the ancients may not be appropriate for society today—is one of the best attested commonplaces in Chinese political philosophy and was certainly well known to Han Fei. The notion of the constant Way of the universe he almost certainly picked up from his teacher, Xunzi. For himself, he did not care to clarify where he stood. All ideas are merely potential themes, to be chosen judiciously by the skilled orator and exploited for their maximum persuasive potential.[14]

*   *   *

One of the greatest defects of the "Legalist" outlook, as Xunzi pointed out in his criticism of Shen Dao, is that it is amoral and admits the possibility of bad laws. It may well have been his sensitivity to this point that induced Han Fei to make his abortive attempt at linking "standards" to the Way. In this manner, he intended to stress that "standards" are not merely regulations that a particular ruler or minister happened to implement: they are in the grain of the cosmos, and so have the same stature as Xunzi's rituals. Recently excavated texts from the philosophical school known as "Huang-Lao" (named after Huangdi, the Yellow Emperor, and Laozi, putative author of the *Daodejing*) display this argumentative strategy even more clearly:

> The Way gave birth to standards. Standards align gain and loss with a marking-line and are what clarifies [the difference] between the curved and the straight. Therefore, whoever grasps the Way produces standards and does not dare violate them. Once the standards are established, he does not dare do away with them. [If] one is able to align oneself with the marking-line, one will see and know all under Heaven and not be deluded. . . . Heaven and Earth have their enduring constancies; the myriad people have their enduring works; the noble and base have their constant positions. There is an enduring Way to tend one's ministers; there are enduring rules for directing the people.[15]

Such language is the hallmark of Huang-Lao: there is a constant Way of the universe, and the ruler who apprehends it can "see and know all under Heaven." In the field of battle, the advantages of following the Way are especially clear: lasting success comes not to the ruler who spends the most on equipping his soldiers, but to the one who "values those who possess the Way." The outcome of warfare is determined by the "Way of Heaven."[16] It is no coincidence that the Huang-Lao conception of warfare is reminiscent of Xunzi's military theory ("Following the Way brings about success; not following it brings about downfall"). It was Xunzi, after all, who first argued so eloquently for this understanding of Heaven and the Way. To be sure, other third-century texts—such as the *Heguanzi*—presented a compatible point of view. But Xunzi, more than anyone else, succeeded in making the idea intellectually respectable.

And yet he would have been horrified to read what the Huang-Lao thinkers did to his philosophy. In delineating their "foundational naturalism,"[17] those writers tore out his notion of the Way from the rest of his philosophy. What distinguishes Xunzi from Han Fei, from the Huang-Lao theoreticians, and from all his epigones is his insistence that the Way comes with moral obligations *for everyone*. All Huang-Lao texts, including such later compilations as the *Huainanzi*, agree that the ruler who best embodies the Way will succeed, whereas the ruler who ignores or abandons it can only fail. There is, consequently, a well-articulated notion of self-cultivation in the Huang-Lao tradition. It is not easy to "see and know all under Heaven";

one must work at it through a rigorous program of meditation and self-perfection.[18] But this possibility is never envisioned for anyone other than the ruler. The rest of humanity exists merely for him to use or to misuse—to "gain" or to "lose."

Xunzi, on the other hand, consciously extends the duty of self-cultivation all the way down to the "man in the street." Every human being is presented with the choice of becoming a *junzi* or a *xiaoren*. This is because every human being has a mind (*xin*). The mind is the foundation for Xunzi's entire humanistic vision. "How does one know the Way?" Xunzi asks. "I say: the mind" (*X* 15.21.263; K 21.5d).

> The mind is the lord of the body and the master of spiritual illumination. It issues commands but does not receive commands. It prohibits on its own; it employs on its own; it considers on its own; it chooses on its own; it acts on its own; it ceases on its own. Thus the mouth can be forced to be silent or to speak; the body can be forced to contract or expand; the mind cannot be forced to change its intention. If it accepts something, it receives it; if it rejects it, it forgoes it. (*X* 15.21.265; K 21.6a)

This may be the closest that any Chinese writer comes to a concept of free will. The mind must be able to observe dispassionately the conduct of the self. It observes that the *xing* is self-destructive because it does not conform to the Way, and it directs the self to begin the arduous process of "transformation" (*hua*). Self-reflection is the key to moral development: we can see ourselves and change what we see if we do not like it. Our "lord" is not our ruler but our mind. We bear the responsibility for our actions for the simple reason that our actions are the consequence of our own choices.

This last—and most important—dimension of Xunzi's piety takes a uniquely Confucian form. The Way may be great and good, *but human beings must make their own contribution*. We must all actively participate in the Way. It is an idea that goes back as far as Confucius: "Man can make the Way great; it is not that the Way makes man great" (*Analects* 15:29). For Xunzi too, Heaven and earth are not the end of philosophy but the beginning: "Heaven and earth give birth to it; the sage completes it" (*X* 6.10.118; K 10.6). In this respect, Confucian spirituality simply does not fit into the familiar models of Western theology. One can see how the "Euthyphro problem" does not apply to the Confucian case. The point is not that the rituals are holy because the sages established them, nor that the sages established the rituals because the rituals were holy, but that the sages were human beings who fulfilled their destiny by spreading the principles of Heaven and earth throughout the world. They affirmed their own humanity by means of a spiritual act.

Notes

1. The following overview of Xunzi's philosophy is taken from my *Rituals of the Way: The Philosophy of Xunzi* (Chicago and La Salle, Ill.: Open Court, 1999). The subsequent discussions of Han Fei and Huang-Lao, as well as that of Xunzi's piety, are written for this essay. In accordance with the aims of this volume, I shall try to keep notes at a minimum, and cite only the most critical works in the field.

2. I. A. Richards suggests that the "sound" refers to "the unpleasant sound of the child thudding down into the well, not the mere rumour or report of what has happened" (*Mencius on the Mind: Experiments in Multiple Definition* [London: Routledge & Kegan Paul, 1932], 19).

3. All translations in this essay are my own.

4. This crucial observation was first made by A. C. Graham, "The Background to the Mencian Theory of Human Nature," *Tsing Hua Journal of Chinese Studies* 6, no. 2 (1967), reprinted in Graham's *Studies in Chinese Philosophy and Philosophical Literature*, SUNY Series in Chinese Philosophy and Culture (Albany: State University of New York Press, 1990), 7–66.

5. References to the *Xunzi* will be cited as follows. "*X*" refers to the Chinese text as presented in Wang Xianqian, *Xunzi jijie*, Zhongguo sixiang mingzhu (Beijing: Guji, 1954; rpt., Taipei: Shijie, 1992). For purposes of comparison, I cite also the relevant paragraph number ("K") in John Knoblock's recent English translation, *Xunzi: A Translation and Study of the Complete Works*, 3 vols. (Stanford: Stanford University Press, 1988–1994), although the translation here will often differ significantly.

6. This observation goes back to Dai Zhen (1724–1777); see his *Mengzi ziyi shuzheng* (Beijing: Zhonghua, 1961), B.25. See also P. J. Ivanhoe, "Thinking and Learning in Early Confucianism," *Journal of Chinese Philosophy* 17, no. 4 (1990): 480ff.

7. This is not to say, however, that the idea started with Xunzi; see e.g. *Mencius* 1A:5.

8. Herbert Fingarette traces this aspect of *li* to the writings of Confucius (*Confucius—The Secular as Sacred* [New York: Harper & Row, 1972]). For a recent discussion of "contractarianism" in Western philosophy, see, e.g., David Gauthier, *Morals by Agreement* (Oxford: Oxford University Press, 1986).

9. Shen Dao's writings are reconstructed in P. M. Thompson, *The Shen-tzu Fragments*, London Oriental Series 29 (Oxford: Oxford University Press, 1979). See, e.g., p. 242: "Though a law be not good, it is still preferable to no law."

10. The "root" is usually taken to mean humanity and righteousness; the "branch," ritual.

11. Li Si is said to have quoted Xunzi once; see *Shiji* (Beijing: Zhonghua, 1959), 87.2547. The apophthegm that Li Si cites is of no philosophical significance and even suggests that he did not learn much from his teacher. Cf. also Léon Vandermeersch, *La formation du légisme: Recherche sur la constitution d'une philosophie caractéristique de la Chine ancienne*, Publications de l'Ecole Française d'Extrême-

Orient 56 (Paris, 1965), 203. Vandermeersch claims further that Xunzi's doctrines were completely abandoned by Han Fei, who, like Li Si, sought in Xunzi nothing more than a good classical education. The following discussion will show why I do not agree.

12. References to the *Han Feizi* ("*H*") are cited according to Chen Qiyou, *Han Feizi jishi* (Beijing: Zhonghua, 1958).

13. Commentators do not agree on the meaning of this phrase.

14. See Paul Rakita Goldin, "Han Fei's Doctrine of Self-Interest," *Asian Philosophy* 11, no. 3 (2001): 153f.

15. This is from the first chapter of the *Jingfa*, one of the four Huang-Lao texts discovered at Mawangdui in 1973. I cite from the edition in Robin D. S. Yates, *Five Lost Classics: Tao, Huang-Lao, and Yin-Yang in Ancient China*, Classics of Ancient China (New York: Ballantine, 1997), 50–52. Compare Yates's translation.

16. See Yates, *Five Lost Classics,* 70 and 132.

17. "Foundational naturalism" is the term used to describe Huang-Lao in R. P. Peerenboom, *Law and Morality in Ancient China: The Silk Manuscripts of Huang-Lao*, SUNY Series in Chinese Philosophy and Culture (Albany: State University of New York Press, 1993). For more on Huang-Lao, see, e.g., Tu Weiming, "The 'Thought of Huang-Lao': A Reflection on the Lao Tzu and Huang Ti Texts in the Silk Manuscripts of Ma-wang-tui," *Journal of Asian Studies* 39 (1979–80): 95–110.

18. See especially Harold D. Roth, "Psychology and Self-Cultivation in Early Taoistic Thought," *Harvard Journal of Asiatic Studies* 51, no. 2 (1991): 599–650.

Suggested Reading List

Fingarette, Herbert. *Confucius—The Secular as Sacred*. New York: Harper & Row, 1972.

Goldin, Paul Rakita. *Rituals of the Way: The Philosophy of Xunzi*. Chicago and La Salle, Ill.: Open Court, 1999.

Graham, A. C. *Disputers of the Tao: Philosophical Argument in Ancient China*. La Salle, Ill.: Open Court, 1989.

Knoblock, John, trans. *Xunzi: A Translation and Study of the Complete Works*. 3 volumes. Stanford: Stanford University Press, 1988–94.

Peerenboom, R. P. *Law and Morality in Ancient China: The Silk Manuscripts of Huang-Lao*. SUNY Series in Chinese Philosophy and Culture. Albany: State University of New York Press, 1993.

Tu Weiming. "The 'Thought of Huang-Lao': A Reflection on the Lao Tzu and Huang Ti Texts in the Silk Manuscripts of Ma-wang-tui." *Journal of Asian Studies* 39 (1979–80): 95–110.

Yates, Robin D. S., trans. *Five Lost Classics: Tao, Huang-Lao, and Yin-Yang in Han China*. Classics of Ancient China. New York: Ballantine, 1997.

15

The Way of the Unadorned King: The Classical Confucian Spirituality of Dong Zhongshu

SARAH A. QUEEN

THIS ARTICLE PRESENTS A TYPOLOGY of classical Confucian spirituality as it was represented in the official writings of one of the most important early reformers within the Confucian tradition—Dong Zhongshu, scholar and statesman of the Han dynasty (206 B.C.E.–220 C.E.). Through his interpretations of the *Gongyang Commentary* associated with the *Spring and Autumn*, Dong sought to reform the Han by reconfiguring the ideal of emperorship, revitalizing the fundamental ethical principles of the Confucian tradition and reconstituting a religious basis for rulership that would have a lasting impact on the Chinese state. Dong's activities were instrumental in terminating imperial patronage for non-Confucian texts and establishing official recognition and support of the Confucian Canon. Henceforth, the Confucian Canon would occupy a prominent position in the religious and political life of the traditional state. It is also important to note that beyond what was officially sanctioned by the central court, the critical spirit of Dong hermeneutics would inspire Confucians of later generations, particularly in the Song (960–1279) and Qing (1644–1911) dynasties, to challenge, reform, and thereby renew Confucian state orthodoxy when political abuses or authoritarian tendencies proliferated and required redress.

In reformulating the institution of emperorship, Dong articulated the ideal of a ruler whose authority and power were both legitimized and limited by the higher authority of Heaven's moral principles, as embodied in the Confucian scriptures and interpreted by Confucian scholars. By linking monarch, text, and interpreter, Dong sought to renegotiate the parameters of political power and textual authority, to redefine the relationship between the ruler and ruled, and to reform the ruler's arbitrary exercise of power, which had become widespread during the preceding Qin dynasty (221–206 B.C.E.). Central to this reformulation was the figure of Confucius as he was portrayed in the *Gongyang Commentary,* the written expression of one interpretive tradition that survived through oral transmission for some three hundred years before the Han. *Gongyang* scholars like Dong Zhongshu believed that Confucius authored the *Spring and Autumn* to catalogue and condemn the ills of his day, leaving his message hidden in an esoteric language invisible to the untrained or uninitiated. Dong elevated this vision of Confucius to messianic heights. Reinvented as the "unadorned king [*suwang*]," Dong argued that Heaven had mandated that Confucius not only correct the faults of his age but also establish institutions for a new ruler and dynasty, though he lacked the power to reign. While in actuality unable to become king, Confucius assumed the historiographical prerogatives of the king and spoke in his place through the Spring and Autumn, adapting each entry to express model judgments on every event and participant he recorded. This "praise and blame" constituted a blueprint for reform that was to sit idle until the coming of a future sage who would decode Confucius's message and institute the new dynasty envisioned therein. Thus, in Dong's reading of the *Spring and Autumn,* Confucius embodied the highest ideal of the sage, while the text he authored recorded an esoteric message by which to establish the perfect state, characterized in Dong's words by an era of Grand Peace (Taiping). Dong perceived his life mission as nothing short of instituting this new dynasty envisioned by Confucius.

What follows is a close reading of the three famous memorials that Dong wrote in response to an imperial inquiry which Emperor Wu initiated shortly after he assumed the throne in 140 B.C.E. Here Dong's vision of Confucius's theocratic utopia, rendered as "The Way of the Unadorned King," finds its most passionate and poetic expression. Indeed, these memorials constitute one of the most moving and powerful arguments in the history of the tradition for the adoption of the Confucian Way as the defining spiritual vision for the Chinese empire.

Methodological Considerations

To explicate Dong's spiritual vision I will take as my point of departure two recent studies that have addressed the question of Confucian spirituality, each of which represents a distinct approach to the challenge of cross-cultural dialogue. Rodney Taylor's *Religious Dimensions of Confucianism* asks to what extent religious categories indigenous to Western religious traditions may be employed to analyze Confucian spirituality. He warns:

"When we examine the Confucian tradition, we are not necessarily going to find those structures of religion that we have grown most accustomed to encountering in the study of religious traditions. We need to be sensitive to different ways in which a religious tradition can express its religious dimension."[1] Tu Weiming, author of *Centrality and Commonality,* speaks to us as a contemporary participant in the ongoing transmission of the Confucian tradition, albeit one who is steeped in the religious and philosophic traditions of both East and West.[2] Adopting an interpretive approach to the *Zhongyong,* a seminal work attributed to Confucius's grandson, Zisi, Tu Weiming explicates the humanistic vision enlivening this text, one that, he maintains, embodies a decidedly religious orientation. Each of these works expands our resources for thinking about the spiritual dimension of the Confucian tradition, thereby enabling us to appreciate the differences as well as the commonalities that define religious life.

Taylor highlights three areas of concern through which we may broadly define religious life. First, there must be a concept of the absolute. In the Classical Confucian tradition this element is identified as Tian, Heaven, which functions as a religious authority or absolute, often theistic in its portrayal. There must also be a provision for a relationship. "For a religious tradition, the absolute must provide for a relationship with the individual, although that relationship can differ widely, whether discussing theistic, monistic, or the spectrum of traditions possible." Moreover, to describe fully the religious aspects of this relationship there must be the possibility of ultimate transformation. "Religion provides not only for a relationship with what is defined as the absolute, but provides as well a way for the individual to move toward that which is identified as the absolute. This movement toward the absolute is a process of transformation, and because the goal is the absolute, the process can be spoken of as ultimate transformation." Finally, the absolute must, in its relation with the individual and perhaps other living things, provide a means of salvation; it must provide a means for ultimate transformation. In Confucianism, the figure of the sage provides the model for such a process of ultimate transformation. As Taylor explains:

> Thus, in the relationship between Heaven as a religious absolute and the sage as a transformed person, we have the identification of a soteriological process and, as a result, the identification of the religious core of the tradition. In turn, the soteriological relationship between Heaven and the sage becomes a religious model for the tradition as a whole. As each person has the capacity to emulate the way of the sage, if not to become a sage, the possibility exists for soteriological transformation of the individual. A life lived within this salvational hope and committed to its achievement is a religious life.[3]

Tu Weiming echoes Taylor's typology in *Centrality and Commonality,* wherein he explains the Confucian way of being religious as "ultimate self-transformation as a communal act and as a faithful dialogical response to the transcendent."[4] Tu complements and adumbrates Taylor's definition in three important ways: he expands on Taylor's notion of ultimate transformation by emphasizing personhood or selfhood as the ontological grounds for ultimate transformation; he reminds us of the Confucian proclivity to underscore the communal, corporate, or social aspects of this process; and he refines Taylor's discussion of the absolute with a provision for a relationship as involving a "dialogue" between self and transcendent defined in the *Zhongyong* by the consummate value of sincerity (*cheng*).

In the discussion to follow I will employ Taylor's and Tu's typologies to clarify Dong's spiritual vision in the following ways. I will suggest that for Dong Zhongshu "ultimate self-transformation" involves the perfection or completion of human beings' Heavenly endowed nature. As "communal act," it entails a vision of politics as a means toward ultimate transformation. Human nature necessitates that this process can begin only when the individual who occupies the throne rules as a sage. As sage-king, the ruler initiates a process of "transformation through moral instruction" that proceeds from his person through the political and social communities, beyond the human realm to the natural world, so that finally all forms of existence mirror that of Heaven. In this sense the central task of governance is profoundly spiritual, as it involves fulfilling the ultimate meaning of human existence. Finally, a "faithful dialogical response to the Transcendent" finds expression in Dong's articulations of the Mandate of Heaven as both Heaven's highly public charge to the ruler, on the one hand, and, on the other, Heaven's deeply personal connection to each human being. Such are the conditions whereby the ruler is fit to rule and human beings are fit to be considered human.

The Kingly Way

Our analysis of Dong's spiritual vision begins with his description of the "Kingly Way" and the closely related "Mandate of Heaven." In utilizing the latter concept, Dong reaffirms the ancient usage of the term in its most politicized sense: Heaven's Mandate denotes one who assumes the position of sovereignty based on the authority of Heaven. Bestowal of the Mandate involves a purposeful intervention by Heaven in the realm of human affairs. As Dong explains to Emperor Wu, "Your humble subject has heard that the king who is appointed by Heaven inevitably possesses something which cannot be brought about by human effort and yet he finds himself in possession of it. This is the auspicious sign that he has indeed received the Mandate" (*HS* 56/2500).[5] The Mandate is granted only to one who possesses outstanding virtue. Echoing Confucius's words, Dong concludes "'Virtue never stands alone. It is bound to have neighbors.' Such is the result of accumulating acts of goodness and participating in virtuous deeds" (ibid.). Should the ruler fail to act virtuously, Heaven's Mandate will be lost. In a further elaboration on Confucius's words, Dong explains to Emperor Wu: "'Human beings are capable of broadening the Way. It is not the Way that broadens human beings.' Thus order or disorder and decline or prosperity rest within your person. It is not the case that the Mandate ordained by Heaven is irrevocable" (ibid.). Indeed, Dong argues, the extent to which the ruler maintains in the forefront of his mind the primacy of the people determines the longevity or brevity of the Mandate:

> Heaven generates the people not on behalf of the king but on the contrary, Heaven establishes the king on behalf of the people. Thus if his virtue is sufficient to provide the people with security and happiness, Heaven grants [the Mandate to him]. If his evil is sufficient to harm or injure the people, Heaven withdraws [the Mandate from him].[6]

Having received the Mandate, the king's call to rectify his subjects must proceed from Heaven at every turn. Dong insists, "Whenever the king wishes to do anything, he must derive his principles from Heaven" (*HS* 56/2501–2). The ruler's relationship to his people must mirror his relationship to Heaven. Just as Heaven serves as model and guide to the ruler, so the ruler must serve as model and guide to his people. Just as Heaven embodies perfect humaneness, so the ruler must embody humaneness in his relations with his subjects. Just as Heaven provides the starting point for the ruler's self-transformation, the ruler must initiate the moral transformation of his people. He must initiate and facilitate "the ultimate self-transformation of the community," the process of correlating the order and values of the human world with those of Heaven. Indeed, Dong maintains, the very morphology of the term *king*, with its three horizontal lines representing Heaven, earth, and humanity, connected through the center by a vertical stroke representing the king's penetration of their interrelated principles, illuminates the ruler's ultimate significance as cosmic pivot uniting the Heavenly and human realms (*CQFL* 11/6a).

The sage-kings of antiquity perfectly expressed this unity. They were the rulers who embodied the Absolute in their governance, emulating Heaven's normative patterns in the natural world when they established the Way among humanity:

With universal love and free from selfish desires, they spread out their bounties and displayed their humaneness to enrich the people. They established righteous principles and set out behavioral norms to guide the people. Spring is the means by which Heaven generates; humaneness is the means by which the ruler extends his love. Summer is the means by which Heaven brings living things to maturity; virtue is the means by which the ruler nourishes. Frost is the means by which Heaven brings death; punishment is the means by which the ruler corrects. Speaking from this perspective, the verifications of Heaven in the human world are the enduring principles from antiquity to the present. (*HS* 56/2515)

Here Heaven's impartial, regulated, and constant role in nature provides the ultimate models for human governance. Yet Heaven is not only the ultimate ground of all that is good, nor simply a remote absolute. Heaven also acts in ways that are expressly responsive to human conduct. We have already seen one expression of this notion in the auspicious signs sent by Heaven when granting the Mandate. Heaven's responsiveness, Dong argues, continues throughout the ruler's reign:

When a state is about to suffer a defeat because [the ruler] has erred from proper principles, Heaven first sends forth anomalies and disasters to reprimand and warn him. If the [ruler] does not know to look into himself, then Heaven again sends forth extraordinary and strange signs to frighten and startle him. If he still does not know to change, only then will ruin and defeat come to him. From this example one observes that Heaven's heart is humane and loving toward the people's ruler and that Heaven desires to keep him from chaos. During those ages when there is no great loss of proper principles, Heaven still desires to support and secure him. His task is simply to exert himself. He must exert himself to learn and inquire, and then what he hears and sees will be pervasive and his knowledge will become increasingly enlightened. He must exert himself to practice proper principles, and then his virtue will increase daily and he will be in possession of great achievements. Such efforts will enable him to quickly achieve results. The Odes states: "From dawn to dusk unceasing." The Documents states: "Make the effort. Make the effort." Both are references to exerting oneself. (*HS* 56/2498–99)

Thus the ruler is subject not only to Heaven's impersonal processes but also to Heaven's personal will. Heaven responds to the ruler, not always according to fixed rules and patterns but often according to the dynamic circumstances of his rule. Possessing the anthropomorphic quality of a "humane heart," Heaven purposely manifests disapproval to assist the ruler. Alerted to the fact that he has strayed from proper principles, the ruler must engage in critical self-reflection and endeavor to rectify his conduct. If necessary, he must be willing to exert himself "from dawn to dusk unceasing." No other trope from the canonical literature captures better the centrality of ethical praxis and self-effort in the ongoing spiritual process of ultimate transformation. Should the ruler fail to make the effort, Heaven's anomalies grow correspondingly more significant and awesome. Even so, Heaven does not abandon the ruler for his transgressions. Heaven's relation to the ruler is not that of "wholly other" to human "creature," but that of father to son. If ruin and defeat ultimately visit the ruler, they are the consequence of his own all-too-human actions, not the outcome of divine wrath.

Conversely the ruler who seeks ever to embody the virtues of the sage-kings will always be assisted by Heaven:

> The *Odes* states: "He treats his people and his officials correctly, and so receives his reward from Heaven." Those who govern by treating the people correctly will certainly be rewarded by Heaven. It is the Five Virtues—Humanity, Righteousness, Propriety, Wisdom and Trustworthiness—that the king should cultivate. When the king cultivates them, he will receive Heaven's protection and be favored by the ghosts and spirits. His virtue will reach beyond the four corners of his empire, extending to all living things. (*HS* 56/2505)

In constant "dialogue" with Heaven, the king who fulfills his role as sage is rewarded, while one who acts like a brigand is punished. When he receives inauspicious omens he knows he has erred from the Way, failed to act as a sage, and consequently must look deep within himself to examine and rectify his thought and conduct. When he receives auspicious omens, he knows that he has fulfilled the Mandate to act as Heaven's son, providing the physical and spiritual resources whereby human beings are able to fulfill their destiny as moral agents.

The starting point of the king's rectification of the world begins with his person as he stands in relation to Heaven. It begins with an awakening to his Heavenly potential. Accordingly Dong implores Emperor Wu as follows:

> If you are aware of your Heavenly endowed nature, you will know that you are superior to all forms of life. Realizing this, you will understand humanity and righteousness. Understanding of these will lead you to attach great importance to ritual and etiquette. Having attached great importance to such matters, you will find contentment in abiding in the good. Having found contentment in abiding in the good, you will delight in conforming to proper principles. When you delight in conforming to proper principles you will be deemed a Gentleman! Therefore Confucius said: "One has no way of becom-

ing a Gentleman unless he understands the Mandate." This captures the essence of what I refer to here. (*HS* 56/2516)

Here, Dong employs the Mandate in yet another important sense: it is the ontological pull toward ethical perfection or the soteriological goal of self-cultivation. The king must first establish his own character; he must morally rectify his own person before he can hope to transform his subjects. Only then, Dong explains, can he become a model of transformation for all to emulate:

> Therefore, the ruler rectifies his heart to rectify those of his court officials; when the hearts of his court officials are rectified, those of his rank and file officers will be rectified; when the hearts of his rank and file officers are rectified, those of his subjects will be rectified and consequently all within the four corners of the world, near and far, will be one with his rectitude, and no evil influences will cause dissension among them. (*HS* 56/2502–3)

Having established moral harmony in the human world, the ruler's influence radiates beyond, to the world of nature, in ever-widening circles to encompass the transformation of all living things and ultimately beyond to affect the cosmic rhythms of Heaven itself. Dong continues:

> Thus yin and yang will be harmonious and wind and rain will arrive in their appropriate season; all living beings will be in harmony and the multitudes will prosper; the Five Cereals will reach fruition and the subsidiary crops will flourish. All within Heaven and Earth will be showered by these blessings and all within the four seas will hear of the ruler's flourishing virtue and flock to him to become his subjects. Of all possible blessings and every conceivable auspicious omen that may be summoned, none will fail to arrive and the Kingly Way will be fulfilled. (*HS* 56/2503)

This process of ultimate transformation is accomplished only gradually through the arduous efforts of the ruler to direct his thoughts and efforts away from such mundane concerns as wealth and power to the steady accumulation of virtue. The process of self-cultivation, although laborious and slow, is sure to succeed if the ruler remains constant in his efforts. In place of the steady accumulation of wealth, the pastime of lesser kings, the sage-king concerns himself with what Dong refers to as "accumulating acts of goodness," ever mindful of his thoughts and deeds:

> Yao appeared among the ranks of the feudal lords while Shun emerged from deep within the mountains. Neither achieved fame in the course of a single day. On the contrary, they achieved it only gradually. Words that derive from the heart cannot be repressed; acts that emanate from the core of one's being cannot be concealed. Speech and conduct are the most vital aspects of

governance. They are the means by which the Gentleman moves Heaven and Earth . . . . Thus Yao trembled as he daily pursued the Way while Shun proceeded fearfully as he daily extended his filiality. Their small acts of goodness accumulated and their reputations became prominent; their virtue became evermore manifest, and their persons revered. Such is the manner in which the Way gradually became illustrious and prosperous. (*HS* 56/2517)

Why must ultimate transformation begin with the king? To understand Dong's emphasis on the political realm as the starting point for spiritual transformation, we must turn to his comments on human nature.

Human Nature as Clay on a Potter's Wheel

In an earlier excerpt addressed to Emperor Wu, we have seen Dong assert the ruler's superiority over all other living beings based on his possession of a "Heavenly endowed nature," that which enables him to exist as a moral agent in the world. As the next excerpt makes clear, such a capacity is not unique to the ruler but the defining characteristic of humanity itself. All human beings differ from the birds and beasts in being endowed with ethical capacities. Dong describes the difference as follows:

> Human beings receive "the Mandate" from Heaven and consequently differ immeasurably from other forms of life. Within their households, they enjoy the feelings of kinship appropriate to father and son or to elder and younger brother. Beyond their households, they participate in the righteousness appropriate to ruler and minister or to superior and inferior. When they gather together with others in social discourse, they practice the various social distinctions appropriate to seniority or youth. With their splendid cultural forms they communicate with one another; with their peaceful sense of compassion they exhibit their love for one another. These are the reasons why human beings are superior to all other forms of life. (*HS* 56/2516)

Thus, while Dong optimistically asserts that all people participate in the Mandate, the personal calling to exist as moral beings in the world, most need assistance in doing so. In fact, Dong writes, this is the very reason why sage-kings came into existence:

> Heaven's command is known as "the Mandate (*ming*)" and can only be put into effect by a sage; the inherent qualities of a human being is known as "the nature (*xing*)" and can only be perfected through transformational instruction (*jiaohua*); human desire is known as "the disposition (*qing*)" and can only be disciplined through regulatory limitations. This is why the king must reverently carry forth Heaven's intentions to comply with 'the Mandate; he must strive to enlighten his people through transformational instruction to

perfect their natures; he must rectify the various laws and measures and maintain the various social distinctions to constrain their desires. When the ruler has attended to these three matters the root of good governance will have been established. (*HS* 56/2515–16)

It is in this sense, Dong explains, that the ruler's personal character is intimately related to the material and spiritual flourishing or decline of the broader human community:

A long or short life, a humane or degenerate character; once ordered and completed by the potter, cannot be refined or improved. Thus human beings possess at birth the seeds of order and disorder and consequently are not uniform. Confucius said: "The virtue of a gentleman is like the wind; the virtue of the small man is like grass. Let the wind blow over the grass and it is sure to bend." When Yao and Shun practiced their virtuous ways, the people were humane and lived out their natural life spans, when Jie and Zhou practiced their violent ways, the people were degenerate and died prematurely. Thus the ruler's transformation of his subjects and his subjects' submission to their ruler resemble clay on a potter's wheel: only a potter can shape it; it resembles metal in a mould: only a smith can cast it. This is precisely what Confucius referred to when he [described the Gentleman as follows]: "Having brought peace to them, they turned to him; having set them tasks, they worked harmoniously." (*HS* 56/2501)

Thus the sage is, at once, both ordinary and exceptional. Like all human beings, he participates in the Mandate, which commands all humans to perfect their natures, yet only he participates in the Mandate from which he derives his political authority because he has surpassed all others in doing so. He is, in the words of Taylor, thus imitable to the extent that that which enables him to become a sage, his human nature, is possessed by all human beings equally. Yet he is also inimitable to the extent that he has transcended other human beings in fulfilling the moral propensities of this nature.[7] This is precisely why he must lead others on to the path of ultimate transformation. His is the role of the potter or smith in molding the character of his people by actualizing the ethical propensities latent in their natures and restraining the unruly desires that constitute their dispositions.

Perfecting Human Nature through Educational Transformation

The means by which the emperor assists the populace in the perfection of their natures is through the transformative influence of moral instruction. Like the sage-kings before him, Dong warns, the ruler must rely on moral suasion rather than harsh punitive measures to rectify his subjects. Once again Heaven provides the ultimate sanction for this model of governance. Accordingly, Dong maintains, Heaven demonstrates this preference for moral suasion over punitive measures in relying more heavily on *yang* than *yin*, in issuing forth the seasonal cycles:

> The greatest aspect of Heaven's Way lies in yin and yang. Yang constitutes virtue and yin constitutes punishments. Punishments preside over death, while virtue presides over life. Therefore yang always occupies the vast summer and devotes itself to the matters of birth, growth, nourishment, and maturation. Yin always occupies the vast winter and accumulates in vacant and useless places. From this we see that Heaven relies on virtue and does not rely on punishments. Heaven causes yang to issue forth and circulate above, presiding over the achievements of the year. Heaven causes yin to retire and lie below, occasionally issuing forth to assist yang. If yang does not obtain the assistance of yin, it cannot complete the year on its own. Ultimately, however, the completion of the year is designated by yang. This is Heaven's intention. The king carries forth Heaven's intention in the conduct of his affairs. Therefore he relies on moral instruction and does not rely on coercive punishments. Coercive punishments cannot bring order to the age, just as yin cannot complete the year. Those who rely on coercive punishments to govern do not comply with Heaven. This is why the former kings did not rely on them. (*HS* 56/2502)

Indeed, when pressed by Emperor Wu to explain why, given his unfailing efforts to rule justly, Heaven has not responded with auspicious signs, Dong responds as follows:

> It is because transformation through moral instruction has not been established and consequently the people are not yet rectified. The people continue to seek after profit as water naturally tends to flow downward. If you do not rely on transformation through moral instruction to damn up this [tendency] you will not be able to stop it. Hence, when moral instruction has been established, evil and corrupt practices cease because the dikes have been perfected. When moral instruction has been neglected, villainy and evil appear but punishments and penalties cannot overcome them because the dikes have deteriorated. The kings of antiquity understood this principle. Therefore when they faced south and ruled the world, they considered transformation through moral instruction their most important undertaking. They set up institutions for study in the country and created schools for transformation in the villages. They saturated the people with humaneness; refined them with upright conduct; and restrained them with ritual. Hence, the reason the prohibitions were not disobeyed although the punishments were light was because transformation through moral instruction was practiced so that morals and customs became good. (*HS* 56/2503–4)

Moral instruction constitutes the basis of reform at all levels of society. Local schools were to be complemented by a Grand Academy at the capital to attract upright and gifted men to serve in the central government.[8] The curriculum from the most elementary schools across the empire to the highest institution of learning at the capital was to be dedicated to the Six Arts of Confucius, while other textual traditions were to be summarily proscribed.[9] The relevancy of the Six Arts did not stop here: the emperor was obligated to follow their strictures in every aspect of imperial administration. Indeed, Dong Zhongshu spent most of his career delineating the ways in which the emperor was to follow the *Spring and Autumn* in his quotidian responsibilities as the supreme religious and legal authority of the empire. Although beyond the scope of this article, Dong's interpretations endowed this text with novel modes of authority in the realms of law, ritual, and cosmology, resulting in the formation of China's first Confucian Canon.[10]

The Unity of Heaven and Humanity as Spiritual Ideal

In sum, as self-proclaimed heir to Confucius and would-be "unadorned king" of his age, Dong tirelessly sought to initiate a spiritual rectification of the Han empire. Hoping to reestablish the golden age of the sage-kings, and thereby institute an era of Grand Peace, Dong followed his Confucian predecessors in reasserting the long-held belief in the unity of Heaven and humanity. This concept, known as *tianren heyi,* literally "Heaven and humanity united as one," captures well the spiritual core of Dong's reformist vision. The quest to become a sage was no less than the existential endeavor to realize this ontological unity between Heaven and humanity; a unity predicated on the belief that humanity was endowed with a nature fundamentally commensurate with that of Heaven. Such an orientation determined, early on, the decidedly secular tone of Confucian thought. Given the immanence of humanity's Heavenly attributes, attention was naturally focused on the human community, wherein the project of self-actualization loomed large.

Yet this very immanence contained within it important transcendent dimensions. It implied something more: the concept of the absolute rendered in Chinese terms as *tian,* or Heaven, and a relationship with that absolute conceived in terms of *tianming* or Heaven's Mandate, which provided the means for ultimate transformation. Indeed, this concept in the Confucian lexicon underscores its propensity to stress the ontological unity between Heaven and humanity and thereby focus on the coincidence of their natures to be realized through human effort. Religious experience in the Confucian context, therefore, consists of the existential struggle to realize this unity. While devoid of any implicit tension between faith and reason, there persists an explicit tension between unity as an ontological ideal and as an existential struggle to realize this unity. While devoid of any implicit tension between faith and reason, there persists an explicit tension between unity as an ontological ideal and as an existential reality.

In considering the spiritual dimensions of the Confucian tradition, therefore, one finds the loci of religious life in the dual processes of divinization and humanization. Human beings possess the capacity to become like Heaven; the extent to which they actualize their Heavenly potential, bringing Heaven into the human world, is the measure of their religious life. We have seen that for Dong Zhongshu this was a highly politicized and textualized process. It could only occur when the individual who occupied the throne ruled as a sage-king and was guided by the normative patterns of Heaven embodied in the written legacy of Confucius. Indeed, Dong Zhongshu's most important contribution as a religious thinker was the idea that knowledge of the Confucian scriptures was indispensable to this spiritual endeavor—in fact, he made it a practically unanimous belief within Confucianism. It was in this sense that Dong Zhongshu left his most profound and durable impressions on the spiritual life of the Confucian tradition.

Notes

1. Rodney Taylor, *The Religious Dimensions of Confucianism* (Albany: State University of New York Press, 1990), 1.

2. Ibid., 2–3.

3. Ibid., 3.

4. Tu Weiming, *Centrality and Commonality* (Albany: State University of New York Press, 1989).

5. *Han Shu*, by Ban Gu (Beijing: Zhonghua Shuju, 1985), 56/2500 (hereafter cited as *HS*).

6. Dong states: "Heaven generates the people not on behalf of the king but on the contrary, Heaven establishes the king on behalf of the people. Thus if his virtue is sufficient to provide the people with security and happiness, Heaven grants [the Mandate to him]. If his evil is sufficient to harm or injure the people, Heaven withdraws [the Mandate from him]" (*Chunqiu fanlu*, by Dong Zhongshu, Sibucongkan edition [Shanghai: Hansulou, 1929], 7/14b [hereafter cited as *CQFL*]).

7. Taylor, *Religious Dimensions of Confucianism*, 52.

8. Dong urges the emperor: "The Grand Academy is an institution to which scholars will attach themselves. It is the root and source of educational transformation. Presently, with the numerous scholars from each commandery and each kingdom, there is a lack of those responding to your edicts. This means that the Kingly Way will gradually become extinct. Your humble minister requests your majesty to establish an Academy and appoint enlightened teachers to nurture the world's scholars. Frequently examine and question them to make the most of their talents, and then it will surely be possible to obtain outstanding candidates." (*HS* 56/2512)

9. Dong writes: "In his ignorance your minister suggests that all that is not in the category of the Six Disciplines or Arts of Confucius should be cut off and not allowed to be promoted. Only after evil and licentious theories are destroyed is it possible to unify rules and regulations and clarify standards and measures so that the people know what to follow" (*HS* 56/2523).

10. For a detailed treatment of this topic see Sarah A. Queen, *From Chronicle to Canon: The Hermeneutics of the Spring and Autumn according to Tung Chung-shu* (New York: Cambridge University Press, 1996).

Determining the Position of Heaven and Earth: Debates over State Sacrifices in the Western Han Dynasty

MICHAEL PUETT

T HROUGHOUT MUCH OF THE LATER imperial history of China, the most important sacrifices offered by the emperor were those given to Heaven and earth. Indeed, the Qing temples to Heaven and earth, located to the south and north respectively of the Forbidden City, can still be visited today.

This cult was first instituted during the latter portion of the Western Han dynasty after a series of extraordinary court debates.[1] Over the course of these debates, a group of Confucian ministers succeeded in eradicating significant portions of the sacrificial system that had been dominant for over two centuries and replacing it with the cults that would ultimately become normative.[2] In this essay, I will analyze how and why these debates took place, seeking to understand what was at stake for the Confucians in question and what significance the final outcome had.

In order to set these debates in context, it will be helpful to trace the development of the sacrificial system in the Han dynasty and to understand why particular sacrifices came to be imbued with such significance. To do so, I will begin with a discussion of the "Fengshan shu" chapter of Sima Qian's *Shiji*. Sima Qian was the court historian during the reign of Han Wudi, the figure who consolidated the sacrificial system against which the Confucians in question would later react. His "Fengshan shu" chapter is an attempt, among other things, to explicate the sacrificial system that Han Wudi had inherited and developed. A close reading of the chapter will therefore give us a glimpse of the various meanings that had become associated with these sacrifices and will put us in position to understand the arguments of the later Confucians.

The "Fengshan shu" Chapter
of Sima Qian

Sima Qian's ruler, Han Wudi, was the figure who consolidated imperial rule in China. To symbolize this consolidation, Han Wudi decided to undertake the *feng* and *shan* sacrifices—sacrifices that symbolized the consolidation of a dynasty. Sima Qian's chapter places this decision within the entire history of cultic activity in China. As many commentators have pointed out, Sima Qian's goal in the work was to criticize Han Wudi's decision.[3] However, there is much more of interest in the chapter than just this criticism. As I will argue, the chapter, if read carefully, gives us a unique and very suggestive glimpse of some of the views at Han Wudi's court concerning sacrifices, and will thus give us crucial clues for explicating the later debates that led to the partial eradication of Han Wudi's sacrificial system.

Early in the chapter, Sima Qian quotes the "Shun dian" chapter of the *Shangshu,* which discusses the sacrificial system of Shun, one of the early sage-kings. Shun is described as sacrificing to the higher gods at his capital and sacrificing from afar to the mountains, rivers, and various spirits. He would then hold audience with the feudal lords. Every five years he would make inspection tours of the Five Mountains. He would begin with the eastern Mount Tai, where he would sacrifice to Heaven, sacrifice from afar to the mountains and rivers, and meet with the feudal lords. He would then travel to the other four mountains (to the south, west, north, and center). This sacrificial system, based on a feudal political arrangement, will continue, with some variations, until the rise of an alternate system under the Qin (*Shiji,* 28.1355–56).[4]

Sima Qian then goes on to narrate the rise of the Xia dynasty under Yu. Yu himself continued the same sacrificial practice as Shun. But problems with the dynasty became apparent in the fourteenth generation:

> Yu accorded with this. After fourteen generations, it came to the reign of Di Kongjia. He made his virtue licentious and was fond of spirits. The spirits were angered, and the two dragons left. (*Shiji,* 28.1356)

The Xia fell three generations later.

A similar structure underlies Sima Qian's presentation of the Shang dynasty. Two rulers are singled out in particular. The first is Di Taiwu. One night a mulberry grew in his courtyard. Although this caused great alarm, his minister Yi Zhi argued: "Evil portents cannot overcome virtue." Di Taiwu then cultivated his virtue, and the mulberry died (*Shiji,* 28.1356).

Fourteen generations later, a decline in the Shang dynasty had set in. But Di Wuding arose and restored the dynasty. A bad portent appeared under Wuding as well, and Wuding was alarmed. But his minister Zu Ji said: "Cultivate virtue." Wuding did so, and his reign was thus long-lasting and peaceful (*Shiji*, 28.1356). Five generations later, however, Di Wuyi "treated the spirits with contempt" and was killed. The dynasty fell three generations later (*Shiji*, 28.1356).

Sima Qian then sums up his argument thus far:

> From this it can be seen that, at the beginning [of a dynasty] there is always reverence and respect, but later it deteriorates into disrespect and contempt. (*Shiji*, 28.1356–57)

Overtly, this is a simple reference to the dynastic cycle: a dynasty begins in virtue and ends in vice. But Sima Qian has set up this claim in a specific way. Virtue is based here on the proper intention of the ruler, involving, among other things, a proper reverence for spirits. Such a virtue, Sima Qian argues, overrides even bad portents sent from the spirits. And vice, so to speak, involves improper reverence, an impropriety that can take the form of *either* being "too fond of the spirits" or of "treating the spirits with contempt."

With this as his frame, the author turns next to the rise and fall of the Zhou dynasty. He begins by quoting from the *Zhouguan*, a text that purports to explicate the ritual system of the Zhou dynasty:

> The *Zhouguan* says: "When the winter solstice arrives, sacrifice to Heaven at the southern suburb in order to welcome the coming of the longer day. When the summer solstice arrives, sacrifice to the spirits of the earth. At both use music and dancing, and the spirits can thereby be obtained and brought into ritual. The Son of Heaven sacrifices to the famous mountains and great rivers under Heaven. The Five Peaks he regards as his ministers, the Four Waterways as his feudal lords. The feudal lords sacrifice to the famous mountains and great rivers within their fiefdoms." (*Shiji*, 28.1357)

The Zhou is thus presented as continuing, with minor variations, the same ritual system as Shun.

The later decline of the Zhou is then connected to the rise of the Qin.

> Fourteen generations after the Zhou conquered the Yin, the generations gradually declined, the rites and music were discarded, and the feudal lords acted on their own. (*Shiji*, 28.1358)

It was in this context that Duke Xiang of Qin was enfeoffed (*Shiji*, 28.1358). Sima Qian thus immediately presents Qin as emerging in a period when the feudal lords were usurping the power of the Zhou.

In the ensuing discussion, Sima Qian presents the emergence of a new sacrificial system in the Qin, a system that would develop and reach its zenith under Han Wudi. The first step was taken soon after the enfeoffment. Since the state of Qin was in the far west, Duke Xiang created an "altar of the west," at which sacrifices to the white god, the god of the west, were given (*Shiji*, 28.1358). As Sima Qian argues elsewhere:

> When Duke Xiang of Qin was enfeoffed as a lord, he made a western altar for use in sacrificing to the higher gods. The beginning of Qin's usurpation is clear to see. The *Liji* says: "The Son of Heaven makes offerings to Heaven and earth, while the lords of the states make offerings to the famous mountains and great rivers within their domains." (*Shiji*, 15.685)

This first sacrificial act, Sima Qian argues, was a usurpation of royal privilege.

Sixteen years later, Duke Wen of Qin had a dream, which his historian Dun interpreted as a sign from the higher gods. Duke Wen thereupon constructed an altar at Yong (*Shiji*, 28.1358). Sima Qian explains the method by which such sacrifices were legitimated:

> Some say that, from ancient times, because the region of Yong is so high, it was a site for spirits and the illustrious. Altars were therefore erected for suburban sacrifices to the higher gods, and the sacrifices to all the spirits were amassed there. Since it was used in the time of Huangdi, even though it was the waning of the Zhou, it could again be used for the suburban sacrifices. However, such words cannot be read in any of the classics, so scholars do not follow them. (*Shiji*, 28.1359)

Defenders of the Yong sacrifices argue that, even though the Zhou had not yet fallen, the antiquity of the Yong altars made their "reinstitution" by the Qin acceptable. In his telling of the narrative, Sima Qian is clearly calling into question the antiquity of the sacrificial system of Yong and casting into doubt such claims of legitimacy. But he is also pointing out that this new form of sacrificial practice was based upon a particular set of claims concerning the figure Huangdi. As I have argued elsewhere,[5] Huangdi had come to be associated during the late Warring States and early Han with centralized statecraft. And, as we shall see, Huangdi was to continue being the main figure invoked to legitimate the new Qin—and, later, Han—sacrificial system.

Sima Qian goes on to present how, over the next several centuries, the rulers of Qin instituted sacrifices at Yong to the gods of the other three directions as well—presumably as part of an increasing claim to universal dominance (*Shiji*, 28.1360, 1364). The most important Qin sacrifices, then, came to consist of the offerings at Yong to the four gods—the white, green, yellow, and red gods—symbolizing Qin control over the land (*Shiji*, 28.1376). During this process, the capital of Qin was also moved to Yong (*Shiji*, 28.1360).

Meanwhile, we are told, the Zhou continued to decline:

> At the same time [as Confucius], Chang Hong used formulas (*fang*) to serve King Ling of the Zhou. None of the feudal lords paid homage at the Zhou court, and the power of the Zhou was limited. Chang Hong thereupon clarified the affairs of ghosts and spirits, and hung up and shot arrows at the head of a wildcat. The wildcat head symbolized the feudal lords' not coming to court. [Chang Hong] depended on the object in wild hopes of thereby summoning the feudal lords. The feudal lords did not follow this, and the Jin captured Chang Hong and put him to death. The talk among the Zhou of formulas and abnormalities began with Chang Hong. (*Shiji*, 28.1364)

The Zhou gradually fell under the sway of magicians overly oriented toward spirits and using formulas to impose their will on the world. The Zhou thus fell into the same pattern of decadence seen in earlier dynasties. By presenting a concern with formulas and an overinterest in the spirit world as a defining moment of Zhou decline, Sima Qian sets the framework for his later presentation of the Qin-Han imperium.

In 221 B.C.E., Qin defeated the other states and created the first empire. The four altars at Yong continued to be the dominant sacrifices of the Qin state (*Shiji*, 28.1376). Not only did Qin maintain these sacrifices, however, but they also made attempts to take control of the significant cults of each local region within the empire. As Sima Qian states: "When Qin united all under heaven, [the First Emperor] commanded the officials of sacrifices to put in order the frequently-performed offerings to Heaven, earth, the famous mountains, the great rivers, the ghosts, and the spirits" (*Shiji*, 28.1371).

The sacrifices to important deities were placed under the jurisdiction of a great invocator, who "offered the sacrifices according to the appropriate time of the year" (*Shiji*, 28.1377). The First Emperor also wished to avoid the potential dangers of such a centralization of ritual activities: if a disaster occurred, he charged a "secret invocator" with the duty of trying to transfer the blame to those below the emperor (*Shiji*, 28.1377).

The First Emperor himself undertook several tours of the lands under his control, personally performing many of the most significant of these sacrifices (*Shiji*, 28.1377). Unlike Shun, these tours were not inspections of feudal lands; they were imperial tours of the emperor's own lands, intended to enhance the personal power of the ruler.

This attempt to secure divine support also helps to explain the rise to prominence of those technical specialists known as "masters of formulas" —figures whose use of particular formulas gave them knowledge about aspects of the spirit world.[6] As Sima Qian describes them: "They practiced formulas (*fang*) and the way of the transcendents. . . . They relied upon the activities of ghosts and spirits" (*Shiji*, 28.1368–69). One of the major jobs these figures were asked to perform under the First Emperor was to seek out transcendents who had achieved long life and to find drugs that would grant immortality to the emperor (*Shiji*, 6.252, 263).

Given his framework of dynastic decline, seen most obviously in his descriptions of Kongjia of the Xia as being too fond of spirits and of the last Zhou kings as falling under the sway of figures with magical formulas, Sima Qian is painting this moment of imperial unification as equally involving the beginning of a fall into decadence. A fall that, as Sima Qian describes it, will reach its culmination with Han Wudi.

After the end of the Qin empire, the rulers of the ensuing Han dynasty simply reinstituted the Qin sacrificial system. Indeed, the only significant change that occurred during the reign of the first Han emperor occurred when Gaozu instituted sacrifices to a fifth god at Yong—the black god (*Shiji*, 28.1378). As Sima Qian states about Han Gaozu: "He summoned the former Qin officials of invocations and restored appointments to the great invocator and great supervisor to perform the rituals as before" (*Shiji*, 28.1378). The Han for Sima Qian is very much a continuation of the Qin.

This particular sacrificial system and mode of dealing with the spirits reached its high point in the reign of Han Wudi, the ruler under whom Sima Qian worked. Wudi was the figure who rebuilt and consolidated the empire that the First Emperor had created. One of Wudi's explicit policies for doing so was to re-create much of the commandery system of the First Emperor by reannexing the territories of the feudal lords. Sima Qian points out how this policy was paralleled by his sacrificial practice. Thus, Wudi worked to gain direct imperial control over the Five Peaks, a series of mountains with important sacrificial traditions. The king of Changshan, for example, was charged with a crime and removed, and Changshan was made into a commandery. As Sima Qian narrates: "As such, the Five Peaks were all situated in the commanderies of the Son of Heaven" (*Shiji*, 28.1387). Such a policy of imperial centralization, in which the Five Peaks were under the direct control of Wudi, is clearly meant to contrast with the feudal system of sacrifices that had begun with Shun.

Indeed, whereas Shun inspected the realm of his feudal lords only every five years, Wudi undertook constant tours of his empire (for example, *Shiji*, 28.1389 and 28.1403). He did this so often, Sima Qian claims, that the officials in charge of the commanderies and kingdoms would constantly clear their roads and repair their palaces and sacrificial sites in anticipation of a visit from the emperor (*Shiji*, 28.1396).

Also like the First Emperor, Wudi strongly supported the masters of formulas out of the hopes that they could increase his access to the world of spirits and ultimately help him gain immortality. Indeed, the most important ritual innovations during his reign were taken on the advice of these masters.

One of these masters, Miu Ji, authored a memorial concerning Taiyi, a deity who Miu Ji claimed to be above the five gods in power:

> The most valued of the Heavenly spirits is Taiyi. The assistants of Taiyi are the five gods. In ancient times the Son of Heaven sacrificed to Taiyi in the spring and autumn at the southeast suburb. (*Shiji*, 28.1386)

Following the advice of Miu Ji, Wudi established offerings to Taiyi (*Shiji*, 28.1386).[7]

At least according to Sima Qian's presentation, it would appear that this addition to the sacrificial system was yet one more step in a long process that had begun with the Qin—a process involving ever more claims to dominance. Just as the Qin rulers had progressively added sacrifices to more gods at Yong until four were receiving cult, and just as Han Gaozu had added sacrifices to a fifth god, so Wudi was making claim to yet a more powerful deity. And Sima Qian's framework is clearly intended to present such a cult, offered in response to the advice of a master of formulas, in a negative light.

Another step in the development of the Han sacrificial system occurred when a certain Shaoweng gained audience with the ruler because of his "formulas for ghosts and spirits" (*Shiji*, 28.1387). In response to Shaoweng's proposals, Wudi built a palace in Ganquan to summon the Heavenly spirits (*Shiji*, 28.1388).

The following year, after performing the suburban sacrifices at Yong, Wudi declared: "Now I have personally performed the suburban sacrifices to the higher gods, but I have not made offerings to the Hou-tu (Lord Earth)" (*Shiji*, 28.1389). In response, Kuan Shu, the Official of Sacrifices who had been asked to continue the formulas of Li Shaojun (*Shiji*, 28.1386), recommended that sacrifices be given at Fenyin. Han Wudi thereupon traveled east and personally performed the sacrifice to Hou-tu at Fenyin (*Shiji*, 28.1389).

The next set of reforms were undertaken under the advice of Gongsun Qing, yet another figure from Qi. Gongsun Qing presented a letter discussing how "Huangdi became a transcendent and ascended to Heaven" (*Shiji*, 28.1393). Gongsun Qing claimed the letter had been given to him by

Shen Gong, also from Qi. Sheng Gong said that "of the seventy-two kings who have attempted the *feng* and *shan*, only Huangdi was able to ascend Tai Shan and give the *feng* sacrifice. The Han ruler who attempts it will also ascend and perform the *feng*. If he does ascend and give the *feng*, he will be able to become a transcendent and climb to Heaven" (*Shiji*, 28.1393).

Gongsun Qing also stated that:

> These five mountains [Hua Shan, Shou Shan, Tai Shi, Tai Shan, and Dong Lai] were where Huangdi often travelled and met with spirits. Huangdi at times fought wars and at times studied to become a transcendent. He was concerned that the hundred families opposed his way, so he thereupon had anyone who opposed ghosts and spirits beheaded. After more than a hundred years he was able to obtain communication with the spirits. (*Shiji*, 28.1393)

Gongsun Qing also explained how Huangdi made contact with myriad numinous beings at Ganquan (*Shiji*, 28.1394). After Gongsun Qing further recounted Huangdi's ascension to Heaven, Wudi expressed his wish to be like Huangdi (*Shiji*, 28.1394).

Wudi then performed the suburban sacrifice at Yong and returned to Ganquan. He ordered his Official of Sacrifices, Kuan Shu, and others to make an altar to Taiyi at Ganquan. The altar was modeled on Miu Ji's Taiyi altar. The first level was dedicated to Taiyi. The level below consisted of five sides, each of which, in the appropriate direction, was dedicated to one of the five gods. The third level was dedicated to the various spirits (*Shiji*, 28.1394).

In 113 B.C.E., Wudi first performed the suburban sacrifice to Taiyi. A beautiful glow appeared that night, and the next day yellow *qi* rose to Heaven (*Shiji*, 28.1395). The Grand Historian, the Official of Sacrifices Kuan Shu, and others argued that an altar to Taiyi should be built to response (*Shiji*, 28.1395).

These sacrifices to Taiyi at Ganquan and to Hou-tu at Fenyin would become among the most important imperial sacrifices for Han Wudi. As Sima Qian is at pains to point out, each stage in the development of Wudi's sacrificial system was undertaken at the instigation of the masters of formulas. These masters of formulas, who played such a strong role at the court of the First Emperor as well, bear a strong resemblance to the figures that came to prominence at the end of the Zhou dynasty, and the rulers in question seem quite comparable to the rulers who were too fond of spirits at the end of the Xia dynasty. In other words, Sima Qian has clearly constructed his narrative to emphasize the degree to which the religious activities of the rulers of his day represent a continuing decadence, and he clearly means to imply that the end of the Han dynasty may be approaching.

But there is another side to his presentation that will be in some ways more important for our understanding of the later debates concerning the Han sacrificial system. Beyond his critiques of Han Wudi, Sima Qian's presentation of the rise of the Qin-Han system of sacrifices is one in which imperial power and a certain mode of religious worship are directly interconnected. The system began with a transgression, in which Duke Xiang of Qin began implementing suburban sacrifices to the god of the east while the Zhou were still in power. The addition of sacrifices to the gods of the other three directions occurred as a growing claim of Qin dominance. Moreover, all of this was, according to Sima Qian, linked with the purported sacrificial system of Huangdi, the figure associated with centralized statecraft.

Sima Qian then links the rise of the Qin imperial state with a continuation of this mode of religious worship. The First Emperor spent much of his life traversing the lands under his control in order to personally perform the sacrifices of local areas and to search for spirits and transcendents who could help him attain personal immortality. This reached its extreme with Han Wudi, who, under the influence of the masters of formulas, instituted cults to deities claimed to be even greater than those worshiped by previous rulers and embarked on lengthy inspection tours to perform personally the sacrifices of local areas. Here too, Huangdi was explicitly invoked as the exemplar. The rise of a particular mode of religious worship and the emergence of centralized state institutions are thus presented as linked.

As we shall see, this linkage of the Qin and Han sacrificial system with imperial control was also very strongly at the heart of the debates that would rage several decades later. The Confucians we will be looking at also viewed these two as directly linked, but their response was quite different from the one espoused by Sima Qian. Sima Qian did not present the rise of the Yong sacrificial system as necessarily wrong, although he did portray it as new. Moreover, he presented the reliance on magicians and the overconcern with spirits and portents as nothing but a recurrent sign of decline in dynasties. It may have been associated in this particular instance with the rise of empire, but Sima Qian's concern in this chapter lies more in showing the degree of the decadence of his own ruler rather than in critiquing Qin-Han imperial system per se. The Confucians we will turn to now, however, take a very different reading of these issues.

The Han Ritual Reforms

In the period following the reign of Wudi, the Han had fallen into a gradual decline. A full discussion of all the causes that led to this is beyond the limits of this essay, but suffice it to note that the Han was suffering from imperial overreach: the military campaigns that defined Wudi's centralization and expansion severely strained the resources of the Han state. These issues came to a head in the reign of Chengdi (33–7 B.C.E.). When Chengdi came to power, two of his Confucian ministers, Kuang Heng and Zhang Tan, used the opportunity to push for a shift in Han policies. Their method of doing so was to call on the emperor to follow the precedents found in the classical texts. Their memorials are filled with references to the *Shi* and the *Shangshu,* and they frequently critique the Han for not following antiquity. Immediately, therefore, it is clear that their perspective is quite different from that of Sima Qian.

The initial argument against the sacrificial system consolidated under Wudi was made in a memorial by Kuang Heng and Zhang Tan:

> In the affairs of emperors and kings, none are greater than supporting the order of Heaven. In supporting the order of Heaven, nothing is more important than sacrifices and offerings. Therefore, sage-kings devoted their hearts and trained their thoughts to the fullest to establish their regulations. They sacrificed to Heaven in the southern suburb, in accordance with the propriety of *yang.* They offered to earth in the northern suburb, in accordance with the image of *yin.* (*Hanshu,* 25B.1253–54)

Kuang Heng and Zhang Tan are arguing in favor of sacrifices to Heaven and earth, with the respective altars to each aligned on a south–north axis. Such a normative order, the memorial claims, was practiced in the past. However, the ritual system in place since the time of Wudi "differs from the regulations of antiquity" (*Hanshu,* 25B.1254). Considering this, Kuang Heng and Zhang Tan argue that the main altars to Taiyi and Hou-tu be moved to the south and north of the capital Chang'an:

> In ancient times, Wen and Wu of Zhou sacrificed at Feng and Hao, and King Cheng sacrificed at the city of Luo. From this it can be seen that Heaven follows the king to where he lives and accepts his offerings. It is fitting that the offerings to Taiyi at Ganquan and to Hou-tu at Hedong be moved and set up at Chang'an in accord with the ancient thearchs and kings. (*Hanshu,* 25B.1254)

Since the Zhou kings offered sacrifices at their capitals, so should the Han emperors sacrifice at their capital.

Of immediate interest here is the fact that Kuang Heng and Zhang Tan have clearly shifted the emphasis in terms of which ancient sages should be followed. Whereas Wudi was modeling himself on Huangdi, Kuang Heng and Zhang Tan are emphasizing the Zhou kings.

Also of interest is the way that Kuang Heng and Zhang Tan are specifying the proper relationship between man and Heaven. The ruler should establish his capital, and the deities should follow him. Kuang Heng and Zhang Tan are thus setting themselves in opposition to one of the basic assumptions behind the Qin-Han imperial system. The emperor should not, according to this argument, travel to Yong, Ganquan, and Fenyin to perform the suburban sacrifices; the deities should rather come to the capital. At issue here is an entirely different relationship between the ruler and spirits, as well as an entirely different relationship of the ruler to his realm.

This memorial by Kuang Heng and Zhang Tan sparked a debate at court. Fifty figures defended the proposals through references to the classical texts. They began with a citation of the "Ji fa" chapter of the *Liji*:

> "Burning victims on the great circular altar is to sacrifice to Heaven; burying victims at the square altar is to sacrifice to Earth." An offering in the southern suburb is the means of determining the position of Heaven. Sacrificing to Earth on the square altar, situated in the northern suburb, fixes the position of *yin*. The position for each of the suburban sacrifices is located to the south and north of where the sage-king resides. (*Hanshu*, 25B.1254)

It is the ruler who should determine the proper positions of Heaven and earth. He does so through his establishment of the capital and through his proper sacrifices to each:

> The *Shangshu* says: "On the third day, *dingsi*, he [the Duke of Zhou] made offerings of two oxen in the suburbs."[8] When the Duke of Zhou raised offerings, it was to announce his moving to a new city. He determined the sacrificial rites at Luo. (*Hanshu*, 25B.1254)

The quotation is from the "Luogao" chapter of the *Shangshu*. The chapter in question narrates the founding of the city of Luoyang by the Duke of Zhou. This is of some interest, because, it should be remembered, the Qin capital was moved to Yong in order to move it closer to the area of spiritual potency. The authors here are claiming that the proper method is for the ruler to choose his capital and then announce it as such to the higher powers. The Zhou did so properly; the Qin, as well as the Han who followed them did not.

As we have seen, much of this rhetoric refers implicitly to the issues concerning empire. A call for the ruler to abandon sacrificial policies that require him to travel throughout the realm is, in essence, a call for the ruler to withdraw from the highly centralized form of imperial statecraft that had been developing since the emergence of the Qin. The authors are calling for a return to the pre-Qin system of the Zhou and, indeed, go so far as to argue that the Han, by instituting this new imperial system, have failed to receive the support of Heaven:

> When enlightened kings and sagely rulers serve Heaven it is illuminated; when they serve earth it is opened. When Heaven and earth are illuminated and opened, then the spiritual brightness (*shen ming*) is arrayed. Heaven and earth take the king as the master. Therefore, when the sages and kings instituted the rites of sacrificing to Heaven and earth, they necessarily did so in the suburbs of the capital. Chang'an is where the sagely ruler dwells, and it is where august Heaven watches him. The sacrifices at Ganquan and Hedong have not been accepted by the spirits and numinous powers; it is fitting to move them to places with the correct *yang* and the great *yin*. We should oppose custom and return to the ancients, accord with the regulations of the sages, and set aright the position of Heaven as the rituals prescribe. (*Hanshu*, 25B.1254)

The ruler must be watched by Heaven in his own capital. The implication of this is that Heaven's support comes only when the ruler has been judged adequate in his daily activities; divine support does not come to the ruler by his seeking out of divinities, and the sacrifices of Ganquan and Fenyin have therefore not been accepted by the spirits.

Kuang Heng and Zhang Tan authored a further memorial in which they elaborated on this point:

> The *Shi* says: "Do not say: 'It [Heaven] is high above.' It ascends and descends in its work; it daily inspects us" (*Shi*, Mao #288). This is to say that Heaven's eyes looked over the place of the king. It also says: "It thereupon looked about and gazed toward the west. Here it is that it gave a settlement" (*Shi*, Mao #241). This is to say that Heaven took the capital of King Wen as his dwelling. It is fitting at Chang'an to determine the southern and northern suburbs as the foundation for ten thousand generations. (*Hanshu*, 25B.1255)

Gone here is any talk of the ruler seeking spiritual beings or ascending to Heaven. The ruler is called upon to stay in his capital, and it is Heaven who will ascend and descend to inspect the ruler. The ruler, in other words, does not try to achieve spiritual powers; he rather centers the kingdom by establishing his capital, and Heaven then judges his actions. The emphasis is moved fully to the virtue of the ruler—and the memorialists are implying that the Qin and Han rulers have not been judged successful.

Kuang Heng then went on to argue against the ornaments of the Ganquan altar, claiming that "one cannot obtain its models in antiquity" (*Hanshu*, 25B.1256). In another memorial, Kuang Heng argued explicitly that much of Han ritual practice was largely a continuation of that instituted by

330 THE FORMATION OF THE CONFUCIAN TRADITION

the Qin feudal lords and was not based on the proper rites of antiquity (*Hanshu*, 25B.1257). Implicit here, of course, is a rejection of the claim that the Qin-Han system is based on the sacrifices of Huangdi.

In 31 B.C.E., Chengdi accepted these arguments. In the first significant rejection of the sacrificial system that had begun with the Qin and had been developed by Han Wudi, Chengdi instituted suburban sacrifices to Heaven south of Chang'an (*Hanshu*, 25B.1257).

Kuang Heng and Zhang Tan went on to critique the numerous sacrifices initially set up by the masters of formulas. Out of the 683 such sacrifices, only 208, they argued, conformed to the rites of antiquity (*Hanshu*, 25B.1257). They called on the emperor to discontinue the remaining 475. The emperor did so. The *Hanshu* states that, of the 203 sacrifices at Yong, only fifteen were maintained. And many of the sacrifices instituted by Gaozu, Wendi, Wudi, and Xuandi were abolished (*Hanshu*, 25B.1257–58).

The debate, however, did not end here. Liu Xiang immediately authored a memorial calling for a restoration of Wudi's sacrificial system. The sacrifices, Liu Xiang argued, were instituted in response to the spirits, and thus should not be abolished:

> Moreover, when Ganquan, Fenyin, and the five altars of Yong were first instituted, it was because there were spirits of the upper and lower realms interacting (*ganying*). Only then were [the altars] built. This was not done lightly. (*Hanshu*, 25B.1258)

In opposition to Kuang Heng and Zhang Tan, who argued that Heaven should follow the king to where he lives, Liu Xiang is claiming that humans must respond to the spirits: if the spirits interact at specific places, then those are the places where the sacrifices must be given. Liu Xiang's memorial ended with a warning of the dire consequences that could occur now that the sacrifices had been discontinued (*Hanshu*, 25B.1258–59).

This memorial is of some interest to our purposes, since it is actually one of the few documents we possess that was written by a defender of the Qin-Han sacrificial system. Moreover, since Liu Xiang would have considered himself a *Ru* as well, the memorial shows the degree to which the debate itself—as well as many of the underlying issues concerning spirits and the empire—cut across numerous divisions at the court. Liu Xiang's argument here is that there are certain sacred sites where the spirits interact, and Yong, Ganquan, and Fenyin are among these sites. The altars at these places, therefore, were simply instituted in response to the spirits. No claim here is made to the antiquity of the sacrifices or to their purported existence during the reign of Huangdi. The only argument is one based on the spirits: if the spirits interact at certain sites, then those are the places where the emperor should build altars.

Chengdi, who had still not had a son, concurred with Liu Xiang's memorial. The sacrificial system that had been consolidated under Wudi was restored (*Hanshu*, 25B.1259).

A strong response to this reversal was made by Gu Yong:

> Your servant has heard that if you are clear about the nature of Heaven and earth, you cannot be deluded by spirits and anomalies. If you understand the dispositions of the myriad things, you cannot be deluded by what does not fit into categories. Those who turn their back on the correct path of humaneness and propriety and do not honor the model sayings of the five classics, but are instead filled with reports about abnormalities, anomalies, ghosts, and spirits, widely revere formulas for sacrifices and offerings, seek to requite sacrifices that bring no fortune, go so far as to say that there exist transcendents in this world, chew and swallow immortality drugs. . . . They all deceive the people and mislead the masses, hold to the left [i.e., wrong] way, embrace falsity and fabrications so as to delude the current ruler. . . . It is for this reason that the enlightened king should resist them and not listen, and the sage would cut them off and not speak [of such things]. (*Hanshu*, 25B.1260)

What becomes particularly clear here is the object of Gu Yong's concern. If one were to follow the arguments of Liu Xiang, he claims, it would mean that inordinate power would be given to those figures—like the masters of formulas—who claim the ability to find sacred sites and interact with spirits. The critique here is similar to that given by Sima Qian, but the solution offered is quite different: Gu Yong is calling on the emperor to accept the nature of Heaven and earth as given in the five classics.

Gu Yong continues: "When the First Emperor united all under Heaven, he was swayed by the way of spirits and transcendents." Gu Yong then criticizes the First Emperor for sending out people to "seek spirits and gather drugs" (*Hanshu*, 25B.1260). The argument is comparable to that seen in Sima Qian, but absent here is Sima Qian's framework of dynastic decline. What we see instead is simply the emphasis on this as a new system, and the Zhou sacrificial system is posited as the norm of antiquity.

This alternation between the two sacrificial systems continued during the reign of Aidi, Chengdi's successor (*Hanshu*, 25B.1263–64). Finally, in response to memorials from Wang Mang, Pingdi fully instituted the reforms initially laid out by Kuang Heng (*Hanshu*, 25B.1266–68). The system established under Wudi was dismantled, and the rituals purportedly in place during the feudalistic kingdom of the Zhou were reinstated.

Conclusion

The debates that we have been tracing concerned two interrelated issues: the nature of the Han state and the relations that the ruler should maintain with the world of spirits. The texts we have discussed—Sima Qian's historical records and the memorials written during the reign of Chengdi—presented these as directly linked, and their critiques of the Qin-Han model played upon both themes.

According to Sima Qian and the ministers associated with Kuang Heng, the Qin-Han sacrificial system, associated with the imperial state, was motivated by an attempt to gain control over sacred sites where spirits would dwell—sites whose sacrificial traditions, it was claimed, could be traced back to Huangdi. The emperor, by (he hoped) communicating with the spirits of each region, attempted to gain both personal immortality and direct control over those regions. Such a system involved several interrelated imperatives. Horizontally, it resulted in a recurrent drive on the part of each emperor to take control of more and more such sacred sites and to visit each one on a recurrent basis. By the time of Han Wudi, this resulted in the emperor making the five mountains into imperial commanderies, undertaking innumerable imperial tours, and adding the sites of Ganquan and Fenyin to the already important cultic area of Yong. Vertically, it meant appealing to ever more powerful deities who could hopefully exercise greater and greater dominance over the spirit pantheon. Socially, it meant granting power to those figures—especially the masters of formulas—who claimed the ability to find and summon spirits for the emperor. In short, it was a system that inherently involved a never-ending process of each emperor attempting to gain ever more direct control over the territorial and spiritual realms.

In contrast to this, the system that, in very different ways and for very different purposes, both Sima Qian and Kuang Heng ascribed to the pre-Qin period, was one in which there is no claim for the sacrality of the primary sites. The emphasis was rather on the ruler providing a center for the kingdom by establishing his capital. No claim was made about the site as having any significance other than simply that it had thus been established. If Heaven and earth accepted the ruler, such a capital would become the place where *yin* and *yang* would properly interact. The ruler would then, from afar, pay obeisance to the spirits of each local region, and would, on a five-year basis, travel to the five mountains to meet with the feudal lords of each locality.

For Sima Qian, the distinction between these systems was far less important than the overall narrative of dynastic decline, a narrative that he utilized to critique Han Wudi's concern with magical formulas and personal immortality. But, for Kuang Heng and those associated with him, the distinction between these two systems was all-important. At stake for them was an assertion of boundaries, an assertion that would result, they hoped, in a radically different (and, in their view, traditional) vision of human rulership. They were calling for a ritual system that would, on the one hand, grant the ruler tremendous power: it was he who would establish the center and determine the position of Heaven and earth. But a further expansion of his power was not built into the system: he would not be asked to gain direct control over local areas and he would not need to appeal to either ever more numerous or ever more powerful deities. On the contrary, Kuang Heng's precise concern was to assert a strict demarcation between humans and spirits, between center and periphery. The ruler could not ascend to Heaven, could not become immortal, and should not seek to gain control over sacred sites where spirits could be summoned to confer such powers.

In ultimately choosing to side with Kuang Heng and his followers, the emperors of the Western Han effected a fundamental shift in the legitimation of the Han state. This did not, of course, result in an eradication of the empire and a reinstitution of feudalism. But it did result in a tremendous increase in the power of Confucians at court: although various Confucian ministers had played important roles at the Han court since its inception, this shift in the sacrificial system marked the point at which Confucians came to far greater prominence. And, indirectly, it may have laid some of the seeds for the later popularity of millenarian movements, many of which would, in their critiques of the Han state, embrace the very notions of divinization and ascension that the reforms pushed by Kuang Heng and others had (in part) driven out of the central court.

Notes

1. By far the best discussion of these debates thus far is to be found in Michael Loewe, *Crisis and Conflict in Han China 104 BC to 9 AD* (London: George Allen & Unwin, 1974), 154–92.

2. It is important here to define precisely what we mean by "Confucian" in the Western Han. The term that is usually translated as "Confucian" is *Ru*, which refers to those figures who advocated the importance of following the views laid out in the classics. Precisely which texts were defined as the classics varied over the course of the Western Han. The *Book of Poetry*, the *Book of Documents*, and the *Spring and Autumn Annals* were strongly supported by most Ruists; the *Book of*

Rites and the *Book of Changes* were incorporated into the canon over the course of the Western Han dynasty. The *Zhouguan* (or *Zhouli*), a text that purported to present the ritual system of the Zhou dynasty, was strongly supported by certain factions of Ruists as well. Since Confucius was frequently posited as the sage who edited—or, in the case of the *Spring and Autumn Annals*, authored—several of these works, he was seen as a crucial figure by the Ruists. But it is important to remember that the defining feature of the Ruists was their commitment to the classics, rather than a reverence for Confucius; indeed, the precise importance accorded to Confucius (whether, for example, he was a transmitter of Zhou traditions or a creator of a new way of thinking) varied from scholar to scholar among the Ruists.

3. For a full discussion of this, as well as my own, somewhat different reading, see ch. 5 of my *The Ambivalence of Creation: Debates Concerning Innovation and Artifice in Early China*, forthcoming from Stanford University Press.

4. All references to the *Shiji* and the *Hanshu* are to the Zhonghua shuju edition.

5. See my "Sages, Ministers, and Rebels: Narratives from Early China Concerning the Initial Creation of the State," *Harvard Journal of Asiatic Studies* 58, no. 2 (1998): 425–79.

6. On the masters of formulas, see Ngo Va Xuyet, *Divination, magie et politique dans la Chine ancienne* (Paris: Presses universitaires de France, 1976).

7. Relatively little is known about Taiyi. He was evidently a god in at least the southern regions during the pre-Han period. He appears, for example, in the Baoshan divination texts from the state of Chu in the fourth century B.C.E. (For an excellent analysis of the paleographic references to Taiyi, see Li Ling "An Archaeological Study of Taiyi (Grand One) Worship," *Early Medieval China* 2 [1995–96]: 1–39.) Taiyi also appears to have had some associations with warfare. For example, when Wudi was later going to attack Nan Yue, he first made an announcement and prayer to Taiyi. A banner was made which the Grand Historian would point at the country about to be attacked (*Shiji*, 28.1395). After Nanyue was defeated, Wudi offered sacrifices of thanks to the god (*Shiji*, 28.1396). Li Ling, in his aforementioned article, discusses possible paleographic precursors to these associations.

8. The quotation is from the "Luogao" chapter of the *Shangshu*.

Glossary

報   Ben/pao—reciprocity, mutuality, mutual regard, reciprocal relations

本   Ben/pen—root, fundamental, essential

本體   Benti/pen-t'i—the essential or fundamental root

本心   Benxin/pen-hsin—fundamental heart-mind

變   Bian/pian—to change gradually across time

不仁   Buren/pu-jen—insensitive, dead, without human feeling

誠   Cheng/ch'eng—sincere, integrity, self-realization, actualization of the true creative potential of human affairs, even of the cosmos

成   Cheng/ch'eng—to complete an action or process; something which is complete

道   Dao/tao—The Way, a path, way of proper conduct, to lead through, matrix of all the things and events of the cosmos

大同   Datong/ta-t'ung—the Great Harmony (political), perfected state of affairs

德   De/te—virtue, potency, excellence, the power of virtue; that which has ethical power

法   Fa—law; also means *dharma* in Buddhism

改   Gai/kai—to correct, reform, improve

感應   Ganying/kan-ying—activity and response; stimulus and response; correlative action and response; often cited as the foundation for correlative cosmology

格物   Gewu/ko-wu—examination of things and events

公   Gong/kung—public good, the public sphere of activity

工夫   Gongfu/kung-fu—effort, action, activity

335

鬼神　Guishen/kuei-shen—spiritual forces of the cosmos; positive and negative spiritual powers or forces; also related to the heavenly and earthly aspects of the human soul; shen is positive and kuei is the negative force of spirit

和　He—harmony of a situation or person

化　Hua—to transform utterly such that A becomes B

幾　Ji/chi—the subtle, incipient

教　Jiao/chiao—teaching or instruction, education

敬　Jing/ching—reverence, respect, reverence, the concentration of reverence on the moral path

君子　Junzi/chün-tzu—gentleman or exemplary person; originally meant the son of a prince or a nobleman; second in virtue only to the sage

理　Li—principle that orders all things, persons, and events, form, pattern, norm, the defining pattern or principle of the cosmos

禮　Li—ritual, civility, proper social order, customs, etiquette, ritual propriety

立　Li—to establish, set up, to make firm (in virtue and conduct)

良知　Liangzhi/liang-chih—innate good knowledge

理一分殊　Liyi fenshu/li-yi fen-shu—principle (pattern, norm) is one, the manifestations are many

立志　Lizhi/li-chih—establish the will, make the will secure

明　Ming—brightness, brilliant, clarity (or person, purpose, or action)

命　Ming—mandate, command, order, destiny, fate

末　Mo—branch (of a plant), something that branches off from the root of a thing, person, event or situation

内外　Nei/wai—inner and outer

氣　Qi/ch'i—vital force, vital energy, matter-energy, vapor, the dynamic element of all that is

器　Qi/ch'in—concrete thing, something of substance

遷　Qian/ch'ien—to change from one place to another

親　Qin/ch'in—relatives or kin

情　Qing/ch'ing—emotions, feelings, desires, the developed nature of a person; the vital force of a person or thing

仁　Ren/jen—humaneness, humanity, human-heartedness, benevolence, first of the Confucian virtues, love

人慾　Renyu/jen-yu—human emotion, human passions, passionate human feelings or emotions

儒	Ru/ju—scholar, ritual specialist, Chinese term for what is called a Confucian
善	Shan—good, perfect, excellent, felicity
善人	Shanren/shan-jen—good, adept person, someone who achieves the good, excellent, or perfect
聖人	Sheng/shengren/sheng-jen—sage, the perfected person
詩	Shi/shih—poetry
士	Shi/shih—scholar, literati, official, member of the gentry
恕	Shu—altruism, reciprocity, empathy, to extend feelings to others
私	Si/ssu—private, personal
四端	Siduan/ssu-tuan—four roots or seeds of virtue
太極	Taiji/t'ai-chi—The Supreme Polarity or the Supreme Ultimate
天	Tian/t'ien—Heaven; sky, the blue sky, the High God of the Zhou people
天下	Tiangxia/t'ien-hsia—All under Heaven, everyone and everything
天理	Tianli/t'ien-li—Heavenly principle, ultimate principle or norm of the good or perfect
天命	Tianming/t'ien-ming—Mandate of Heaven
體認	Tiren/t'i-jen—realization through personal experience
體用	Tiyong—/t'i-yung—substance and function
未發	Weifa/wei-fa—not yet manifested
文	Wen—culture, what the sage and worthies seek to create for human society
無	Wu—nonbeing, nothingness
五常	Wuchang/wulun/wu-ch'ang—five constant virtues: humaneness, righteousness, ritual/civility, wisdom or discernment, and faithfulness
無極	Wuji/wu-chi—the Ultimate of Non-polarity, the infinite
物事	Wushi/wu-shih—things and events
無為	Wuwei—/wu-wei—uncontrived action; non-action
五行	Wuxing/wu-hsing—five phases of the vital force and yin-yang modalities; air, wood, fire, earth, and metal
孝	Xiao/hsiao—filial piety, filiality, deference, respect
信	Xin/hsin—faithfulness, honesty, integrity of thought, word, and action; virtue of friendship, credibility
心	Xin/hsin—heart-mind; seat of the intelligence; most refined aspect of the vital force
性	Xing/hsing—human nature, natural tendencies, nature as principle, norm or pattern

形 而 上
　　　 Xingershang/Hsing-er-shang—what is above (shape); incorporeal
形 而 下
　　　 Xingerxia/hsing-er-hsia—what is below (shape); corporeal
形 名　 Xingming/hsing-ming—actuality and name
修 身　 Xiushen/hsiu-shen—self-cultivation of the mind-heart of the person
虛　　 Xu/hsü—vacuous, blank, empty
玄　　 Xuan/hsüan—profound, mysterious, deep
學　　 Xue/hsüeh—study; the study or cultivation of the Dao is education
易　　 Yi/i—change or transformation, processive
意　　 Yi/i—intentions, motivations
義　　 Yi/i—righteousness, moral, appropriateness, second of the cardinal virtues
已 發　 Yifa/I-fa—already manifested (as certain qualities or objects and events)
陰 陽　 Yin-yang—yin-yang forces; positive and negative, light and dark, male and female
有　　 You/yu—being present, having, existing, to have certain qualities, being in a certain state
慾　　 Yu/yü—desire, passion, emotion
正　　 Zheng/cheng—rectification, to make correct, to bring order
正 心　 Zhengxin/cheng-hsin—established or rectified mind-heart
志　　 Zhi/chih—will, fortitude of character
至　　 Zhi/chih—fully develop, cultivate, to reach a goal
致　　 Zhi/chih—government, the public realm
知　　 Zhi/chih—knowledge, intelligence, to realize, discernment, wisdom
至 知　 Zhizhi/chih-chih—the extension of knowledge or capacity to know
中　　 Zhong/Chung—centrality, focus, equilibrium, being centered in proper virtue
忠　　 Zhong/chung—loyalty, being completely committed
忠 恕　 Zhongshu/chung-shu—conscientiousness and altruism
中 庸　 Zhongyong/Chung-yung—Centrality and Commonality, locus for achieving harmony; title of one of the Four Books
自 然　 Ziran/tzu-jan—spontaneity, uncontrived action, complete freedom

General Bibliography

General Reference Works: Asian and Chinese Thought

Ames, Roger T., Wimal Dissanayke, Thomas P. Kasulis, eds.
  1994   *Self as Person in Asian Theory and Practice*. Albany: State University of New York Press.

Chan, Wing-tsit
  1953   *Religious Trends in Modern China*. New York: Columbia University Press; Octagon Books, reprint 1969.
  1963   *A Source Book in Chinese Philosophy*. Princeton, N.J.: Princeton University Press.

Chang, Kang-I, and Huan Saussy, eds.
  1999   *Women Writers of Traditional China: An Anthology of Poetry and Criticism*. Stanford, Calif.: Stanford University Press.

Ch'en, Kenneth K. S.
  1964   *Buddhism in China: A Historical Survey*. Princeton, N.J.: Princeton University Press.
  1973   *The Chinese Transformation of Buddhism*. Princeton, N.J.: Princeton University Press.

Ching, Julia
  1993   *Chinese Religions*. Maryknoll, N.Y.: Orbis Books.

de Bary, Wm. Theodore, et al., eds.
  1999,   *Sources of Chinese Tradition*. 2 vols. 2nd ed. New York:
  2000   Columbia University Press.
  2001   *Sources of Japanese Tradition*. 2 vols. 2nd ed. New York: Columbia University Press.

Fung, Yu-lan
  1947   *The Spirit of Chinese Philosophy*. Translated by E. R. Hughes. Boston: Beacon Press.

1952,   *A History of Chinese Philosophy.* 2 vols. Translated by Derk
    1953   Bodde. Princeton, N.J.: Princeton University Press.
Jochim, Christian
    1986   *Chinese Religions: A Cultural Perspective.* Englewood Cliffs,
            N.Y.: Prentice-Hall, Inc.
Lee, Peter H.
    1997,   *Sourcebook of Korean Civilization.* 2 vols. New York: Colum-
    2000   bia University Press.
Liu, Shu-hsien, and Robert E. Allinson, eds.
    1988   *Harmony and Strife: Contemporary Perspectives, East & West.*
            Hong Kong: Chinese University Press.
Loewe, Michael
    1993   *Early Chinese Texts: A Bibliographic Guide.* Early China Special
            Monograph Series 2. Berkeley, Calif.: Institute of East Asian
            Studies.
Lopez, Donald S., Jr.
    1996   *Religions of China in Practice.* Princeton, N.J.: Princeton Uni-
            versity Press.
Martinson, Paul Varo
    1987   *A Theology of World Religions: Interpreting God, Self, and World
            in Semitic, Indian, and Chinese Thought.* Minneapolis, Minn.:
            Augsburg Publishing House.
Moore, Charles A.
    1967   *The Chinese Mind: Essentials of Chinese Philosophy and Culture.*
            Honolulu: University of Hawaii Press.
Mote, Frederick W.
    1989   *Intellectual Foundations of China.* 2nd ed. New York: McGraw-
            Hill Publishing Company.
Nakamura, Hajime
    1965   *Ways of Thinking of Eastern Peoples: India, China, Tibet, and
            Japan.* Honolulu: East-West Center Press.
    1975   *Parallel Developments: A Comparative History of Ideas.* Tokyo:
            Kodansha.
Overmeyer, Daniel L.
    1986   *Religions of China: The World as Living System.* San Francisco:
            Harper & Row.
Schirokauer, Conrad
    1990   *A Brief History of Chinese Civilization.* 2nd ed. Fort Worth,
            Tex.: Harcourt Brace Publishers.
    1993   *A Brief History of Japanese Civilization.* 2nd ed. Fort Worth,
            Tex.: Harcourt Brace Publishers.

Shahar, Meir, and Robert P. Weller
  1996   *Unruly Gods: Divinity and Society in China*. Honolulu: University of Hawaii Press.
Smith, Jonathan Z., ed.
  1995   *The HarperCollins Dictionary of Religion*. William Scott Green, Associate Editor with the American Academy of Religion. San Francisco: HarperCollins.
Sommer, Deborah, ed.
  1995   *Chinese Religion: An Anthology of Sources*. New York and Oxford: Oxford University Press.
Thompson, Laurence
  1989   *Chinese Religion*. 4th ed. Belmont, Calif.: Wadsworth Publishing.
Tsunoda, Ryusaku, ed.
  1958   *Sources of the Japanese Tradition*. New York: Columbia University Press.
Tu Weiming, ed.
  1996   *Confucian Traditions in East Asian Modernity: Moral Education and Economic Culture in Japan and the Four Mini-Dragons*. Cambridge, Mass.: Harvard University Press.
Tucker, Mary Evelyn, and John Berthrong, eds.
  1998   *Confucianism and Ecology: The Interrelationship of Heaven, Earth, and Humans*. Cambridge, Mass.: Harvard University Center for the Study of World Religions.
Weller, Robert P.
  1987   *Unities and Diversities in Chinese Religion*. Seattle: University of Washington Press.
Yang, C. K.
  1967   *Religion in Chinese Society*. Berkeley: University of California Press.
Yao, Xinzhong
  2000   *An Introduction to Confucianism*. Cambridge: Cambridge University Press.

Monographs: China

Allan, Sarah
  1991   *The Shape of the Turtle: Myth, Art, and Cosmos in Early China*. Albany: State University of New York Press.
  1997   *The Way of Water and the Sprouts of Virtue*. Albany: State University of New York Press.

Alitto, Guy S.
1979   *The Last Confucian: Liang Shu-ming and the Chinese Dilemma of Modernity*. Berkeley: University of California Press.

Ames, Roger, and David L. Hall
2001   *Focusing the Familiar: A Translation and Philosophical Interpretation of the Zhongyong*. Honolulu: University of Hawaii Press.

Barrett, T. H.
1992   *Li Ao: Buddhist, Taoist, or Neo-Confucian?* Oxford: Oxford University Press.

Bauer, Wolfgang
1976   *China and the Search for Happiness: Recurring Themes in Four Thousand Years of Chinese Cultural History*. Translated by Michael Shaw. New York: Seabury Press.

Berling, Judith A.
1980   *The Syncretic Religion of Lin Chao-en*. New York: Columbia University Press.

Berthrong, John H.
1994   *All under Heaven: Transforming Paradigms in Confucian-Christian Dialogue*. Albany: State University of New York Press.
1998   *Transformations of the Confucian Way*. Boulder, Colo.: Westview Press.

——, and Evelyn Nagai Berthrong
2000   *Confucianism: A Short Introduction*. Oxford: Oneworld.

Birdwhistell, Anne D.
1989   *Transition to Neo-Confucianism: Shao Yung on Knowledge and Symbols of Reality*. Stanford, Calif.: Stanford University Press.
1996   *Li Yong (1627–1705) and Epistemological Dimensions of Confucian Philosophy*. Stanford, Calif.: Stanford University Press.

Black, Alison Harley
1989   *Man and Nature in the Philosophical Thought of Wang Fu-chih*. Seattle: University of Washington Press.

Bloom, Irene
1987   *Knowledge Painfully Acquired: The K'un-chih chi by Lo Ch'in-shun*. New York: Columbia University Press.

——, and Joshua A. Fogel, eds.
1997   *Meetings of Minds: Intellectual and Religious Interaction in East Asian Traditions of Thought*. New York: Columbia University Press.

Bodde, Derk
1981   *Essays on Chinese Civilization*. Edited by Charles Le Blanc and Dorothy Borei. Princeton, N.J.: Princeton University Press.

Bol, Peter K.
1992   "This Culture of Ours": Intellectual Transition in T'ang and Sung China. Stanford, Calif.: Stanford University Press.

Bruce, J. Percy
1973   Chu Hsi and His Masters: An Introduction to Chu Hsi and the Sung School of Chinese Philosophy. London: Probsthain & Co., 1923; New York: AMS Press Edition.

Chan, Alan K. L.
1991   Two Visions of the Way: A Study of Wang Pi and the Ho-shang Kung Commentaries on the Lao Tzu. Albany: State University of New York Press.

Chan, Hok-lam, and Wm. Theodore de Bary, eds.
1982   Yüan Thought: Chinese Thought and Religion under the Mongols. New York: Columbia University Press.

Chan, Wing-tsit
1986   Chu Hsi and Neo-Confucianism. Honolulu: University of Hawaii Press.
1987   Chu Hsi: Life and Thought. Hong Kong: Chinese University Press.
1989   Chu Hsi: New Studies. Honolulu: University of Hawaii Press.
1986   Neo-Confucian Terms Explained (The Pei-hsi tzu-i) by Ch'en Ch'un, 1159–1223. New York: Columbia University Press.

Chang, Carsun
1957,   The Development of Neo-Confucian Thought. 2 vols. New York:
1962   Bookman Associates.
1970   Wang Yang-ming: Idealist Philosopher of Sixteenth-Century China. New York: St. John's University Press.

Chang, Hao
1971   Liang Ch'i-ch'ao and Intellectual Transition in China (1890–1907). Cambridge, Mass.: Harvard University Press.

Chaves, Jonathan
1993   Sing of the Source: Nature and Gospel in the Poetry of the Chinese Painter Wu Li. Honolulu: SHAPS Library of Translations, University of Hawaii Press.

Chen, Charles K. H., compiler
1969   Neo-Confucianism, Etc.: Essays by Wing-tsit Chan. Hanover, N.H.: Oriental Society.

Chen, Jo-shui
1992   Liu Tsung-yüan and Intellectual Change in T'ang China, 773–819. Cambridge: Cambridge University Press.

Chen, Li-Fu
  1948   *Philosophy of Life.* New York: Philosophical Library.
  1972   *The Confucian Way: A New and Systematic Study of the "Four Books."* Translated by Liu Shih Shun. Taipei: Commercial Press.
Cheng, Chung-ying, trans.
  1971   *Tai Chen's Inquiry into Goodness.* Honolulu: East-West Center Press.
  1991   *New Dimensions of Confucian and Neo-Confucian Philosophy.* Albany: State University of New York Press.
Ch'ien, Edward T.
  1986   *Chiao Hung and the Restructuring of Neo-Confucianism in the Late Ming.* New York: Columbia University Press.
Chin, Ann-ping, and Mansfield Freedman
  1990   *Tai Chen on Mencius: Explorations in Words and Meaning.* New Haven, Conn.: Yale University Press.
Ching, Julia, trans.
  1972   *The Philosophical Letters of Wang Yang-ming.* Columbia: University of South Carolina Press.
  1976   *To Acquire Wisdom: The Way of Wang Yang-ming.* New York: Columbia University Press.
  1977   *Confucianism and Christianity: A Comparative Study.* Tokyo: Kodansha International.
  1990   *Probing China's Soul: Religion, Politics, and Protest in the People's Republic.* San Francisco: Harper & Row.
  1997   *Mysticism and Kingship in China: The Heart of Chinese Wisdom.* Cambridge: Cambridge University Press.
  2000   *The Religious Thought of Chu Hsi.* Oxford and New York: Oxford University Press.
———, and Hans Küng.
  1989   *Christianity and Chinese Religion.* New York: Doubleday.
Chow, Kai-wing
  1995   *The Rise of Confucian Ritualism in Late Imperial China: Ethics, Classics, and Lineage Discourse.* Stanford, Calif.: Stanford University Press.
Chow, Kai-wing, On-cho Ng, and John B. Henderson, eds.
  1999   *Imagining Boundaries: Changing Confucian Doctrines, Texts, and Hermeneutics.* Albany: State University of New York Press.
Chu Hsi
  1973   *The Philosophy of Human Nature.* Translated by J. Percy Bruce. London: Probsthain & Co., 1922; New York: AMS Press Edition.

1991   *Chu Hsi's Family Rituals: A Twelfth-Century Chinese Manual for the Performance of Cappings, Weddings, Funerals, and Ancestral Rites.* Translated and edited by Patricia Buckley Ebrey. Princeton, N.J.: Princeton University Press.

———, and Lü Tsu-ch'ien
1967   *Reflections on Things at Hand: The Neo-Confucian Anthology.* Translated by Wing-tsit Chan. New York: Columbia University Press.

Clarke, J. J.
1997   *Oriental Enlightenment: The Encounter Between Asian and Western Thought.* London: Routledge.
2000   *The Tao of the West: Western Transformations of Taoist Thought.* London: Routledge.

Confucius
1992   *Confucius: The Analects (Lun yü).* Translated by D. C. Lau. Hong Kong: Chinese University Press.

Creel, H. G.
1949   *Confucius and the Chinese Way.* New York: Harper & Row.
1970   *What Is Taoism? And Other Studies in Chinese Cultural History.* Chicago: University of Chicago Press.

Cua, A. S.
1982   *The Unity of Knowledge and Action: A Study of Wang Yang-ming's Moral Psychology.* Honolulu: University Press of Hawaii.
1985   *Ethical Argumentation: A Study in Hsün Tzu's Moral Epistemology.* Honolulu: University Press of Hawaii.
1998   *Moral Vision and Tradition: Essays in Chinese Ethics.* Washington, D.C.: Catholic University of America Press.

———, ed.
2003   *Encyclopedia of Chinese Philosophy.* New York and London: Routledge.

Dardess, John W.
1973   *Conquerors and Confucians: Aspects of Political Change in Late Yüan China.* New York: Columbia University Press.
1983   *Confucianism and Autocracy: Professional Elites in the Founding of the Ming Dynasty.* Berkeley: University of California Press.
1996   *A Ming Society: T'ai-ho Country, Kiangsi, Fourteenth to Seventeenth Centuries.* Berkeley: University of California Press.

de Bary, Wm. Theodore
1981   *Neo-Confucian Orthodoxy and the Learning of the Mind-and-Heart.* New York: Columbia University Press.

1983   *The Liberal Tradition in China*. New York: Columbia University Press.

1988   *East Asian Civilizations: A Dialogue in Five Stages*. Cambridge: Harvard University Press.

1989   *The Message of the Mind in Neo-Confucianism*. New York: Columbia University Press.

1991a   *The Trouble with Confucianism*. Cambridge, Mass.: Harvard University Press.

1991b   *Learning for One's Self: Essays on the Individual in Neo-Confucian Thought*. New York: Columbia University Press.

——, ed.

1970   *Self and Society in Ming Thought*. New York: Columbia University Press.

1975   *The Unfolding of Neo-Confucianism*. New York: Columbia University Press.

——, trans.

1993   *Waiting for the Dawn: A Plan for the Prince-Huang Tsung-hsi's Ming-i-tai-fang lu*. New York: Columbia University Press.

——, and John Chaffee, eds.

1989   *Neo-Confucian Education: The Formative Stage*. Berkeley: University of California Press.

Dimberg, Ronald G.

1974   *The Sage and Society: The Life and Thought of Ho Hsin-yin*. Honolulu: University of Hawaii Press.

Eber, Irene, ed.

1986   *Confucianism: The Dynamics of Tradition*. New York: Macmillan.

Ebrey, Patricia Buckley.

1991   *Confucianism and Family Rituals in Imperial China: A Social History of Writing about Rites*. Princeton, N.J.: Princeton University Press.

1993   *The Inner Quarters: Marriage and the Lives of Chinese Women in the Sung Period*. Berkeley: University of California Press.

Elman, Benjamin A.

1984   *From Philosophy to Philosophy: Intellectual and Social Aspects of Change in Late Imperial China*. Cambridge, Mass.: Harvard University Press.

1990   *Classicism, Politics and Kinship: The Ch'ang-Chou School of New Test Confucianism in Later Imperial China*. Berkeley: University of California Press.

Eno, Robert
1990   *The Confucian Creation of Heaven: Philosophy and the Defense of Ritual Mastery.* Albany: State University of New York Press.

Fairbank, John K., ed.
1957   *Chinese Thought and Institutions.* Chicago: University of Chicago Press.

Fang, Thome H.
n.d.   *The Chinese View of Life: The Philosophy of Comprehensive Harmony.* Hong Kong: Union Press.

Fingarette, Herbert
1972   *Confucius—The Secular as Sacred.* New York: Harper & Row, Publishers.

Gardner, Daniel K.
1986   *Chu Hsi and the Ta-hsüeh: Neo-Confucian Reflection the Confucian Canon.* Cambridge: Harvard University Press.
2003   *Zhu Xi's Reading of the Analects.* New York: Columbia University Press.

———, trans.
1990   *Learning to Be a Sage: Selections from the Conversations of Master Chu, Arranged Topically.* Berkeley: University of California Press.

Geaney, Jane
2002   *On the Epistemology of the Senses in Early Chinese Philosophy.* Honolulu: University of Hawaii Press.

Gernet, Jacques
1985   *China and the Christian Impact.* Translated by Janet Lloyd. Cambridge: Cambridge University Press.

Graham, A. C.
1986a   *Studies in Chinese Philosophy and Philosophical Literature.* Singapore: Institute for East Asian Philosophy.
1986b   *Yin-yang and the Nature of Correlative Thinking.* Singapore: The Institute of East Asian Philosophy.
1989   *Disputers of the Tao: Philosophical Argument in Ancient China.* La Salle, Ill.: Open Court.
1992   *Two Chinese Philosophers: The Metaphysics of the Brothers Ch'eng.* La Salle, Ill.: Open Court.

Granet, Marcel
1968   *La pensée Chinoise.* Paris: Editions Albin Michel.
1975   *The Religion of the Chinese People.* Translated by Maurice Freedman. New York: Harper & Row.

Grant, Beata
  1994   *Mount Lu Revisited: Buddhism in the Life of Su Shih*. Honolulu: University of Hawaii Press.
Gregory, Peter N.
  1991   *Tsung-mi and the Sinification of Buddhism*. Princeton, N.J.: Princeton University Press.
———, trans.
  1995   *Inquiry in the Origin of Humanity: An Annotated Translation of Tsung-mi's Yüan jen lun with a Modern Commentary*. Honolulu: University of Hawaii Press.
Hall, David L., and Roger T. Ames
  1987   *Thinking Through Confucius*. Albany: State University of New York Press.
  1995   *Anticipating China: Thinking Through the Narratives of Chinese and Western Culture*. Albany: State University of New York Press.
  1998   *Thinking from the Han: Self, Truth and Transcendence in Chinese and Western Culture*. Albany: State University of New York Press.
Handlin, Joanna
  1983   *Action in Late Ming Thought: The Reorientation of Lu K'un and Other Scholar-Officials*. Berkeley: University of California Press.
Hansen, Chad
  1992   *A Daoist Theory of Chinese Thought: A Philosophic Interpretation*. Oxford: Oxford University Press.
Hartman, Charles
  1986   *Han Yü and the T'ang Search for Unity*. Princeton, N.J.: Princeton University Press.
Henderson, John B.
  1984   *The Development and Decline of Chinese Cosmology*. New York: Columbia University Press.
  1991   *Scripture, Canon, and Commentary: A Comparison of Confucian and Western Exegesis*. Princeton, N.J.: Princeton University Press.
  1998   *The Construction of Orthodoxy and Heresy: Neo-Confucian, Islamic, Jewish, and Early Christian Patterns*. Albany: State University of New York Press.
Henke, Frederick Goodrich
  1964   *The Philosophy of Wang Yang-ming*. 2nd ed. New York: Paragon Boo Reprint Co.

Hoobler, Thomas, and Dorothy Hoobler
1993　*Confucianism: World Religions*. New York: Facts On File, Inc.
Hocking, William Ernest
1936　"Chu Hsi's Theory of Knowledge." *Harvard Journal of Asiatic Studies* 1 (1936): 109–27.
Hsiao, Kung-chuan
1975　*A Modern China and New World: K'ang Yu-wei, Reformer and Utopian, 1854–1927*. Seattle: University of Washington Press.
1979　*A History of Chinese Political Thought*. Vol. I: *From the Beginnings to the Sixth Century A.D.* Translated by F. W. Mote. Princeton, N.J.: Princeton University Press.
Hsieh, Shan-yuan
1979　*The Life and Thought of Li Kou (1009–1069)*. San Francisco: Chinese Materials Center.
Huang, Chin-shing
1995　*Philosophy, Philology, and Politics in Eighteenth-Century China: Li Fu and the Lu-Wang School Under the Ch'ing*. Cambridge: Cambridge University Press.
Huang, Chun-chieh
2001　*Mencian Hermeneutics: A History of Interpretations in China*. New Brunswick and London: Transaction Publishers.
Huang, Siu-chi
1968　"Chang Tsai's Concept of *Ch'i*." *Philosophy East & West* 18 (October 1968): 247–60.
1971　"The Moral Point of View of Chang Tsai." *Philosophy East & West* 21 (April 1971): 141–56.
1977　*Lu Hsiang-shan: A Twelfth Century Chinese Idealist Philosophy*. Westport, CT: Hyperion Press.
Huang Tsung-hsi
1987　*The Records of Ming Scholars*. Edited by Julia Ching with the collaboration of Chaoying Fang. Honolulu: University of Hawaii Press.
Ivanhoe, Philip J.
1990　*Ethics in the Confucian Tradition: The Thought of Mencius and Wang Yang-ming*. Atlanta: Scholars Press.
1991　"A Happy Symmetry: Xunzi's Ethical Thought." *Journal of the American Academy of Religions* 59.2 (Summer): 309–22.
2000　*Confucian Moral Self Cultivation*. 2nd ed. Indianapolis: Hackett Publishing Company.
——, ed.
1996　*Chinese Language, Thought, and Culture: Nivison and His Critics*. Chicago, Ill.: Open Court.

——, and Bryan Van Nordon, eds.
2001   *Readings in Classical Chinese Philosophy.* New York: Seven Bridges Press.

——, and Xiusheng Liu, eds.
2002   *Essays in the Moral Philosophy of Mengzi.* Indianapolis: Hackett Publishing Company.

Jensen, Lionel M.
1997   *Manufacturing Confucianism: Chinese Traditions and Universal Civilizations.* Durham, N.C.: Duke University Press.

Jiang, Paul Yun-Ming
1980   *The Search for Mind: Ch'ien Pai-sha, Philosopher-Poet.* Singapore: Singapore University Press, 1980.

Kasoff, Ira E.
1984   *The Thought of Chang Tsai.* Cambridge: Cambridge University Press.

Kim, Sung-Hae
1985   *The Righteous and the Sage: A Comparative Study on the Ideal Images of Man in Biblical Israel and Classical China.* Seoul: Sogang University Press.

Kim, Yung Sik
2000   *The Natural Philosophy of Chu Hsi (1130–1200).* Philadelphia: American Philosophical Society.

Knoblock, John
1988–   *Xunzi: A Translation and Study of the Complete Works.* 3 vols.
1994   Stanford, Calif.: Stanford University Press.

Ko, Dorothy
1994   *Teachers of the Inner Chambers: Women and Culture in Seventeenth-Century China.* Stanford, Calif.: Stanford University Press.

Kohn, Livia
1991   *Early Chinese Mysticism: Philosophy and Soteriology in the Taoist Tradition.* Princeton, N.J.: Princeton University Press.
1995   *Laughing at the Tao: Debates among Buddhists and Taoists in Medieval China.* Princeton, N.J.: Princeton University Press.

Kuhn, Philip A.
1990   *Soulstealers: The Chinese Sorcery Scare of 1768.* Cambridge, Mass.: Harvard University Press.

Lee, Peter K. H., ed.
1991   *Confucian-Christian Encounter in Historical and Contemporary Perspective.* Lewiston, N.Y.: Edwin Mellen Press.

Lee, Thomas H. C.
1985   *Government Education and Examinations in Sung China*. Hong Kong: Chinese University Press.

Legge, James, trans.
1960   *The Chinese Classics*. 5 vols. Hong Kong: Hong Kong University Press.
1968   *The Li Ki*. 2 vols. Delhi: Motilal Barnarsidass.

Leibniz, Gottfried Wilhelm
1977   *Discourse on the Natural Theology of the Chinese*. Translated by Henry Rosemont and Daniel J. Cook. Honolulu: University of Hawaii Press.
1994   *Writings on China*. Translated by Daniel J. Cook and Henry Rosemont, Jr. Chicago: Open Court.

Levenson, Joseph R.
1968   *Confucian China and Its Modern Faith: A Trilogy*. 3 vols. Berkeley: University of California Press.

Lewis, Mark Edward
1990   *Sanctioned Violence in Early China*. Albany: State University of New York Press.

Leys, Simon, trans.
1997   *The Analects of Confucius*. New York: W. W. Norton & Company.

Liang Ch'i-ch'ao
1959   *Intellectual Trends in the Ch'ing Period*. Translated by Immanuel C. Y. Hsü. Cambridge, Mass.: Harvard University Press.

Liu, James T. C.
1959   *Reform in Sung China: Wang An-shih (1021–1086) and His New Policies*. Cambridge, Mass.: Harvard University Press.
1967   *Ou-yang Hsiu: An Eleventh-Century Neo-Confucianist*. Palo Alto, Calif.: Stanford University Press.
1988   *China Turning Inward: Intellectual Changes in the Early Twelfth Century*. Cambridge, Mass.: Harvard University Press.

Liu, Shu-hsien
1971   "The Religious Import of Confucian Philosophy: Its Traditional Outlook and Contemporary Significance." *Philosophy East & West* 21 (April 1971): 157–75.
1978   "The Functions of the Mind in Chu Hsi's Philosophy." *Journal of Chinese Philosophy* 5 (1978): 204.
1989   "Postwar Neo-Confucian Philosophy: Its Development and Issues." In *Religious Issues and Interreligious Dialogues*. Edited

by Charles Wei-hsun Fu and Gerhard E. Spiegler. New York: Greenwood Press.

1990   "Some Reflections on the Sung-Ming Understanding of Mind, Nature, and Reason." *The Journal of the Institute of Chinese Studies of the Chinese University of Hong Kong* 21 (1990): 331–43.

1998   *Understanding Confucian Philosophy: Classical and Sung-Ming.* Westport, Conn.: Praeger.

Lo, Winston Wan

1974   *The Life and Thought of Yeh Shih.* Hong Kong: Chinese University of Hong Kong.

Loden, Torbjon, trans.

1988   "Dai Zhen's Evidential Commentary on the Meaning of the Words of Mencius." *Bulletin of the Museum of Far Eastern Antiquities* [Stockholm] no. 60 (1988): 165–313.

Loewe, Michael

1979   *Ways to Paradise: The Chinese Quest for Immortality.* London: George Allen & Unwin Ltd.

1982   *Chinese Ideas of Life and Death: Faith, Myth and Reason in the Han Period (202 B.C.–A.D. 220).* London: George Allen & Unwin Ltd.

1994   *Divination, Mythology and Monarch in Han China.* Cambridge: Cambridge University Press.

Lufrano, Richard

1997   *Honorable Merchants: Commerce and Self-Cultivation in Later Imperial China.* Honolulu: University of Hawaii Press.

Lynn, Richard John, trans.

1994   *The Classic of Changes: A New Translation of the I Ching as Interpreted by Wang Bi.* New York: Columbia University Press.

Machle, Edward J.

1993   *Nature and Heaven in the Xunzi: A Study of Tien Lun.* Albany: State University of New York Press.

Major, John

1993   *Heaven and Earth in Early Han Thought.* Albany: State University of New York Press.

Makeham, John

1995   *Name and Actuality in Early Chinese Thought.* Albany: State University of New York Press.

Malebranche, Nicolas

1980   *Dialogue Between a Christian Philosopher and a Chinese Philosopher on the Existence and Nature of God.* Translated by

Dominick A. Iorio. Washington, D.C.: University Press of America.

Mann, Susan
1997   *Precious Records: Women in China's Long Eighteenth Century.* Stanford, Calif.: Stanford University Press.

Maspero, Henri
1978   *China in Antiquity.* Translated by Frank A. Kierman, Jr. N.P: University of Massachusetts Press.

Mencius
1984   Translated by D. C. Lau. 2 vols. Hong Kong: Chinese University Press.

Metzger, Thomas A.
1977   *Escape from Predicament: Neo-Confucianism and China's Evolving Political Culture.* New York: Columbia University Press.

Minamiki, George, S.J.
1985   *The Chinese Rites Controversy from Its Beginning to Modern Times.* Chicago: Loyola University Press.

Moran, Patrick Edwin
1993   *Three Smaller Wisdom Books: Lao Zi's Dao De Jing, The Great Learning (Da Xue), and the Doctrine of the Mean (Zhong Yong).* Lanham, Md.: University Press of America.

Mungello, David E.
1977   *Leibniz and Confucianism: The Search for Accord.* Honolulu: University of Hawaii Press.
1985   *Curious Land: Jesuit Accommodation and the Origins of Sinology.* Stuttgart: Franz Steiner Verlag.

Munro, Donald J.
1969   *The Concept of Man in Early China.* Stanford, Calif.: Stanford University Press.
1977   *The Concept of Man in Contemporary China.* Ann Arbor: University of Michigan Press.
1988   *Images of Human Nature: A Sung Portrait.* Princeton, N.J.: Princeton University Press.

Murata, Sachiko
2000   *Chinese Gleams of Sufi Light.* Albany: State University of New York Press.

Needham, Joseph
1954–   *Science and Civilisation in China.* 8 vols. Cambridge: Cambridge University Press.

Neville, Robert C.
2000   *Boston Confucianism.* Albany: State University of New York Press.

Ni, Peimin
  2002   *On Confucius.* Belmont, Calif.: Wadsworth/Thompson Learning, Inc.
Nivison, David S.
  1966   *The Life and Thought of Chang Hsüeh-ch'eng (1738–1801).* Stanford, Calif.: Stanford University Press.
  1996   *The Ways of Confucianism: Investigations in Chinese Philosophy.* Edited by Bryan W. Van Norden. Chicago and La Salle: Open Court.
———, and Arthur F. Wright, eds.
  1959   *Confucianism in Action.* Stanford, Calif.: Stanford University Press.
Obenchain, Diane B., ed.
  1994   "Feng Youlan: Something Happens." *Journal of Chinese Philosophy* 21, nos. 3/4 (September–December 1994).
Paper, Jordan
  1987   *The Fu-Tzu: A Post-Han Confucian Text.* Leiden: E. J. Brill.
  1995   *The Spirits Are Drunk: Comparative Approaches to Chinese Religion.* Albany: State University of New York Press.
Pines, Yuri
  2002   *Foundations of Confucian Thought: Intellectual Life in the Chunqiu Period, 722–453 B.C.E.* Honolulu: University of Hawaii Press.
Prazniak, Roxann
  1996   *Dialogues Across Civilizations: Sketches in World History from the Chinese and European Experiences.* Boulder, Colo.: Westview Press.
Puett, Michael J.
  2000   *The Ambivalence of Creation: Debates Concerning Innovation and Artifice in Early China.* Stanford, Calif.: Stanford University Press.
  2002   *To Become a God: Cosmology, Sacrifice, and Self-Divinization in Early China.* Cambridge: Harvard University Press.
Queen, Sarah A.
  1996   *From Chronicle to Canon: The Hermeneutics of the Spring and Autumn, According to Tung Chung-shu.* Cambridge: Cambridge University Press.
Raphals, Lisa
  1992   *Knowing Words: Wisdom and Cunning in the Classical Traditions of China and Greece.* Ithaca, N.Y., and London: Cornell University Press.

1998 *Sharing the Light: Representations of Women and Virtue in Early China.* Albany: State University of New York Press.

Ricci, Matteo, S.J.
1985 *The True Meaning of the Lord of Heaven (T'ien-chu Shih-i).* Translated by Douglas Lancashire and Peter Hu Kuo-chen, S.J. Taipei: Ricci Institute.

Roetz, Heiner
1993 *Confucian Ethics of the Axial Age: A Reconstruction under the Aspect of the Breakthrough Toward Postconventional Thinking.* Albany: State University of New York Press.

Rosemont, Henry, Jr., ed.
1991 *Chinese Texts and Philosophical Contexts: Essays Dedicated to Angus C. Graham.* La Salle, Ill.: Open Court.

Rowley, Harold Henry
1956 *Prophecy and Religion in Ancient China and Israel.* London: University of London, The Athlone Press.

Rozman, Gilbert, ed.
1991 *The East Asian Region: Confucian Heritage and Its Modern Adaptation.* Princeton, N.J.: Princeton University Press.

Rubin, Vitaly A.
1976 *Individual and State in Ancient China: Essays on Four Chinese Philosophers.* Translated by Steven I. Levine. New York: Columbia University Press.

Schwartz, Benjamin I.
1985 *The World of Thought in Ancient China.* Cambridge, Mass.: Belknap Press of Harvard University.

Shao Yung
1986 *Dialogue Between a Fisherman and a Wood-Cutter.* Translated by Knud Lundbaek. Hamburg: C. Bell Verlag.

Shaughnessy, Edward L.
1996 *I Ching: The Classic of Changes.* New York: Ballantine Books.
1997 *Before Confucius: Studies in the Creation of the Chinese Classics.* Albany: State University of New York Press.

Shryock, J. K.
1937 *The Study of Human Abilities: The Jen wu chih of Liu Shao.* New Haven, Conn.: American Oriental Society.

Shun, Kwong-loi
1997 *Mencius and Early Chinese Thought.* Stanford, Calif.: Stanford University Press.

Smith, D. Howard
1968 *Chinese Religions.* New York: Holt, Rinehart and Winston.

1973 *Confucius.* New York: Charles Scribner's Sons.
Smith, Kidder, Jr., et al.
1990 *Sung Dynasty Uses of the I Ching.* Princeton, N.J.: Princeton University Press.
Smith, Richard J.
1991 *Fortune-Tellers and Philosophers: Divination in Traditional Chinese Society.* Boulder, Calif.: Westview Press.
1994 *China's Cultural Heritage: The Ch'ing Dynasty, 1644-1912.* 2nd ed. Boulder, Colo.: Westview Press.
——, and D. W. Y. Kwok, eds.
1993 *Cosmology, Ontology, and Human Efficacy.* Honolulu: University of Hawaii Press.
Som, Tjan Tjoe
1973 *The Comprehensive Discussions in the White Tiger Hall.* 2 vols. Westport, Conn.: Hyperion Press. Leiden: E. J. Brill, 1949. Reprint.
Standaert, N.
1988 *Yang Tingyun, Confucian and Christian in Late Ming China.* Leiden: E. J. Brill.
Swann, Nancy Lee
1968 *Pan Chao: Foremost Woman Scholar of China.* New York: Russell and Russell.
T'an, Ssu-t'ung
1984 *An Exposition of Benevolence: The Jen-hsüeh of T'an Ssu-t'ung.* Translated by Chan Sin-wai. Hong Kong: Chinese University of Hong Kong Press.
T'ang, Chün-i
1956 "Chang Tsai's Theory of Mind and Its Metaphysical Basis." *Philosophy East & West* 6 (1956): 113–36.
1974 "The Spirit and Development of Neo-Confucianism." In *Invitation to Chinese Philosophy,* edited by A. Naess and A. Hanny. Oslo: Scandinavian University Press.
Taylor, Rodney L.
1978 *The Cultivation of Sagehood as a Religious Goal in Neo-Confucianism: A Study of Selected Writings of Kao P'an-lung, 1562–1626.* Missoula, Mont.: Scholars Press.
1990 *The Religious Dimensions of Confucianism.* Albany: State University of New York Press.
Thompson, Laurence G.
1958 *The One-World Philosophy of K'ang Yu-wei.* London: George Allen & Unwin Ltd.

Tillman, Hoyt Cleveland

1982   *Utilitarian Confucianism: Ch'en Liang's Challenge to Chu Hsi.* Cambridge, Mass.: Harvard University Press.

1992   *Confucian Discourse and Chu Hsi's Ascendancy.* Honolulu: University of Hawaii Press.

1994   *Ch'en Liang on Public Interest and the Law.* Honolulu: University of Hawaii Press.

Ts'ai, Y. C.

1950   "The Philosophy of Ch'eng I: A Selection from the Complete Works." Ph.D. dissertation. Columbia University.

Tsai, Yen-zen

1994   "*Ching* and *Chuan*: Towards Defining the Confucian Scriptures in Han China (206 BCE–220 CE)." Unpublished Manuscript.

Tu, Weiming

1971   Review of *Hsin-t'i yü hsing-t'i* [Mind and Nature], by Mou Tsung-san. *Journal of Asian Studies* 30 (May 1971): 642–47.

1974   "Reconstituting the Confucian Tradition." *Journal of Asian Studies* 33 (May 1974): 441–54.

1976   *Neo-Confucian Thought in Action: Wang Yang-ming's Youth (1472–1509).* Berkeley: University of California Press.

1979   *Humanity and Self-Cultivation: Essays in Confucian Thought.* Berkeley, Calif.: Asian Humanities Press.

1985   *Confucian Thought: Self-hood as Creative Transformation.* Albany: State University of New York Press.

1989   *Centrality and Commonality: An Essay on Confucian Religiousness.* Albany: State University of New York Press.

1993   *Way, Learning, and Politics: Essays on the Confucian Intellectual.* Albany: State University of New York Press.

——, ed.

1994a   *China in Transformation.* Cambridge, Mass.: Harvard University Press.

1994b   *The Living Tree: The Changing Meaning of Being Chinese Today.* Stanford, Calif.: Stanford University Press.

——, Milan Hejtmanek, and Alan Wachman, eds.

1992   *The Confucian World Observed: A Contemporary Discussion of Confucian Humanism in East Asia.* Honolulu: University of Hawaii Press.

Van Zoeren, Steven

1991   *Poetry and Personality: Reading, Exegesis and Hermeneutics in Traditional China.* Stanford, Calif.: Stanford University Press.

Waley, Arthur
1938   *The Analects of Confucius*. London: George, Allen & Unwin, Ltd.
1939   *Three Ways of Thought in Ancient China*. Garden City, N.Y.: Doubleday.

Wang, Aihe
2000   *Cosmology and Political Culture in Early China*. Cambridge: Cambridge University Press.

Wang, Y. C.
1966   *Chinese Intellectuals and the West: 1872-1949*. Chapel Hill: University of North Carolina Press.

Wang Yang-ming
1963   *Instructions for Practical Living and Other Neo-Confucian Writings*. Translated by Wing Tsit-chan. New York: Columbia University Press.

Watson, Burton, trans.
1967   *Basic Writings of Mo Tzu, Hsün Tzu, and Han Fei Tzu*. New York: Columbia University Press.

Weber, Max
1951   *The Religion of China: Confucianism and Taoism*. Translated by Hans H. Gerth. New York: Macmillan.

Williamson, H. R.
1973   *Wang An Shih: A Chinese Statesman and Educationalist of the Sung Dynasty*. 2 vols. Westport, Conn.: Hyperion Press.

Wilson, Thomas A.
1995   *Genealogy of the Way: The Construction and Uses of the Confucian Tradition in Late Imperial China*. Stanford, Calif.: Stanford University Press.
———, ed.
2003   *On Sacred Grounds: Culture, Society, Politics and the Formation of the Cult of Confucius*. Cambridge, Mass.: Harvard University Asia Center.

Wittenborn, Allen, trans.
1991   *Further Reflections on Things at Hand: A Reader, Chu Hsi*. Lanham, Md.: University Press of America.

Wood, Alan T.
1995   *Limits to Autocracy: From Sung Neo-Confucianism to a Doctrine of Political Rights*. Honolulu: University of Hawaii Press.

Wright, Arthur F., ed.
1953   *Studies in Chinese Thought*. Chicago: University of Chicago Press.

1960   *The Confucian Persuasion.* Stanford, Calif.: Stanford University Press.

———, and Denis Twichett, eds.
1962   *Confucian Personalities.* Stanford, Calif.: Stanford University Press.

Wu, Pei-yi
1990   *The Confucian's Progress: Autobiographical Writings in Traditional China.* Princeton, N.J.: Princeton University Press.

Wyatt, Don J.
1996   *The Recluse of Loyang: Shao Yung and the Moral Evolution of Early Sung Thought.* Honolulu: University of Hawaii Press.

Yang Hsiung
1993   *The Canon of Supreme Mystery: A Translation with Commentary of the T'ai Hsüan Ching.* Translated and edited by Michael Nylan. Albany: State University of New York Press.
1994   *The Elemental Changes: The Ancient Chinese Companion to the I Ching, The T'ai Hsüan Ching of Master Yang Hsiung.* Translated and edited by Michael Nylan. Albany: State University of New York Press.

Yang, Lien-sheng
1957   "The Concept of *Pao* as a Basis for Social Relations in China." In *Chinese Thought and Institutions,* edited by J. K. Fairbank. Chicago: University of Chicago Press.

Yearley, Lee H.
1990   *Mencius and Aquinas: Theories of Virtue and Conceptions of Courage.* Albany: State University of New York Press.

Yeh, Theodore T. Y.
1969   *Confucianism, Christianity and China.* New York: Philosophical Library.

Yen Yüan
1972   *Preservation of Learning.* Translated by Maurice Freeman. Los Angeles: Monumenta Serica.

Young, John D.
1983   *Confucianism and Christianity: The First Encounter.* Hong Kong: Hong Kong University Press.

Yü, Chün-fang
1981   *The Renewal of Buddhism in China: Chu-hung and the Late Ming Synthesis.* New York: Columbia University Press.

Zaehner, R. C.
1970   *Concordant Discord: The Interdependence of Faiths.* Oxford: Oxford University Press.

Monographs: Korea

Choi, Ming-hong
1980   *A Modern History of Korean Philosophy.* Seoul: Seong Moon Sa.
Choung Haechang, and Han Hyong-jo, eds.
1996   *Confucian Philosophy in Korea.* Kyonggi-do: The Academy of Korean Studies.
Chung Chai-Sik
1995   *A Korean Confucian Encounter with the Modern World: Yi Hang-no and the West.* Berkeley: Institute for East Asian Studies, University of California, Berkeley.
Chung, Edward Y. J.
1995   *The Korean Neo-Confucianism of Yi T'oegye and Yi Yulgok: A Reappraisal of the "Four-Seven Thesis" and Its Practical Implications for Self-Cultivation.* Albany: State University of New York Press.
de Bary, Wm. Theodore, and JaHyun Kim Haboush, eds.
1985   *The Rise of Neo-Confucianism in Korea.* New York: Columbia University Press.
Deuchler, Martina
1992   *The Confucian Transformation of Korea: A Study of Society and Ideology.* New York: Columbia University Press.
Grayson, James Huntley
1989   *Korea: A Religious History.* Oxford: Clarendon Press.
Haboush, JaHyun Kim
1988   *A Heritage of Kings: One Man's Monarchy in the Confucian World.* New York: Columbia University Press.
1996   *The Memoirs of Lay Hyegyong: The Autobiographical Writings of a Crown Princess of Eighteenth-Century Korea.* Berkeley: University of California Press.
Kalton, Michael C., trans.
1988   *To Become a Sage: The Ten Diagrams on Sage Learning by Yi T'oegye.* New York: Columbia University Press.
Kalton, Michael, et al.
1994   *The Four Seven Debate: An Annotated Translation of the Most Famous Controversy in Korean Neo-Confucian Thought.* Albany: State University of New York Press.
Kendall, Laurel, and Griffin Dix, eds.
1987   *Ritual and Religion in Korean Society.* Berkeley: Institute of East Asian Studies, University of California, Berkeley Center for Korean Studies.

Kim, Sung-Hae
  1985   *The Righteous and the Sage: A Comparative Study on the Ideal Images of Man in Biblical Israel and Classical China.* Seoul: Sogang University Press.
Phillips, Earl H., and Eui-young Yu, eds.
  1982   *Religions in Korea: Beliefs and Cultural Values.* Los Angeles: Center for Korean-American and Korean Studies, California State University.
Ro, Young-chan
  1989   *The Korean Neo-Confucianism of Yi Yulgok.* Albany: State University of New York Press.
Setton, Mark
  1997   *Chong Yagyong: Korea's Challenge to Orthodox Neo-Confucianism.* Albany: State University of New York Press.

Monographs: Japan

Ackroyd, Joyce, trans.
  1979   *Told Round a Brushwood Fire: The Autobiography of Arai Hakuseki.* Princeton, N.J.: Princeton University Press and University of Tokyo Press.
Bellah, Robert N.
  1957   *Tokugawa Religion: The Values of Pre-Industrial Japan.* Boston: Beacon Press.
Craig, Albert, and Donald Shively, eds.
  1970   *Personality in Japanese History.* Berkeley: University of California Press.
Davis, Winston
  1992   *Japanese Religion and Society: Paradigms of Structure and Change.* Albany: State University of New York Press.
de Bary, Wm. Theodore, and Irene Bloom, eds.
  1979   *Principle and Practicality: Essays in Neo-Confucianism and Practical Learning.* New York: Columbia University Press.
Elison, George
  1973   *Deus Destroyed: The Image of Christianity in Early Modern Japan.* Cambridge, Mass.: Harvard University Press.
Irokawa, Daikichi
  1985   *The Culture of the Meiji Period.* Translation edited by Marius B. Jansen. Princeton, N.J.: Princeton University Press.
Kassel, Marleen
  1996   *Tokugawa Confucian Education: The Kangien Academy of Hirose Tanso (1782–1856).* Albany: State University of New York Press.

Kitagawa, Joseph M.
1987   *On Understanding Japanese Religion*. Princeton, N.J.: Princeton University Press.
Lidin, Olof, trans.
1970   *Ogyu Sorai's Distinguishing the Way*. Tokyo: Sophia University Press.
1973   *The Life of Ogyu Sorai: A Tokugawa Confucian Philosopher*. Lund: Scandinavian Institute of Asian Studies.
Maruyama, Masao
1974   *Studies in the Intellectual History of Tokugawa Japan*. Translated by Mikiso Hane. Princeton, N.J.: Princeton University Press.
McEwan, J. R., trans.
1969   *The Political Writings of Ogyu Sorai*. Cambridge: Cambridge University Press.
Mercer, Rosemary, trans.
1991   *Deep Words: Miura Baien's System of Natural Philosophy*. Leiden: E. J. Brill.
Najita, Tetsuo
1987   *Visions of Virtue in Tokugawa Japan: The Kaitokudo Merchant Academy of Osaka*. Chicago: University of Chicago Press.
——, and Irwin Scheiner, eds.
1978   *Japanese Thought in the Tokugawa Period 1600–1868: Methods and Metaphors*. Chicago: University of Chicago Press.
Nakai, Kate Wildman
1980   "The Naturalization of Confucianism in Tokugawa Japan: The Problem of Sinocentrism." *Harvard Journal of Asian Studies* 40 (1980): 157–99.
Nakamura, Hajime
1969   *A History of the Development of Japanese Thought from A. D. 592 to 1868*. Tokyo: Japan Cultural Society.
Nosco, Peter, ed.
1984   *Confucianism and Tokugawa Culture*. Princeton, N.J.: Princeton University Press.
Ooms, Herman
1985   *Tokugawa Ideology: Early Constructs, 1570–1680*. Princeton, N.J.: Princeton University Press.
Pollack, David
1986   *The Fracture of Meaning: Japan's Synthesis of China from the Eighth to the Eighteenth Centuries*. Princeton, N.J.: Princeton University Press.

Sawada, Janine Anderson
1993   *Confucian Values and Popular Zen: Sekimon Shingaku in Eighteenth-Century Japan.* Honolulu: University of Hawaii Press.
Smith, Warren W.
1973   *Confucianism in Modern Japan: A Study of Conservatism in Japanese Intellectual History.* 2nd ed. Tokyo: Hokuseido Press.
Spae, Joseph
1967   *Ito Jinsai: A Philosopher, Educator and Sinologist of the Tokugawa Period.* New York: Paragon.
Taylor, Rodney L.
1988   *The Confucian Way of Contemplation: Okada Takehiko and the Tradition of Quiet-Sitting.* Columbia: University of South Carolina Press.
Tominaga, Nakamoto
1990   *Emerging from Meditation.* Translated with introduction by Michael Pye. London: Duckworth.
Totman, Conrad
1993   *Early Modern Japan.* Berkeley: University of California Press.
Tucker, Mary Evelyn
1989   *Moral and Spiritual Cultivation in Japanese Neo-Confucianism: The Life and Thought of Kaibara Ekken (1630–1714).* Albany: State University of New York Press.
Yamashita, Samuel H.
1994   *Master Sorai's Responsals: Annotated Translation of Sorai Sensi Tomonsho.* Honolulu: University of Hawaii Press.
Yasunaga, Toshinobu
1992   *Ando Shoeki: Social and Ecological Philosopher in Eighteenth Century Japan.* New York: Weatherhill.
Yoshikawa, Kojiro.
1983   *Jinsai, Sorai, Norinaga: Three Classical Philologists of Mid-Tokugawa.* Tokyo: Toho Gakkai.

Contributors

ROGER T. AMES is Professor of Chinese philosophy at the University of Hawaii where he directs its Center for Chinese Studies. He is a translator of Chinese classics such as *Sun-tzu, The Art of Warfare, Sun Pin: The Art of Warfare* (with D. C. Lau), *The Analects of Confucius: A Philosophical Translation* (with H. Rosemont, Jr.), and is the co-author of several interpretative studies of classical Chinese philosophy: *Thinking Through Confucius, Anticipating China,* and *Thinking from the Han* (all with D. Hall).

THOMAS BERRY received his Ph.D. from The Catholic University of America in European intellectual history with a thesis on Giambattista Vico. Widely read in Western history and theology, he also spent many years studying and teaching the cultures and religions of Asia. He has lived in China and traveled to other parts of Asia. He has authored two books on Asian religions, *Buddhism* and *Religions of India,* both of which are distributed by Columbia University Press. For some twenty years, he directed the Riverdale Center of Religious Research, along the Hudson River. During this period he taught at Fordham University, where he chaired the history of religions program and directed twenty-five doctoral theses. His major contributions to the discussions on the environment are in his books *The Dream of the Earth* (Sierra Club Books, 1988) and, with Brian Swimme, *The Universe Story* (HarperSan Francisco, 1992). His latest book, *The Great Work: Our Way into the Future,* was published by Random House in 1999.

JOHN BERTHRONG, educated in sinology at the University of Chicago, is the Associate Dean for Academic and Administrative Affairs and Director of the Institute for Dialogue among Religious Traditions at the Boston University School of Theology. Active in interfaith dialogue projects and programs, his teaching and research interests are in the areas of interreligious dialogue, Chinese religions, and comparative theology. His most recent books are *All under Heaven: Transforming Paradigms in Confucian-Christian Dialogue, The Transformations of the Confucian Way,* and *Concerning Creativity* (on the thought of Chu Hsi, A. N. Whitehead, and R. C. Neville). He is co-editor with Mary Evelyn Tucker of the volume on *Confucianism and Ecology* published by the Center for the Study of World Religions and Harvard University Press in 1998.

IRENE BLOOM is Emeritus Professor of Asian and Middle Eastern Cultures at Barnard College and is interested in the areas of Confucian ethics and human rights. She is co-editor, with Wm. Theodore de Bary, of *Sources of Chinese Tradition*, vol. 1 (revised ed., 1999), *Eastern Canons: Approaches to the Asian Classics* (1990), and *Principle and Practicality* (1979), and co-editor with Wayne Proudfoot and J. Paul Martin of *Religious Diversity and Human Rights* (1996). With Joshua Fogel she co-edited *Meeting of Minds—Religious and Intellectual Interaction in East Asian Traditions of Thought: Essays in Honor of Wing-tsit Chan and Wm. Theodore de Bary* (1997). She is editor and translator of *Knowledge Painfully Acquired: The K'un-chih chi by Lo Ch'in-shun* (1987).

JULIA CHING was University Professor of Religion, Philosophy, and East Asian Studies at the University of Toronto, and a Fellow of the Royal Society of Canada. Born in Shanghai, she was a specialist in Chinese philosophy and religion and was the author of numerous books, including *Christianity and Chinese Religions*, with Hans Küng (Doubleday, 1989), *Probing China's Soul: Religion, Politics, and Protest in the People's Republic* (Harper and Row, 1990), *Chinese Religions* (Orbis, 1993), *Mysticism and Kingship in China* (Cambridge, University Press, 1997), and *The Religious Thought of Chu Hsi* (Oxford, 2000). She received her Ph.D. from the Australian National University, where she lectured until 1974. She also taught in the United States, Taiwan, Germany, and France.

CHENG CHUNG-YING is a professor of philosophy at the University of Hawaii, Manoa. He is the editor of the *Journal of Chinese Philosophy* and the author of *Perce's and Lewis' Theories of Induction* (Martinus Nijhoff, 1969), *Tai Chen's Inquiry into Goodness* (The East-West Center Press, 1971), *Philosophical Aspects of the Mind-Body Problem* (University of Hawaii Press, 1975), *New Dimensions of Confucian and Neo-Confucian Philosophy* (State University of New York Press, 1991), and, in Chinese, *C Theory: Philosophy of Management in the I Ching* (Sanmin, 1995) and *On Spirits of Chinese and Western Philosophies* (Dongfang, 1997).

ANTONIO S. CUA is Professor Emeritus of Philosophy at The Catholic University of America. He is the author of *Reason and Virtue: A Study in the Ethics of Richard Price*; *Dimensions of Moral Creativity: Paradigms, Principles, and Ideals; The Unity of Knowledge and Action: A Study in Wang Yang-ming's Moral Psychology; Ethical Argumentation: A Study in Hsun Tzu's Moral Epistemology; Moral Vision and Tradition: Essays in Chinese Ethics;* and *Two Lectures on Confucian Ethics: Tradition and Conceptual Framework*. Professor Cua is the editor of the *Encyclopedia of Chinese Philosophy* (Routledge, 2003), co-editor of the *Journal of Chinese Philosophy*, an associate editor of the *International Journal of the Philosophy of Religion*, and a member of the editorial boards of the *American Philosophical Quarterly* and *Philosophy East and West*.

PAUL RAKITA GOLDIN received his Ph.D. from Harvard University. He teaches Chinese history and philosophy at the University of Pennsylvania. He is the author of *Rituals of the Way: The Philosophy of Xunzi* (Open Court, 1999) and *The Culture of Sex in Ancient China* (University of Hawaii, 2002).

PHILIP J. IVANHOE has special interest in Chinese religious and ethical thought. His work focuses on Chinese views on character, self-cultivation, virtue, moral agency, environmental philosophy, relativism, and skepticism. He is the author of *Ethics in the Confucian Tradition: The Thought of Mencius and Wang Yang-ming* (1990) and *Confucian Moral Self Cultivation* (1993). He has edited and contributed to *Chinese Language, Thought and Culture* (1996) and co-edited and contributed to *Essays on Skepticism, Relativism and Ethics in the Zhuangzi* (1996) and *Religious and Philosophical Aspects of the Laozi* (1999). *Readings in Classical Chinese Philosophy* (contributor and co-editor with Bryan W. Van Norden) was published in 2002. His forthcoming publications include *The Sense of Anti-Rationalism: Zhuangzi and Kierkegaard's Religious Thought* (co-authored with Karen L. Carr), *Virtue, Nature and Agency in the Xunzi* (contributor and co-editor with Thornton C. Kline). Professor Ivanhoe is Associate Professor in the Department of Asian Languages and Cultures as well as in the Department of Philosophy at the University of Michigan, Ann Arbor.

MICHAEL PUETT is John L. Loeb Associate Professor of Humanities at Harvard University. He is the author of *The Ambivalence of Creation: Debates Concerning Innovation and Artifice in Early China* (Stanford University Press, 2001) and *To Become a God: Cosmology, Sacrifice, and Self-Divinization in Early China* (Harvard University Press, 2002).

SARAH A. QUEEN is currently Associate Professor of History and Director of Asian Studies at Connecticut College, where she teaches courses on the history of Confucianism and Daoism with special attention to their spiritual dimensions. She has published *From Chronicle to Canon: The Hermeneutics of the Spring and Autumn Annals according to Tung Chung-shu* (Cambridge University Press, 1996) and a number of articles on Chinese intellectual history. She received her M.A. and Ph.D. from Harvard University and her B.A. from Wellesley College.

HENRY ROSEMONT, JR., is George B. and Willma Reeves Distinguished Professor of the Liberal Arts at St. Mary's College of Maryland, and Senior Consulting Professor at Fudan University in Shanghai. He has written *A Chinese Mirror* and the forthcoming *A Confucian Alternative* and has edited and/or translated seven other works, the most recent of which, with Roger T. Ames, is *The Analects of Confucius: A Philosophical Translation*.

BENJAMIN I. SCHWARTZ was the Leroy B. Williams Professor of History and Political Science, Harvard University. He authored numerous books, including *The World of Thought in Ancient China* (Harvard University Press, 1985) and *China and Other Matters* (Harvard University Press, 1996).

DEBORAH SOMMER is currently Associate Professor in the Department of Religion at Gettysburg College. She received her Ph.D. from Columbia University. Her areas of research include the religious aspects of the literati tradition, especially sacrifice and ritual and the use of images in ritual contexts. She is the editor of *Chinese Religion: An Anthology of Sources* (Oxford, 1995) and is currently working on a book on the religious significance of the iconography of Confucius.

TU WEIMING is Professor of Chinese History and Philosophy and of Confucian Studies at Harvard. He is also the director of the Harvard-Yenching Institute. He is the author of *Neo-Confucian Thought in Action: Wang Yang-ming's Youth* (1976), *Centrality and Commonality: An Essay on Confucian Religiousness* (1989), *Confucian Thought: Selfhood as Creative Transformation* (1985), *Way, Learning, and Politics: Essays on the Confucian Intellectual* (1993), and the editor of *The Living Tree: The Changing Meaning of Being Chinese Today* (1994), *China in Transformation* (1994), and *Confucian Traditions in East Asian Modernity* (1996).

MARY EVELYN TUCKER is Professor of Religion at Bucknell University, where she teaches courses in world religions, Asian religions, and religion and ecology. She received her Ph.D. from Columbia University in the history of religions, specializing in Confucianism in Japan. She has published *Moral and Spiritual Cultivation in Japanese Neo-Confucianism* (State University of New York Press, 1989). She co-edited *Worldviews and Ecology* (Orbis Books, 1994), *Buddhism and Ecology* (Harvard University Press, 1997), *Confucianism and Ecology* (Harvard University Press, 1998), and *Hinduism and Ecology* (Harvard University Press, 2000). She and her husband, John Grim, have directed the series of ten conferences on religions of the world and ecology at the Harvard University Center for the Study of World Religions from 1996–1998. They are also editors of the book series from these conferences.

LEE H. YEARLEY is the Walter Y. Evans-Wenz Professor of Oriental Philosophies, Religions, and Ethics in the Department of Religious Studies at Stanford University. A graduate of Haverford College, he received his Ph.D. from the University of Chicago. He is the author of *Mencius and Aquinas: Theories of Virtues and Conceptions of Courage* (1990), and many other works in comparative religious ethics and in both Western and Chinese religious thought. In 1992, he was awarded the Peter S. Bing Teaching Award for Excellence in Undergraduate Education.

YÜ YING-SHIH is the Gordon Wu Professor of Chinese Studies and Professor of History of Princeton University. He received his B.A. from New Asia College, Hong Kong, and Ph.D. from Harvard University. He has taught at Harvard and Yale and served as President of New Asia College, the Chinese University of Hong Kong in 1973–75 while on leave from Harvard. Among his many publications are *Trade and Expansion in Han China*, *Intellectual Elite and Chinese Culture*, *Religious Ethnic and the Merchant Class in Early Modern China*, and *The Historical World of Zhu Xi*.

Photo Credits

THE EDITORS AND PUBLISHER thank the suppliers of the following photographs:

1. Image of Confucius, Mount Ni. Courtesy of Deborah Sommer.
2. Grave of Confucius, Qufu. Courtesy of Deborah Sommer.
3. Spirit tablet of Confucius, Confucian Temple, Zhanghua, Taiwan. Courtesy of Deborah Sommer.
4. Main hall of Confucian Temple, Beijing. Courtesy of Deborah Sommer.
5. Main hall of Confucian Temple, Ilan, Taiwan. Courtesy of Deborah Sommer.
6. Spirit tablets of local female worthies, Ilan Confucian Temple, Taiwan. Courtesy of Deborah Sommer.
7. Image of Confucius, Confucian academy, Ilan, Taiwan. Courtesy of Deborah Sommer.
8. Shrine to the *Great Learning*, Confucian Temple, Tainan, Taiwan. Courtesy of Deborah Sommer.
9. Offerings to Confucius, Confucian Temple, Jiali, Taiwan. Courtesy of Chu Ronguey.
10. Ritual presentation of food offerings, Confucian Temple, Jiali, Taiwan. Courtesy of Chu Ronguey.
11. Spirit tablets of famous literati, Confucian Temple, Tainan, Taiwan. Courtesy of Deborah Sommer.
12. Diagram illustrating proper construction of a spirit tablet. Collection Cheng Dexiang.
13. Offering the sacrificial eulogy, Confucian Temple, Tainan, Taiwan. Courtesy of Chu Ronguey.
14. Musical instruments for commemorative rites to Confucius, Confucian Temple, Seoul. Courtesy of Chu Ronguey.

15. Statue of Mencius, Qufu. Courtesy of Deborah Sommer.
16. Ancestral offerings, Cheng clan graveyard, Henan. Courtesy of Cheng Dexiang.
17. Sacrificial food offerings, Cheng clan graveyard. Courtesy of Cheng Dexiang.
18. Calling for the return of the soul of the deceased, border of Yichuan and Song counties, Henan. Courtesy of Cheng Dexiang.
19. Entrance to a Qing dynasty imperial tomb. Courtesy of Deborah Sommer.
20. Rites commemorating visiting scholars and relatives, Cheng family graveyard. Courtesy of Cheng Dexiang.
21. Ritual at a shrine in a local academy, central Korea. Courtesy of Cheng Dexiang.
22. Shrine to the Cheng brothers, Korea. Courtesy of Cheng Dexiang.
23. Hall of Prayer for Good Harvests, Temple of Heaven, Beijing. Courtesy of Deborah Sommer.
24. Mount Hua. Courtesy of Deborah Sommer.

Index

action
  intelligent guidance of, 148
  See also non-action
Adams, Robert M., 232n. 19
Adler, Felix, 166
Adler, Joseph, 35n. 106
affectivity
  in classical Confucian tradition, 96–112
age of decay, 64
Age of Yu and Shun, 54
Aidi, 331
Alexander, Jon, 217n. 1
Allan, Sarah, 30n. 41
Allinson, Robert E., 280n. 22
Ames, Roger, 26n. 2, 27n. 4, 28n. 6, 29nn. 21, 22, 31; 33n. 73, 35n. 96, 178n. 2, 194n. 7, 195n. 15, 251n. 23
amor fati, 176, 180n. 19
Analects (*Lunyu*), 19, 57, 186–92
  death and dying in, 220–32
  on friendship, 101–2
ancestor worship, 204, 210–12
  See also sacrifice(s)
ancestral spirit
  transformation into, at death, 205
  See also spirits
Arendt, Hannah, 79, 80n. 19
asceticism, 86–87, 147–48
Augustinus Niphus, 281n. 37
Austin, J. L., 273, 283n. 55
authenticity. *See cheng*
Axial Age/Axial Period, 3, 66
  communication with Heaven in, 73

Axial breakthrough, 66–68
  directed against shamanistic component of ritual system, 71
  and individualism, 70
  and ritual breakdown, 68
  as spiritual revolt, 70

bao (response), 4
beauty (*mei*), 258
Becker, Ernest, 230n. 2
Beginnings, Four, 30n. 40, 288, 290
belief, 148
Bell, Daniel, 32n. 61
ben (foundation), 259, 335
Berkeley, George, 267, 281n. 37
Berling, Judith, 30n. 34
Berry, Thomas, 19, 35n. 101
Berthrong, John, 28n. 9, 29nn. 21, 31; 30nn. 35, 38; 33n. 76, 35n. 103, 135
bian (encompassing) sacrifice, 204
  See also sacrifice(s)
Bloom, Irene, 31n. 53, 148, 151
Bodde, Derk, 79n. 3
Boethius, 54n. 2
Bol, Peter K., 32n. 63, 35n. 106
Bo Niu
  death of, 222–23, 224, 229
Boodberg, Peter, 187
Book of Changes (*Yijing*), 6, 44, 45, 88, 97, 114, 198, 333n. 2
  as divination handbook, 200
  on friendship, 101–2

Great Appendix of, 8, 45, 282n. 43
  on *shen*, 268
Book of Documents (*Shujing*), 8, 73, 88, 92, 125, 236, 243, 333n. 2
Book of History (*Shangshi*), 44–45, 97, 98, 198
  central moments of, 99
Book of Poetry (*Shijing*), 8, 92, 99, 125, 126, 186, 198, 297, 333n. 2
  on friendship, 102–3
  Heaven in, 203
  shi in, 187
Book of Ritual (*Liji*), 8, 44, 45, 97, 110, 184, 198, 204, 253, 278n. 5, 291, 333n. 2
  concern with ethical justification in, 254
  on serving parents, 107
  ten normal of, 201
  on triad of Heaven, earth, and humans, 98–99
  See also li; sacrifice(s)
boundary situations, 273
Bo Yi, 223
Brashier, K. E., 217n. 8
brilliant virtues (*mingde*), 73
  as precondition for *tian-ming*, 74
  See also virtues
Brooks, Bruce E., 230n. 3
Brooks, Taeko A., 195n. 10, 230n. 3
Buddhism
  Chan, 77
  Chinese, 124

371

Buddhism (*cont.*)
  and Confucianism, 7
  Four Noble Truths of, 145
  introducing deities to China,
    76
  view of change in, 11
Burke, Edmund, 43

Cairns, H., 194n. 4
cai (capacities), 257
can tianti
  forming a triad with Heaven
    and earth, 263, 264, 267,
    270, 276, 278
  See also Heaven
Chaffee, John, 33n. 70, 34n. 79
Chan, Wing-tsit, 30n. 43, 31n.
  44, 35n. 97, 95nn. 13, 16;
  194n. 3, 280n. 18, 281n.
  42, 283nn. 48, 54
Chang, Carsun, 33n. 75
Chang, K. C., 79n. 3
change
  Buddhist view of, 11
  Neo-Confucian view of, 11
  as source of transformation,
    11
  and suffering, 11
Chaos (Hundun), 65
  death of, 65
Chen Daqi, 279n. 14, 280nn. 22,
  26
Chen Duxiu, 16
cheng (co-creativity), 167–69,
  176, 264–65
  as righteousness, 177–78
  and *zhongyong*, 169
  as religiousness, 177–78
cheng (sincerity), 47, 269, 270,
  280n. 18, 307, 335
  and *li*, 259–60
  as pristine source of divin-
    ity), 113
  as root source of all beings,
    131
  of rulers, 203
Cheng Chung-ying, 29n. 21
Chengdi, 327, 330, 331
Cheng Hao, 263, 277
  inscription of, 93
Cheng Yi, 231n. 12
chengyi, 280n. 18?
Chen Hsi-yuan, 32n. 65

Chen Kuying, 132n. 2
chi (terrestrial powers), 202
China
  Confucianism in, 13–17
  Cultural Revolution of, 33n.
    73
  human rights in, 32n. 61
  May Fourth movement of
    1919, 13
  New Culture movement of,
    13, 16–17
  repudiation of Confucian-
    ism in, 13
  schools of philosophy in, 65
Chinese tradition
  absence of theology in, 76
  individualism and holism in,
    39–55
Ching, Julia, 29n. 21, 30n. 41,
  31nn. 44, 45; 33n. 68,
  194n. 5
Chin Yueh-lin, 63
Chong Yu, 250n. 13
chu (host), 270, 271
Chung-ying Cheng, 133n. 3
Clarke, J. J., 33n. 68
*Classic of Changes. See Book of
  Changes*
*Classic of Documents. See Book of
  Documents*, 236, 243
Classic of Filial Piety (*Xiaojing*),
  48, 105, 106
co-creativity. *See cheng*
Collcutt, Martin, 31n. 53
community
  of earth, 99–101
  of family, 105–7
  of friendship, 101–5
  of Heaven, earth, and
    humanity, 98–99
  individual person as, 107–9
Confucianism
  and aesthetic arts, 21
  and Buddhism, 7
  in China, 13–17
  and civil service examina-
    tions, 10, 15, 19
  classical, 7–10, 100–101
    atheistic religiousness of,
      165–78
    as religion, 165
  and communitarian ethics,
    3–4, 20

  cosmological orientation of,
    3, 4, 20, 23–24
  and microcosm and
    macrocosm, 4
  and Daoism, 7
  divinity without theology
    in, 129
  early, 197–216
  economic, 19–20
  educational, 19
  elite, 18
  ethics and, 56–61
  Four Books of, 10, 19
  Han, 6, 8 (*see also* Han
    dynasty)
  and immanence, 1
  imperial, 7, 17
  influence of, 8
  in Japan, 6, 7, 12, 30n. 33 (*see
    also* Japan)
  kinds of, 17–20
  in Korea, 7, 12 (*see also*
    Korea)
  mass, 18
  merchant-house, 18
  and Neo-Confucianism, 8
  as philosophical system, 18
  political and social aspects
    of, 18–19
  reform, 17–18
  and religion, 2, 34n. 89
  religious dimensions of,
    14–15, 18, 20–21
  repudiation of, in China, 12
  ritual dimensions of, 21 (*see
    also li;* sacrifice[s])
  self-cultivation in, 6, 27n. 4
  self-transformational dimen-
    sions, 21, 27n. 4
  and Shinto, 7, 30n. 33
  six periods of, 30n. 35
  social, 19
  spiritual dimensions of,
    21–23 (*see also* spirituality,
    Confucian)
  and theism, 2
  and Zen monasteries, 12
Confucian Canon, 315
Confucian spirituality. *See* spirituality, Confucian
Confucius (Kongzi), 8, 13, 65
  Analects of, 6, 8, 19, 46 (*see
    also Analects*)

Confucius (*cont.*)
  on death and the dead,
    221–32, 274
  ethics of, 57
  life of, 49
  on ghosts and spirits, 204–5,
    230nn. 4, 5; 273, 274
  on Heaven, 273–74
  on manifestation of spirits,
    206
  and Mencius, 235
  on mourning for three
    years, 95n. 11
  presacrificial vigils of, 211
  reinterpretation of ritual
    practice, 71
  on ritual, 149
  self-affirming righteousness
    of, 178
  significance of, 108
  spirituality of, 82–83
  as teacher of disciples, 83
  on *zhi* (wisdom), 273–74
  and Zhou tradition, 274 (*see*
    also Zhou dynasty)
contractarianism, 302n. 8
Cosmic Person
  metaphor of, 46
cosmology
  and cultivation, 24–25
  organismic, 23–24
  in Zhou period, 201–2
cosmos
  as macrophase of humans,
    97
  ordering of, 29n. 29
courage
  and *qi*, 147
creatio ex nihilo, 167
creativity
  versus power, 166–68
Creel, Herrlee, 15, 33n. 69
Cua, Antonio S., 29n. 21,
    278nn. 3, 4; 279nn. 5,
    12–14; 280nn. 15, 17–22,
    24, 27, 29, 30; 281nn. 33,
    36, 40; 282n. 43; 283nn.
    46, 47, 50, 56, 63
cui (purity), 265

da (to break through), 179n. 10
Dai Zhen, 302n. 6

Dao/*dao* (the Way), 43, 51, 59,
    79, 114, 176, 193, 294
  dialectic in, 53
  ethical duty to, 224
  explanation of, 120–21
  functions of, 124
  Heaven as, 73
  preexistence of, 121
  primeval oneness of, 65
  sacrificing one's life for, 223
  as self-transformation, 121
  as symbol of transcendental
    world, 67
  taiji and, 114, 117–19 (*see*
    also taiji)
  as tenuous and indistinct,
    211
  as void or empty, 122
  wholeness of, 65
  and *wu* and *you*, 124
  See also Daoism
Daodejing, 69, 123, 300
  process of "fall," in, 69
  theory of reality in, 119–24
Daoism
  and Confucianism, 7
  depersonalization of *tian* in,
    126
  divinity without theology
    in, 129
  transcendence of, 69
  two worlds of, 67, 69
  view of reality in, 113,
    123–24
daijiao (Daoism), 172
daoquan, 282n. 43
daotong weiyi (interpenetrating
    power of oneness), 121
Daoist School of Laozi, 114–15
da ren (great persons), 186
Daxue. See Great Learning
de (Lord on High), 125
  and *tian*, 125–26
de (virtue), 4, 70, 335
  change toward inwardness,
    74–75
  of rulers, 203
  as written character, 75, 80n.
    12
  See also brilliant virtues
death
  in *Analects*, 220–32
  life after, 221

  See also li; mourning prac-
    tices; ritual
de Bary, Wm. Theodore, 27n.
    6, 29nn. 21, 22, 25, 26, 27,
    31; 31nn. 48, 49, 53, 56;
    32nn. 57, 60, 66; 33nn. 73,
    75; 34nn. 79, 80; 55n. 14
deities
  venerable celestial (*tianzun*),
    76
Dewey, John, 33n. 73, 165, 166,
    178n. 1
dhyāna (meditation), 89
Di (Lord or high god), 199, 202
diminution, language of, 86–87
Disheng Li, 279n. 5
Di Taiwu, 319
divination, 199, 200
  associated with moral
    behavior, 200
divinity (*shen*), 113
  cheng as pristine source of,
    113
  classical Chinese views of,
    113–33
  meaning of, in Chinese phi-
    losophy, 126–27
  without theology, 124–28
  See also Confucianism
Di Wuding, 320
Di Wuyi, 320
Doctrine of the Mean
    (*Zhongyong*), 45, 67, 97,
    128–32, 165, 306, 338
  on *cheng*, 169
  on divination, 200–201
  on education, 171
  on harmony, 175
  as one of Four Books, 177
  on *qing*, 176
  as record of Han court
    debate, 180n. 22
  on *ren*, 107, 110
  on triad of *tian,* earth, and
    humanity, 270
Dong Zhongshu, 35n. 98, 46,
    62, 97
  Gongyang Commentary of,
    304
  on Heaven, 314
  on Mandate of Heaven,
    307–13
  on *ren*, 98

Dong Zhongshu (*cont.*)
   spirituality of, 304–17
Dore, Ronald, 34n. 82
Dubs, Homer H., 94n. 4, 253,
   278n. 2, 281n. 41
   on *li*, 254
Du Fu
   on friendship, 103
   as model of goodness, 104
Durkheim, Emile, 22

earth (*di*), 202, 203
   creativity of, 6
   as panhuman community,
   99–101
   triad of, 3, 98–99
   vitalism of, 25–26
   See also Heaven
Ebrey, Patricia, 34n. 88
education, 170–71
   process and content of,
   172–74
   and perfecting human
   nature, 313–15
Eight Trigrams (*bagua*), 114,
   117
Ekken, Kaibara, 12
Eliade, Mircea, 212, 217n. 13
Elman, Benjamin, 32n. 63
empire
   root of, in state, 107
enlightenment, 92
Eno, Robert, 35n. 107, 250nn.
   5, 16
equilibrium, psychic
   doctrine of, 84–85
ethics
   in Chinese high cultural
   thought, 56–61
   communitarian, 3–4, 7, 20,
   23–24
   Confucian
   reciprocity and, 4
Euthyphro problem, 287–88

family
   as center of Confucian religious experience, 178n. 7
   as community, 105–7
   as governing metaphor,
   171–72
   root of, in person, 107
   root of state in, 107

fan (reversion), 123, 124
fear
   overcoming, 140, 147
fen (social or class distinction),
   256
Feng Youlan (Fung Yu-lan), 63,
   79n. 2, 81, 94nn. 1, 2
fiduciary community, 4
filial piety. *See xiao*
Fingarette, Herbert, 180n. 16,
   195n. 18, 259, 283n. 57,
   302n. 8
   on *li*, 275
First Emperor, 322–24, 326, 331
Fisher, Galen, 55n. 15
Five Peaks, 323
Five Sacrificials, 207
Four Beginnings, 30n. 40, 288,
   290
Four Books, 19, 153
   Zhongyong as one of, 177
Four Forms (*shixiang*), 114, 117
Four Noble Truths, 145
Freud, Sigmund, 230n. 1
friendship
   as human community,
   101–5
fu (return), 123
Fu Hao, 198–99
   tomb of, 200
Fung Yu-lan. *See* Feng Youlan
Fu Sinian, 80n. 13

gao (sacrificial announcements),
   215
Gao Panlong
   on mysticism, 92
Gaozi, 246
Gaozong, King, 86
Gardner, Daniel, 153
Gauthier, David, 302n. 8
Geertz, Clifford, 35n. 92
   on religion as a cultural sys-
   tem, 22–23
Giles, Lionel, 259
Girardot, Norman J., 32n. 67
Golden Rule, 280n. 22
Goldin, Paul Rakita, 30n. 42,
   302n. 1, 303n. 14
gong (respectfulness), 335
   and *li*, 260
Gongsun Chou, 246
Gongsun Qing, 324–25

Gongyang Commentary
   Confucius in, 305
Graham, A. C., 175, 180nn. 15,
   18; 270, 281n. 43, 282n.
   43, 302n. 4
Great Learning (*Daxue*), 10, 19,
   45–46, 97, 107, 180n. 15,
   259
   tree metaphor in, 52
Great Tao. *See* Tao
growth, language of, 87
guantong, 255, 277
gui (ghost), 127, 202
   relationship to spirit, cloud
   and material souls, vital
   energy, and refined
   essence, 204–5
Guodian
   Confucian texts from, 75
   zisizi documents discovered
   at, 175
Gu Yong, 331

Halder, Alois, 55n. 2
Hall, David, 26n. 2, 27n. 4, 28n.
   6, 29nn. 21, 31; 33n. 73,
   35n. 96, 166–67, 178nn. 2,
   3; 195n. 15
Hamilton, E., 194n. 4
Hampshire, Stuart, 157n. 2
Han dynasty, 8, 62
   Confucianism, 6, 8, 35n. 93
   ritual reforms of, 326–31
   sacrificial system of, 318,
   323, 324
Han Fei, 297–99, 302n. 1, 303n.
   11
Han Fei Tzu, 7
Han Gaozu, 323, 324
Han Wudi, 318, 319, 330, 331,
   321, 323–27
Hardacre, Helen, 30n. 33
harmony
   emotional, doctrine of,
   84–85
   See also he
Hawkes, David, 217n. 9
he (harmony), 131, 132, 165,
   170, 336
   See also harmony
heart. *See xin*
Heaven (*tian*), 34n. 89, 43, 59,
   176, 294, 337

Heaven (*cont.*)
  in classical Confucianism, 1
  in Confucius, 273–74
  creativity of, 6
  depersonalization of, 126
  and *dao,* 125
  and *de,* 125–26
  early Confucian attitudes to, 203
  and earth
    and humanity, 252
    myth of separation of, 64, 69
  and human reality, 59
  identified with Lord on High, 202
  interaction with humans, 62, 63
  king having access to, 64
  and humans
    unity of (*tianrenheyi*), 62, 63, 65, 70, 174, 263, 315
    and communication between Heaven and humans, 70–73
    inward transcendence and, 69
    as spiritual ideal, 315–16
    and *tianming,* 73–74
  in the *Mencius,* 236–45
  as most powerful numina for Zhou, 202–3
  as plurisign, 281n. 32
  as Providence, 98
  reinterpretation of, 75
  and *ren,* 264
  as social environment, 180n. 23
  spirit realm located in, 201–2
  triad of, 3
  in Zhou period, 202–3
  See also earth; Heavenly Mandate; Heavenly principle; Supreme Ultimate
Heavenly Mandate (*tianming*), 49, 70, 238–39, 294–95, 337
  change toward inwardness, 74–75
  conferred on individuals, 70
  origin of term, 73
  and *tianrenheyi,* 73–74

Heavenly principle (*tianli*), 63, 84, 337
  ren as equivalent of, 87, 98
Hegel, G. W. F., 77, 80n. 17, 228–29
Heguanzi, 300
Henderson, John, 28n. 12, 35n. 107
Heraclitus, 43, 50
hexagram, 123
He Yan, 63
  commentary, 231n. 10
Hobbes, Thomas, 42, 55n. 3, 283n. 52, 292
  covenant theory of, 44
  doctrine of universal antagonism of human beings, 44
  on language, 272
holism
  in Chinese tradition, 39–55
Hsu Cho-yun, 217 n. 6
Hsun Tzu. *See* Xunzi
hua (transformation), 301, 336
Huangdi (emperor), 300, 321, 325–26, 330
Huang-Lao (philosophical school), 300, 302n. 1, 303n. 17
Huang Tsung-hsi. *See* Huang Zongxi
Huang Zongxi, 86–87, 94–95n. 8
Hui, King, 234, 235
Huineng, 77
human desires (*renyü*), 63, 336
humaneness. *See* ren
human nature. *See* xing
human person(s)
  becoming spirits after death, 202
  and communitarian ethics, 4
  as community, 107–9
  cultural and political order resting on, 107
  and immortality, 273
  individual
    role of, 97–98
  levels of existence of, 127
  as microphase of cosmos, 97–98
  as mixture of pure and gross *qi,* 71–72
  moral transformation of, 4

  mortality of, 273
  numinous aspects of, 202
  relationships of, 185
  roles of, 186
  root of family in, 107
  triad of humans, Heaven, and earth, 3, 98–99
Hume, David, 261, 280n. 23, 281n. 32
humility, 260
hun (cloud "soul"), 237
  as numinous aspect of human being, 202
  relationship to spirit, ghost, material soul, vital energy, and refined essence, 204–5
Hu Shi, 15–16, 34n. 89, 279nn. 8, 10
  on *li,* 254
Hutton, Eric, 30n. 42
Huxley, Thomas, 42–43

ideology
  as oppressive force, 14
individualism
  and Axial breakthrough, 70
  in Chinese tradition, 43–55
  sources of, in Western civilization, 40–43
immanence, 1, 2
immortality, 273
imperialism, Western
  impact of, on China, 16
integrity, 168
International Confucian Society, 8
Irwin, Terence, 157n. 5
Ivanhoe, P. J., 4, 5, 28nn. 6, 15, 18, 20; 29nn. 21, 22; 30n. 42, 31n. 48, 195n. 11, 250nn. 4, 14; 302n. 6

James, William, 139, 155, 157n. 6, 160n. 28, 194n. 6, 206, 267
Japan
  Confucianism in, 6, 12, 19, 30n. 33
  Shinto in, 7
  Tokugawa period in, 6
Jaspers, Karl, 28n. 8, 66, 80n. 5
  and Axial Age, 3

Jaspers, Karl (*cont.*)
    and concept of "break-
        through," 66, 70
Jensen, Lionel, 32n. 63
ji (powers of growing crops),
    203, 336
Ji Lu, 225
jiao (education or teaching),
    172, 181n. 28, 336
jing (reverence), 47–48, 88, 143,
    149, 336
    essence of life, 127
    and *li,* 260
    as numinous aspect of
        human being, 202
    relationship to spirit, ghost,
        cloud and material souls,
        and vital energy, 204–5
Joachim, Harold H., 283n. 45
Job
    suffering of, 243–44
Joken Kato, 279nn. 7, 8
junzi (noble person), 4, 8, 11,
    129, 165, 171, 174, 257,
    296, 336
    attainment of moral
        integrity by, 272
    contrasted with petty per-
        son (*xiaoren*), 174
    functioning as name,
        186–88, 190–93
    relation to *sheng,* 191
    relation to *shi,* 191
    role of, in ethical education,
        262
    shift from political to moral
        designation, 108

Kang Youwei, 15, 32n. 65
Kant, Immanuel, 194n. 5
Karlgren, Bernhard, 55n. 4,
    179n. 14, 194n. 3
Keightley, David, 5, 29n. 23,
    217n. 3
Kierkegaard, Søren, 227–28
Kim Kyong-Dong, 18, 33n. 78,
    34n. 82
king
    character designating, 308
    See also Kingly Way; ruler
Kingly Way, 307–12
    See also ruler
Kline, T. C., 30n. 42

Knoblock, John, 270, 279n. 5,
    281nn. 41, 43; 282n. 43
knowledge
    extension of, 90–91
    as understanding heart, 97
Kongzi. *See* Confucius
Korea
    civil service exam in, 19
    Confucianism in, 12, 19,
        31n. 51
    Koryo dynasty of, 12, 19
    shamanism in, 7
    Yi dynasty of, 12, 19
Koryo dynasty, 12
Kuang Heng, 327, 328, 332–33
Kuan Shu, 325

Lao Tzu, 264
Laozi, 65, 67, 122, 300
    on *dao,* 119
    Daodejing, 119, 123
    Daoist School of, 114
Lau, D. C., 70, 75–76, 195n. 13,
    249n. 1, 250n. 4
LeBlanc, Charles, 28n. 12
Leclerq, Jacques, 88–89
Legalism, 60, 155, 295, 299
Legalists, 7, 282n. 43
    view of individual of, 43
Legge, James, 15, 158n. 16,
    159n. 17, 176–77, 180nn.
    15, 21; 194n. 3, 225, 253,
    278n. 5
Levenson, Joseph, 194n. 5
li (civility; rituals), 8–9, 30n. 38,
    68, 124, 138, 166, 171,
    181n. 28, 192, 336
    analyses of, 252–59
    cheng and, 260
    communicative function of,
        71
    delimiting function of, 256
    earliest use of, 254
    educational and nourishing
        function of, 257
    ennobling function of,
        258–59
    ethical and religious dimen-
        sions of, 254–86
    etymology of, 254, 273
    foundation of, 259–64
    gong and, 260

    and growth and extension,
        174–75
    and human mortality, 273
    as innate tendency, 250n. 5
    and *jing,* 260
    meaning of, 82–83, 172–74
    as medium of religious
        expression for Confucius,
        180n. 16
    of mourning and sacrifice,
        275
    as one of Four Beginnings,
        288
    origin of, 68–69
    and reality, 133n. 5
    relationship to *qi,* 12
    religious dimension of,
        273–76
    and *ren,* 68, 260, 262
    scope and evolution of,
        253–55
    significance of, 255–59
    supportive function of,
        256–58
    three layers of, 279n. 14
    as virtue, 144–45
    and *yi,* 254–55, 260
li (profit), 234
li (wraiths), 202, 205
li* (reason), 254, 275, 279n. 12
Liang Shuming, 17
liangzhi (innate knowledge), 78,
    336
Liji. See Book of Rituals
Li Ling, 334n. 7
Linduff, Katheryn M., 217n. 6
Lin Yu-sheng, 33n. 73
liquan, 282n. 43
Li Si, 297, 302n. 11
Liu Shu-hsien, 26n. 2, 27n. 3,
    29n. 21
Liu Xiang, 330, 331
Liu Zhiji, 62
liyi (meaning of rites), 69
    See also li
Li Xueqin, 217n. 6
long
    and *li,* 280n. 25
Loewe, Michael, 333n. 1
Lufrano, Richard, 33n. 75
Lu Jiuyuan, 91
Lu Xun, 33n. 73
Lu Zuxian, 10

Machle, Edward, 28n. 19, 30n. 42, 270, 271, 280n. 31, 281nn. 34, 38, 43; 282nn. 43, 44
Mao Chang, 297
Mao Heng, 297
Maspero, Henri, 180n. 15
Mawangdui
    zisizi documents discovered at, 175
May Fourth movement of 1919, 13, 33n. 73, 194n. 5
Mazzotta, Giuseppe, 158n. 16
Mean (*Zhongyong*), 10, 19, 45
    profound person of, 44
    See also Doctrine of the Mean
meat
    as votive offering, 207–8
meditation (*jingzuo*), 89–90
Meiji Restoration, 12, 19
Mencius/*The Mencius*, 6, 8, 9, 19, 46, 159n. 17, 198
    concept of *haoran zhi qi* (floodlike *qi*), 72, 73
    confidence and doubt in, 234–36
    and Confucius, 235
    controversy with Xunzi, 142
    on the divine, 129
    on goodness of human nature, 104
    Heaven in, 236–45
    on human suffering, 103
    on ideal society, 101
    idea of benevolent government, 74
    on knowledge, 92
    on Learning of the Mind and Heart, 77
    on the mean, 261
    parable of child and well, 288
    practicality and spirituality in, 233–51
    on *qi*, 246–47
    sagehood and, 235–36
    self-transcendence in, 247–48
    this-worldliness in, 236–38
    and "unmoved heart and mind," 231n. 7
    on *xing*, 288–89

Merton, Robert, 280n. 16
Metzger, Thomas, 32n. 57
ming, 181nn. 24, 25, 28, 336
ming (decree; destiny), 238, 242
    as "insight," 270, 336
ming (visible realm), 201
mingde. See brilliant virtues
Ming Gao, 279n. 6
Ming period, 7
Miu Ji, 324
moderation, 147–48
modesty, 261
Mo Di, 65
Mohism, 60, 155
Mohists, 282n. 43
morality
    roots of, 288
mortality
    of human beings, 273
mourning practices, 214, 222–23, 231n. 9
    and boundary situations, 273
    See also death; ritual; sacrifice(s)
Mou Zongsan, 17, 29n. 21
Mozi, 69, 281n. 33
Muller, Max, 55n. 2
mysticism, 91–93

Nakae Toju, 48
Nan Huaijin, 281n. 39
nature
    organismic order of, 59
Needham, Joseph, 35n. 94
neizhi, 80n. 12
Neo-Confucianism, 8, 10
    contributions of, to Confucian spirituality, 85–87
    schools of, 15
    of Song-Ming, 63, 124
    and spiritual practice, 11
    view of change in, 11
Neo-Daoistic philosophy, 63, 124
Neville, Robert, 28n. 19, 29n. 31, 32n. 59, 34n. 83, 135, 150
New Culture movement, 13, 16–17, 30n. 39
    See also China
Ngo Va Xuyet, 334n. 6

Nietzsche, Friedrich, 176, 180n. 20
Nine Tripods
    as ritual symbol, 74
Nishitani, Ken, 178n. 4, 180nn. 19, 20
noble person. *See junzi*
non-action (*wuwei*), 58
north
    darkness and obscurity associated with, 201
Nussbaum, Martha, 158n. 9

Ogden, Schubert M., 159n. 24
Onozawa Seiichi, 70, 80n. 11
ontocosmology, 114, 117, 120, 125
optimism
    Confucian, 145
Otto, Rudolf, 22, 212, 217n. 12
Owen, Stephen, 167, 178n. 5
Oxtoby, Willard, 33n. 68

Pang Pu
    on education, 181n. 28
    on *tian*, 180n. 23
Parsons, Talcott, 80n. 7
particularism, 186
Peerenboom, R. P., 303n. 17
Pelikan, Jaroslav, 76–77, 80n. 16
personator
    in funerary rites, 213
pi (obsession), 141
po (material "soul"), 202, 237
    relationship to spirit, ghost, cloud soul, vital energy, and refined essence, 204–5
Potter, Charles Francis, 166
power
    creativity versus, 166–68
practicality
    in the *Mencius*, 233–51
    religious, 238–45
pre-Axial period
    communication between Heaven and king in, 71
    ritual tradition of, 72
presacrificial vigils, 212
psyche
    Hellenic concept of, 41, 49
pu (method of divination), 132n. 1

Puett, Michael, 334nn. 3, 5
Pusey, James, 31n. 55, 32n. 65,
    33n. 73

quan (integrity), 265
qi (material force or vital
    energy), 4, 25, 124, 127,
    138, 336
  cosmology of, 71–72
  and courage, 147
  gross, 71–72
  in the Mencius, 246–47
  as numinous aspect of
    human being, 202
  of person and of cosmos, 11
  pure, 71–71
  and reality, 133n. 5
  relationship to li, 12
  relationship to spirit, ghost,
    cloud and material souls,
    and refined essence, 204–5
qi (prayers), 215
Qian Mu, 262–63, 280n. 28
qin, 105, 336
Qin dynasty, 305, 320–21
  sacrificial system of, 321–22,
    324
qing, 175–76, 336
Qing dynasty, 7, 304
qiongli (pursuit of principle), 90
Queen, Sarah, 35n. 107, 317n.
    10

Radcliffe-Brown, A. R., 283n.
    58
reality
  classical Chinese views of,
    113–33
  Daoist view of, 113, 119–24
  depersonalized, 126
  as inexhaustible origination,
    115
  as multi-interactive har-
    mony, 116–17
  as organismic totality,
    118–19
  as polar-generative process,
    115–16
  as recursive but limitless
    regenerativity, 117–18
  as virtual hierarchization,
    117
  Yijing view of, 113

Yizhuan approach to, 119,
    120, 123–24
reciprocity
  as key to Confucian ethics, 4
Reese, Curtis W., 166
relations
  five, 8, 28n. 13
religion
  Confucianism as, 2
religiousness, Confucian
  entailing transformation,
    165
  li-centered, 165
ren (authoritativeness), 189
ren (humaneness), 8–9, 47, 103,
    106, 158–59n. 16, 165,
    234, 270
  communicative power of, 71
  defined by Confucius, 86
  dependence of ethical signifi-
    cance of li on, 253
  and divinity, 131
  as equivalent of Heavenly
    principle, 87, 98
  as greatest of virtues, 107
  and li, 260, 262
  and love of others, 281n. 35
  and New Confucianism, 17,
    87
  as one of Four Beginnings,
    288
  as process of spiritual
    growth, 87
  qualities of, 108, 110
  as source of fecundity and
    growth, 11
  as spiritual kernel of li, 68,
    71
  and tian, 264
  as utopian, 111
  viewing life in terms of, 275
ren ren (authoritative persons),
    186
renyü. See human desires
response. See bao
return. See fu
reverence. See jing
reversion. See fan
Richard of St. Victor, 55n. 2
Richards, I. A., 302n. 2
Riegel, Jeffrey, 180nn. 15, 22;
    181nn. 23, 26

righteousness
  co-creativity as, 177–78
  See also yi
Rites of Zhou (Zhouli), 198, 214,
    253
ritual, 7, 20, 149–50
  functionaries of, 214
  funerary rites, 213 (see also
    death; mourning prac-
    tices)
  and human emotion, 5
  inconsequential, 135
  music (yue) serving function
    of, 84
  and sacrifice, 197–216
  and thresholds, 149
  vigils of purification, 210–11
  See also li; sacrifice(s)
rituals of origin, 158n. 15
Rosemont, Henry, 172
Ross, W. D., 283n. 60
Roth, Harold D., 303n. 18
Royce, Josiah, 232n. 20
Rozman, Gilbert, 17, 18
Ru (Confucian), 333n. 2, 337
ru (scholar), 133n. 4, 198, 234,
    337
Rubinger, Richard, 29n. 24
rujiao (Confucianism), 172,
    179n. 11
ruler, 298
  authority of, legitimized by
    Heaven, 304
  and Heaven, 308
  political power of, 129
  role of, 99–101
  sage-king as, 307
  See also king; Kingly Way
rushen, 269, 270, 281n. 41
Ryle, Gilbert, 281n. 32

sacrifice(s)
  to ancestral spirits, 210–12
  Encompassing (bian), 204
  feng, 319, 325
  of humans, 208
  offered by emperor, 318
  presacrificial vigils, 212
  and ritual, 197–216
  shan, 319, 325
  of Shun, 319
sage (sheng), 11, 21, 28n. 18, 131,
    191–93, 257, 306, 337

sage (*cont.*)
   as archetypal personality, 43–44
   relation of, to *junzi*, 191
sage (*shengren*), 165, 186–87, 191–93, 270, 288, 337
sagehood
   and Mencius, 235–36
   quest for, 91
      as heart of Confucianism, 93
sage-kings, 59, 290, 293–95, 298, 319, 327, 328
sageliness (*sheng*), 129, 186
Schleiermacher, Friedrich, 165
School of Mind (*xin-xue*), 15
School of Names (Mingjia), 263
School of Principle (*li-xue*), 15
Schuessler, Axel, 194n. 3
Schwarz, Benjamin I., 66, 80nn. 6, 8, 137, 259
science
   and individualism, 51
seeds, four, 30n. 40
self-cultivation, 6–7
   ritual and, 10
   See also Confucianism; *li*
self-denial, 86–87
self-reflection
   as key to moral development, 301
self-transcendence
   in the *Mencius*, 247–48
self-transformation (*zihua*), 1, 6–7, 20
   dao as, 121
Separation of Heaven and Earth
   myth of, 64, 69, 75
shamanism, 7
shamans. *See wu*-shamans
shame, 261–62, 280n. 24
shan (human excellence; good), 252, 261, 337
   as product of *wei* , 265
Shangdi (Lord on High), 34n. 89, 43, 82, 99
   Heaven identified with, 202
Shang dynasty, 64, 68, 99–100, 235
   sacrificial system of, 319–20
Shang people, 126
   early tradition of, 198–200
   spirituality of, 199–200

Shangshi. See Book of History
Shangshu, 319, 327
Shaoweng, 324
she (powers of the land)
   ritual offerings to, 203
shen (divinity), 113, 126, 165, 281n. 43
   as body, or physical reality of existence, 127
   definitions of, 180n. 17
   as "godlike," 270
   as numinous aspect of human being, 202
   (spirituality), 174
shen (spirits), 202
   categories of, 204
   characteristics of, 209
   as numinous aspect of human being, 204
   relationship to ghost, cloud and material souls, vital energy, and refined essence, 204–5
   Shang belief in, 199
   and *shenming*, 268–72, 277
   Zhou belief in, 200–216
   See also spirit world
Shen Dao, 293, 298, 302n. 9
   refutation of, by Xunzi, 295, 299
shendu (vigilance in solitude), 88, 180n. 15
sheng. See sage; sageliness
Shen Gong, 325
shengren. See sage
shenming, 282nn. 43, 44
   and *shen*, 268–72, 277
shen ren (good persons), 186
shensheng (divine and sagely), 129
Shi, 327
shi (scholar-apprentice), 167, 178n. 5, 186, 337
   functioning as name, 186–92
   relation to *junzi*, 191
shi (timeliness), 260
shifei (fact; value), 175
shih (scholar), 257, 337
Shijing. See Book of Poetry
Shinto
   and Confucianism, 7, 30n. 33
   See also Japan

Shotoku, Prince, 12, 19
shoulian (collecting together), 89
shu,
   embracing modesty and humility, 267, 337
   and Golden Rule, 280n. 22
shuai, meaning of, 181n. 25
Shujing. See Book of Documents
Shun (sage-king), 58, 100, 143–44, 250n. 7, 280n. 24, 322–24
   sacrificial system of, 319
Shun Kwong-loi, 280n. 24
Shu Qi, 223
Sima Qian, 62, 63, 179n. 11, 318
   History, 62
   Shiji, 318–26
Six Arts of Confucius, 315
Slote, Michael, 227–28, 232n. 17
Smith, Kidder, 35n. 106
Smith, Wilfred Cantwell, 22, 27n. 4, 34n. 89, 249, 251n. 25
social darwinism, 42–43, 50
society
   five relations of, 4
   ideal, 101
   ordering of, 29n. 29
Song dynasty, 304
Song-Ming Neo-Confucianism, 6, 63, 187, 270
soul
   material (*see po*)
Spencer, Herbert, 42–43
spirits. *See shen* (spirits)
spirituality
   Confucian, 81–94
      cosmological orientation of, 20
      development of, 83–84
      dimensions of, 3–5, 21–23
      earth-based aspects of, 203–5
      ethical dimensions of, 20–21
      explanation of, 2–3
      forms of, 20–21
      in the *Mencius*, 233–51
      modern applicability of, 152
      Neo-Confucian, 91

spirituality (*cont.*)
  Neo-Confucian contributions to, 85–87
  self-transformational dimensions of, 21
  virtues and, 134–62
  of Shang people, 199–200
  See also Confucianism: spiritual dimensions of
spiritual practice
  and realization of cosmological being, 11
spirit world
  communicating with, 204–16
  as other dimension, 202
  See also divination; *shen*
spontaneity. *See ziran*
Spring and Autumn Annals (*Chunqiu*), 8, 198, 305, 315, 333n. 2
state
  root of empire in, 107
Sterckx, Roel, 217n. 11
Streng, Frederick, 27n. 4
suffering
  and change, 11
  as preparation for refinement of intelligence, 243
Supreme Ultimate
  in Neo-Confucianism, 1
  See also Heaven; *taiji*

taiji (Supreme Ultimate), 43, 114, 123, 337
  and *dao*, 114, 117–19
  as root source of reality, 115
Taiping (era of Grand Peace), 305
Tang Chun-I, 29n. 21
Tang Junyi, 29n. 21, 277, 283n. 59
Tao. *See* Dao
Tao Qian
  on friendship, 102–3
Taylor, Charles, 79, 80n. 20
Taylor, Rodney, 28n. 18, 29n. 21, 34nn. 83, 87; 35n. 105, 305–7, 313, 316nn. 1, 7
technology
  and individualism, 51
Tetsuo Najita, 34n. 81

theism
  and Confucianism, 2
  See also Confucianism
theology
  absence of, in Chinese tradition, 76
  divinity without, 124–28
  origin of, in Western philosophy, 76
Thomas Aquinas, 54nn. 1, 2
Thompson, P. M., 302n. 9
Three Dynasties (Xia, Shang, Zhou), 64, 68
  ritual tradition and, 72
Three Kingdoms period, 12
thresholds, 149
ti (substance), 16
tian. See Heaven
tian (ancestral legacy), 172
tiandao (Way of Heaven), 126
tianli. See Heavenly principle
tianming. See Heavenly Mandate
tianrenheyi. See Heaven: and humans, unity of
tianren polarity, 62, 63
tian xia (all under Heaven), 57, 185
tianzun. See deities: venerable celestial
Tillich, Paul, 27n. 4
Tillman, Hoyt, 32n. 63
Tokugawa period, 6, 12
transcendence, 1, 2, 195n. 15
  Chinese, 66
  inward, 71–72
  See also self-transcendence
transcendent, the, 245, 250n. 8
transcendental values. *See* values: transcendental
tree, metaphor of, 46, 52
trigram, 123
Tucker, Mary Evelyn, 29n. 21, 31nn. 53, 54
Turbayne, Colin Murray, 283n. 53
Turner, Victor, 280n. 16
Tu Weiming, 26n. 2, 27nn. 5, 6; 28nn. 10, 14, 16; 29nn. 21, 28, 31; 30n. 35; 32n. 58, 34nn. 82, 84, 86; 35nn. 95, 99, 108; 181n. 23, 283n.

62, 303n. 17, 306, 307, 316n. 4
  on anthropocosmic vision, 278
  and cosmological orientation of Confucianism, 20, 23–24
  and self-transformation in Confucianism, 21
  and social Confucianism, 19
  and term "anthropocosmic," 4
Two Norms (*liangyi*), 114

values
  Asian, 183
  and *li*, 276
  transcendental, 245
Vandermeersch, Léon, 302n. 11
vigils
  presacrificial, 212
  of purification, 210–11
virtue, 134–62
virtues
  beautiful (*meide*), 258
  brilliant (*mingde*), 73–74
  character of, 136–39
  corrective, 140, 158n. 8
  four central, 30n. 40, 139–45, 147–50
  Neo-Confucian, 157n. 3
  ordinary versus religious, 145–50
  perfected, 149
  religious, in Confucianism, 145–46, 150–52
  significance of, 152–56
von Falkenhausen, Lothar, 217n. 14
votive offerings
  types of, 207–8

Waley, Arthur, 187, 254, 279n. 10
Walsh, Vivian Charles, 281n. 33
Wang Bi, 63
wang (Distant) sacrifices, 203
Wang Yangming, 8, 13, 80n. 18, 91, 97, 103, 263, 277, 279n. 12, 283n. 61
  on Learning of the Mind and Heart, 78

Wang Yangming (*cont.*)
  and School of Mind, 15
Warring States, period of, 129
Watson, Burton, 80nn. 4, 12;
    180n. 15, 232n. 16, 264,
    279n. 5, 281n. 41
Watts, Alan, 194n. 6
Weber, Max, 22, 32n. 57, 69,
    80n. 10, 237, 245, 251n.
    20
wei (the artificial), 265, 290
Wei-Jin Neo-Taoism, 63
wen (cultural refinement), 275,
    337
wen (form), 258, 266
Wen, Duke, 321
Wen, King, 99, 100, 103, 209,
    274
Western tradition
  individualism in, 40–43
Wheelwright, Philip, 281n. 32
Whitehead, Alfred North,
    178n. 5, 179n. 15
Wilhelm, Hellmut, 35n. 102
William of Ockham, 42, 44
  and doctrine of atomistic
    realism, 42
Williams, Bernard, 157n. 3,
    231n. 13
Wilson, Thomas, 33n. 71
Wittgenstein, Ludwig, 151,
    159n. 22
wu (emptiness; void; non-
    being), 119, 122, 337
  and *dao*, 119, 122
  and *yu*, 122
Wu (emperor), 305, 307–9, 312
Wu Hung, 217n. 10
wu-shamans, 64, 69, 79n. 3
  and communication with
    Heaven, 71, 75
  male and female, 214
  performing rites for
    deceased, 205
Wu Ding, 199, 214
wuyu (desires), 122
wuji (ultimateness), 119, 123,
    337
wuwei (actions), 122
wuwei (non-coercive action),
    58, 168, 337
Wyatt, Don, 35n. 106

Xia dynasty, 64, 68, 99–100,
    125, 132n. 1
  sacrificial system of, 319
Xiang, Duke, 320–21, 326
xianzhi (foreknowledge), 130
xiao (filial piety), 8–9, 47–49,
    158n. 15, 188
  as supreme dynamic of uni-
    verse, 105–6
*Xiaojing. See Classic of Filial
    Piety*
xiaoren (petty person), 174
  versus *junzi*, 301
xin (heart-mind), 185, 261, 337
  as medium of communica-
    tion between Heaven and
    humans, 69–75
  as part of *de*, 80n. 12
xing (human nature), 111, 175,
    176, 181nn. 24, 28, 257,
    258–59, 288, 290, 312–13,
    337
  goodness of, 9
  perfecting of, through edu-
    cation, 313–15
xingxing (mindful alertness), 88
xinxue (Learning of the Mind
    and Heart), 77–78
Xiong Shili, 17
xiu (shame), 148
  meaning of, 181n. 27
xu (empty), 211, 338
  dao as, 122
Xuan, King, 234, 235, 239–40,
    289
xue (learning), 90–91, 338
Xu Fuguan, 17
Xunzi (Hsun Tzu)/*Xunzi*, 5, 9,
    10, 30n. 42, 62, 148, 159n.
    18, 160n. 28, 192, 195n.
    14, 198, 252
  concern with ethical justifi-
    cation in, 254
  controversy with Mencius,
    142
  and distinction between
    generic and specific terms
    of, 253
  on economic scarcity, 281n.
    33
  and Euthyphro problem,
    288–301

  on funeral rites, 274 (*see also*
    mourning practices)
  on Heaven (*tian*), 216,
    264–66, 281n. 32
  on Heaven's Mandate, 294
  on human nature (*xing*),
    258–59, 265, 288, 290
  on humans as good, 290
  ideal of *can tianti* in, 264
  on *junzi*, 296
  on *li*, 255–56, 257, 263, 276,
    279n. 12
  piety of, 287–303
  qing in, 175
  reinterpretation of virtues
    of, 151
  and respect for linguistic
    practices, 272
  on rituals, 84, 236, 291
  on *shen* and *shenming*,
    267–72, 277, 281n. 43
  on social conflict, 256
  use of *long* (magnifying), 272
  on *wen*, 275
  on *xin* (mind), 267, 301
Xu Qinting, 281n. 39

yan, 181n. 28
yang, 257, 258
Yang, C. K., 16, 33n. 71
Yang Huijie, 280n. 30
Yan Hui, 70, 171, 179n. 9
  death of, 222–23, 224, 229,
    231 n. 7, 232n. 15
Yates, Robin D. S., 303nn. 15,
    16
Yearley, Lee, 29n. 21, 238,
    240–41, 250nn. 10, 15
yi (appropriateness), 174
yi (change), 132n. 1, 338
yi (oneness), 180n. 15
yi (righteousness; rightness),
    147, 234, 270, 338
  dependence of ethical signifi-
    cance of *li* on, 253
  and *li*, 254–55, 260
  as one of Four Beginnings,
    288
Yi Ching. See Book of Changes
Yi dynasty, 12
Yijing. See Book of Changes
Yijing view of reality, 113

Yili (*Ceremonies and Rites*), 253, 291
yin-yang
  cosmology, 62, 76
  opposition, 40–41, 116–18, 122, 123, 126, 268, 269, 332, 338
  and Heaven's Way, 314
Yi T'oegye, 12
Yi Yulgok, 12
Yizhuan, 113, 114, 119
  approach to reality, 123–24
  and *dao*, 133n. 2
yong (familiar), 178n. 7
yong (function), 16
you (invisible realm), 201
you (having-things), 338
  dao and, 122
Young Chan Ro, 29n. 21, 31n. 52
Yu, 47, 48, 100 (emperor), 319
yu (desire), 122, 338
Yucai Duan, 279n. 9
yue (music), 68, 83–84
  serving the function of ritual, 84
Yueh-lin Chin, 79n. 1
Yung Sik Kim, 31n. 47
Yü Ying-shih, 217n. 8, 231n. 5

Zang
  on friendship, 102
Zarathustra, 167
Zeng Yunqian, 80n. 14
Zengzi, 83, 189, 232n. 14
Zen monasteries
  Confucianism and, 12
Zhang Junmai, 17
Zhang Xuecheng, 62
Zhang Zai, 97
  on human suffering, 103
Zhuanxu (sage-ruler), 64
zhengming (rectifying terms or names)
  as task of sage-king, 272

Zheng Tan, 327, 328
Zheng Xuan (Han dynasty commentator), 181n. 27
Zheng Yi, 89
Zheng Zhenxiang, 217n. 3
zhi (straight)
  as part of *de*, 80n. 12
zhi (wisdom), 273, 338
  as one of Four Beginnings, 288
zhicheng (utmost sincerity), 130
zhiqi (intelligent vital energy), 205
zhong (centrality; equilibrium; mean), 131, 170, 261, 338
zhongyong (co-creativity), 165, 166, 176–77
  as staying centered in familiar affairs, 169
Zhongyong. See Doctrine of the Mean
Zhou, Duke, 99, 328
Zhou Dunyi, 97, 103, 119, 123
  Taiji Tushuo (Discourse on the Diagram of the Great Ultimate), 123
Zhou dynasty/period, 64, 68, 99, 198, 320–22
  chaos in, 240
  religious beliefs in, 200–216
  sacrificial system of, as norm of antiquity, 331
Zhouguan (or *Zhouli*), 320, 334n. 2
Zhouli. See Rites of Zhou
Zhou tradition
  adopted by Confucius, 274
Zhouyi (Book of Changes), 125, 132n. 1
  influence of, on *Daodejing*, 120
  influence of, on *Yizhuan*, 120
  pragmatism of, 120
  Xici Commentary of, 114

Zhuangzi/*Zhuangzi*, 58–59, 62, 65, 66, 67, 68, 70, 71, 76, 115, 160n. 28, 264–67, 282n. 43
  and communication with Heaven, 73
  on *de*, 80n. 12
  on death, 226–27
  death of, 226–27
  on Learning of the Mind and Heart, 77
  as main source of other-worldliness, 69
  process of "salvation" in, 69
  on sitting and forgetting (*zuowang*), 89
  theory of *xin-zhai* (fasting of the heart), 72
Zhu Gaozheng, 133n. 4
Zhu Xi, 8, 10, 13, 61, 231n. 12, 280n. 18
  and canon of Four Books, 19
  on Daoist *tianzun*, 76
  on *jing*, 87–88
  on learning, 90–91
  on Learning of the Mind and Heart, 77–78
  on *li*, 254
  on *qiongli*, 271
  and School of Principle, 15
  on *shoulian*, 89
  on spiritual growth, 87–88
  view of change of, 11
Zigong, 188
zihua (self-transformation), 121
Zilu, 188
ziran (spontaneity), 58–59, 176
Zisi, 306
Zisizi Confucian documents, 175
Zizhang, 188
Zuo Commentary (*Zuozhuan*), 74, 198
  on wraiths, 205